10 Best College Majors for Your Personality

Second Edition

Part of JIST's Best Jobs® Series

Laurence Shatkin, Ph.D.

Also in JIST's Best Jobs® Series

- ❋ *Best Jobs for the 21st Century*
- ❋ *200 Best Jobs for College Graduates*
- ❋ *300 Best Jobs Without a Four-Year Degree*
- ❋ *200 Best Jobs Through Apprenticeships*
- ❋ *50 Best Jobs for Your Personality*
- ❋ *40 Best Fields for Your Career*
- ❋ *225 Best Jobs for Baby Boomers*

- ❋ *250 Best-Paying Jobs*
- ❋ *150 Best Jobs for Your Skills*
- ❋ *150 Best Jobs Through Military Training*
- ❋ *150 Best Jobs for a Better World*
- ❋ *200 Best Jobs for Introverts*
- ❋ *150 Best Low-Stress Jobs*

JIST Works
America's Career Publisher®

10 Best College Majors for Your Personality, Second Edition

© 2011 by JIST Publishing

Published by JIST Works, an imprint of JIST Publishing
7321 Shadeland Station, Suite 200
Indianapolis, IN 46256-3923

Phone: 800-648-JIST   Fax: 877-454-7839
E-mail: info@jist.com   Web site: www.jist.com

Some Other Books by the Author

Best Jobs for the 21st Century	40 Best Fields for Your Career
200 Best Jobs for College Graduates	225 Best Jobs for Baby Boomers
300 Best Jobs Without a Four-Year Degree	250 Best-Paying Jobs
200 Best Jobs Through Apprenticeships	150 Best Jobs for a Better World
50 Best Jobs for Your Personality	200 Best Jobs for Introverts

Quantity discounts are available for JIST products. Please call our sales department at 800-648-JIST for a free catalog and more information.

Visit www.jist.com for information on JIST, free job search information, tables of contents, sample pages, and ordering information on our many products.

Acquisitions Editor: Susan Pines
Development Editor: Stephanie Koutek
Cover and Interior Designer: Aleata Halbig
Cover Photo: Adam Kaz, iStock
Interior Layout: Aleata Halbig
Proofreaders: Laura Bowman, Jeanne Clark
Indexer: Kelly D. Henthorne

Printed in the United States of America

16 15 14 13 12 11   9 8 7 6 5 4 3 2 1

Library of Congress Cataloging-in-Publication Data

Shatkin, Laurence.
   10 best college majors for your personality / Laurence Shatkin. -- 2nd ed.
      p. cm.
   Includes index.
   ISBN 978-1-59357-863-3 (alk. paper)
   1. College majors--United States. 2. Vocational guidance--United
States. I. Title.
   LB2361.5.S528 2011
   378.2'41--dc22

                        2011010829

ISBN 978-1-59357-863-3

This Is a Big Book, But It Is Very Easy to Use

Psychologists often use the concept of personality as a convenient way of summarizing many characteristics of a person. It can be especially useful when you're making decisions about your education and your career.

What kind of personality do you have? Forget about common labels such as "happy-go-lucky," "dependable," "even-tempered," "friendly," or "funny." These might help you get a date on Saturday night, but they're not much help in choosing a college major.

That's where this book can help. Learn about the personality types that many psychologists and guidance practitioners use to describe people, college majors, and careers. Take a quick assessment to help you clarify your dominant personality type. Then dig into a gold mine of facts about the college majors that are the best fit for your personality type—and that are the best for other reasons, such as their potential for income and job openings. Lists of "best majors" will suggest promising majors that you may never have considered. Turn to the descriptive profiles of the majors to learn what courses to expect, what specializations you may choose from, and what jobs may be open to you when you graduate. Get detailed facts about these jobs, based on the latest government data.

You're probably expecting college to improve your earning potential. So why not find a major that suits your personality and has outstanding economic potential? This book can show you the way.

Some Things You Can Do with This Book

- ✸ Explore and select a college major that relates to a career objective that suits your personality.
- ✸ Learn about college majors that previously were unfamiliar to you.
- ✸ Understand what majors are good preparation for a career you already have in mind.
- ✸ Learn key facts about jobs that may be a good fit for your personality.

These are a few of the many ways you can use this book. I hope you find it as interesting to browse as I did to put together. I have tried to make it easy to use and as interesting as possible.

When you are done with this book, pass it along or tell someone else about it. I wish you well in your education, in your career, and in your life.

Credits and Acknowledgments: While the author created this book, it is based on the work of many others. The occupational information is based on data obtained from the U.S. Department of Labor and the U.S. Census Bureau. These sources provide the most authoritative occupational information available. The noneconomic job-related information is from the O*NET database, which was developed by researchers and developers under the direction of the U.S. Department of Labor. They, in turn, were assisted by thousands of employers who provided details on the nature of work in the many thousands of job samplings used in the database's development. We used the most recent version of the O*NET database, release 15. We appreciate and thank the staff of the U.S. Department of Labor for their efforts and expertise in providing such a rich source of data. The taxonomy of college majors (the Classification of Instructional Programs) is from the U.S. Department of Education.

Table of Contents

Summary of Major Sections

Introduction. A short overview to help you better understand and use the book. Starts on page 1.

Part I. Your Personality and Your Major. Provides an overview of personality and of personality types. This section also explores the relationship between personality and college majors. Starts on page 15.

Part II. What's Your Personality Type? Take An Assessment. Helps you discover your personality type with a short, easy-to-complete assessment. Starts on page 21.

Part III. The Best Majors Lists. Very useful for exploring college majors! Lists are arranged into easy-to-use groups based on personality types. The first group of lists presents the 10 best majors for each personality type. Other lists identify, for each personality type, majors linked to jobs with the highest earnings, the fastest job growth, and the most job openings. More-specialized lists follow, ranking majors related to jobs by education level, majors linked to best jobs by worker demographics, and majors that prepare for jobs requiring either high or low math and verbal skills. The column starting on the right presents all the list titles. Starts on page 31.

Part IV. Descriptions of the Best College Majors for Your Personality. Provides complete descriptions of the majors that appear on the lists in Part III, plus five related majors. Each description contains information on specializations and college and high school courses, plus definitions and key facts for related jobs. Starts on page 91.

Appendix A. Resources for Further Exploration. Starts on page 283.

Appendix B. Majors Sorted by Three-Letter Personality Code. Starts on page 285.

Appendix C. The Career Clusters and Pathways. Starts on page 287.

Appendix D. Definitions of Skills Used in Descriptions of Majors. Starts on page 297.

Detailed Table of Contents

Introduction

Choosing a major can be scary. It's not a simple either/or decision, like choosing a car with either stick shift or automatic. It means a commitment of several years and, in most cases, a great amount of money. Although it's a personal decision, your friends and relatives will probably feel free to second-guess it. How can you sort out all of the possible choices and pick one that's right for you?

This book can help. It won't *tell* you what to do, but it will guide you to the information you need to make an intelligent choice—information about yourself, about majors, and about careers.

Many successful careers begin with an associate (two-year) degree, but workers with a bachelor's have 26 percent higher earnings and 23 percent less unemployment, so this book focuses on majors that require four or more years of education beyond high school.

Factors to Consider When You Choose a Major

When you're trying to choose a major, a good place to start is to think about why you're going to college at all. Some people have trivial reasons for going to college, and choosing a major is easy for them. For example, if you're going to college because all of your friends are going, then choose the same major that your best friends choose. If you're going because you think that's where the really cool social scene is, study whatever's easiest for you so your coursework won't interfere with your social life.

But most people who go to college have a more important reason: making themselves more employable in the future. They view college as an investment of time and money that will pay off through future employment opportunities. Whether they are planning for a specific job goal or a general area of employment, they expect that a college degree will result in higher earnings and less time spent unemployed. And they're right about this. In fact, the economic value of a college education continues to grow.

Therefore, an important factor to consider when you choose a college major is the **potential economic rewards of the major**. Different majors promise different earnings and job opportunities. This book can help with your decision because it ranks majors in terms of their potential economic rewards, based on the latest information available from the U.S. Department of Labor.

But money alone can't buy happiness. It would not be wise to decide on how to invest the time, money, and energy you're devoting to college simply by selling them to the highest bidder. Instead, you should consider the following additional factors when you think about choosing a college major:

* What majors are **interesting** to you?

* What majors are consistent with your **skills**?

* What majors match your preferences for **styles and locations of learning**?

This is a lot to consider, but fortunately there is a shortcut that can summarize these various noneconomic factors: **personality**. Career professionals and academic advisors often use an analysis of personality that focuses on six major types, referred to by the six-letter abbreviation RIASEC. Developed by occupational researcher John L. Holland, RIASEC stands for the personality types that he identified: Realistic, Investigative, Artistic, Social, Enterprising, and Conventional. (Part I discusses this scheme in detail.) Once you identify your personality type and match it to college majors, as this book will help you do, you can identify majors that suit your interests, your skills, and how and where you enjoy learning.

How to Use This Book

This is a book that you can dive right into:

* **If you don't know much about what personality types are,** you'll want to read Part I, which is an overview of the theory behind using personality types as a way of making choices about college majors and careers. You'll also see definitions of the six personality types that are used in this book.

* **If you want to understand your own personality type,** you'll want to do the assessment in Part II. It takes only 20 or 30 minutes to complete and can guide you to majors that suit you.

* **If you like lists and want an easy way to compare majors,** you should turn to Part III. Here you can browse lists showing the 10 majors for each personality type that are linked to jobs with the best pay, the fastest growth, and the most job openings. You can see these "best majors" broken down in various ways, such as by amount of education required.

❋ **For detailed information about majors,** turn to Part IV and read the profiles of the majors. I include 57 majors and itemize their specializations, their course requirements, characteristics of related jobs, and other facts that go beyond what you can learn from the lists in Part III. Because the descriptions are organized by personality type, you may find it helpful to browse within a section that fits you and become acquainted with unfamiliar majors that may deserve consideration. The information about related jobs may also open your eyes to options that are new to you.

On the other hand, if you like to do things in a methodical way, you may want to read the sections in order:

❋ Part I will give you useful background on **how personality type can be a guide** in choosing a major and career.

❋ The assessment in Part II will help you **identify your dominant personality type**.

❋ With a clearer understanding of your personality type, you can **browse the appropriate lists of "best majors"** in Part III and take notes on the majors that have the greatest appeal for you. If you find yourself bordering between two personality types, as many people do (for example, Investigative and Artistic), you may look at the lists for both types or turn to Appendix B for a complete list of majors by three-letter (primary and secondary) codes.

❋ Then you can **look up the descriptions of these majors** in Part IV and narrow down your list. Ask yourself these questions: Do the required courses interest me? Do the related jobs look rewarding? Can I handle the amount of education that these jobs will require?

Of course, no single book can tell you everything you need to know about college majors and careers. That's why you will probably want to confirm your tentative choices by using some of the resources listed in Appendix A. Other appendixes will help you understand some of the terms used in the Part IV descriptions.

Where the Information Came From

Because this book is about both college majors and the jobs they are related to, it uses information from a variety of sources.

The Classification of Instructional Programs, developed by the U.S. Department of Education, provided a standard title and definition for each major.

The information for the "Typical Sequence of College Courses" is derived from research into course requirements listed on college Web sites. The courses are those that appeared on several sites and were commonly required for the majors. The number of courses listed often varies. Some majors have fairly standard requirements that can be listed in detail; in some cases, a professional association mandates that certain courses be included. For other majors, notably the interdisciplinary subjects (such as Humanities or American Studies, which straddle several departments), requirements are either so minimal or so varied that it is difficult to list more than a handful of typical courses.

The "Typical Sequence of High School Courses" sections are based on a general understanding of which high school courses are considered prerequisites for the college-level courses required by the major.

You should be aware that course requirements and prerequisites for majors vary widely from one college to another. The descriptions outline average requirements, but before you declare a major you need to be aware of *all* the courses that your college (or your intended college) requires. For example, most colleges do not require a course in thermodynamics as part of their bachelor's degree program in electrical engineering. However, Iowa State University does, and so do some other colleges. Some colleges require *all* students to take certain core courses in writing, public speaking, math, or religion, and these core courses often are not reflected in this book's descriptions of majors.

The job-related information came from databases and books created by the U.S. Department of Labor and the U.S. Census Bureau. The definitions, work tasks, personality (RIASEC) types, skills (including verbal and math), and work conditions are derived from the Department of Labor's O*NET (Occupational Information Network) database, which is now the primary source of detailed information on occupations. The Labor Department updates the O*NET on a regular basis, and I used the most recent one available—O*NET release 15.

The information about earnings; growth; number of openings; and workers who are self-employed, urban, rural, male, and female is based on figures from the U.S. Bureau of Labor Statistics (BLS) and the U.S. Census Bureau.

As you look at the economic and demographic figures, keep in mind that they are estimates. They give you a general idea about the number of workers employed, annual earnings, rate of job growth, annual job openings, and composition of the workforce.

When you see these figures, you may sometimes wonder how to interpret them: Is $60,000 a good yearly salary? Is 15 percent job growth considered slow or fast? What number of job openings represents a good job market? It helps to compare these figures for any one occupation to the national averages. For all workers in all occupations, the median earnings (half earned more and half less) were $33,190 in May 2009. For the 92 occupations linked to the majors described in this book, the average earnings were about $78,000. (Later in this introduction, I explain how averages for earnings were computed.)

For the 782 occupations for which the Bureau of Labor Statistics projects job growth over the 10-year period ending in 2018, the average figure is 10.1 percent, but for the 92 occupations described in this book, the average is 14.0 percent.

For these same 782 occupations, the average number of job openings each year is about 6,400, whereas for the 92 occupations in this book, the average is about 4,200. If that difference surprises you, think about what you find when you read the help-wanted advertisements. Most of the jobs require considerably less than a bachelor's degree. On the other hand, most of these non–college-level jobs also are not as rewarding or fulfilling as you want; that's why you're reading this book.

When you see figures in this book describing jobs, remember that they always describe an average and therefore have limitations. Just as there is no precisely average person, there is no such thing as a statistically average example of a particular job. I say this because data, while helpful, can also be misleading.

Take, for example, the yearly earnings information about related jobs in this book. The employment security agency of each state gathers information on earnings for various jobs and forwards it to the U.S. Bureau of Labor Statistics. This information is organized in standardized ways by a BLS program called Occupational Employment Statistics, or OES. To keep the earnings for the various jobs and regions comparable, the OES screens out certain types of earnings and includes others, so the OES earnings I use in this book represent straight-time gross pay exclusive of premium pay. More specifically, the OES earnings include the job's base rate; cost-of-living allowances; guaranteed pay; hazardous-duty pay; incentive pay, including commissions and production bonuses; on-call pay; and tips but do not include back pay, jury duty pay, overtime pay, severance pay, shift differentials, non-production bonuses, or tuition reimbursements. Also, self-employed workers are not included in the estimates, and they can be a significant segment in certain occupations.

This OES-derived information on earnings is very accurate for identifying the median, but remember that half of all people in the occupation earn less than the median. For example, people who are new to the occupation or with only a few years of work experience often earn much less than the median amount. People who live in rural areas or who work for smaller employers typically earn less than those who do similar work in cities (where the cost of living is higher) or for bigger employers. People in certain areas of the country earn less than those in others. Other factors also influence how much you are likely to earn in a given job in your area. For example, dentists in the New York metropolitan area earn an average of $101,480 per year, whereas dentists in six metropolitan areas in North Carolina earn an average of more than $129,631 per year. Although the cost of living tends to be higher in the New York area, North Carolina until recently had only one dentistry school, and therefore dentists there experience less competition for patients and can command higher fees. So you can see that many factors can cause earnings to vary widely.

It's especially tricky to assign an average earnings figure to college majors, as I did to create the lists in Part I of this book. Understand that this figure is not based on the *actual* earnings of people who have completed the major, but rather on the earnings of people in the occupations that graduates are most likely to enter. Most majors prepare graduates to enter more than one occupation, so I needed to compute an earnings figure that would represent an average among these occupations. One factor I wanted to take into account was the size of the workforce, giving greater weight to occupations with larger workforces. However, I also wanted to diminish the weight of an occupation if graduates from the major are less likely to enter that occupation. Therefore, I ranked each occupation by its likelihood as an outcome of the major, based on a general understanding of how people prepare for the occupation, and I divided the workforce size by the square of this ranking. (For example, I divided the workforce of the second-ranked occupation by 4.) I used this weighting, rather than the raw workforce size, in computing the average.

Another limitation of the earnings figures is that the OES survey does not report annual earnings figures for some occupations with highly irregular income, such as Actors, so I could not factor their earnings into an average for the associated majors. OES reports only "more than $166,400" for certain highly paid jobs, such as Anesthesiologists, so I used the figure $166,400 in computing the average for the majors linked to these occupations.

To reflect the imprecision of the earnings averages for majors, I rounded the dollar figures to the nearest $1,000.

The figures for job growth and number of openings for occupations are projections by labor economists—their best guesses about what we can expect between now and 2018. They are not guarantees. A major economic downturn, war, or technological breakthrough could change the actual outcome. These figures also are averages for the 10-year period preceding 2018; at various times during that period, occupations may be growing faster or more slowly than the average.

Computing the average growth and total job openings for college majors presented the same problem as computing average earnings, so I used the same solution: I weighted the figures by dividing the occupation's workforce size by the square of its ranking as a likely outcome of the major. Less-likely occupations counted for less of the projected growth or openings.

Finally, don't forget that the job market for the occupations described here consists of both job openings and job seekers. The figures on job growth and openings don't tell you how many people will be competing with you to be hired. The Department of Labor does not publish figures on the supply of job candidates, so I can't tell you about the level of competition you can expect. Competition is an important issue that you should research for any tentative career goal. In some cases, the *Occupational Outlook Handbook* provides informative statements. You should speak to people who educate or train tomorrow's workers; they probably have a good idea of how many of their graduates find rewarding employment and how quickly. People in the workforce also can provide insights into this issue. Use your critical thinking skills to evaluate what people tell you. For example, recruiters for training programs are highly motivated to get you to sign up, whereas people in the workforce may be trying to discourage you from competing. Get a variety of opinions to balance out possible biases.

So, in reviewing the information in this book, please understand the limitations of the data. You need to use common sense in making decisions about education and careers as in most other things in life. I hope that, using that approach, you find the information helpful and interesting.

How the Majors in This Book Were Selected

Study the catalog or Web site of any large university and you'll find dozens of majors listed. I wanted to save you time by identifying the best commonly offered majors associated with each personality type.

Here is the procedure I followed to select the 51 majors (10 for each personality type, with some appearing on multiple lists) that I included in the lists in this book:

1. I began with the descriptions of 120 college majors that were developed for an earlier book, *Panicked Student's Guide to Choosing a College Major* (JIST Publishing). These covered the most commonly offered programs at the bachelor's or professional level. I matched these 120 majors to O*NET occupations by using the recommended matches made by the National Center for O*NET Development, with one slight modification: I removed the postsecondary teaching jobs. Theoretically, students in any major can go on to teach the subject in college—for example, some Electrical Engineering majors aspire to do what their professors are doing rather than work in industry—but this number is difficult to determine and usually quite small. Furthermore, job-outlook information is not available for each of the 36 postsecondary teaching jobs included in O*NET; it is available only for the combined occupation Postsecondary Teachers. Therefore, it made sense to create the pseudo-major "Graduate Study for College Teaching" as an option for those who want to use their education for that career goal. I linked "Graduate Study for College Teaching" to the combined occupation Postsecondary Teachers.

2. O*NET provides two kinds of information on RIASEC personality types: It identifies the dominant RIASEC type or types for every job and it gives every job a numerical

rating on all six RIASEC types. When a major was linked to a single job, I used the dominant RIASEC type or types that O*NET assigned to the related job. When a major was linked to more than one job, I averaged the numerical ratings of each of the six RIASEC types for all of the related jobs. (I determined a weighted average, using a formula based on the size of the workforce and the likelihood of the occupation as an outcome of the major, as explained earlier in this introduction.) I used the highest-rated RIASEC type as the primary type. I subtracted the rating for the second-highest-rated RIASEC type from the rating for the highest type and calculated the ratio of this remainder to the sum of all six ratings. If this ratio was higher than 0.17, I used the two highest-rated types. I performed the same calculation for the third-highest-rated type and applied the same cutoff of 0.17 to determine whether to use all three highest-rated types. These were the same rules that the O*NET developers used to identify the top RIASEC type(s) for individual occupations.

3. Based on the O*NET data, I created lists of majors for each of the six RIASEC types. For the Investigative, Artistic, Social, and Enterprising types, I was able to create sufficiently large pools of majors on the basis of the primary type. On the other hand, only a few majors had Realistic or Conventional as their primary type, so the pool of R and C majors also needed to include those with Realistic or Conventional as their second-highest-rated type. As a result, a few majors ended up on more than one list. For example, the top-rated Conventional major, Pharmacy, actually has Conventional as its secondary personality type. Its primary type is Investigative, so it also appears as the fourth-ranked major on the list of Investigative majors.

4. To be able to sort these preliminary lists and determine the "best" majors, I computed the economic potential of each major by assembling three kinds of economic information about the jobs related to majors: the annual earnings, the job growth projected for a 10-year period ending in 2018, and the average number of job openings expected annually during that same time span. When more than one job was linked to a major, I computed a weighted average for earnings and job growth in related jobs and computed the total number of annual openings in related jobs. My method of weighting is explained earlier in this introduction.

5. I ranked the majors in each of the six lists on each of these three measures of economic potential: by earning potential, by potential job growth, and by potential job openings. I then added the numerical ranks for each major in each list to produce an overall score. To emphasize majors leading to jobs with the best economic rewards, I selected the 10 majors from each list with the best numerical

scores. These majors are the focus of this book. Because some majors appeared on two lists, the total number of unique majors was 51 rather than 60.

Here's an example of how I combined the three measures of economic potential: Nursing (R.N. Training) is the Social major with the best combined score for earnings, growth, and number of job openings—based on the related job Registered Nurses. Therefore, Nursing (R.N. Training) is listed first in my "10 Best Social Majors" list even though it is not the Social major with the best earning potential (which is Physician Assisting) or the best potential for job growth (also Physician Assisting). It ranked #1 among the Social majors on only one measure of economic potential, job openings, but its *combined* ranking on all three measures put it in first place.

All 51 of these majors appear not only on the lists in Part III of this book but also in the descriptions in Part IV. Japanese also appears among the descriptions in Part IV. It was excluded from the 10 best Artistic majors because there was room for only 7 language majors, and alphabetical ordering would have excluded the much more popular Spanish major. Five additional majors are described in Part IV but could not be included in the Part III lists because they are not linked to any particular job except college teaching, which is already represented in the lists by the pseudo-major Graduate Study for College Teaching. For example, American Studies is one such major that appears in Part IV but not in Part III. People with a degree in this subject sometimes go on to careers in law, marketing, or politics, but this major is not the obvious one to link to these jobs, so it would be a mistake to calculate the economic rewards of the major on the basis of these or any other jobs. On the other hand, American Studies is a popular major and could be combined with postgraduate study in law, social work, library science, or several other fields covered by this book, so I decided that this major and four others—African-American Studies, Area Studies, Humanities, and Women's Studies—should be included in the Part IV descriptions. Thus a total of 57 majors are described in this book.

A Sample Description of a Major

The 57 descriptions of majors in this book all have the same data elements. Following is a sample, together with explanations of how to interpret the information.

Title →

Social Majors

Personality Type →

African-American Studies

→ **Personality Type:** Social–Investigative–Artistic

Useful Facts About the Major →

Useful Facts About the Major

→ Focuses on the history, sociology, politics, culture, and economics of the North American peoples descended from the African diaspora; focusing on the United States, Canada, and the Caribbean, but also including reference to Latin American elements of the diaspora.

Related CIP Program →

→ **Related CIP Program:** 05.0201 African-American/Black Studies

Specializations in the Major →

Specializations in the Major: History and culture, behavioral and social inquiry, literature, language, and the arts.

Typical Sequence of College Courses →

Typical Sequence of College Courses: English composition, foreign language, American history, introduction to African American studies, African American literature, African American history, African Diaspora studies, research methods in African American studies, seminar (reporting on research).

Typical Sequence of High School Courses →

Typical Sequence of High School Courses: English, algebra, foreign language, history, literature, public speaking, social science.

Career Snapshot →

Career Snapshot

→ African-American studies draws on a number of disciplines, including history, sociology, literature, linguistics, and political science. Usually you can shape the program to emphasize whichever appeals most to you. Graduates frequently pursue higher degrees as a means of establishing a career in a field such as college teaching or the law.

Useful Averages for the Related Jobs

← *Useful Averages for the Related Jobs*

- Annual Earnings: $65,000
- Growth: 15.1%
- Openings: Roughly 200
- Self-Employed: No data available
- Verbal Skill Rating: 84
- Math Skill Rating: 39

Other Details About the Related Jobs

← *Career Clusters and Pathways*

Career Clusters: 05 Education and Training; 10 Human Service. **Career Pathways:** 05.3 Teaching/Training; 10.2 Counseling and Mental Health Services.

← *Skills*

Skills: Science, writing, operations analysis, learning strategies, speaking, reading comprehension, active learning, active listening. **Work Conditions:** Indoors; sitting; exposed to disease or infections.

← *Work Conditions*

Related Jobs

← *Related Jobs*

Area, Ethnic, and Cultural Studies Teachers, Postsecondary

Personality Type: Social–Investigative–Artistic

Earnings: $65,030
Growth: 15.1%
Annual Openings: 200

Most Common Education/Training Level: Doctoral degree

Teach courses pertaining to the culture and development of an area (e.g., Latin America), an ethnic group, or any other group (e.g., women's studies, urban affairs). Keep abreast of developments in their field by reading current literature,

Here are some details on each of the major parts of the descriptions you will find in Part IV:

❋ Title—This is a commonly used title for the major. Sometimes the major may also be known under other names. For example, Humanities is sometimes called Liberal Arts.

❋ Personality Type—This consists of the one, two, or three RIASEC types that describe this major, based on the jobs linked to the major. If more than one type is listed, they appear in descending order of importance. Only the first one or two types are used to assign the major to the lists in Part III.

❋ Useful Facts About the Major—This section begins with a definition of the major derived from the Classification of Instructional Programs (CIP), a database created by the U.S. Department of Education.

❋ Related CIP Program—This is the title of the CIP program that provided the definition used in the previous data element.

❋ Specializations in the Major—These are the most commonly available concentrations that may be offered in the major. In some cases, these are job specializations rather than educational pathways.

❋ Typical Sequence of College Courses—These courses are ordered roughly as they might be taken to complete the major. Survey courses and introductory courses, especially in supporting disciplines (for example, a writing course within a science major), are usually ordered near the beginning, whereas specialized and advanced courses are usually ordered near the end. Some of these titles may represent multiple-semester courses or even separate courses with different names collapsed into one title.

❋ Typical Sequence of High School Courses—These are the courses that are most commonly expected to provide secondary-level preparation for the college major. Additional courses are required by almost all high schools and are expected for college admission.

❋ Career Snapshot—This is an overview of the jobs that the major leads to. It usually indicates the level of education the employers expect for new hires, as well as the job outlook.

❋ Useful Averages for the Related Jobs—The economic information here, as well as the Total Annual Job Openings figure, comes from various U.S. Department of Labor and Census databases for this occupation, and weighted averages were computed as explained elsewhere in this introduction. The figures for verbal and math skills are derived from the O*NET database, as explained in Part III (where you'll find lists of majors linked to jobs that require high and low levels of these skills). Note that these skill ratings are based on the *requirements of the related jobs* and may not indicate the level of achievement necessary for admission to the major or the level of ability required for completion of the courses.

❋ Career Clusters and Pathways—This information assigns each related job to one or more clusters and pathways within the career cluster scheme developed by the U.S. Department of Education's Office of Vocational and Adult Education around 1999. You can find the full outline of the career clusters and pathways in Appendix C. Because the clustering scheme is more detailed than the six RIASEC personality types, it may help you identify majors that relate to your specific interests.

❋ Skills—The O*NET database provides data on many skills; I decided to list only those that were most important for the jobs related to the major rather than list pages of unhelpful details. For each major, I computed the weighted average skill ratings for all related jobs. I then identified any skill that is rated at a level higher than the average rating for that skill for all jobs and that also is not rated as an unimportant skill. If there are more than eight, I include only the eight with the highest ratings, and I present them from highest to lowest score (that is, in terms of by how much its score exceeds the average score). I include up to 10 skills if scores were tied for eighth place. If no skill has a rating higher than the average for all jobs, I say "None met the criteria." If the names of the skills are not clear to you, you can find definitions in Appendix D. Note that the skills are based on the requirements of the jobs and may not correspond exactly to the skills needed for academic success in the major.

❋ Work Conditions—This entry, also derived from O*NET data about the related jobs, mentions aspects of the work settings that some people may want to avoid, such as exposure to loud noises or the necessity of standing for long periods of time. I determined the dominant work conditions by using the same method as I used for skills, except that the ordering of these environmental factors is not significant. Like the other work-related characteristics, the work conditions may not accurately describe the environment where the major is studied, unless the major involves a lot of workplace learning (for example, clinical practice in health-care majors).

❋ Related Jobs—The jobs described here are linked to the major according to matches made by the O*NET Development Center, with modifications as noted earlier in this introduction. The information on earnings, growth, job openings, and most common level of education or training is derived from the U.S. Department of Labor. Note that in some cases an occupation may require less education than a college degree, but graduates of the major are commonly hired into this job. For example, one of the jobs linked to Physical Education is Coaches and Scouts, which can be learned through long-term on-the-job training. Nevertheless, some employers prefer applicants with a college degree, and in fact slightly more than half the Coaches and Scouts currently employed have a bachelor's degree or higher, so this is a logical career choice to link to the Physical Education major. The occupations that are linked to the majors are derived from the taxonomy called Standard Occupational Classification (SOC), and usually each SOC occupation is the exact equivalent of an O*NET occupation. In those cases where a SOC occupation corresponds to two or more O*NET occupations, the facts for the multiple O*NET occupations are listed under the heading "Job Specializations." Where necessary, statements of work tasks are edited to avoid exceeding 2,000 characters.

PART I

Your Personality and Your Major

People often use the term "personality" to refer to various aspects of people they know. When describing their friends, their classmates, or even themselves, they may refer to aspects of personality such as sense of humor, optimism, ambition, irritability, or decisiveness.

Many such concepts of personality are interesting to know about a person but not very useful in helping someone decide on a college major. Fortunately, psychologists have found other aspects of personality that can be valuable to consider when making educational and career plans. In this part of the book, you'll learn about the relationship between personality and college majors, and you will gain a working understanding of the most commonly used scheme for describing personality types in this context.

Why Personality Is Useful for Choosing a Major

Personality theorists believe that people with similar personality types naturally tend to associate with one another in the workplace, the classroom, and other places. As they do so, they create an environment that is hospitable to their personality type. For example, a workplace or classroom with a lot of Artistic types tends to reward creative thinking and behavior. Therefore, your personality type not only predicts how well your skills will match the demands of the tasks in a particular major or job; it also predicts how well you will fit in with the culture of the classroom or work site as shaped by the people who will surround you and interact with you. Your personality type thus is a key to career choice because it affects your satisfaction with the job, your productivity in it, and the likelihood that you will persist in this type of work. Likewise, your personality indicates which majors might be good choices for you because most college students choose their majors to help advance their careers.

One of the advantages of using personality as a key to choosing a major and a career is that it is economical—it provides a tidy summary of many aspects of people, majors, and careers. Consider how knotty the decision about a major could get if you were to consider each related job and reflect on how well you might fit into each specific component of the work environment. For example, you could focus on the skills required and your ability to meet them. Next you could analyze the kinds of knowledge that are used on the job and decide how much you enjoy working with those topics. Then you could consider a broad array of satisfactions, such as variety, creativity, and independence; for each one, you would evaluate its importance to you and then determine the potential of various majors to lead to career options that could satisfy this need. You can see that, when looked at under a microscope like this, the choice of a major gets extremely complex.

But the personality-based approach allows you to view the alternatives from 40,000 feet. When you compare yourself or a major to certain basic personality types, you encounter much less complexity. With fewer ideas and facts to sort through and consider, the task of deciding becomes much easier.

The RIASEC Personality Types

During the 1950s, the career guidance researcher John L. Holland was trying to find a meaningful new way to arrange the output of an interest inventory and relate it to college majors, based on the relationship between the majors and the jobs they prepare for. He devised a set of six personality types that would differentiate well between different majors and different people and would have neutral connotations, neither positive nor negative. He called his six types Realistic, Investigative, Artistic, Social, Enterprising, and Conventional. (The acronym *RIASEC* is a convenient way to remember them.)

The following table shows how these labels apply to both people and work:

Personality Type	How It Applies to People	How It Applies to Work
Realistic	Realistic personalities like work activities that include practical, hands-on problems and solutions. They enjoy dealing with plants; animals; and real-world materials such as wood, tools, and machinery. They enjoy outside work. Often they do not like occupations that mainly involve doing paperwork or working closely with others.	Realistic occupations frequently involve work activities that include practical, hands-on problems and solutions. They often deal with plants; animals; and real-world materials such as wood, tools, and machinery. Many of the occupations require working outside and do not involve a lot of paperwork or working closely with others.

Personality Type	How It Applies to People	How It Applies to Work
Investigative	Investigative personalities like work activities that have to do with ideas and thinking more than with physical activity. They like to search for facts and figure out problems mentally rather than to persuade or lead people.	Investigative occupations frequently involve working with ideas and require an extensive amount of thinking. These occupations can involve searching for facts and figuring out problems mentally.
Artistic	Artistic personalities like work activities that deal with forms, designs, and patterns. They often require self-expression and the work can be done without following a clear set of rules.	Artistic occupations frequently involve working with the artistic side of things, such as forms, designs, and patterns. They like self-expression in their work. They prefer settings where work can be done without following a clear set of rules.
Social	Social personalities like work activities that assist others and promote learning and personal development. They prefer to communicate more than to work with objects, machines, or data.	Social occupations frequently involve working with, communicating with, and teaching people. These occupations often involve helping or providing service to others. They like to teach, to give advice, to help, or otherwise to be of service to people.
Enterprising	Enterprising personalities like work activities having to do with starting up and carrying out projects, especially business ventures. They like persuading and leading people and making decisions. They like taking risks for profit. These personalities prefer action rather than thought.	Enterprising occupations frequently involve starting up and carrying out projects. These occupations can involve leading people and making many decisions. They sometimes require risk taking and often deal with business.
Conventional	Conventional personalities like work activities that follow set procedures and routines. They prefer working with data and details rather than with ideas. They prefer work in which there are precise standards rather than work in which you have to judge things by yourself. These personalities like working where the lines of authority are clear.	Conventional occupations frequently involve following set procedures and routines. These occupations can include working with data and details more than with ideas. Usually there is a clear line of authority to follow.

Holland went further by arranging these six personality types on a hexagon:

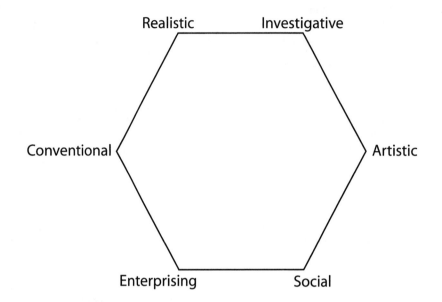

He used this diagram to explain that people tend to resemble one type primarily, but they may also have aspects of one or more adjacent types. Each personality type tends to have little in common with the types on the opposite side of the hexagon. Therefore, for example, a person might be primarily Enterprising, with an additional but smaller resemblance to the Conventional type. Such a person would be described by the two-letter code EC and might be well suited to work in the jobs linked to the college majors Business Management and Marketing (both coded EC). This person would have much less in common with Investigative or Artistic personality types and likely would not be very happy or productive in the physician jobs linked to the Medicine major (coded ISR) or in jobs related to the Art major. But this person could get along well with both Enterprising and Conventional personalities and, to a lesser extent, possibly with Realistic or Social personalities.

The Holland hexagon can be a little misleading in its neat symmetrical shape, especially when you look at jobs for which a college education is appropriate preparation. Most people prepare for Realistic or Conventional jobs by getting on-the-job training rather than a college degree. College is more suited for preparing people for jobs located at the other points on the hexagon, and graduate school is especially designed to teach Investigative skills. It's no accident that of the 57 majors described in this book, only one has Realistic as its first personality code and only three have Conventional in that position.

But that doesn't mean that people who have Realistic or Conventional personalities should forget about pursuing a college-level career. A large number of college-level jobs have Realistic or Conventional as their *second* personality type, meaning that the jobs have a significant representation of work tasks and situations that these personality types will find suitable. The majors related to these jobs also have R or C as their second personality type. In assembling the lists of best majors for each personality type, I added these majors to the pool of majors coded as R or C, and therefore I was able to identify 10 outstanding majors for the R and C types, as for the other four types.

Very few of the majors included in this book represent only one personality type, so when you read the description of a major, be sure to look at the full personality type, which may cover two or even three RIASEC types. For each related job, look at the personality types, the work tasks, and the skills and decide whether the job is a good fit for your personality.

Since Holland did his pioneering work, a number of career decision-making assessments have been developed to help people determine what personality type best describes them (and perhaps an additional adjacent type or types that are also important). You can find one such assessment in Part II of this book. Others are available online (there's a good one at www.mynextmove.org) or in the offices of career professionals, sometimes for a fee.

Keep in mind that although all of these assessments produce outputs with RIASEC codes and some of them also link these codes to college majors, they will not necessarily produce the exact same output. Assessment of personality is not as exact a science as, say, chemistry. Neither is the task of linking personalities to majors.

You should not regard the output of any personality assessment as the final word on what college major or career will suit you best. Use a variety of approaches to decide what kind of person you are and narrow down the kinds of learning and work you enjoy. Actual work experience is probably the best way to test a tentative career choice, and experience in introductory college courses can often give a good indication of how well a related major would satisfy you.

PART II

What's Your Personality Type? Take an Assessment

In this section, you can take a personality type inventory that will help you determine your primary RIASEC personality type and perhaps one or two secondary RIASEC personality types. It asks if you like or dislike various activities and then lets you score your responses. You can use your scores in the following sections of the book to identify specific highly rewarding majors to explore.

It's easy to use the personality type inventory—just turn the page and follow the directions beginning with Step 1. This is not a test, so there are no right or wrong answers. There is also no time limit for completing this inventory.

If someone else will be using this book, you should photocopy the inventory pages and mark your responses on the photocopy. This inventory is for your personal use. Any other use, including reproduction or distribution, is prohibited by U.S. copyright law.

Note: This inventory is based on the O*NET Interest Profiler, Version 3.0, developed by the U.S. Department of Labor (DOL). The DOL's edition consists of several components, including the Interest Profiler Instrument, Interest Profiler Score Report, and Interest Profiler O*NET Occupations Master List. The DOL provides a separate Interest Profiler User's Guide with information on the profiler's development and validity as well as tips for professionals using it in career counseling and academic advisement. Additional information on these items is available at www.onetcenter.org, which is maintained by the DOL. This Personality Type Inventory is a version of the DOL's O*NET Interest Profiler that uses its work activity items and scoring system but has shorter directions, format changes, and additional content.

Restrictions for use: This and any other form of the O*NET Interest Profiler should be used for career exploration, career planning, and vocational counseling purposes only, and no other use has been authorized or is valid. Results should not be used for employment or hiring decisions or for applicant screening for jobs or training programs.

Please see the DOL's separate "O*NET User's Agreement" at www.onetcenter.org/agree/ tools for additional details on restrictions and use. The word "O*NET" is a trademark of the U.S. Department of Labor, Employment and Training Administration.

JIST Publishing offers a color foldout version of this assessment. It is called the *O*NET Career Interests Inventory*, and it is sold in packages of 25.

Step 1: Respond to the Statements

Carefully read each work activity (items 1 through 180). For each item, fill in just one of the three circles as follows:

If you think you would LIKE the activity, fill in the circle containing the L, like this:

If you think you would DISLIKE the activity, fill in the circle containing the D, like this:

If you are UNSURE whether you would like the activity, fill in the circle with the ?, like this:

As you respond to each activity, don't consider whether you have the education or training needed for it or how much money you might earn if it were part of your job. Simply fill in the circle based on whether you would like, would dislike, or aren't sure about the activity.

After you respond to all 180 activities, you'll score your responses in Step 2.

Would you LIKE the activity or DISLIKE the activity, or are you UNSURE?

1. Build kitchen cabinets   L ? D
2. Guard money in an armored car   L ? D
3. Operate a dairy farm   L ? D
4. Lay brick or tile   L ? D
5. Monitor a machine on an assembly line   L ? D
6. Repair household appliances   L ? D
7. Drive a taxicab   L ? D
8. Install flooring in houses   L ? D
9. Raise fish in a fish hatchery   L ? D
10. Build a brick walkway   L ? D
11. Assemble electronic parts   L ? D
12. Drive a truck to deliver packages to offices and homes   L ? D
13. Paint houses   L ? D
14. Enforce fish and game laws   L ? D
15. Operate a grinding machine in a factory   L ? D
16. Work on an offshore oil-drilling rig   L ? D
17. Perform lawn-care services   L ? D
18. Assemble products in a factory   L ? D
19. Catch fish as a member of a fishing crew   L ? D
20. Refinish furniture   L ? D
21. Fix a broken faucet   L ? D
22. Do cleaning or maintenance work   L ? D
23. Maintain the grounds of a park   L ? D
24. Operate a machine on a production line   L ? D
25. Spray trees to prevent the spread of harmful insects   L ? D
26. Test the quality of parts before shipment   L ? D
27. Operate a motorboat to carry passengers   L ? D
28. Repair and install locks   L ? D
29. Set up and operate machines to make products   L ? D
30. Put out forest fires   L ? D

_____ **Page Score for R**

Would you LIKE the activity or DISLIKE the activity, or are you UNSURE?

		L	?	D
31.	Study space travel	Ⓛ	Ⓩ	Ⓓ
32.	Make a map of the bottom of an ocean	Ⓛ	Ⓩ	Ⓓ
33.	Study the history of past civilizations	Ⓛ	Ⓩ	Ⓓ
34.	Study animal behavior	Ⓛ	Ⓩ	Ⓓ
35.	Develop a new medicine	Ⓛ	Ⓩ	Ⓓ
36.	Plan a research study	Ⓛ	Ⓩ	Ⓓ
37.	Study ways to reduce water pollution	Ⓛ	Ⓩ	Ⓓ
38.	Develop a new medical treatment or procedure	Ⓛ	Ⓩ	Ⓓ
39.	Determine the infection rate of a new disease	Ⓛ	Ⓩ	Ⓓ
40.	Study rocks and minerals	Ⓛ	Ⓩ	Ⓓ
41.	Diagnose and treat sick animals	Ⓛ	Ⓩ	Ⓓ
42.	Study the personalities of world leaders	Ⓛ	Ⓩ	Ⓓ
43.	Conduct chemical experiments	Ⓛ	Ⓩ	Ⓓ
44.	Conduct biological research	Ⓛ	Ⓩ	Ⓓ
45.	Study the population growth of a city	Ⓛ	Ⓩ	Ⓓ
46.	Study whales and other types of marine life	Ⓛ	Ⓩ	Ⓓ
47.	Investigate crimes	Ⓛ	Ⓩ	Ⓓ
48.	Study the movement of planets	Ⓛ	Ⓩ	Ⓓ
49.	Examine blood samples using a microscope	Ⓛ	Ⓩ	Ⓓ
50.	Investigate the cause of a fire	Ⓛ	Ⓩ	Ⓓ
51.	Study the structure of the human body	Ⓛ	Ⓩ	Ⓓ
52.	Develop psychological profiles of criminals	Ⓛ	Ⓩ	Ⓓ
53.	Develop a new way to better predict the weather	Ⓛ	Ⓩ	Ⓓ
54.	Work in a biology lab	Ⓛ	Ⓩ	Ⓓ
55.	Invent a replacement for sugar	Ⓛ	Ⓩ	Ⓓ
56.	Study genetics	Ⓛ	Ⓩ	Ⓓ
57.	Study the governments of different countries	Ⓛ	Ⓩ	Ⓓ
58.	Do research on plants or animals	Ⓛ	Ⓩ	Ⓓ
59.	Do laboratory tests to identify diseases	Ⓛ	Ⓩ	Ⓓ
60.	Study weather conditions	Ⓛ	Ⓩ	Ⓓ

____ **Page Score for I**

Would you LIKE the activity or DISLIKE the activity, or are you UNSURE?

61.	Conduct a symphony orchestra	L ? D
62.	Write stories or articles for magazines	L ? D
63.	Direct a play	L ? D
64.	Create dance routines for a show	L ? D
65.	Write books or plays	L ? D
66.	Play a musical instrument	L ? D
67.	Perform comedy routines in front of an audience	L ? D
68.	Perform as an extra in movies, plays, or television shows	L ? D
69.	Write reviews of books or plays	L ? D
70.	Compose or arrange music	L ? D
71.	Act in a movie	L ? D
72.	Dance in a Broadway show	L ? D
73.	Draw pictures	L ? D
74.	Sing professionally	L ? D
75.	Perform stunts for a movie or television show	L ? D
76.	Create special effects for movies	L ? D
77.	Conduct a musical choir	L ? D
78.	Act in a play	L ? D
79.	Paint sets for plays	L ? D
80.	Audition singers and musicians for a musical show	L ? D
81.	Design sets for plays	L ? D
82.	Announce a radio show	L ? D
83.	Write scripts for movies or television shows	L ? D
84.	Write a song	L ? D
85.	Perform jazz or tap dance	L ? D
86.	Direct a movie	L ? D
87.	Sing in a band	L ? D
88.	Design artwork for magazines	L ? D
89.	Edit movies	L ? D
90.	Pose for a photographer	L ? D

_____ **Page Score for A**

Would you LIKE the activity or DISLIKE the activity, or are you UNSURE?

91. Teach an individual an exercise routine · L · ? · D
92. Perform nursing duties in a hospital · L · ? · D
93. Give CPR to someone who has stopped breathing · L · ? · D
94. Help people with personal or emotional problems · L · ? · D
95. Teach children how to read · L · ? · D
96. Work with mentally disabled children · L · ? · D
97. Teach an elementary school class · L · ? · D
98. Give career guidance to people · L · ? · D
99. Supervise the activities of children at a camp · L · ? · D
100. Help people with family-related problems · L · ? · D
101. Perform rehabilitation therapy · L · ? · D
102. Do volunteer work at a nonprofit organization · L · ? · D
103. Help elderly people with their daily activities · L · ? · D
104. Teach children how to play sports · L · ? · D
105. Help disabled people improve their daily living skills · L · ? · D
106. Teach sign language to people with hearing disabilities · L · ? · D
107. Help people who have problems with drugs or alcohol · L · ? · D
108. Help conduct a group therapy session · L · ? · D
109. Help families care for ill relatives · L · ? · D
110. Provide massage therapy to people · L · ? · D
111. Plan exercises for disabled students · L · ? · D
112. Counsel people who have a life-threatening illness · L · ? · D
113. Teach disabled people work and living skills · L · ? · D
114. Organize activities at a recreational facility · L · ? · D
115. Take care of children at a day-care center · L · ? · D
116. Organize field trips for disabled people · L · ? · D
117. Assist doctors in treating patients · L · ? · D
118. Work with juveniles on probation · L · ?
119. Provide physical therapy to people recovering from an injury · L · ? · D
120. Teach a high school class · L · ? · D

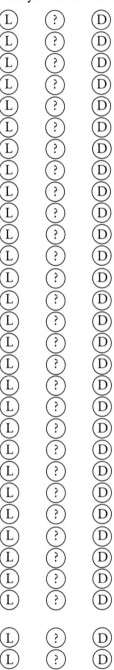

____ **Page Score for S**

Would you LIKE the activity or DISLIKE the activity, or are you UNSURE?

121. Buy and sell stocks and bonds   (L)   (?)   (D)
122. Manage a retail store   (L)   (?)   (D)
123. Sell telephone and other communication equipment   (L)   (?)   (D)
124. Operate a beauty salon or barber shop   (L)   (?)   (D)
125. Sell merchandise over the telephone   (L)   (?)   (D)
126. Run a stand that sells newspapers and magazines   (L)   (?)   (D)
127. Give a presentation about a product you are selling   (L)   (?)   (D)
128. Buy and sell land   (L)   (?)   (D)
129. Sell compact discs at a music store   (L)   (?)   (D)
130. Run a toy store   (L)   (?)   (D)
131. Manage the operations of a hotel   (L)   (?)   (D)
132. Sell houses   (L)   (?)   (D)
133. Sell candy and popcorn at sports events   (L)   (?)   (D)
134. Manage a supermarket   (L)   (?)   (D)
135. Manage a department within a large company   (L)   (?)   (D)
136. Sell a soft drink product line to stores and restaurants   (L)   (?)   (D)
137. Sell refreshments at a movie theater   (L)   (?)   (D)
138. Sell hair-care products to stores and salons   (L)   (?)   (D)
139. Start your own business   (L)   (?)   (D)
140. Negotiate business contracts   (L)   (?)   (D)
141. Represent a client in a lawsuit   (L)   (?)   (D)
142. Negotiate contracts for professional athletes   (L)   (?)   (D)
143. Be responsible for the operation of a company   (L)   (?)   (D)
144. Market a new line of clothing   (L)   (?)   (D)
145. Sell newspaper advertisements   (L)   (?)   (D)
146. Sell merchandise at a department store   (L)   (?)   (D)
147. Sell automobiles   (L)   (?)   (D)
148. Manage a clothing store   (L)   (?)   (D)
149. Sell restaurant franchises to individuals   (L)   (?)   (D)
150. Sell computer equipment in a store   (L)   (?)   (D)

____ **Page Score for E**

Would you LIKE the activity or DISLIKE the activity, or are you UNSURE?

151. Develop a spreadsheet using computer software   L   ?   D

152. Proofread records or forms   L   ?   D

153. Use a computer program to generate customer bills   L   ?   D

154. Schedule conferences for an organization   L   ?   D

155. Keep accounts payable/receivable for an office   L   ?   D

156. Load computer software into a large computer network   L   ?   D

157. Transfer funds between banks using a computer   L   ?   D

158. Organize and schedule office meetings   L   ?   D

159. Use a word processor to edit and format documents   L   ?   D

160. Operate a calculator   L   ?   D

161. Direct or transfer phone calls for a large organization   L   ?   D

162. Perform office filing tasks   L   ?   D

163. Compute and record statistical and other numerical data   L   ?   D

164. Generate the monthly payroll checks for an office   L   ?   D

165. Take notes during a meeting   L   ?   D

166. Keep shipping and receiving records   L   ?   D

167. Calculate the wages of employees   L   ?

168. Assist senior-level accountants in performing
bookkeeping tasks   L   ?   D

169. Type labels for envelopes and packages   L   ?   D

170. Inventory supplies using a hand-held computer   L   ?   D

171. Develop an office filing system   L   ?   D

172. Keep records of financial transactions for an organization   L   ?   D

173. Record information from customers applying for
charge accounts   L   ?   D

174. Photocopy letters and reports   L   ?   D

175. Record rent payments   L   ?   D

176. Enter information into a database   L   ?   D

177. Keep inventory records   L   ?   D

178. Maintain employee records   L   ?   D

179. Stamp, sort, and distribute mail for an organization   L   ?   D

180. Handle customers' bank transactions   L   ?   D

____ **Page Score for C**

Step 2: Score Your Responses

Do the following to score your responses:

1. **Score the responses on each page.** On each page of responses, go from top to bottom and add the number of "L's you filled in. Then write that number in the "Page Score" box at the bottom of the page. Go on to the next page and do the same there.

2. **Determine your primary interest area.** Which Page Score has your highest score: **R, I, A, S, E**, or **C**? Enter the letter for that personality type in the space below.

    My Primary Personality Type: ____

    You will use your Primary Personality Type *first* to explore college majors. (If two Page Scores are tied for the highest scores or are within 5 points of each other, use both of them for your Primary Personality Type. You are equally divided between two types.)

    * R = Realistic
    * I = Investigative
    * A = Artistic
    * S = Social
    * E = Enterprising
    * C = Conventional

3. **Determine your secondary interest areas.** Which Page Score has your next highest score? Which has your third highest score? Enter the letters for those areas in the spaces below.

    My Secondary Personality Types: ____ ____

    If you do not find many interesting majors that you like using your Primary Personality Type, you can use your Secondary Personality Types to look at more educational options.

Step 3: Find College Majors that Suit Your Personality Type

Start with your Primary Personality Type. Turn to Part III and look at the Best Majors lists for your type. Find lists that suit your particular priorities and see what majors appear there. Don't rule out a major just because the title is not familiar to you.

When you find majors that interest you or that you want to learn more about, turn to Part IV. The descriptions of majors there are grouped by Primary Personality Types and are listed alphabetically within each type. Of course, you can also look at majors that are linked to one of your Secondary Personality Types.

If you want to find majors that *combine* your Primary Personality Type and a Secondary Personality Type, turn to Appendix B. All 57 majors in this book are listed there by their one-, two-, or three-letter RIASEC codes. For example, if your Primary Personality Type is Social and your Secondary Personality Type is Investigative, you would look in Appendix B for the letter S and then for majors coded SI, such as Nursing (R.N. Training), Occupational Therapy, and Graduate Study for College Teaching. This set of majors includes those coded SI_, such as Physical Therapy (SIR) and Speech-Language Pathology and Audiology (SIA).

You may also want to consider majors that combine your Primary Personality Type and a Secondary Personality Type in some other order. To continue the example using SI, you might want to consider majors coded ISR (such as Medicine) or even IRS (such as Dentistry). Using reverse order can be especially helpful if your Primary Personality Type is R or C. Only one major in Appendix B has R as its first code, but 18 others have R as their second or third code. Only two majors in Appendix B have C as their first code, but 16 others have C as their second or third code.

You may discover that you can't find an appealing major in your Primary Personality Type that *also* is coded for one of your Secondary Personality Types. That is not necessarily a problem. John Holland himself has remarked, "You cannot expect a single job to satisfy all aspects of your personality." This is also true for majors. While you're in college, use elective courses to explore interests related to your Secondary Personality Types. Later, when you're in the workforce, use recreational time for the same purpose. At any age, volunteer work can be another outlet for these interests and abilities.

PART III

The Best Majors Lists

This part contains a lot of interesting lists, and it's a good place for you to start using the book. Here are some suggestions for using the lists to explore college majors that may suit your personality type:

❊ The table of contents at the beginning of this book presents a complete listing of the list titles in this section. You can browse the lists or use the table of contents to find those that interest you most.

❊ I gave the lists clear titles, so most require little explanation. I provide comments for each group of lists.

❊ As you review the lists of majors, one or more of the majors may appeal to you enough that you want to seek additional information. As this happens, mark that major (or, if someone else will be using this book, write it on a separate sheet of paper) so that you can look up the description of the major and its related jobs in Part IV.

❊ Keep in mind that all majors in these lists meet my basic criteria for being included in this book, as explained in the introduction. All lists consist of majors that are offered at many colleges and universities, with emphasis on majors leading to jobs with high pay, high growth, or large numbers of openings. These measures are easily quantified and are often presented in lists of best jobs in the newspapers and other media, so I decided they would be useful for evaluating college majors. While earnings, growth, and openings are important, there are other factors to consider in your educational and career planning. Obviously you are considering the personality types that characterize college majors; that's why you're reading this book. Other examples of factors to consider are availability of the major at a nearby college, your qualifications to enter the major (some have high entry requirements), and your comfort level with specific course requirements for the major. Many other factors that may help define the ideal major for you are difficult or impossible to quantify and thus are not used in this book, so you will need to consider the importance of these issues yourself.

❋ All data used to create these lists comes from the U.S. Department of Labor and the Census Bureau. The earnings figures are based on the average annual pay received by full-time workers in jobs related to the major. Because the earnings represent the national averages, actual pay rates can vary greatly by location, amount of previous work experience, and other factors. Figures for projected job growth and job openings are also national averages but can vary by location and industry. Many of the majors can lead to more than one career, and in some cases one career option may have much higher average pay, faster job growth, or more job openings than another option. In these lists I use the average pay and average job growth for *all* the related jobs, using a formula that gives extra weight to the jobs with the largest workforces and that are the most likely career paths for graduates of the majors. I also computed the *total* number of annual job openings for all related jobs, again with the assumption that some jobs are more likely career paths than others. The descriptions of majors in Part IV list the average figures for earnings, job growth, and job openings for *each* related job.

Some Details on the Lists

The sources of the information I used in constructing these lists are presented in this book's introduction. Here are some additional details on how I created the lists:

❋ Some majors have the same scores for one or more data elements. There was no way to avoid ties between the scores, so simply understand that the difference of a few positions on a list may not mean as much as it seems. For example, all the foreign-language majors (Chinese, French, German, and so forth) are linked to the same job, Interpreters and Translators, so all of these majors are rated identically on all data elements. Therefore, in all of the lists in this section, I ordered these majors alphabetically, and their order has no other significance. If you notice lists that include some but not all of the foreign-language majors, understand that the list is limited to a certain number of majors; Chinese may appear but not Spanish simply because of alphabetical ordering.

❋ One of the majors listed here in Part III, Graduate Study for College Teaching, represents a wide variety of subject areas. In reality, *all* of the majors listed here can be studied at the graduate level as preparation for a postsecondary teaching career. For example, you might get a bachelor's degree in Civil Engineering and then get a master's and perhaps a doctorate in the same field in order to land a job teaching the subject in college. However, only a very small fraction of people who major in Civil Engineering have college teaching as their career goal. Therefore, when I matched college majors with the jobs they prepare for, I decided it would be misleading to match *every* major to a postsecondary teaching career. Instead, I created a generic major called Graduate Study for College Teaching and linked it to the job Postsecondary Teachers. In Part IV you can see a description of this major and its related job. You'll also find descriptions of five majors (such as Humanities) that are not included in the Part III lists because they often are studied with the goal of postgraduate study—either in the same field as preparation for college teaching or in another field, such as Medicine or Law, as preparation for a profession.

Here is a reminder of the personality type that each code letter represents: R=Realistic, I=Investigative, A=Artistic, S=Social, E=Enterprising, C=Conventional.

Best Majors Overall for Each Personality Type: Majors Related to Jobs with the Highest Pay, Fastest Growth, and Most Openings

The four sets of lists that follow are the most important lists in this book. The first set of lists presents, for each personality type, the majors related to jobs with the highest combined scores for pay, growth, and number of openings. These are very appealing lists because they represent majors that prepare you for jobs with the very highest quantifiable measures from our labor market. The 51 majors in these six lists, plus six related majors, are the ones that are described in detail in Part IV.

The three additional sets of lists present, for each personality type, majors linked to jobs with the highest scores in each of three measures: annual earnings, projected percentage growth, and largest number of openings.

The 10 Best Majors for Each Personality Type

These are the lists that most people want to see first. For each personality type, you can see the majors that prepare for jobs with the highest overall combined ratings for earnings, projected growth, and number of openings. (The section in the introduction called "How the Majors in This Book Were Selected" explains in detail how I linked majors to jobs and rated the majors so I could assemble this list.)

Although the majors on each list share an affinity with one personality type, you'll notice some variety in the majors. This is particularly true for the majors on the Realistic and Conventional lists, because these majors have R or C as their **first or second** RIASEC code. For example, the top-ranked major on the Realistic list, Computer Engineering, is coded IRC, which means that Realistic is actually its secondary type; Investigative is its primary type. (As the introduction explains, I used this approach because otherwise this list would contain only six majors.)

A look at one list will clarify how I ordered the majors—take the Social list as an example. Nursing (R.N. Training) was linked to an occupation with outstanding figures for income, growth, and job openings: Registered Nurses. This highly promising linked job caused Nursing (R.N. Training) to be the major with the best total score, and it is at the top of the list. The other majors follow in descending order based on their total scores. Several majors had tied scores (for example, Graduate Study for College Teaching and Health Information Systems Administration) and are simply listed one after another, so there are often only very small or even no differences between the scores of majors that are near each other on the list. All the other lists of Social majors in this book consist of majors selected from this list. You can find descriptions for each of these majors in Part IV, beginning on page 91.

Remember that the figures for earnings, growth, and job openings are based on specific related jobs that are entered by many graduates of these majors; however, some graduates enter nontraditional jobs (for example, an English major who goes into advertising), so the figures do not indicate the economic rewards of *all* graduates of these majors. Figures on earnings in related jobs are sometimes limited; see the comments that precede the next set of lists.

The 10 Best Realistic Majors

Major	Annual Earnings of Related Jobs	Percent Growth of Related Jobs	Annual Openings of Related Jobs	Personality Types
1. Computer Engineering	$92,000	23.1%	10,109	IRC
2. Civil Engineering	$83,000	21.7%	12,678	RIC
3. Dentistry	$142,000	15.3%	5,180	IRS
4. Environmental Science	$59,000	28.0%	5,470	IRC
5. Veterinary Medicine	$81,000	32.9%	3,020	IR
6. Oceanography	$90,000	17.0%	2,085	IR
7. Geophysics	$90,000	17.0%	2,042	IR
8. Microbiology	$83,000	21.6%	1,988	IR
9. Aeronautical/Aerospace Engineering	$103,000	8.7%	3,448	IRE
10. Geology	$85,000	17.3%	1,858	IR

Note: Because few majors have Realistic as their primary personality type, this list includes majors with Realistic as their secondary type.

The 10 Best Investigative Majors

Major	Annual Earnings of Related Jobs	Percent Growth of Related Jobs	Annual Openings of Related Jobs	Personality Types
1. Medicine	$164,000	21.8%	26,050	ISR
2. Computer Science	$99,000	23.6%	7,023	ICR
3. Computer Engineering	$92,000	23.1%	10,109	IRC
4. Pharmacy	$109,000	17.0%	10,580	ICS
5. Biochemistry	$82,000	36.9%	3,498	IAR
6. Dentistry	$142,000	15.3%	5,180	IRS
7. Optometry	$96,000	24.4%	2,010	ISR
8. Veterinary Medicine	$81,000	32.9%	3,020	IR
9. Environmental Science	$59,000	28.0%	5,470	IRC
10. Economics	$65,000	24.1%	4,081	IEC

The 10 Best Artistic Majors

Major	Annual Earnings of Related Jobs	Percent Growth of Related Jobs	Annual Openings of Related Jobs	Personality Types
1. Architecture	$86,000	13.8%	5,898	AIE
2. Classics	$41,000	22.4%	2,452	AS
3. Graphic Design, Commercial Art, and Illustration	$46,000	12.0%	13,796	ARE
4. Chinese	$41,000	22.2%	2,340	AS
5. French	$41,000	22.2%	2,340	AS
6. German	$41,000	22.2%	2,340	AS
7. Interior Design	$46,000	19.4%	3,590	AE
8. Modern Foreign Language	$41,000	22.2%	2,340	AS
9. Russian	$41,000	22.2%	2,340	AS
10. Spanish	$41,000	22.2%	2,340	AS

Majors 4, 5, 6, 8, 9, and 10 share a link to a job with 2,340 job openings.

The 10 Best Social Majors

Major	Annual Earnings of Related Jobs	Percent Growth of Related Jobs	Annual Openings of Related Jobs	Personality Types
1. Nursing (R.N. Training)	$64,000	22.2%	103,900	SI
2. Physical Therapy	$74,000	30.3%	7,860	SIR
3. Physician Assisting	$84,000	39.0%	4,280	SIR
4. Communications Studies/Speech	$52,000	23.3%	14,170	SAE
5. Graduate Study for College Teaching	$63,000	15.1%	55,290	SI
6. Occupational Therapy	$70,000	25.6%	4,580	SI
7. Elementary Education	$51,000	15.8%	59,650	SAC
8. Chiropractic	$68,000	19.5%	1,820	SIR
9. Speech-Language Pathology and Audiology	$65,000	18.7%	4,525	SIA
10. Physical Education	$44,000	16.0%	23,020	SE

The 10 Best Enterprising Majors

Major	Annual Earnings of Related Jobs	Percent Growth of Related Jobs	Annual Openings of Related Jobs	Personality Types
1. Law	$112,000	13.0%	24,392	EI
2. Business Management	$116,000	2.1%	28,909	EC
3. Bioengineering	$108,000	23.2%	2,708	EIR
4. Management Information Systems	$106,000	14.6%	11,712	ECI
5. International Business	$121,000	−0.7%	23,805	ECS
6. Human Resources Management	$49,000	26.7%	12,528	ESC
7. Public Relations	$54,000	23.1%	13,762	EAS
8. Biology	$115,000	15.5%	2,010	EI
9. Botany	$115,000	15.5%	2,010	EI
10. Health Information Systems Administration	$82,000	16.0%	9,940	ESC

Majors 8 and 9 share links to two jobs with 2,010 openings.

The 10 Best Conventional Majors

Major	Annual Earnings of Related Jobs	Percent Growth of Related Jobs	Annual Openings of Related Jobs	Personality Types
1. Pharmacy	$109,000	17.0%	10,580	ICS
2. Computer Science	$99,000	23.6%	7,023	ICR
3. Accounting	$60,000	21.5%	50,818	CEI
4. Management Information Systems	$106,000	14.6%	11,712	ECI
5. Business Management	$116,000	2.1%	28,909	EC
6. Finance	$81,000	16.1%	14,512	CEI
7. International Business	$121,000	–0.7%	23,805	ECS
8. Marketing	$107,000	12.2%	7,639	EC
9. Public Administration	$95,000	–0.1%	53,888	ECS
10. Actuarial Science	$87,000	21.4%	1,000	CIE

Note: Because few majors have Conventional as their primary personality type, this list includes majors with Conventional as their secondary type.

The 5 Majors with the Best Income Potential for Each Personality Type

On the following six lists you'll find, for each personality type, the five majors meeting my criteria for this book that have the best income potential. These are appealing lists, for obvious reasons.

If you compare these six lists, you may notice that some personality types have better income possibilities than others. For example, the five Enterprising majors listed here are linked to jobs that command much higher incomes than those linked to the five Artistic majors listed here. Keep in mind that these figures are only averages; there are a few graduates of Interior Design programs who are earning more than some graduates of a Medical program, whereas other Interior Design grads are barely scraping by. The average earnings for Physicians and Surgeons are probably somewhat *higher* than the figures given here, because five of the eight linked jobs (for example, Anesthesiologists) have earnings that the Department of Labor reports as "more than $166,400." I had to use the figure of $166,400 to compute the averages, but for five of the linked jobs, the actual earnings are probably considerably higher.

In conclusion, if a major interests you, look at its description in Part IV and note the earnings figures for the related jobs, paying special attention to those jobs you'd *actually consider* as career goals. Also remember what I said earlier about how earnings can vary by region of the country, by amount of experience, and because of many other factors.

The 5 Realistic Majors with the Best Income Potential

Major	Annual Earnings of Related Jobs	Personality Types
1. Dentistry	$142,000	IRS
2. Aeronautical/Aerospace Engineering	$103,000	IRE
3. Computer Engineering	$92,000	IRC
4. Geophysics	$90,000	IR
5. Oceanography	$90,000	IR

The 5 Investigative Majors with the Best Income Potential

Major	Annual Earnings of Related Jobs	Personality Types
1. Medicine	$164,000	ISR
2. Dentistry	$142,000	IRS
3. Pharmacy	$109,000	ICS
4. Computer Science	$99,000	ICR
5. Optometry	$96,000	ISR

Earnings for Job 1 are based on limited data about related occupations and are probably too low.

The 5 Artistic Majors with the Best Income Potential

Major	Annual Earnings of Related Jobs	Personality Types
1. Architecture	$86,000	AIE
2. Graphic Design, Commercial Art, and Illustration	$46,000	ARE
3. Interior Design	$46,000	AE
4. German	$41,000	AS
5. Modern Foreign Language	$41,000	AS

The 5 Social Majors with the Best Income Potential

Major	Annual Earnings of Related Jobs	Personality Types
1. Physician Assisting	$84,000	SIR
2. Physical Therapy	$74,000	SIR
3. Occupational Therapy	$70,000	SI
4. Chiropractic	$68,000	SIR
5. Speech-Language Pathology and Audiology	$65,000	SIA

The 5 Enterprising Majors with the Best Income Potential

Major	Annual Earnings of Related Jobs	Personality Types
1. International Business	$121,000	ECS
2. Business Management	$116,000	EC
3. Biology	$115,000	EI
4. Botany	$115,000	EI
5. Law	$112,000	EI

The 5 Conventional Majors with the Best Income Potential

Major	Annual Earnings of Related Jobs	Personality Types
1. International Business	$121,000	ECS
2. Business Management	$116,000	EC
3. Pharmacy	$109,000	ICS
4. Marketing	$107,000	EC
5. Management Information Systems	$106,000	ECI

The 5 Majors with the Best Job-Growth Potential for Each Personality Type

From the six lists of 10 majors that met my criteria for this book, these six lists show the five majors for each personality type that are linked to jobs projected to have the highest percentage increase in the numbers of people employed through 2018.

You will notice that just as income opportunities vary among the lists of majors for various personality types, job opportunities also vary. The jobs linked to the top Investigative and Social majors have better opportunities than do the jobs linked to the top majors in the other groups. This is partly because an aging population with greater need for medical and personal care is going to need many workers trained in Investigative and Social subjects. In addition, the kind of work done in Investigative and Social occupations typically cannot be done by computers or by overseas workers.

The 5 Realistic Majors with the Best Job-Growth Potential

Major	Percent Growth of Related Jobs	Personality Types
1. Veterinary Medicine	32.9%	IR
2. Environmental Science	28.0%	IRC
3. Computer Engineering	23.1%	IRC
4. Civil Engineering	21.7%	RIC
5. Microbiology	21.6%	IR

The 5 Investigative Majors with the Best Job-Growth Potential

Major	Percent Growth of Related Jobs	Personality Types
1. Biochemistry	36.9%	IAR
2. Veterinary Medicine	32.9%	IR
3. Environmental Science	28.0%	IRC
4. Optometry	24.4%	ISR
5. Economics	24.1%	IEC

The 5 Artistic Majors with the Best Job-Growth Potential

Major	Percent Growth of Related Jobs	Personality Types
1. Classics	22.4%	AS
2. Chinese	22.2%	AS
3. French	22.2%	AS
4. German	22.2%	AS
5. Spanish	22.2%	AS

The 5 Social Majors with the Best Job-Growth Potential

Major	Percent Growth of Related Jobs	Personality Types
1. Physician Assisting	39.0%	SIR
2. Physical Therapy	30.3%	SIR
3. Occupational Therapy	25.6%	SI
4. Communications Studies/Speech	23.3%	SAE
5. Nursing (R.N. Training)	22.2%	SI

The 5 Enterprising Majors with the Best Job-Growth Potential

Major	Percent Growth of Related Jobs	Personality Types
1. Human Resources Management	26.7%	ESC
2. Bioengineering	23.2%	EIR
3. Public Relations	23.1%	EAS
4. Health Information Systems Administration	16.0%	ESC
5. Biology	15.5%	EI

The 5 Conventional Majors with the Best Job-Growth Potential

Major	Percent Growth of Related Jobs	Personality Types
1. Computer Science	23.6%	ICR
2. Accounting	21.5%	CEI
3. Actuarial Science	21.4%	CIE
4. Pharmacy	17.0%	ICS
5. Finance	16.1%	CEI

The 5 Majors with the Best Job-Opening Potential for Each Personality Type

From the six lists of 10 majors that met my criteria for this book, these six lists show the five majors for each personality type whose related occupations are projected to have the largest number of job openings per year through 2018.

Majors linked to jobs with many openings present several advantages that may be attractive to you. Because there are many openings, these jobs can be easier to obtain, particularly when you first enter the job market after completing your major. These majors may also create more opportunities for you to move from one employer to another with relative ease. Though a few of the majors lead to jobs with unimpressive pay, most lead to jobs that pay quite well and can provide good long-term career opportunities or the ability to move up to more responsible roles.

It is interesting that the top majors in the Artistic list are linked to jobs in applied arts. This field is where the most Artistic job openings will be, rather than in the fine or performing arts, where keen competition for jobs is the rule. The three personality types with the highest figures for job openings are Social, Conventional, and Enterprising, reflecting the many job opportunities in the health-care and business fields.

The 5 Realistic Majors with the Best Job-Opening Potential

Major	Total Annual Openings of Related Jobs	Personality Types
1. Civil Engineering	12,678	RIC
2. Computer Engineering	10,109	IRC
3. Environmental Science	5,470	IRC
4. Dentistry	5,180	IRS
5. Aeronautical/Aerospace Engineering	3,448	IRE

The 5 Investigative Majors with the Best Job-Opening Potential

Major	Total Annual Openings of Related Jobs	Personality Types
1. Medicine	26,050	ISR
2. Pharmacy	10,580	ICS
3. Computer Engineering	10,109	IRC
4. Computer Science	7,023	ICR
5. Environmental Science	5,470	IRC

The 5 Artistic Majors with the Best Job-Opening Potential

Major	Total Annual Openings of Related Jobs	Personality Types
1. Graphic Design, Commercial Art, and Illustration	13,796	ARE
2. Architecture	5,898	AIE
3. Interior Design	3,590	AE
4. Classics	2,452	AS
5. Chinese	2,340	AS

Major 5 and five other majors not included in this list share a link to a job with 2,340 openings.

The 5 Social Majors with the Best Job-Opening Potential

Major	Total Annual Openings of Related Jobs	Personality Types
1. Nursing (R.N. Training)	103,900	SI
2. Elementary Education	59,650	SAC
3. Graduate Study for College Teaching	55,290	SI
4. Physical Education	23,020	SE
5. Communications Studies/Speech	14,170	SAE

The 5 Enterprising Majors with the Best Job-Opening Potential

Major	Total Annual Openings of Related Jobs	Personality Types
1. Business Management	28,909	EC
2. Law	24,392	EI
3. International Business	23,805	ECS
4. Public Relations	13,762	EAS
5. Human Resources Management	12,528	ESC

The 5 Conventional Majors with the Best Job-Opening Potential

Major	Total Annual Openings of Related Jobs	Personality Types
1. Public Administration	53,888	ECS
2. Accounting	50,818	CEI
3. Business Management	28,909	EC
4. International Business	23,805	ECS
5. Finance	14,512	CEI

Best Majors Lists by Demographic

I decided it would be interesting to include lists in this section that feature majors linked to jobs in which different types of people dominate. For example, what majors are associated with jobs that have the highest percentage of male workers? I'm not saying that men should consider these majors over others, but it is interesting information to know.

In some cases, the lists can give you ideas for majors to consider that you might otherwise overlook. For example, perhaps women should consider some majors that prepare for jobs that traditionally have high percentages of men in them. Although these are not obvious ways of using these lists, the lists may give you some good ideas about majors to consider. The lists may also help you identify majors that work well for others in your situation—for example, majors that lead to plentiful opportunities for self-employment, if that is something you want to do at this stage of your career.

All of the lists in this section were created using a similar process. For each personality type, I sorted the 10 best majors according to a demographic criterion and discarded those whose related jobs did not have a high percentage of that criterion. For example, I sorted the majors based on the percentage of female workers in related jobs from highest to lowest percentage and discarded those with a figure less than 60 percent. I then ranked this subset of majors according to the usual economic criteria applied to related jobs—income, job growth, and job openings.

I used the same basic process for all six personality types and for five demographic characteristics (self-employed, urban, rural, women, and men). Some lists are much shorter than others because few majors met the criteria I set for them. For example, I found only one Conventional major related to jobs with a high percentage of women. The lists based on demographic characteristics are very interesting, and I hope you find them helpful.

Best Majors Related to Jobs with a High Percentage of Self-Employed Workers

About 8 percent of all working people are self-employed. Although you may think of the self-employed as having similar jobs, they actually work in an enormous range of situations, fields, and work environments that you may not have considered.

However, only 24 of the best college majors—and, from this group, only one Realistic major—are linked to jobs with an above-average percentage of self-employed workers.

In this set of lists, the fact that a major appears here at all is more important than the rank of the major on the list, because the figures for earnings used to sort the list are especially unreliable. The survey that the figures are based on *does not include self-employed workers,* so the median earnings for self-employed workers in these occupations may be significantly higher or lower.

The following lists contain the best majors linked to jobs in which more than 8 percent of the workers are self-employed.

Best Realistic Majors Related to Jobs with a High Percentage of Self-Employed Workers

Major	Percentage of Self-Employed Workers in Related Jobs	Annual Earnings of Related Jobs	Percent Growth of Related Jobs	Annual Openings of Related Jobs	Personality Types
1. Dentistry	28.0%	$142,000	15.3%	5,180	IRS

Best Investigative Majors Related to Jobs with a High Percentage of Self-Employed Workers

Major	Percentage of Self-Employed Workers in Related Jobs	Annual Earnings of Related Jobs	Percent Growth of Related Jobs	Annual Openings of Related Jobs	Personality Types
1. Medicine	11.7%	$164,000	21.8%	26,050	ISR
2. Dentistry	28.0%	$142,000	15.3%	5,180	IRS
3. Optometry	24.6%	$96,000	24.4%	2,010	ISR

Best Artistic Majors Related to Jobs with a High Percentage of Self-Employed Workers

Major	Percentage of Self-Employed Workers in Related Jobs	Annual Earnings of Related Jobs	Percent Growth of Related Jobs	Annual Openings of Related Jobs	Personality Types
1. Classics	25.4%	$41,000	22.4%	2,452	AS
2. Chinese	26.1%	$41,000	22.2%	2,340	AS
3. French	26.1%	$41,000	22.2%	2,340	AS
4. German	26.1%	$41,000	22.2%	2,340	AS
5. Spanish	26.1%	$41,000	22.2%	2,340	AS

Majors 2, 3, 4, and 5 and two other majors not included in this list share a link to a job with 2,340 openings.

Best Social Majors Related to Jobs with a High Percentage of Self-Employed Workers

Major	Percentage of Self-Employed Workers in Related Jobs	Annual Earnings of Related Jobs	Percent Growth of Related Jobs	Annual Openings of Related Jobs	Personality Types
1. Physical Therapy	8.0%	$74,000	30.3%	7,860	SIR
2. Communications Studies/Speech	8.0%	$52,000	23.3%	14,170	SAE
3. Chiropractic	44.5%	$68,000	19.5%	1,820	SIR
4. Speech-Language Pathology and Audiology	8.8%	$65,000	18.7%	4,525	SIA

Best Enterprising Majors Related to Jobs with a High Percentage of Self-Employed Workers

Major	Percentage of Self-Employed Workers in Related Jobs	Annual Earnings of Related Jobs	Percent Growth of Related Jobs	Annual Openings of Related Jobs	Personality Types
1. Business Management	12.4%	$116,000	2.1%	28,909	EC
2. Law	26%	$112,000	25.9%	24,392	EI
3. International Business	10.8%	$121,000	−0.7%	23,805	ECS

Best Conventional Majors Related to Jobs with a High Percentage of Self-Employed Workers

Major	Percentage of Self-Employed Workers in Related Jobs	Annual Earnings of Related Jobs	Percent Growth of Related Jobs	Annual Openings of Related Jobs	Personality Types
1. Accounting	7.9%	$60,000	21.5%	50,818	CEI
2. Business Management	12.4%	$116,000	2.1%	28,909	EC
3. International Business	10.8%	$121,000	−0.7%	23,805	ECS

Best Majors Related to Jobs with a High Percentage of Urban Workers

Some people have a strong preference for an urban setting. They want to live and work where there's more energy and excitement, more access to the arts, more diversity, more really good restaurants, and better public transportation. On the other hand, some prefer the open spaces, closeness to nature, quiet, and inexpensive housing of rural locations. If you're strongly attracted to either setting, you'll be interested in the following lists.

I identified the majors linked to jobs for which 60 percent or more of the workforce is located in the 38 most populous metropolitan areas of the United States. (This means the total workforce, not just those with a college education.) These 38 metro areas—the most populous 10 percent of all U.S. metro areas, according to the Census Bureau—consist primarily of built-up communities, unlike smaller metro areas, which consist of a core city surrounded by a lot of countryside. In the following lists of majors related to urban jobs, you'll see a figure called the "urban ratio" for each major. This figure is based on the percentage of the total U.S. workforce for the related jobs that is located in those 38 huge metro areas. When more than one job is linked to the major, the figure is an average for all the jobs, weighted by the usual factors: the size of the workforce and its likelihood as a career outcome.

The Census Bureau also identifies 173 nonmetropolitan areas—areas that have no city of 50,000 people and a total population of less than 100,000. I identified the majors related to jobs for which 6 percent or more of the total U.S. workforce is located in these nonmetropolitan areas. In the following lists of majors related to rural jobs, you'll see a figure called the "rural ratio" that represents the average percentage (again, weighted) of the total U.S. workforce for the jobs that are located in nonmetropolitan areas.

You'll find a few majors, such as Accounting and Human Resources Management, that appear linked to both urban *and* rural jobs. These jobs are well represented in all kinds of communities, so if your major leads you to one of these jobs and you tire of either the urban or the rural lifestyle, you can probably relocate to the opposite setting and still find job opportunities.

Both lists are ordered by the usual three economic measures: earnings, growth, and openings.

Best Realistic Majors Related to Jobs Employing 60 Percent or More Urban Workers

Major	Urban Ratio of Related Jobs	Annual Earnings of Related Jobs	Percent Growth of Related Jobs	Annual Openings of Related Jobs	Personality Types
1. Computer Engineering	59.7%	$92,000	23.1%	10,109	IRC
2. Civil Engineering	61.3%	$83,000	21.7%	12,678	RIC
3. Microbiology	67.0%	$83,000	21.6%	1,988	IR

Best Investigative Majors Related to Jobs Employing 60 Percent or More Urban Workers

Major	Urban Ratio of Related Jobs	Annual Earnings of Related Jobs	Percent Growth of Related Jobs	Annual Openings of Related Jobs	Personality Types
1. Computer Science	71.3%	$99,000	23.6%	7,023	ICR
2. Computer Engineering	59.7%	$92,000	23.1%	10,109	IRC
3. Biochemistry	72.4%	$82,000	36.9%	3,498	IAR
4. Economics	70.1%	$65,000	24.1%	4,081	IEC

Best Artistic Majors Related to Jobs Employing 60 Percent or More Urban Workers

Major	Urban Ratio of Related Jobs	Annual Earnings of Related Jobs	Percent Growth of Related Jobs	Annual Openings of Related Jobs	Personality Types
1. Architecture	70.2%	$86,000	13.8%	5,898	AIE
2. Graphic Design, Commercial Art, and Illustration	64.7%	$46,000	12.0%	13,796	ARE
3. Interior Design	69.3%	$46,000	19.4%	3,590	AE

Best Social Majors Related to Jobs
Employing 60 Percent or More Urban Workers

Major	Urban Ratio of Related Jobs	Annual Earnings of Related Jobs	Percent Growth of Related Jobs	Annual Openings of Related Jobs	Personality Types
1. Communications Studies/Speech	65.5%	$52,000	23.3%	14,170	SAE

Best Enterprising Majors Related to Jobs
Employing 60 Percent or More Urban Workers

Major	Urban Ratio of Related Jobs	Annual Earnings of Related Jobs	Percent Growth of Related Jobs	Annual Openings of Related Jobs	Personality Types
1. Bioengineering	63.6%	$108,000	23.2%	2,708	EIR
2. Biology	59.9%	$115,000	15.5%	2,010	EI
3. Botany	59.9%	$115,000	15.5%	2,010	EI
4. Human Resources Management	62.1%	$49,000	26.7%	12,528	ESC
5. Law	71.2%	$112,000	13.0%	24,392	EI
6. Public Relations	65.3%	$54,000	23.1%	13,762	EAS
7. Management Information Systems	71.3%	$106,000	14.6%	11,712	ECI

Majors 2 and 3 share links to two jobs with 2,010 openings.

Best Conventional Majors Related to Jobs Employing 60 Percent or More Urban Workers

Major	Urban Ratio of Related Jobs	Annual Earnings of Related Jobs	Percent Growth of Related Jobs	Annual Openings of Related Jobs	Personality Types
1. Accounting	63.2%	$60,000	21.5%	50,818	CEI
2. Computer Science	71.3%	$99,000	23.6%	7,023	ICR
3. Management Information Systems	71.3%	$106,000	14.6%	11,712	ECI
4. Finance	70.6%	$81,000	16.1%	14,512	CEI
5. Marketing	70.0%	$107,000	12.2%	7,639	EC
6. Actuarial Science	69.1%	$87,000	21.4%	1,000	CIE

Best Majors Related to Jobs with a High Percentage of Rural Workers

If the rural lifestyle appeals to you, you may want to consider the majors in the following six lists. The introduction to the preceding six lists explains how the following lists were created.

Best Realistic Majors Related to Jobs Employing 6 Percent or More Rural Workers

Major	Rural Ratio of Related Jobs	Annual Earnings of Related Jobs	Percent Growth of Related Jobs	Annual Openings of Related Jobs	Personality Types
1. Civil Engineering	6.7%	$83,000	21.7%	12,678	RIC
2. Dentistry	8.4%	$142,000	15.3%	5,180	IRS
3. Environmental Science	7.1%	$59,000	28.0%	5,470	IRC
4. Veterinary Medicine	12.2%	$81,000	32.9%	3,020	IR

Best Investigative Majors Related to Jobs Employing 6 Percent or More Rural Workers

Major	Rural Ratio of Related Jobs	Annual Earnings of Related Jobs	Percent Growth of Related Jobs	Annual Openings of Related Jobs	Personality Types
1. Medicine	6.3%	$164,000	21.8%	26,050	ISR
2. Pharmacy	13.3%	$109,000	17.0%	10,580	ICS
3. Environmental Science	7.1%	$59,000	28.0%	5,470	IRC
4. Veterinary Medicine	12.2%	$81,000	32.9%	3,020	IR
5. Dentistry	8.4%	$142,000	15.3%	5,180	IRS
6. Optometry	9.7%	$96,000	24.4%	2,010	ISR

Best Artistic Majors Related to Jobs Employing 6 Percent or More Rural Workers

Major	Rural Ratio of Related Jobs	Annual Earnings of Related Jobs	Percent Growth of Related Jobs	Annual Openings of Related Jobs	Personality Types
1. Graphic Design, Commercial Art, and Illustration	6.6%	$46,000	6.6%	13,796	ARE

Best Social Majors Related to Jobs Employing 6 Percent or More Rural Workers

Major	Rural Ratio of Related Jobs	Annual Earnings of Related Jobs	Percent Growth of Related Jobs	Annual Openings of Related Jobs	Personality Types
1. Physical Therapy	11.7%	$74,000	30.3%	7,860	SIR
2. Physician Assisting	10.3%	$84,000	39.0%	4,280	SIR
3. Occupational Therapy	9.6%	$70,000	25.6%	4,580	SI
4. Communications Studies/Speech	6.6%	$52,000	23.3%	14,170	SAE
5. Elementary Education	16.8%	$51,000	15.8%	59,650	SAC
6. Chiropractic	8.1%	$68,000	19.5%	1,820	SIR
7. Physical Education	15.8%	$44,000	16.0%	23,020	SE
8. Speech-Language Pathology and Audiology	12.5%	$65,000	18.7%	4,525	SIA

Best Enterprising Majors Related to Jobs Employing 6 Percent or More Rural Workers

Major	Rural Ratio of Related Jobs	Annual Earnings of Related Jobs	Percent Growth of Related Jobs	Annual Openings of Related Jobs	Personality Types
1. Business Management	11.2%	$116,000	2.1%	28,909	EC
2. International Business	12.2%	$121,000	–0.7%	23,805	ECS
3. Public Relations	6.8%	$54,000	23.1%	13,762	EAS
4. Human Resources Management	5.5%	$49,000	26.7%	12,528	ESC
5. Health Information Systems Administration	12.8%	$82,000	16.0%	9,940	ESC

Best Conventional Majors Related to Jobs Employing 6 Percent or More Rural Workers

Major	Rural Ratio of Related Jobs	Annual Earnings of Related Jobs	Percent Growth of Related Jobs	Annual Openings of Related Jobs	Personality Types
1. Accounting	7.5%	$60,000	21.5%	50,818	CEI
2. Business Management	11.2%	$116,000	2.1%	28,909	EC
3. Public Administration	11.7%	$95,000	–0.1%	53,888	ECS
4. International Business	12.2%	$121,000	–0.7%	23,805	ECS
5. Pharmacy	13.3%	$109,000	17.0%	10,580	ICS

Best Majors Related to Jobs Employing a High Percentage of Women

To create the six lists that follow, I sorted the 10 best majors for each personality type according to the percentages of women and men in the workforces of the related jobs. These are the most controversial lists in the book, and we JIST editors knew we would create some controversy when we first included similar lists in our *Best Jobs* books. But these lists are not meant to restrict women or men from considering options for majors or jobs—these lists are intended to have exactly the opposite effect. That is, I hope the lists help people see possibilities that they might not otherwise have considered.

The fact is that jobs with high percentages (60 percent or higher) of women or high percentages of men offer good opportunities for both men and women if they want to do one of these jobs. So I suggest that women browse the lists of majors leading to jobs that employ high percentages of men and that men browse the lists of majors leading to jobs with high percentages of women. There are majors among both lists that have high income potential, and women or men who are interested in them should consider them.

It is interesting to compare the two sets of jobs related to the best majors—jobs with the highest percentage of men and jobs with the highest percentage of women—in terms of the economic measures that I use to rank these lists. The male-dominated jobs have much higher average earnings ($108,000) than the female-dominated jobs ($60,000). This is unfortunate but consistent with most other books in the *Best Jobs* series that look at jobs by the sex of the workers. On the other hand, the female-dominated occupations have potential for greater job growth: 21 percent versus 9 percent. The average number of annual job openings projected for the female-dominated occupations is also larger: 18,000 compared to 13,000.

Another reality of the workplace is that Realistic and Investigative jobs tend to be dominated by men, and the Enterprising and Conventional jobs that are dominated by women tend to be service and clerical jobs, for which a college degree is unnecessary. As a result, the following set of lists covers only four of the six RIASEC types: Artistic, Social, Enterprising, and Conventional.

Best Artistic Majors Related to Jobs with a High Percentage of Women

Major	Percentage of Female Workers in Related Jobs	Annual Earnings of Related Jobs	Percent Growth of Related Jobs	Annual Openings of Related Jobs	Personality Types
1. Classics	63.4%	$41,000	22.4%	2,452	AS
2. Chinese	63.5%	$41,000	22.2%	2,340	AS
3. French	63.5%	$41,000	22.2%	2,340	AS
4. German	63.5%	$41,000	22.2%	2,340	AS
5. Modern Foreign Language	63.5%	$41,000	22.2%	2,340	AS
6. Russian	63.5%	$41,000	22.2%	2,340	AS
7. Spanish	63.5%	$41,000	22.2%	2,340	AS

Majors 2, 3, 4, 5, 6, and 7 share a link to a job with 2,340 openings.

Best Social Majors Related to Jobs with a High Percentage of Women

Major	Percentage of Female Workers in Related Jobs	Annual Earnings of Related Jobs	Percent Growth of Related Jobs	Annual Openings of Related Jobs	Personality Types
1. Physical Therapy	59.6%	$74,000	30.3%	7,860	SIR
2. Nursing (R.N. Training)	90.7%	$64,000	22.2%	103,900	SI
3. Occupational Therapy	81.7%	$70,000	25.6%	4,580	SI
4. Elementary Education	81.3%	$51,000	15.8%	59,650	SAC
5. Speech-Language Pathology and Audiology	97.2%	$65,000	18.7%	4,525	SIA

Best Enterprising Majors Related to Jobs with a High Percentage of Women

Major	Percentage of Female Workers in Related Jobs	Annual Earnings of Related Jobs	Percent Growth of Related Jobs	Annual Openings of Related Jobs	Personality Types
1. Human Resources Management	67.2%	$49,000	26.7%	12,528	ESC
2. Health Information Systems Administration	68.9%	$82,000	16.0%	9,940	ESC

Best Conventional Majors Related to Jobs with a High Percentage of Women

Major	Percentage of Female Workers in Related Jobs	Annual Earnings of Related Jobs	Percent Growth of Related Jobs	Annual Openings of Related Jobs	Personality Types
1. Accounting	60.9%	$60,000	21.5%	50,818	CEI

Best Majors Related to Jobs Employing a High Percentage of Men

If you have not already read the introduction to the previous group of lists, Best Majors Related to Jobs with a High Percentage of Women, consider doing so. Much of the discussion there applies to these lists as well. The previous set of lists includes no jobs for the Realistic and Investigative personality types, and the following set of lists includes only one job each for the Artistic and Social types. This simply reflects the realities of the jobs that attract female and male college graduates, respectively.

I did not include these groups of lists with the assumption that men should consider only majors leading to jobs with high percentages of men or that women should consider only majors leading to jobs with high percentages of women. Instead, these lists are here because I think they are interesting and perhaps helpful in considering nontraditional career options. For example, some men would do very well in and enjoy some jobs that have high percentages of women but may not have considered the associated majors seriously. In a similar way, some women would very much enjoy and do well in some jobs that traditionally have been held by high percentages of men. I hope that these lists help you consider college majors that you previously did not consider seriously because of gender stereotypes.

Best Realistic Majors Related to Jobs with a High Percentage of Men

Major	Percentage of Male Workers in Related Jobs	Annual Earnings of Related Jobs	Percent Growth of Related Jobs	Annual Openings of Related Jobs	Personality Types
1. Computer Engineering	83.2%	$92,000	23.1%	10,109	IRC
2. Civil Engineering	91.6%	$83,000	21.7%	12,678	RIC
3. Environmental Science	67.9%	$59,000	28.0%	5,470	IRC
4. Aeronautical/Aerospace Engineering	89.8%	$103,000	8.7%	3,448	IRE
5. Oceanography	66.5%	$90,000	17.0%	2,085	IR
6. Geophysics	66.4%	$90,000	17.0%	2,042	IR
7. Geology	68.5%	$85,000	17.3%	1,858	IR

Best Investigative Majors Related to Jobs with a High Percentage of Men

Major	Percentage of Male Workers in Related Jobs	Annual Earnings of Related Jobs	Percent Growth of Related Jobs	Annual Openings of Related Jobs	Personality Types
1. Medicine	65.7%	$164,000	21.8%	26,050	ISR
2. Computer Science	74.7%	$99,000	23.6%	7,023	ICR
3. Computer Engineering	83.2%	$92,000	23.1%	10,109	IRC
4. Environmental Science	67.9%	$59,000	28.0%	5,470	IRC
5. Optometry	60.0%	$96,000	24.4%	2,010	ISR

Best Artistic Majors Related to Jobs with a High Percentage of Men

Major	Percentage of Male Workers in Related Jobs	Annual Earnings of Related Jobs	Percent Growth of Related Jobs	Annual Openings of Related Jobs	Personality Types
1. Architecture	79.6%	$86,000	13.8%	5,898	AIE

Best Social Majors Related to Jobs with a High Percentage of Men

Major	Percentage of Male Workers in Related Jobs	Annual Earnings of Related Jobs	Percent Growth of Related Jobs	Annual Openings of Related Jobs	Personality Types
1. Chiropractic	70.0%	$68,000	19.5%	1,820	SIR

Best Enterprising Majors Related to Jobs with a High Percentage of Men

Major	Percentage of Male Workers in Related Jobs	Annual Earnings of Related Jobs	Percent Growth of Related Jobs	Annual Openings of Related Jobs	Personality Types
1. Business Management	71.6%	$116,000	2.1%	28,909	EC
2. Law	62.9%	$112,000	13.0%	24,392	EI
3. International Business	73.5%	$121,000	−0.7%	23,805	ECS
4. Bioengineering	90.5%	$108,000	23.2%	2,708	EIR
5. Management Information Systems	72.6%	$106,000	14.6%	11,712	ECI

Best Conventional Majors Related to Jobs with a High Percentage of Men

Major	Percentage of Male Workers in Related Jobs	Annual Earnings of Related Jobs	Percent Growth of Related Jobs	Annual Openings of Related Jobs	Personality Types
1. Business Management	71.6%	$116,000	2.1%	28,909	EC
2. International Business	73.5%	$121,000	−0.7%	23,805	ECS
3. Management Information Systems	72.6%	$106,000	14.6%	11,712	ECI
4. Computer Science	74.7%	$99,000	23.6%	7,023	ICR
5. Public Administration	71.3%	$95,000	−0.1%	53,888	ECS

Best Majors Related to Jobs at Different Levels of Education

The lists in this section organize the best majors associated with all six personality types into six groups based on the education, training, or experience typically required for entry to related jobs. For each level of preparation, I provide one list that includes *all* related majors—not just the best 5 or 10, and not just those related to one personality type. Nevertheless, the list identifies the personality type or types for each major, and the majors are ranked by their total combined score for the earnings, growth, and number of openings for all related jobs.

These lists can help you when you plan your education. For example, you might be thinking about a particular college major because the expected pay is very good, but the lists may help you identify a major that interests you more and offers even better potential for the same general educational requirements.

You may notice that many majors appear in more than one list. These double listings occur when a major is related to two or more jobs that require different levels of education. For example, Business Management appears in the list for the bachelor's degree because it is linked to Construction Managers and to two other jobs at that level, and it also appears in the list for work experience plus degree because it is linked to Sales Managers and to three other jobs at that level. Law appears on the list for the bachelor's degree because many people who work as Arbitrators, Mediators, and Conciliators have law degrees, but many others enter the occupation with only a suitable bachelor's.

Best Majors Related to Jobs that Require Long-Term On-the-Job Training

Eight of the 51 majors covered in Part 3 are linked to occupations that require long-term on-the-job training. Seven of these majors are in languages and are linked to Interpreters and Translators; the eighth major is Physical Education, which is linked to Coaches and Scouts. For some workers in these fields, training alone would be sufficient for getting a job. This might be the case for someone who grew up speaking two languages or who had a lot of experience playing a sport. On the other hand, about half of the people who enter these occupations are trained *after* earning a bachelor's degree, often in a related major. As in all the lists, the RIASEC types of the majors are represented by their initials because the full names would take up too much space.

The following list shows the eight majors linked to jobs requiring long-term on-the-job training.

Best Majors Related to Jobs that Require Long-Term On-the-Job Training

Major	Annual Earnings of Related Jobs	Percent Growth of Related Jobs	Annual Openings of Related Jobs	Personality Types
1. Classics	$41,000	22.4%	2,452	AS
2. Chinese	$41,000	22.2%	2,340	AS
3. French	$41,000	22.2%	2,340	AS
4. German	$41,000	22.2%	2,340	AS
5. Modern Foreign Language	$41,000	22.2%	2,340	AS
6. Russian	$41,000	22.2%	2,340	AS
7. Spanish	$41,000	22.2%	2,340	AS
8. Physical Education	$44,000	16.0%	23,020	SE

Majors 2, 3, 4, 5, 6, and 7 share a link to a job with 2,340 openings.

Best Majors Related to Jobs that Require a Bachelor's Degree

Of the 51 majors that appear on the lists in this book, 19 are linked to jobs that most commonly require a bachelor's degree. A bachelor's degree usually requires 120 to 130 semester hours to complete. A full-time student usually takes four to five years to complete a bachelor's degree, depending on the complexity of courses. Traditionally, people have thought of the bachelor's degree as a four-year degree. Some bachelor's degrees—such as the Bachelor of Architecture—are considered a first professional degree and take five or more years to complete.

The following list shows the majors linked to jobs requiring the bachelor's degree. Although the personality types for these jobs include the Conventional and Enterprising types most frequently, all of the RIASEC types are represented at least once among these majors.

Best Majors Related to Jobs that Require a Bachelor's Degree

Major	Annual Earnings of Related Jobs	Percent Growth of Related Jobs	Annual Openings of Related Jobs	Personality Types
1. Law	$112,000	13.0%	24,392	EI
2. Business Management	$116,000	2.1%	28,909	EC
3. Computer Science	$99,000	23.6%	7,023	ICR
4. Accounting	$60,000	21.5%	50,818	CEI
5. Bioengineering	$108,000	23.2%	2,708	EIR
6. Communications Studies/Speech	$52,000	23.3%	14,170	SAE
7. Computer Engineering	$92,000	23.1%	10,109	IRC
8. Finance	$81,000	16.1%	14,512	CEI
9. Public Administration	$95,000	–0.1%	53,888	ECS
10. Civil Engineering	$83,000	21.7%	12,678	RIC
11. Elementary Education	$51,000	15.8%	59,650	SAC
12. Human Resources Management	$49,000	26.7%	12,528	ESC
13. Management Information Systems	$106,000	14.6%	11,712	ECI
14. Economics	$65,000	24.1%	4,081	IEC
15. Public Relations	$54,000	23.1%	13,762	EAS
16. Physical Education	$44,000	16.0%	23,020	SE
17. Architecture	$86,000	13.8%	5,898	AIE
18. Aeronautical/Aerospace Engineering	$103,000	8.7%	3,448	IRE
19. Graphic Design, Commercial Art, and Illustration	$46,000	12.0%	13,796	ARE

Best Majors Related to Jobs that Require Work Experience Plus Degree

Of the 51 best majors, 30 lead to jobs that require some work experience in addition to a bachelor's or master's degree. Most commonly these are managerial jobs. For example, Engineering Managers is a job linked to several engineering majors, but it is seldom an option for new graduates. Instead, the usual entry route is to get a job in engineering following a bachelor's degree in an engineering major, acquire work experience over some years, and then advance to management after demonstrating relevant knowledge and skills in managerial work assignments.

The presence of several managerial jobs causes the Enterprising personality type to dominate this list.

Best Majors Related to Jobs that Require Work Experience Plus Degree

Major	Annual Earnings of Related Jobs	Percent Growth of Related Jobs	Annual Openings of Related Jobs	Personality Types
1. Business Management	$116,000	2.1%	28,909	EC
2. Computer Science	$99,000	23.6%	7,023	ICR
3. Bioengineering	$108,000	23.2%	2,708	EIR
4. Computer Engineering	$92,000	23.1%	10,109	IRC
5. Law	$112,000	13.0%	24,392	EI
6. International Business	$121,000	−0.7%	23,805	ECS
7. Civil Engineering	$83,000	21.7%	12,678	RIC
8. Human Resources Management	$49,000	26.7%	12,528	ESC
9. Management Information Systems	$106,000	14.6%	11,712	ECI
10. Public Administration	$95,000	−0.1%	53,888	ECS
11. Public Relations	$54,000	23.1%	13,762	EAS
12. Biochemistry	$82,000	36.9%	3,498	IAR
13. Biology	$115,000	15.5%	2,010	EI
14. Botany	$115,000	15.5%	2,010	EI
15. Marketing	$107,000	12.2%	7,639	EC
16. Finance	$81,000	16.1%	14,512	CEI
17. Oceanography	$90,000	17.0%	2,085	IR
18. Geophysics	$90,000	17.0%	2,042	IR
19. Health Information Systems Administration	$82,000	16.0%	9,940	ESC
20. Aeronautical/Aerospace Engineering	$103,000	8.7%	3,448	IRE
21. Actuarial Science	$87,000	21.4%	1,000	CIE
22. Architecture	$86,000	13.8%	5,898	AIE
23. Microbiology	$83,000	21.6%	1,988	IR
24. Geology	$85,000	17.3%	1,858	IR

Majors 13 and 14 share links to two jobs with 2,010 openings.

Best Majors Related to Jobs that Require a Master's Degree

Only 10 majors that meet the criteria for this book are linked to jobs that most commonly require a master's degree. This degree usually requires 33 to 60 semester hours beyond the bachelor's degree. An academic master's degree, such as a Master of Arts in Environmental Science, usually requires 30 to 36 hours. A first professional degree in Occupational Therapy usually requires two and one-half years of full-time work, including supervised clinical training. Note that although Physical Therapy currently appears on this list, by 2020 the first professional degree required for this occupation will rise to the doctoral level. The doctorate is also becoming the required credential for Audiologists.

The following list, in which the Social and Investigative types dominate, ranks these 10 majors by the usual three economic criteria.

Best Majors Related to Jobs that Require a Master's Degree				
Major	Annual Earnings of Related Jobs	Percent Growth of Related Jobs	Annual Openings of Related Jobs	Personality Types
1. Physical Therapy	$74,000	30.3%	7,860	SIR
2. Physician Assisting	$84,000	39.0%	4,280	SIR
3. Occupational Therapy	$70,000	25.6%	4,580	SI
4. Environmental Science	$59,000	28.0%	5,470	IRC
5. Economics	$65,000	24.1%	4,081	IEC
6. Oceanography	$90,000	17.0%	2,085	IR
7. Speech-Language Pathology and Audiology	$65,000	18.7%	4,525	SIA
8. Geophysics	$90,000	17.0%	2,042	IR
9. Geology	$85,000	17.3%	1,858	IR
10. Classics	$41,000	22.4%	2,452	AS

Best Majors Related to Jobs that Require a Doctoral Degree

The doctoral degree normally requires two or more years of full-time academic work beyond the bachelor's degree, including writing a dissertation that demonstrates mastery of research methods. Because of this emphasis on research, doctoral-level jobs tend to suit the Investigative personality type, but programs in the sciences often appeal additionally to the Realistic type.

Only five majors that meet the criteria for this book are linked to jobs requiring a doctoral degree. (Speech-Language Pathology and Audiology is included for the sake of Audiologists; as of 2009, 18 states required the doctorate for new Audiologists.) The majors are ranked here by the earnings, job growth, and job openings of related jobs.

Best Majors Related to Jobs that Require a Doctoral Degree

Major	Annual Earnings of Related Jobs	Percent Growth of Related Jobs	Annual Openings of Related Jobs	Personality Types
1. Computer Science	$99,000	23.6%	7,023	ICR
2. Biochemistry	$82,000	36.9%	3,498	IAR
3. Graduate Study for College Teaching	$63,000	15.1%	55,290	SI
4. Microbiology	$83,000	21.6%	1,988	IR
5. Speech-Language Pathology and Audiology	$65,000	18.7%	4,525	SIA

Best Majors Related to Jobs that Require a First Professional Degree

The first professional degree normally requires a minimum of two years of education beyond the bachelor's degree and frequently requires three or more years. Programs that lead to health-care careers teach problem solving at both the theoretical and hands-on levels. As a result, these programs are attractive to people with the Investigative personality type.

Eight majors that meet the criteria for this book are linked to jobs requiring a first professional degree and are ranked here.

Best Majors Related to Jobs that Require a First Professional Degree

Major	Annual Earnings of Related Jobs	Percent Growth of Related Jobs	Annual Openings of Related Jobs	Personality Types
1. Medicine	$164,000	21.8%	26,050	ISR
2. Dentistry	$142,000	15.3%	5,180	IRS
3. Law	$112,000	13.0%	24,392	EI
4. Pharmacy	$109,000	17.0%	10,580	ICS
5. Veterinary Medicine	$81,000	32.9%	3,020	IR
6. Optometry	$96,000	24.4%	2,010	ISR
7. Speech-Language Pathology and Audiology	$65,000	18.7%	4,525	SIA
8. Chiropractic	$68,000	19.5%	1,820	SIR

Best Majors Lists by Verbal and Math Skills

If you have ever applied for admission to a college, you are probably very aware of the verbal and math abilities you demonstrated on a standardized test. But have you thought about the relationship between verbal and math abilities and the different majors that are available in college?

One way to look at that relationship is to compare people's *intended* majors with their verbal and math scores on standardized tests. According to the College Board, the students in the high school class of 2010 who had the highest average scores in the two verbal scales (critical reading and writing) were those who intended to major in Multi/Interdisciplinary Studies; English Language and Literature/Letters; Foreign Languages, Literatures, and Linguistics; Social Sciences; and Liberal Arts and Sciences, General Studies, and Humanities. Those with the highest math SAT scores intended to major in Mathematics and Statistics, Multi/Interdisciplinary Studies, Physical Sciences, Engineering, and Biological and Biomedical Sciences. These findings are not at all surprising (except maybe for the presence of Multi/Interdisciplinary Studies in both lists), because people tend to plan enrollment in majors that seem consistent with their standardized test scores.

Another way to look at these abilities is to consider the verbal and math skills that are required for academic *success* when you're in the major. I don't have access to good data on this for a variety of majors, but you can make some inferences by looking at the Typical Sequence of College Courses listed for each major in Part IV. If you notice several courses related to writing, literature, or public speaking, the major probably requires a high level of verbal ability. For other majors, you may find that the curriculum is rich in mathematical courses.

A third way to consider the relationship of these skills to college majors is to look at the *jobs* that people are preparing for by enrolling in the majors. The O*NET database provides good information about the skill requirements of jobs, and therefore, for each major described in Part IV, you can find the verbal and math skills required by related jobs. I use a scale from 0 to 100, and I compute it using a formula that gives extra weight to the jobs with the largest workforces and the highest likelihood of being a career goal for graduates of the major. (I used the O*NET ratings for knowledge of English Language and Mathematics, because these produced a wider range of values than O*NET's ratings for the equivalent skills.)

Based on these job-related ratings, I compiled the sets of lists that follow. For each of the six personality types, I identified the majors linked to jobs that require a high level of verbal skill. First I list these highly verbal majors ordered by the level of verbal skill. Then I list them ordered by the standard "best jobs" criteria: earnings, job growth, and job openings. Finally, I list the majors linked to jobs that require a *low* level of verbal skills, also ranked by the three economic criteria. Those lists based on verbal skills are followed by another set of lists, similarly ordered, showing the majors linked to jobs that require high and low levels of mathematical skill.

The relationship between skills required in the major and skills required on the job is not exact. Students sometimes complain that they are required to study math at a level that they're never going to use on the job. Conversely, employers sometimes complain that graduates with excellent academic records are deficient in verbal skills they need at work. Nevertheless, the job-related skills are useful to know because one of the chief reasons you enroll in a major is to prepare for a job.

Best Majors Related to Jobs that Require a High Level of Verbal Skills

To rank the majors by their verbal skills, I looked at the ratings that O*NET gives for knowledge of the English language. I represented it as a figure on a scale ranging from 0 to 100 and eliminated all majors linked to jobs scoring lower than 65.

Realistic Majors Related to Jobs that Require the Highest Level of Verbal Skills		
Major	Level of Verbal Skills in Related Jobs	Personality Types
1. Environmental Science	70	IRC
2. Microbiology	70	IR
3. Civil Engineering	66	RIC
4. Aeronautical/Aerospace Engineering	65	IRE

Investigative Majors Related to Jobs that Require the Highest Level of Verbal Skills		
Major	Level of Verbal Skills in Related Jobs	Personality Types
1. Economics	71	IEC
2. Environmental Science	70	IRC
3. Biochemistry	69	IAR
4. Pharmacy	69	ICS
5. Medicine	66	ISR

Artistic Majors Related to Jobs that Require the Highest Level of Verbal Skills

Major	Level of Verbal Skills in Related Jobs	Personality Types
1. Chinese	71	AS
2. Classics	71	AS
3. French	71	AS
4. German	71	AS
5. Modern Foreign Language	71	AS
6. Russian	71	AS
7. Spanish	71	AS

Social Majors Related to Jobs that Require the Highest Level of Verbal Skills

Major	Level of Verbal Skills in Related Jobs	Personality Types
1. Speech-Language Pathology and Audiology	90	SIA
2. Graduate Study for College Teaching	80	SI
3. Communications Studies/Speech	74	SAE
4. Nursing (R.N. Training)	66	SI

Enterprising Majors Related to Jobs that Require the Highest Level of Verbal Skills

Major	Level of Verbal Skills in Related Jobs	Personality Types
1. Law	84	EI
2. Public Relations	74	EAS
3. Health Information Systems Administration	69	ESC
4. Bioengineering	65	EIR
5. Human Resources Management	65	ESC

Conventional Majors Related to Jobs that Require the Highest Level of Verbal Skills

Major	Level of Verbal Skills in Related Jobs	Personality Types
1. Pharmacy	69	ICS
2. Marketing	68	EC
3. Finance	66	CEI

The following lists rank the highly verbal majors by the earnings, job growth, and job openings of related jobs.

Best Realistic Majors Related to Jobs that Require a High Level of Verbal Skills

Major	Level of Verbal Skills in Related Jobs	Annual Earnings of Related Jobs	Percent Growth of Related Jobs	Annual Openings of Related Jobs	Personality Types
1. Civil Engineering	66	$83,000	21.7%	12,678	RIC
2. Environmental Science	70	$59,000	28.0%	5,470	IRC
3. Aeronautical/Aerospace Engineering	65	$103,000	8.7%	3,448	IRE
4. Microbiology	70	$83,000	21.6%	1,988	IR

Best Investigative Majors Related to Jobs that Require a High Level of Verbal Skills

Major	Level of Verbal Skills in Related Jobs	Annual Earnings of Related Jobs	Percent Growth of Related Jobs	Annual Openings of Related Jobs	Personality Types
1. Medicine	66	$164,000	21.8%	26,050	ISR
2. Biochemistry	69	$82,000	36.9%	3,498	IAR
3. Pharmacy	69	$109,000	17.0%	10,580	ICS
4. Environmental Science	70	$59,000	28.0%	5,470	IRC
5. Economics	71	$65,000	24.1%	4,081	IEC

Best Artistic Majors Related to Jobs that Require a High Level of Verbal Skills

Major	Level of Verbal Skills in Related Jobs	Annual Earnings of Related Jobs	Percent Growth of Related Jobs	Annual Openings of Related Jobs	Personality Types
1. Classics	71	$41,000	22.4%	2,452	AS
2. Chinese	71	$41,000	22.2%	2,340	AS
3. French	71	$41,000	22.2%	2,340	AS
4. German	71	$41,000	22.2%	2,340	AS
5. Russian	71	$41,000	22.2%	2,340	AS
6. Modern Foreign Language	71	$41,000	22.2%	2,340	AS
7. Spanish	71	$41,000	22.2%	2,340	AS

Majors 2, 3, 4, 5, 6, and 7 share a link to a job with 2,340 openings.

Best Social Majors Related to Jobs that Require a High Level of Verbal Skills

Major	Level of Verbal Skills in Related Jobs	Annual Earnings of Related Jobs	Percent Growth of Related Jobs	Annual Openings of Related Jobs	Personality Types
1. Nursing (R.N. Training)	66	$64,000	22.2%	103,900	SI
2. Communications Studies/Speech	74	$52,000	23.3%	14,170	SAE
3. Speech-Language Pathology and Audiology	90	$65,000	18.7%	4,525	SIA
4. Graduate Study for College Teaching	80	$63,000	15.1%	55,290	SI

Best Enterprising Majors Related to Jobs that Require a High Level of Verbal Skills

Major	Level of Verbal Skills in Related Jobs	Annual Earnings of Related Jobs	Percent Growth of Related Jobs	Annual Openings of Related Jobs	Personality Types
1. Law	84	$112,000	13.0%	24,392	EI
2. Bioengineering	65	$108,000	23.2%	2,708	EIR
3. Human Resources Management	65	$49,000	26.7%	12,528	ESC
4. Public Relations	74	$54,000	23.1%	13,762	EAS
5. Health Information Systems Administration	69	$82,000	16.0%	9,940	ESC

Best Conventional Majors Related to Jobs that Require a High Level of Verbal Skills

Major	Level of Verbal Skills in Related Jobs	Annual Earnings of Related Jobs	Percent Growth of Related Jobs	Annual Openings of Related Jobs	Personality Types
1. Pharmacy	69	$109,000	17.0%	10,580	ICS
2. Finance	66	$81,000	16.1%	14,512	CEI
3. Marketing	68	$107,000	12.2%	7,639	EC

Best Majors Related to Jobs that Require a Low Level of Verbal Skills

Maybe verbal ability is not one of your strengths, and you'd prefer a major that is compatible with your personality type but requires a relatively low level of verbal skills. To create the following list, I took the majors with a verbal score of less than 60 and ranked them by their economic potential. The results suggest that careers in business or health care may be good choices for people who want to use verbal abilities at a comparatively low level.

Best Majors Related to Jobs that Require a Low Level of Verbal Skills

Major	Level of Verbal Skills in Related Jobs	Annual Earnings of Related Jobs	Percent Growth of Related Jobs	Annual Openings of Related Jobs	Personality Types
1. Business Management	58	$116,000	2.1%	28,909	EC
2. Computer Engineering	58	$92,000	23.1%	10,109	IRC
3. International Business	58	$121,000	–0.7%	23,805	ECS
4. Physical Therapy	59	$74,000	30.3%	7,860	SIR
5. Public Administration	50	$95,000	–0.1%	53,888	ECS
6. Accounting	59	$60,000	21.5%	50,818	CEI
7. Optometry	57	$96,000	24.4%	2,010	ISR
8. Veterinary Medicine	57	$81,000	32.9%	3,020	IR
9. Biology	58	$115,000	15.5%	2,010	EI
10. Botany	58	$115,000	15.5%	2,010	EI
11. Occupational Therapy	56	$70,000	25.6%	4,580	SI
12. Architecture	58	$86,000	13.8%	5,898	AIE
13. Graphic Design, Commercial Art, and Illustration	59	$46,000	12.0%	13,796	ARE

Majors 9 and 10 share links to two jobs with 2,010 openings.

Best Majors Related to Jobs that Require a High Level of Math Skills

All jobs in the O*NET database are rated on knowledge of math, so I was able to use these ratings to assign math skill levels to each of the best majors. I eliminated majors that scored less than 59 on a scale from 0 to 100. This was a lower cutoff level than I used for verbal skills, but I needed to set the bar lower to ensure a reasonable number of majors from each personality type. Even at that level, only one Artistic and one Social major made the cut. The lists consist mostly of majors linked to business, science, and engineering.

Realistic Majors Related to Jobs that Require the Highest Level of Math Skills

Major	Level of Math Skills in Related Jobs	Personality Types
1. Civil Engineering	81	RIC
2. Aeronautical/Aerospace Engineering	76	IRE
3. Geology	72	IR
4. Geophysics	71	IR
5. Oceanography	71	IR
6. Environmental Science	70	IRC
7. Computer Engineering	69	IRC
8. Microbiology	68	IR

Investigative Majors Related to Jobs that Require the Highest Level of Math Skills

Major	Level of Math Skills in Related Jobs	Personality Types
1. Biochemistry	70	IAR
2. Environmental Science	70	IRC
3. Computer Engineering	69	IRC
4. Computer Science	66	ICR
5. Pharmacy	65	ICS
6. Economics	64	IEC
7. Optometry	64	ISR

Artistic Majors Related to Jobs that Require the Highest Level of Math Skills

Major	Level of Math Skills in Related Jobs	Personality Types
1. Architecture	60	AIE

Social Majors Related to Jobs that Require the Highest Level of Math Skills

Major	Level of Math Skills in Related Jobs	Personality Types
1. Graduate Study for College Teaching	60	SI

Enterprising Majors Related to Jobs that Require the Highest Level of Math Skills

Major	Level of Math Skills in Related Jobs	Personality Types
1. Bioengineering	77	EIR
2. Biology	65	EI
3. Botany	65	EI
4. International Business	63	ECS
5. Management Information Systems	63	ECI
6. Business Management	61	EC

Conventional Majors Related to Jobs that Require the Highest Level of Math Skills

Major	Level of Math Skills in Related Jobs	Personality Types
1. Actuarial Science	97	CIE
2. Finance	71	CEI
3. Accounting	67	CEI
4. Computer Science	66	ICR
5. Pharmacy	65	ICS
6. Public Administration	64	ECS
7. International Business	63	ECS
8. Management Information Systems	63	ECI
9. Business Management	61	EC

The following lists rank the highly mathematical majors by the earnings, job growth, and job openings of related jobs.

Best Realistic Majors Related to Jobs that Require a High Level of Math Skills

Major	Level of Math Skills in Related Jobs	Annual Earnings of Related Jobs	Percent Growth of Related Jobs	Annual Openings of Related Jobs	Personality Types
1. Computer Engineering	69	$92,000	23.1%	10,109	IRC
2. Civil Engineering	81	$83,000	21.7%	12,678	RIC
3. Environmental Science	70	$59,000	28.0%	5,470	IRC
4. Aeronautical/Aerospace Engineering	76	$103,000	8.7%	3,448	IRE
5. Oceanography	71	$90,000	17.0%	2,085	IR
6. Geophysics	71	$90,000	17.0%	2,042	IR
7. Microbiology	68	$83,000	21.6%	1,988	IR
8. Geology	72	$85,000	17.3%	1,858	IR

Best Investigative Majors Related to Jobs that Require a High Level of Math Skills

Major	Level of Math Skills in Related Jobs	Annual Earnings of Related Jobs	Percent Growth of Related Jobs	Annual Openings of Related Jobs	Personality Types
1. Pharmacy	65	$109,000	17.0%	10,580	ICS
2. Computer Science	66	$99,000	23.6%	7,023	ICR
3. Biochemistry	70	$82,000	36.9%	3,498	IAR
4. Computer Engineering	69	$92,000	23.1%	10,109	IRC
5. Environmental Science	70	$59,000	28.0%	5,470	IRC
6. Optometry	64	$96,000	24.4%	2,010	ISR
7. Economics	64	$65,000	24.1%	4,081	IEC

Best Artistic Majors Related to Jobs that Require a High Level of Math Skills

Major	Level of Math Skills in Related Jobs	Annual Earnings of Related Jobs	Percent Growth of Related Jobs	Annual Openings of Related Jobs	Personality Types
1. Architecture	60	$86,000	13.8%	5,898	AIE

Best Social Majors Related to Jobs that Require a High Level of Math Skills

Major	Level of Math Skills in Related Jobs	Annual Earnings of Related Jobs	Percent Growth of Related Jobs	Annual Openings of Related Jobs	Personality Types
1. Graduate Study for College Teaching	60	$63,000	15.1%	55,290	SI

Best Enterprising Majors Related to Jobs that Require a High Level of Math Skills

Major	Level of Math Skills in Related Jobs	Annual Earnings of Related Jobs	Percent Growth of Related Jobs	Annual Openings of Related Jobs	Personality Types
1. Business Management	61	$116,000	2.1%	28,909	EC
2. International Business	63	$121,000	–0.7%	23,805	ECS
3. Bioengineering	77	$108,000	23.2%	2,708	EIR
4. Biology	65	$115,000	15.5%	2,010	EI
5. Botany	65	$115,000	15.5%	2,010	EI
6. Management Information Systems	63	$106,000	14.6%	11,712	ECI

Majors 4 and 5 share links to two jobs with 2,010 openings.

Best Conventional Majors Related to Jobs that Require a High Level of Math Skills

Major	Level of Math Skills in Related Jobs	Annual Earnings of Related Jobs	Percent Growth of Related Jobs	Annual Openings of Related Jobs	Personality Types
1. Business Management	61	$116,000	2.1%	28,909	EC
2. Accounting	67	$60,000	21.5%	50,818	CEI
3. Computer Science	66	$99,000	23.6%	7,023	ICR
4. International Business	63	$121,000	–0.7%	23,805	ECS
5. Pharmacy	65	$109,000	17.0%	10,580	ICS

Best Conventional Majors Related to Jobs that Require a High Level of Math Skills

Major	Level of Math Skills in Related Jobs	Annual Earnings of Related Jobs	Percent Growth of Related Jobs	Annual Openings of Related Jobs	Personality Types
6. Public Administration	64	$95,000	–0.1%	53,888	ECS
7. Management Information Systems	63	$106,000	14.6%	11,712	ECI
8. Finance	71	$81,000	16.1%	14,512	CEI
9. Actuarial Science	97	$87,000	21.4%	1,000	CIE

Best Majors Related to Jobs with a Low Level of Math Skills

If you find math uninteresting or too challenging and want to avoid it in your work, the following list may suggest majors that can suit this preference and also fit your personality type. These majors all scored lower than 55 on the scale for mathematical skills, and they are ranked according to the usual economic criteria. The lists are dominated by Artistic, Social, and Enterprising majors.

Don't assume from this list that you can enter every one of these majors without a good background in math or complete them by taking only low-level math courses. Some of these majors typically include courses in statistics or even calculus! However, the *jobs* that these majors usually lead to generally do not require workers to use a high level of math skill.

You may wonder why there can be such a disconnect between course requirements and work tasks. The curriculum developers who design the majors want you to be able to understand the people you'll work with. In many jobs, you do not use a lot of math but work with people who do, so with a background in mathematical concepts you can understand how these other workers produce their results and can tell the difference between meaningful and misleading results. You can challenge the output of those workers and ask them intelligent questions. For example, Market Research Managers need to understand the procedures of the statisticians who design market surveys. A background in math also makes it possible for you to specialize in research—although, if you are looking at this list, you probably are not interested in such math-intense pursuits.

Best Majors Related to Jobs that Require a Low Level of Math Skills

Major	Level of Math Skills in Related Jobs	Annual Earnings of Related Jobs	Percent Growth of Related Jobs	Annual Openings of Related Jobs	Personality Types
1. Medicine	52	$164,000	21.8%	26,050	ISR
2. Physical Therapy	39	$74,000	30.3%	7,860	SIR
3. Nursing (R.N. Training)	52	$64,000	22.2%	103,900	SI
4. Physician Assisting	52	$84,000	39.0%	4,280	SIR
5. Communications Studies/Speech	44	$52,000	23.3%	14,170	SAE
6. Occupational Therapy	34	$70,000	25.6%	4,580	SI
7. Public Relations	45	$54,000	23.1%	13,762	EAS
8. Human Resources Management	44	$49,000	26.7%	12,528	ESC
9. Law	43	$112,000	13.0%	24,392	EI
10. Dentistry	44	$142,000	15.3%	5,180	IRS
11. Dentistry	44	$142,000	15.3%	5,180	IRS
12. Elementary Education	53	$51,000	15.8%	59,650	SAC
13. Marketing	50	$107,000	12.2%	7,639	EC
14. Physical Education	51	$44,000	16.0%	23,020	SE
15. Speech-Language Pathology and Audiology	49	$65,000	18.7%	4,525	SIA
16. Classics	32	$41,000	22.4%	2,452	AS
17. Chinese	31	$41,000	22.2%	2,340	AS
18. French	31	$41,000	22.2%	2,340	AS
19. German	31	$41,000	22.2%	2,340	AS
20. Modern Foreign Language	31	$41,000	22.2%	2,340	AS
21. Russian	31	$41,000	22.2%	2,340	AS
22. Spanish	31	$41,000	22.2%	2,340	AS
23. Graphic Design, Commercial Art, and Illustration	37	$46,000	12.0%	13,796	ARE
24. Chiropractic	43	$68,000	19.5%	1,820	SIR
25. Interior Design	49	$46,000	19.4%	3,590	AE

Majors 17, 18, 19, 20, 21, and 22 share a link to a job with 2,340 openings.

Bonus Lists: Best Majors that May Appeal to Other Aspects of Your Personality

The six Holland types provide a convenient way of describing personalities, but most of us are familiar with other aspects of personality, many of which are arguably relevant to career choice. The O*NET database provides ratings that allowed me to compile several lists based on these other dimensions of personality. All of the following lists are based on the 51 majors that met the criteria for being listed in this book. For each major in these lists, I also list the one, two, or three Holland types that characterize the major.

Best Majors for Introverts and Extroverts

The psychologist Carl Jung described two kinds of people: **extroverts,** whose psychic energy flows inward, gained from other people, and **introverts,** whose psychic energy flows outward, gained from solitude. Nowadays the concept of psychic energy is not taken literally, but psychologists continue to recognize that some people are stimulated by social settings and feel most comfortable there, whereas others are more energetic and productive when they can escape distractions caused by other people. So psychologists still speak of introverts and extroverts, and in the field of career development it can be useful to consider whether you lean toward one of these personality types.

For example, if you are an introvert, you are likely to fit better in a job where you can focus on the task without being distracted by ringing telephones, office chit-chat, and frequent meetings. On the other hand, if you are an extrovert, you probably don't mind multitasking and enjoy chatting up your coworkers and clients. (For a detailed look at introversion and its relationship to career choice, see *200 Best Jobs for Introverts* from JIST Publishing.)

These two personality types align with the six Holland types to some extent: Extroverts have much in common with Social personalities and introverts have much in common with Realistic personalities.

The O*NET database does not rate jobs for extroversion and introversion as it does for the six Holland types. Nevertheless, I was able to compute extroversion and introversion ratings for jobs related to majors by looking at the O*NET ratings for two aspects of the jobs: the work style Social Orientation, which is defined as preferring to work with others rather than alone and being personally connected with others on the job, and the work-context feature called Contact with Others, which represents how much the job requires workers to be in contact with others—face-to-face, by telephone, or otherwise. O*NET provides ratings for both features on a scale of 1 to 5, so to compute an extroversion score, I took the average of the two ratings and then represented that average on a scale from 0 to 100. For an introversion score, I subtracted the extroversion score from 100.

These scores for major-related jobs enabled me to identify the 20 most introverted majors and the 20 most extroverted majors, and I then used the three standard economic measures to rank each set and produce the following two lists. If you tend toward introversion or extroversion, the majors on one of these lists may appeal to you. Keep in mind that the scores for introversion and extroversion are based on the work situations in related jobs rather than on what happens while you're still in college.

Best Majors for Introverts

Major	Rating for Introversion	Annual Earnings of Related Jobs	Percent Growth of Related Jobs	Annual Openings of Related Jobs	Personality Types
1. Computer Science	34	$99,000	23.6%	7,023	ICR
2. Computer Engineering	36	$92,000	23.1%	10,109	IRC
3. Bioengineering	34	$108,000	23.2%	2,708	EIR
4. Law	27	$112,000	13.0%	24,392	EI
5. Civil Engineering	39	$83,000	21.7%	12,678	RIC
6. Biochemistry	26	$82,000	36.9%	3,498	IAR
7. Management Information Systems	33	$106,000	14.6%	11,712	ECI
8. Accounting	36	$60,000	21.5%	50,818	CEI
9. Environmental Science	30	$59,000	28.0%	5,470	IRC
10. Economics	38	$65,000	24.1%	4,081	IEC
11. Biology	32	$115,000	15.5%	2,010	EI
12. Botany	32	$115,000	15.5%	2,010	EI
13. Finance	27	$81,000	16.1%	14,512	CEI
14. Oceanography	35	$90,000	17.0%	2,085	IR
15. Geophysics	35	$90,000	17.0%	2,042	IR
16. Aeronautical/Aerospace Engineering	32	$103,000	8.7%	3,448	IRE
17. Microbiology	32	$83,000	21.6%	1,988	IR
18. Actuarial Science	48	$87,000	21.4%	1,000	CIE
19. Geology	36	$85,000	17.3%	1,858	IR
20. Graphic Design, Commercial Art, and Illustration	43	$46,000	12.0%	13,796	ARE

Majors 11 and 12 share links to two jobs with 2,010 openings.

Best Majors for Extroverts

Major	Rating for Extroversion	Annual Earnings of Related Jobs	Percent Growth of Related Jobs	Annual Openings of Related Jobs	Personality Types
1. Medicine	85	$164,000	21.8%	26,050	ISR
2. Nursing (R.N. Training)	87	$64,000	22.2%	103,900	SI
3. Physical Therapy	85	$74,000	30.3%	7,860	SIR
4. Physician Assisting	83	$84,000	39.0%	4,280	SIR
5. Veterinary Medicine	86	$81,000	32.9%	3,020	IR
6. Human Resources Management	85	$49,000	26.7%	12,528	ESC
7. Occupational Therapy	88	$70,000	25.6%	4,580	SI
8. Business Management	82	$116,000	2.1%	28,909	EC
9. International Business	82	$121,000	−0.7%	23,805	ECS
10. Dentistry	88	$142,000	15.3%	5,180	IRS
11. Elementary Education	92	$51,000	15.8%	59,650	SAC
12. Marketing	81	$107,000	12.2%	7,639	EC
13. Physical Education	89	$44,000	16.0%	23,020	SE
14. Speech-Language Pathology and Audiology	94	$65,000	18.7%	4,525	SIA
15. Chinese	81	$41,000	22.2%	2,340	AS
16. French	81	$41,000	22.2%	2,340	AS
17. German	81	$41,000	22.2%	2,340	AS
18. Modern Foreign Language	81	$41,000	22.2%	2,340	AS
19. Russian	81	$41,000	22.2%	2,340	AS
20. Spanish	81	$41,000	22.2%	2,340	AS
21. Chiropractic	86	$68,000	19.5%	1,820	SIR

Majors 15, 16, 17, 18, and 19 and another major not included in this list share a link to a job with 2,340 openings.

Best Majors for Persistent People

Some people tend to stick to a task even in the face of obstacles. Whether you call them dedicated or pig-headed, they seem to represent a distinct personality type. Because the O*NET database rates jobs on Persistence (as a work style), I was able to compute scores for majors based on their related jobs and to identify the 20 majors most hospitable to persistent people. I then ranked these majors by the usual three economic criteria to produce the following list.

Best Majors for Persistent People

Major	Rating for Persistence	Annual Earnings of Related Jobs	Percent Growth of Related Jobs	Annual Openings of Related Jobs	Personality Types
1. Medicine	85	$164,000	21.8%	26,050	ISR
2. Business Management	85	$116,000	2.1%	28,909	EC
3. Dentistry	88	$142,000	15.3%	5,180	IRS
4. Law	90	$112,000	13.0%	24,392	EI
5. Biochemistry	91	$82,000	36.9%	3,498	IAR
6. Bioengineering	81	$108,000	23.2%	2,708	EIR
7. International Business	85	$121,000	−0.7%	23,805	ECS
8. Elementary Education	85	$51,000	15.8%	59,650	SAC
9. Finance	84	$81,000	16.1%	14,512	CEI
10. Public Administration	81	$95,000	−0.1%	53,888	ECS
11. Veterinary Medicine	88	$81,000	32.9%	3,020	IR
12. Economics	81	$65,000	24.1%	4,081	IEC
13. Graduate Study for College Teaching	81	$63,000	15.1%	55,290	SI
14. Marketing	83	$107,000	12.2%	7,639	EC
15. Architecture	84	$86,000	13.8%	5,898	AIE
16. Microbiology	83	$83,000	21.6%	1,988	IR
17. Speech-Language Pathology and Audiology	84	$65,000	18.7%	4,525	SIA
18. Physical Education	87	$44,000	16.0%	23,020	SE
19. Aeronautical/Aerospace Engineering	84	$103,000	8.7%	3,448	IRE
20. Chiropractic	83	$68,000	19.5%	1,820	SIR

Best Majors for Sensitive People

Another work style used to rate jobs in O*NET is Concern for Others, which is defined as being sensitive to others' needs and feelings and being understanding and helpful on the job. I used these ratings to identify the 20 majors most suited to sensitive people, and then I ranked this set of majors by the earnings, job growth, and job openings of the related occupations.

As you might expect, the sensitive personality type has a lot in common with the Social personality type, and all but two of the majors listed here have Social as a primary or secondary type.

Best Majors for Sensitive People

Major	Rating for Concern for Others	Annual Earnings of Related Jobs	Percent Growth of Related Jobs	Annual Openings of Related Jobs	Personality Types
1. Medicine	91	$164,000	21.8%	26,050	ISR
2. Nursing (R.N. Training)	94	$64,000	22.2%	103,900	SI
3. Physician Assisting	90	$84,000	39.0%	4,280	SIR
4. Physical Therapy	88	$74,000	30.3%	7,860	SIR
5. Business Management	74	$116,000	2.1%	28,909	EC
6. Pharmacy	82	$109,000	17.0%	10,580	ICS
7. Veterinary Medicine	82	$81,000	32.9%	3,020	IR
8. International Business	74	$121,000	–0.7%	23,805	ECS
9. Public Administration	74	$95,000	–0.1%	53,888	ECS
10. Dentistry	93	$142,000	15.3%	5,180	IRS
11. Human Resources Management	77	$49,000	26.7%	12,528	ESC
12. Occupational Therapy	96	$70,000	25.6%	4,580	SI
13. Optometry	88	$96,000	24.4%	2,010	ISR
14. Health Information Systems Administration	81	$82,000	16.0%	9,940	ESC
15. Elementary Education	92	$51,000	15.8%	59,650	SAC
16. Graduate Study for College Teaching	77	$63,000	15.1%	55,290	SI
17. Speech-Language Pathology and Audiology	98	$65,000	18.7%	4,525	SIA
18. Physical Education	85	$44,000	16.0%	23,020	SE
19. Chiropractic	91	$68,000	19.5%	1,820	SIR
20. Chinese	73	$41,000	22.2%	2,340	AS

Major 20 and five other majors not included in this list share a link to a job with 2,340 openings.

Best Majors for People with Self-Control

The O*NET database rates jobs on a work style called Self-Control, which is defined as maintaining composure, keeping emotions in check, controlling anger, and avoiding aggressive behavior, even in very difficult situations. This tendency to stay as cool as the other side of the pillow may be regarded as a personality type, so I thought it would be interesting to see which majors are a good fit.

I identified the 20 majors with related jobs rated highest on Self-Control, and it's interesting to note that the six highest-rated are in either education or health care. Then I sorted the 20 majors by the three usual economic measures to produce the following list.

Best Majors for People with Self-Control

Major	Rating for Self-Control	Annual Earnings of Related Jobs	Percent Growth of Related Jobs	Annual Openings of Related Jobs	Personality Types
1. Medicine	88	$164,000	21.8%	26,050	ISR
2. Nursing (R.N. Training)	91	$64,000	22.2%	103,900	SI
3. Physical Therapy	79	$74,000	30.3%	7,860	SIR
4. Business Management	82	$116,000	2.1%	28,909	EC
5. Pharmacy	83	$109,000	17.0%	10,580	ICS
6. Veterinary Medicine	91	$81,000	32.9%	3,020	IR
7. Law	83	$112,000	13.0%	24,392	EI
8. Human Resources Management	88	$49,000	26.7%	12,528	ESC
9. Occupational Therapy	89	$70,000	25.6%	4,580	SI
10. Public Administration	84	$95,000	–0.1%	53,888	ECS
11. Dentistry	84	$142,000	15.3%	5,180	IRS
12. International Business	83	$121,000	–0.7%	23,805	ECS
13. Elementary Education	93	$51,000	15.8%	59,650	SAC
14. Health Information Systems Administration	87	$82,000	16.0%	9,940	ESC
15. Graduate Study for College Teaching	80	$63,000	15.1%	55,290	SI
16. Speech-Language Pathology and Audiology	92	$65,000	18.7%	4,525	SIA
17. Chiropractic	90	$68,000	19.5%	1,820	SIR
18. Physical Education	87	$44,000	16.0%	23,020	SE
19. Interior Design	80	$46,000	19.4%	3,590	AE
20. Chinese	78	$41,000	22.2%	2,340	AS

Major 20 and five other majors not included in this list share a link to a job with 2,340 openings.

Best Majors for Stress-Tolerant People

Workplace stress can be emotionally draining and can even have serious consequences for your health. But some people have a personality that allows them to tolerate stressful work situations, and I thought that they deserve a list of majors especially suitable for them. (I also thought that the rest of us deserve a whole book about careers that lack these pressures, *150 Best Low-Stress Jobs* from JIST Publishing.)

To create the list, I identified the 20 majors with related jobs that are rated highest on the O*NET work style Stress Tolerance, which is defined as accepting criticism and dealing calmly and effectively with high-stress situations. The major rated highest for requiring stress tolerance (with a score of 92) is Nursing (R.N. Training), which is not at all surprising if you know what nurses do. As in the other lists in this section, I ordered the 20 majors by three economic criteria so you can see which are best overall.

Best Majors for Stress-Tolerant People

Major	Rating for Stress Tolerance	Annual Earnings of Related Jobs	Percent Growth of Related Jobs	Annual Openings of Related Jobs	Personality Types
1. Medicine	87	$164,000	21.8%	26,050	ISR
2. Nursing (R.N. Training)	92	$64,000	22.2%	103,900	SI
3. Business Management	88	$116,000	2.1%	28,909	EC
4. Pharmacy	85	$109,000	17.0%	10,580	ICS
5. Law	91	$112,000	13.0%	24,392	EI
6. Physician Assisting	83	$84,000	39.0%	4,280	SIR
7. International Business	89	$121,000	−0.7%	23,805	ECS
8. Public Administration	84	$95,000	−0.1%	53,888	ECS
9. Dentistry	85	$142,000	15.3%	5,180	IRS
10. Biochemistry	82	$82,000	36.9%	3,498	IAR
11. Elementary Education	90	$51,000	15.8%	59,650	SAC
12. Finance	83	$81,000	16.1%	14,512	CEI
13. Human Resources Management	84	$49,000	26.7%	12,528	ESC
14. Health Information Systems Administration	88	$82,000	16.0%	9,940	ESC
15. Veterinary Medicine	87	$81,000	32.9%	3,020	IR
16. Marketing	81	$107,000	12.2%	7,639	EC
17. Architecture	81	$86,000	13.8%	5,898	AIE
18. Speech-Language Pathology and Audiology	84	$65,000	18.7%	4,525	SIA
19. Physical Education	85	$44,000	16.0%	23,020	SE
20. Interior Design	85	$46,000	19.4%	3,590	AE

Best Majors for Flexible People

Our rapidly changing economy has made flexibility a very useful personality trait in the workplace. Some jobs are particularly demanding of flexibility, and the O*NET database provides guidance on this matter by rating all occupations on a work style called Adaptability/Flexibility. This trait is defined as being open to change (positive or negative) and to considerable variety in the workplace. Using these ratings, I was able to identify the 20 majors leading to jobs with the highest need for flexible people. I ordered these 20 majors by the economic rewards of the related jobs and produced the following list.

Best Majors for Flexible People

Major	Rating for Flexibility	Annual Earnings of Related Jobs	Percent Growth of Related Jobs	Annual Openings of Related Jobs	Personality Types
1. Occupational Therapy	90	$70,000	25.6%	4,580	SI
2. Speech-Language Pathology and Audiology	89	$65,000	18.7%	4,525	SIA
3. Elementary Education	89	$51,000	15.8%	59,650	SAC
4. Management Information Systems	89	$106,000	14.6%	11,712	ECI
5. Interior Design	89	$46,000	19.4%	3,590	AE
6. Nursing (R.N. Training)	87	$64,000	22.2%	103,900	SI
7. Health Information Systems Administration	87	$82,000	16.0%	9,940	ESC
8. Public Relations	87	$54,000	23.1%	13,762	EAS
9. Physical Education	87	$44,000	16.0%	23,020	SE
10. Communications Studies/Speech	86	$52,000	23.3%	14,170	SAE
11. Human Resources Management	86	$49,000	26.7%	12,528	ESC
12. Business Management	84	$116,000	2.1%	28,909	EC
13. International Business	83	$121,000	−0.7%	23,805	ECS
14. Computer Science	83	$99,000	23.6%	7,023	ICR
15. Veterinary Medicine	82	$81,000	32.9%	3,020	IR
16. Biochemistry	81	$82,000	36.9%	3,498	IAR
17. Marketing	81	$107,000	12.2%	7,639	EC
18. Graphic Design, Commercial Art, and Illustration	81	$46,000	12.0%	13,796	ARE
19. Public Administration	81	$95,000	−0.1%	53,888	ECS
20. Finance	81	$81,000	16.1%	14,512	CEI

Best Majors for Detail-Oriented People

Some workers tend to be careful about detail and thorough in completing work tasks. These workers are attracted to jobs where it is important to get the fine points right. Such jobs can be identified in the O*NET database by their high ratings on a work style called Attention to Detail, so I used these ratings to extract the 20 majors whose related jobs are most detail-oriented.

Dentistry is the major with the highest rating on Attention to Detail, which should give you some comfort the next time you're in the dentist's chair. All the personality types except Realistic are represented on this list at least once, and several majors have Realistic as a secondary type. Like the other lists in this section, this one is ordered to show which majors are best in terms of economic criteria.

Best Majors for Detail-Oriented People

Major	Rating for Attention to Detail	Annual Earnings of Related Jobs	Percent Growth of Related Jobs	Annual Openings of Related Jobs	Personality Types
1. Medicine	93	$164,000	21.8%	26,050	ISR
2. Nursing (R.N. Training)	89	$64,000	22.2%	103,900	SI
3. Physician Assisting	89	$84,000	39.0%	4,280	SIR
4. Law	92	$112,000	13.0%	24,392	EI
5. Pharmacy	93	$109,000	17.0%	10,580	ICS
6. Accounting	94	$60,000	21.5%	50,818	CEI
7. Public Administration	88	$95,000	−0.1%	53,888	ECS
8. Dentistry	99	$142,000	15.3%	5,180	IRS
9. Communications Studies/Speech	88	$52,000	23.3%	14,170	SAE
10. Veterinary Medicine	97	$81,000	32.9%	3,020	IR
11. Finance	93	$81,000	16.1%	14,512	CEI
12. Public Relations	87	$54,000	23.1%	13,762	EAS
13. Economics	91	$65,000	24.1%	4,081	IEC
14. Architecture	91	$86,000	13.8%	5,898	AIE
15. Actuarial Science	91	$87,000	21.4%	1,000	CIE
16. Speech-Language Pathology and Audiology	90	$65,000	18.7%	4,525	SIA
17. Chiropractic	92	$68,000	19.5%	1,820	SIR
18. Aeronautical/Aerospace Engineering	87	$103,000	8.7%	3,448	IRE
19. Graphic Design, Commercial Art, and Illustration	94	$46,000	12.0%	13,796	ARE
20. Interior Design	95	$46,000	19.4%	3,590	AE

Best Majors for Innovators

Some workers like to develop new ideas and solve work-related problems by thinking in creative and unorthodox ways. This tendency is considered to be an aspect of the Artistic personality type, but it also can be useful in the scientific and business fields. I used the O*NET database to discover the 20 majors linked to jobs with the highest ratings for the work style Innovation. Then I ordered the majors by earnings, job growth, and job openings to produce the following list. It comes as no surprise that Artistic majors are more prominent in this list than in any other list in this section.

Best Majors for Innovators

Major	Rating for Innovation	Annual Earnings of Related Jobs	Percent Growth of Related Jobs	Annual Openings of Related Jobs	Personality Types
1. Computer Engineering	74	$92,000	23.1%	10,109	IRC
2. Business Management	75	$116,000	2.1%	28,909	EC
3. International Business	76	$121,000	–0.7%	23,805	ECS
4. Management Information Systems	74	$106,000	14.6%	11,712	ECI
5. Occupational Therapy	77	$70,000	25.6%	4,580	SI
6. Biochemistry	81	$82,000	36.9%	3,498	IAR
7. Marketing	76	$107,000	12.2%	7,639	EC
8. Economics	74	$65,000	24.1%	4,081	IEC
9. Elementary Education	79	$51,000	15.8%	59,650	SAC
10. Graduate Study for College Teaching	78	$63,000	15.1%	55,290	SI
11. Oceanography	78	$90,000	17.0%	2,085	IR
12. Speech-Language Pathology and Audiology	83	$65,000	18.7%	4,525	SIA
13. Architecture	79	$86,000	13.8%	5,898	AIE
14. Geophysics	78	$90,000	17.0%	2,042	IR
15. Microbiology	74	$83,000	21.6%	1,988	IR
16. Physical Education	78	$44,000	16.0%	23,020	SE
17. Geology	79	$85,000	17.3%	1,858	IR
18. Interior Design	95	$46,000	19.4%	3,590	AE
19. Aeronautical/Aerospace Engineering	81	$103,000	8.7%	3,448	IRE
20. Graphic Design, Commercial Art, and Illustration	91	$46,000	12.0%	13,796	ARE

Best Majors for Analytical Thinkers

Maybe you know someone who likes to analyze information and use logic to address work-related issues and problems. This trait is one aspect of the Investigative personality type, but, according to O*NET, it also characterizes many jobs that attract Enterprising and Conventional workers. I isolated the 20 majors with related jobs rated highest on the measure Analytical Thinking and sorted them by the usual economic criteria.

Best Majors for Analytical Thinkers

Major	Rating for Analytical Thinking	Annual Earnings of Related Jobs	Percent Growth of Related Jobs	Annual Openings of Related Jobs	Personality Types
1. Medicine	88	$164,000	21.8%	26,050	ISR
2. Physician Assisting	85	$84,000	39.0%	4,280	SIR
3. Bioengineering	85	$108,000	23.2%	2,708	EIR
4. Civil Engineering	87	$83,000	21.7%	12,678	RIC
5. Biochemistry	88	$82,000	36.9%	3,498	IAR
6. Law	94	$112,000	13.0%	24,392	EI
7. Economics	92	$65,000	24.1%	4,081	IEC
8. Accounting	88	$60,000	21.5%	50,818	CEI
9. Veterinary Medicine	89	$81,000	32.9%	3,020	IR
10. Biology	86	$115,000	15.5%	2,010	EI
11. Botany	86	$115,000	15.5%	2,010	EI
12. Architecture	88	$86,000	13.8%	5,898	AIE
13. Oceanography	91	$90,000	17.0%	2,085	IR
14. Geophysics	91	$90,000	17.0%	2,042	IR
15. Graduate Study for College Teaching	87	$63,000	15.1%	55,290	SI
16. Aeronautical/Aerospace Engineering	86	$103,000	8.7%	3,448	IRE
17. Actuarial Science	96	$87,000	21.4%	1,000	CIE
18. Microbiology	89	$83,000	21.6%	1,988	IR
19. Interior Design	85	$46,000	19.4%	3,590	AE
20. Geology	92	$85,000	17.3%	1,858	IR

Majors 10 and 11 share links to two jobs with 2,010 openings.

Best Majors Related to Jobs Not Behind a Desk

Some people have what might be called an antsy personality. They don't like being stuck behind a desk and they enjoy work that involves physical activity. JIST created an entire book for these people, *175 Best Jobs Not Behind a Desk,* based on the O*NET ratings for Physical Activity and (lack of) Sitting. The following list identifies the 20 majors that are linked to jobs with the highest level of activity and ranks them by the usual economic criteria.

It's worth noting that the major on this list rated highest on physical activity, Dentistry, has an activity score of only 66 on a scale of 0 to 100. Many majors on the list are rated in the low 50s. We live in an information-based economy, with much of the growth in

Dilbert-type settings, so any list of the best jobs or best majors includes many options that are not highly active. Nevertheless, a list such as the following can help you avoid the most sedentary choices.

Best Majors Related to Jobs Not Behind a Desk

Major	Rating for Activity	Annual Earnings of Related Jobs	Percent Growth of Related Jobs	Annual Openings of Related Jobs	Personality Types
1. Computer Science	56	$99,000	23.6%	7,023	ICR
2. Computer Engineering	51	$92,000	23.1%	10,109	IRC
3. Human Resources Management	50	$49,000	26.7%	12,528	ESC
4. Environmental Science	56	$59,000	28.0%	5,470	IRC
5. Economics	51	$65,000	24.1%	4,081	IEC
6. Accounting	50	$60,000	21.5%	50,818	CEI
7. Management Information Systems	59	$106,000	14.6%	11,712	ECI
8. Dentistry	66	$142,000	15.3%	5,180	IRS
9. Classics	52	$41,000	22.4%	2,452	AS
10. Architecture	51	$86,000	13.8%	5,898	AIE
11. Chinese	52	$41,000	22.2%	2,340	AS
12. French	52	$41,000	22.2%	2,340	AS
13. German	52	$41,000	22.2%	2,340	AS
14. Modern Foreign Language	52	$41,000	22.2%	2,340	AS
15. Russian	52	$41,000	22.2%	2,340	AS
16. Spanish	52	$41,000	22.2%	2,340	AS
17. Graphic Design, Commercial Art, and Illustration	51	$46,000	12.0%	13,796	ARE
18. Oceanography	54	$90,000	17.0%	2,085	IR
19. Geophysics	54	$90,000	17.0%	2,042	IR
20. Geology	55	$85,000	17.3%	1,858	IR

Majors 11, 12, 13, 14, 15 and 16 share a link to a job with 2,340 openings.

Best Majors Related to World-Improving Jobs

Some people want to do work that makes the world a better place by easing suffering, increasing knowledge, promoting safety and security, improving the natural environment, or creating things of beauty. The O*NET database does not provide ratings that are useful in identifying world-improving jobs, but the editors at JIST used the criteria in the previous sentence to create a list that became the centerpiece of the book *150 Best Jobs for a Better World*. I used this same list to identify majors related to world-improving jobs; 30 majors met these criteria. I then sorted these majors by their economic potential to produce the following list of the 20 highest-ranking majors.

Best Majors Related to World-Improving Jobs				
Major	Annual Earnings of Related Jobs	Percent Growth of Related Jobs	Annual Openings of Related Jobs	Personality Types
1. Computer Science	$99,000	23.6%	7,023	ICR
2. Physician Assisting	$84,000	39.0%	4,280	SIR
3. Physical Therapy	$74,000	30.3%	7,860	SIR
4. Nursing (R.N. Training)	$64,000	22.2%	103,900	SI
5. Biochemistry	$82,000	36.9%	3,498	IAR
6. Business Management	$116,000	2.1%	28,909	EC
7. Law	$112,000	13.0%	24,392	EI
8. Pharmacy	$109,000	17.0%	10,580	ICS
9. Veterinary Medicine	$81,000	32.9%	3,020	IR
10. Communications Studies/Speech	$52,000	23.3%	14,170	SAE
11. Occupational Therapy	$70,000	25.6%	4,580	SI
12. Environmental Science	$59,000	28.0%	5,470	IRC
13. Public Administration	$95,000	−0.1%	53,888	ECS
14. Dentistry	$142,000	15.3%	5,180	IRS
15. Finance	$81,000	16.1%	14,512	CEI
16. Optometry	$96,000	24.4%	2,010	ISR
17. Architecture	$86,000	13.8%	5,898	AIE
18. Elementary Education	$51,000	15.8%	59,650	SAC
19. Physical Education	$44,000	16.0%	23,020	SE
20. Speech-Language Pathology and Audiology	$65,000	18.7%	4,525	SIA

PART IV

Descriptions of the Best College Majors for Your Personality

T his part provides descriptions for all the majors included in one or more of the lists in Part III, plus the jobs related to these majors. The introduction gives more details on how to use and interpret the descriptions of majors, but here is some additional information:

❈ The descriptions are divided into six sections, based on the primary RIASEC code of the majors. Within each section, majors are arranged in alphabetical order by name. This approach allows you to find a description quickly if you know the major's correct title from one of the lists in Part III. It also allows you to browse easily among majors with a similar primary personality type.

❈ Six additional majors are described here: African-American Studies, American Studies, Area Studies, Humanities, and Women's Studies are similar to Graduate Study for College Teaching in that many people who major in these fields go on to graduate study. However, unlike that pseudo-major, these are specific majors linked to specific college teaching jobs. (Some graduates of these programs go into fields other than college teaching, often by earning a degree in a different field such as library science or law.) Japanese is included because there was room for only 7 language majors in the 10 best Artistic majors list, but ordering the majors with tied scores alphabetically would have eliminated the much more popular Spanish major.

❈ Consider the descriptions of majors in this section as a first step in exploring educational options. When you find a major that interests you, turn to Appendix A for suggestions about resources for further exploration.

❋ Appendix C can give you more context to understand the career clusters and career pathways referred to in the descriptions; you'll find the complete outline of the career clustering taxonomy there. The skills referenced in the job descriptions are defined in Appendix D.

❋ If you are using this section to browse for interesting options, we suggest you begin with the table of contents. Part III features many interesting lists that will help you identify titles of majors to explore in more detail. If you have not browsed the lists in Part III, consider spending some time there. The lists are interesting and will help you identify majors you can find described in the material that follows. The titles of majors in Part III are also listed in the table of contents.

Realistic Majors

Aeronautical/Aerospace Engineering

Personality Type:
Investigative–Realistic–Enterprising

Useful Facts About the Major

Prepares individuals to apply mathematical and scientific principles to the design, development, and operational evaluation of aircraft, missiles, space vehicles, and their systems; applied research on flight and orbital characteristics; and the development of systems and procedures for the launching, guidance, and control of air and space vehicles.

Related CIP Program: 14.0201 Aerospace, Aeronautical, and Astronautical/Space Engineering

Specializations in the Major: Propulsion, airframes and aerodynamics, testing, spacecraft.

Typical Sequence of College Courses: English composition, technical writing, calculus, differential equations, introduction to computer science, general chemistry, general physics, thermodynamics, introduction to electric circuits, introduction to aerospace engineering, statics, dynamics, materials engineering, fluid mechanics, aircraft systems and propulsion, flight control systems, aerodynamics, aircraft structural design, aircraft stability and control, experimental aerodynamics, senior design project.

Typical Sequence of High School Courses: English, algebra, geometry, trigonometry, pre-calculus, calculus, chemistry, physics, computer science.

Career Snapshot

Engineers apply scientific principles to real-world problems, finding the optimal solution that balances elegant technology with realistic cost.

Aeronautical/aerospace engineers need to learn the specific principles of air flow and resistance and the workings of various kinds of propulsion systems. Most enter the job market with a bachelor's degree. Some later move into managerial positions. New technologies and new designs for commercial and military aircraft and spacecraft should spur demand for aerospace engineers. Job outlook is good because new grads are needed to replace aerospace engineers who are retiring or leaving the occupation for other reasons.

Useful Averages for the Related Jobs

* Annual Earnings: $103,000
* Growth: 8.7%
* Openings: 3,448
* Self-Employed: 2.2%
* Verbal Skill Rating: 65
* Math Skill Rating: 76

Other Details About the Related Jobs

Career Clusters: 02 Architecture and Construction; 11 Information Technology; 15 Science, Technology, Engineering, and Mathematics. **Career Pathways:** 02.1 Design/Pre-Construction; 11.4 Programming and Software Development; 15.1 Engineering and Technology; 15.2 Science and Mathematics.

Skills: Operations analysis, science, mathematics, technology design, quality control analysis, reading comprehension, systems analysis, systems evaluation. **Work Conditions:** Indoors; sitting; common protective or safety equipment.

Related Jobs

1. Aerospace Engineers

Personality Type: Investigative–Realistic

Earnings: $94,780
Growth: 10.4%
Annual Openings: 2,230

Most Common Education/Training Level:
Bachelor's or higher degree plus work experience

Perform a variety of engineering work in designing, constructing, and testing aircraft, missiles, and spacecraft. May conduct basic and applied research to evaluate adaptability of materials and equipment to aircraft design and manufacture. May recommend improvements in testing equipment and techniques. Direct and coordinate activities of engineering or technical personnel designing, fabricating, modifying, or testing aircraft or aerospace products. Formulate conceptual design of aeronautical or aerospace products or systems to meet customer requirements. Plan and coordinate activities concerned with investigating and resolving customers' reports of technical problems with aircraft or aerospace vehicles. Plan and conduct experimental, environmental, operational, and stress tests on models and prototypes of aircraft and aerospace systems and equipment. Analyze project requests and proposals and engineering data to determine feasibility, productibility, cost, and production time of aerospace or aeronautical product. Evaluate product data and design from inspections and reports for conformance to engineering principles, customer requirements, and quality standards. Maintain records of performance reports for future reference. Write technical reports and other documentation, such as handbooks and bulletins, for use by engineering staff, management, and customers. Develop design criteria for aeronautical or aerospace products or systems, including testing methods, production costs, quality standards, and completion dates. Review performance reports and documentation from customers and field engineers and inspect malfunctioning or damaged products to determine problem. Formulate mathematical models or other methods of computer analysis to develop,

evaluate, or modify design according to customer engineering requirements. Direct research and development programs. Evaluate and approve selection of vendors by study of past performance and new advertisements.

2. Engineering Managers
Personality Type:
Enterprising–Realistic–Investigative

Earnings: $117,000
Growth: 6.2%
Annual Openings: 4,870

Most Common Education/Training Level:
Bachelor's degree

Plan, direct, or coordinate activities or research and development in such fields as architecture and engineering. Confer with management, production, and marketing staff to discuss project specifications and procedures. Coordinate and direct projects, making detailed plans to accomplish goals and directing the integration of technical activities. Analyze technology, resource needs, and market demand to plan and assess the feasibility of projects. Plan and direct the installation, testing, operation, maintenance, and repair of facilities and equipment. Direct, review, and approve product design and changes. Recruit employees; assign, direct, and evaluate their work; and oversee the development and maintenance of staff competence. Prepare budgets, bids, and contracts and direct the negotiation of research contracts. Develop and implement policies, standards, and procedures for the engineering and technical work performed in the department, service, laboratory, or firm. Review and recommend or approve contracts and cost estimates. Perform administrative functions such as reviewing and writing reports, approving expenditures, enforcing rules, and making decisions about the purchase of materials or services. Present and explain proposals, reports, and findings to clients. Consult or negotiate with clients to prepare project specifications. Set scientific and technical goals within broad outlines provided by top management. Administer highway planning, construction, and maintenance. Direct the engineering of water control, treatment, and distribution projects. Plan, direct, and coordinate survey work with other staff activities, certifying survey work and writing land legal descriptions. Confer with and report to officials and the public to provide information and solicit support for projects.

Job Specialization

Biofuels/Biodiesel Technology and Product Development Managers. Define, plan, or execute biofuel/biodiesel research programs that evaluate alternative feedstock and process technologies with near-term commercial potential. Develop lab scale models of industrial-scale processes, such as fermentation. Develop computational tools or approaches to improve biofuels research and development activities. Develop carbohydrates arrays and associated methods for screening enzymes involved in biomass conversion. Provide technical or scientific guidance to technical staff in the conduct of biofuels research or development. Prepare, or oversee the preparation of, experimental plans for biofuels research or development. Prepare biofuels research and development reports for senior management or technical professionals. Perform protein functional analysis and engineering for processing of feedstock and creation of biofuels. Develop separation processes to recover biofuels. Develop methods to recover ethanol or other fuels from complex bioreactor liquid and gas streams. Develop methods to estimate the efficiency of biomass pretreatments. Design or execute solvent or product recovery experiments in laboratory or field settings. Design or conduct applied biodiesel or biofuels research projects on topics such as transport, thermodynamics, mixing, filtration, distillation, fermentation, extraction, and separation. Design chemical conversion processes, such as etherification, esterification, interesterification,

transesterification, distillation, hydrogenation, oxidation or reduction of fats and oils, and vegetable oil refining. Conduct experiments on biomass or pretreatment technologies. Conduct experiments to test new or alternate feedstock fermentation processes. Analyze data from biofuels studies, such as fluid dynamics, water treatments, or solvent extraction and recovery processes. Oversee biodiesel/biofuels prototyping or development projects. Propose new biofuels products, processes, technologies, or applications based on findings from applied biofuels or biomass research projects.

Civil Engineering

Personality Type:
Realistic–Investigative–Conventional

Useful Facts About the Major

Prepares individuals to apply mathematical and scientific principles to the design, development, and operational evaluation of structural, load-bearing, material moving, transportation, water resource, and material control systems and environmental safety measures.

Related CIP Program: 14.0801 Civil Engineering, General

Specializations in the Major: Transportation engineering, geotechnical engineering, environmental engineering, water resources, structural engineering.

Typical Sequence of College Courses: English composition, technical writing, calculus, differential equations, general chemistry, introduction to computer science, general physics, introduction to electric circuits, engineering graphics, statics, dynamics, materials engineering, introduction to civil engineering, numerical analysis, fluid mechanics, engineering surveying and measurement, environmental engineering and design, soil mechanics, engineering economics, analysis of

Realistic

structures, highway and transportation engineering, reinforced concrete design, steel design, water resources and hydraulic engineering, senior design project.

Typical Sequence of High School Courses: English, algebra, geometry, trigonometry, pre-calculus, calculus, chemistry, physics, computer science.

Career Snapshot

Civil engineers design and supervise construction of roads, buildings, bridges, dams, airports, water-supply systems, and many other projects that affect the quality of our environment. They apply principles of physics and other sciences to devise engineering solutions that are technically effective, as well as being economically and environmentally sound. A bachelor's degree is the usual way to enter the field. Engineering is also a good way to prepare for a later position in management. Employment opportunities tend to rise and fall with the economy.

Useful Averages for the Related Jobs

⁂ Annual Earnings: $83,000

⁂ Growth: 21.7%

⁂ Openings: 12,678

⁂ Self-Employed: 3.8%

⁂ Verbal Skill Rating: 66

⁂ Math Skill Rating: 81

Other Details About the Related Jobs

Career Clusters: 02 Architecture and Construction; 11 Information Technology; 15 Science, Technology, Engineering, and Mathematics. **Career Pathways:** 02.1 Design/Pre-Construction; 11.4 Programming and Software Development; 15.1 Engineering and Technology; 15.2 Science and Mathematics.

Skills: Operations analysis, mathematics, science, management of financial resources, management of material resources, systems evaluation, systems analysis, quality control analysis. **Work Conditions:** More often indoors than outdoors; in a vehicle; sitting; high places; wear specialized protective or safety equipment; climbing ladders, scaffolds, or poles.

Related Jobs

1. Civil Engineers

Personality Type:
Realistic–Investigative–Conventional

Earnings: $76,590
Growth: 24.3%
Annual Openings: 11,460

Most Common Education/Training Level:
Bachelor's degree

Perform engineering duties in planning, designing, and overseeing construction and maintenance of building structures and facilities, such as roads, railroads, airports, bridges, harbors, channels, dams, irrigation projects, pipelines, power plants, water and sewage systems, and waste disposal units. Includes architectural, structural, traffic, ocean, and geo-technical engineers. Manage and direct staff members and construction, operations, or maintenance activities at project site. Provide technical advice regarding design, construction, or program modifications and structural repairs to industrial and managerial personnel. Inspect project sites to monitor progress and ensure conformance to design specifications and safety or sanitation standards. Estimate quantities and cost of materials, equipment, or labor to determine project feasibility. Test soils and materials to determine the adequacy and strength of foundations, concrete, asphalt, or steel. Compute load and grade requirements, water flow rates, and material stress factors to determine design specifications. Plan and design transportation or hydraulic systems and structures, following construction and government standards and using design software and drawing tools. Analyze survey reports, maps, drawings, blueprints, aerial photography, and other topographical or geologic data to plan projects. Prepare or present public reports on topics such as bid proposals, deeds, environmental impact statements, or property and right-of-way descriptions. Direct or participate in surveying to lay out installations and establish reference points, grades, and elevations to guide construction. Conduct studies of traffic patterns or environmental conditions to identify engineering problems and assess the potential impact of projects.

Job Specializations

Transportation Engineers. Develop plans for surface transportation projects according to established engineering standards and state or federal construction policy. Prepare plans, estimates, or specifications to design transportation facilities. Plan alterations and modifications of existing streets, highways, or freeways to improve traffic flow. Prepare data, maps, or other information at construction-related public hearings and meetings. Review development plans to determine potential traffic impact. Prepare administrative, technical, or statistical reports on traffic-operation matters such as accidents, safety measures, and pedestrian volume and practices. Evaluate transportation systems or traffic control devices and lighting systems to determine need for modification or expansion. Evaluate traffic control devices or lighting systems to determine need for modification or expansion. Develop, or assist in the development of, transportation-related computer software or computer processes. Prepare project budgets, schedules, or specifications for labor and materials. Prepare final project layout drawings that include details such as stress calculations. Plan alteration and modification of existing transportation structures to improve safety

or function. Participate in contract bidding, negotiation, or administration. Model transportation scenarios to evaluate the impacts of activities such as new development or to identify possible solutions to transportation problems. Investigate traffic problems and recommend methods to improve traffic flow and safety. Investigate or test specific construction project materials to determine compliance to specifications or standards. Inspect completed transportation projects to ensure safety or compliance with applicable standards or regulations. Direct the surveying, staking, and laying out of construction projects. Estimate transportation project costs. Confer with contractors, utility companies, or government agencies to discuss plans, specifications, or work schedules. Check construction plans, design calculations, or cost estimations to ensure completeness, accuracy, and conformity to engineering standards and practices. Analyze environmental impact statements for transportation projects.

Water/Wastewater Engineers. Design or oversee projects involving provision of fresh water, disposal of wastewater and sewage, or prevention of flood-related damage. Prepare environmental documentation for water resources, regulatory program compliance, data management and analysis, and fieldwork. Perform hydraulic modeling and pipeline design. Write technical reports or publications related to water resources development or water use efficiency. Review and critique proposals, plans, or designs related to water and wastewater treatment systems. Provide technical support on water resource or treatment issues to government agencies. Provide technical direction or supervision to junior engineers, engineering or computer-aided design (CAD) technicians, or other technical personnel. Identify design alternatives for the development of new water resources. Develop plans for new water resources or water efficiency programs. Design or select equipment for use in wastewater processing to ensure compliance with government standards. Conduct water quality studies to identify and characterize water pollutant sources. Perform mathematical modeling of underground or surface water resources, such as floodplains, ocean coastlines, streams, rivers, and wetlands. Perform hydrological analyses, using three-dimensional simulation software, to model the movement of water or forecast the dispersion of chemical pollutants in the water supply. Perform hydraulic analyses of water supply systems or water distribution networks to model flow characteristics, test for pressure losses, or identify opportunities to mitigate risks and improve operational efficiency. Oversee the construction of decentralized and on-site wastewater treatment systems, including reclaimed water facilities. Gather and analyze water use data to forecast water demand. Conduct feasibility studies for the construction of facilities such as water supply systems, run-off collection networks, water and wastewater treatment plants, or wastewater collection systems. Conduct environmental impact studies related to water and wastewater collection, treatment, or distribution. Conduct cost-benefit analyses for the construction of water supply systems, run-off collection networks, water and wastewater treatment plants, or wastewater collection systems.

2. Engineering Managers

Personality Type:
Enterprising–Realistic–Investigative

Earnings: $117,000
Growth: 6.2%
Annual Openings: 4,870

Most Common Education/Training Level:
Bachelor's degree

Plan, direct, or coordinate activities or research and development in such fields as architecture and engineering. Confer with management, production, and marketing staff to discuss project specifications and procedures. Coordinate and direct projects, making detailed plans to accomplish goals and directing the integration of technical activities. Analyze technology, resource needs, and market demand to plan and assess the feasibility of projects. Plan and direct the installation, testing, operation, maintenance, and repair of facilities and equipment. Direct, review, and approve product design and changes. Recruit employees; assign, direct, and evaluate their work; and oversee the development and maintenance of staff competence. Prepare budgets, bids, and contracts and direct the negotiation of research contracts. Develop and implement policies, standards, and procedures for the engineering and technical work performed in the department, service, laboratory, or firm. Review and recommend or approve contracts and cost estimates. Perform administrative functions such as reviewing and writing reports, approving expenditures, enforcing rules, and making decisions about the purchase of materials or services. Present and explain proposals, reports, and findings to clients. Consult or negotiate with clients to prepare project specifications. Set scientific and technical goals within broad outlines provided by top management. Administer highway planning, construction, and maintenance. Direct the engineering of water control, treatment, and distribution projects. Plan, direct, and coordinate survey work with other staff activities, certifying survey work and writing land legal descriptions. Confer with and report to officials and the public to provide information and solicit support for projects.

Job Specialization

Biofuels/Biodiesel Technology and Product Development Managers. Define, plan, or execute biofuel/biodiesel research programs that evaluate alternative feedstock and process technologies with near-term commercial potential. Develop lab-scale models of industrial-scale processes such as fermentation. Develop computational tools or approaches to improve biofuels research and development activities. Develop carbohydrates arrays and associated methods for screening enzymes involved in biomass conversion. Provide technical or scientific guidance to technical staff in the conduct of biofuels research or development. Prepare, or oversee the preparation of, experimental plans for biofuels research or development. Prepare biofuels research and development reports for senior management or technical professionals. Perform protein functional analysis and engineering for processing of feedstock and creation of biofuels. Develop separation processes to recover biofuels. Develop methods to recover ethanol or other fuels from complex bioreactor liquid and gas streams. Develop methods to estimate the efficiency of biomass pretreatments. Design or execute solvent or product recovery experiments in laboratory or field settings. Design or conduct applied biodiesel or biofuels research projects on topics such as transport, thermodynamics, mixing, filtration, distillation, fermentation, extraction, and separation. Design chemical conversion processes, such as etherification, esterification, interesterification, transesterification, distillation, hydrogenation, oxidation or reduction of fats and oils, and vegetable oil refining. Conduct experiments on biomass or pretreatment technologies. Conduct experiments to test new or alternate feedstock fermentation processes. Analyze data from biofuels studies, such as fluid dynamics, water treatments, or solvent extraction and recovery processes. Oversee biodiesel/biofuels prototyping or development projects. Propose new biofuels products, processes, technologies or applications based on findings from applied biofuels or biomass research projects.

Computer Engineering

See **Investigative**

Dentistry

See **Investigative**

Environmental Science

See **Investigative**

Geology

Personality Type: Investigative–Realistic

Useful Facts About the Major

Focuses on the scientific study of the Earth; the forces acting upon it; and the behavior of the solids, liquids, and gases comprising it.

Related CIP Program: 40.0601 Geology/Earth Science, General

Specializations in the Major: Petroleum geology, stratigraphy, engineering geology, mineralogy, paleontology, volcanology, geophysics, oceanography.

Typical Sequence of College Courses: English composition, calculus, introduction to computer science, general chemistry, general physics, introduction to geology, invertebrate paleontology, summer field geology, structural geology, mineralogy, optical mineralogy, igneous and metamorphic petrology, sedimentary petrology, stratigraphy.

Typical Sequence of High School Courses: English, algebra, geometry, trigonometry, chemistry, physics, pre-calculus, computer science, calculus.

Career Snapshot

Geology is the study of the physical makeup, processes, and history of the Earth. Geologists use knowledge of this field to locate water, mineral, and petroleum resources; to protect the environment; and to offer advice on construction and land-use projects. A bachelor's degree opens the door for many entry-level jobs, but a master's degree helps for advancement and is thought to be the degree that now leads to the best opportunities. Many research jobs in universities and the government require a Ph.D. Some field research requires going to

Realistic

remote places, but it is also possible to specialize in laboratory sciences.

Useful Averages for the Related Jobs

❋ Annual Earnings: $85,000

❋ Growth: 17.3%

❋ Openings: 1,858

❋ Self-Employed: 2.1%

❋ Verbal Skill Rating: 61

❋ Math Skill Rating: 72

Other Details About the Related Jobs

Career Clusters: 04 Business, Management, and Administration; 15 Science, Technology, Engineering, and Mathematics. **Career Pathways:** 04.2 Business, Financial Management, and Accounting; 04.4 Business Analysis; 15.2 Science and Mathematics.

Skills: Science, operations analysis, reading comprehension, mathematics, writing, systems evaluation, systems analysis, active listening. **Work Conditions:** More often indoors than outdoors; sitting; in a vehicle.

Related Jobs

1. Geoscientists, Except Hydrologists and Geographers

Personality Type: Investigative–Realistic

Earnings: $81,220
Growth: 17.5%
Annual Openings: 1,540

Most Common Education/Training Level: Master's degree

Study the composition, structure, and other physical aspects of Earth. May use knowledge of geology, physics, and mathematics in exploration for oil, gas, minerals, or underground water or in waste disposal, land reclamation, or other environmental problems. May study Earth's internal composition, atmospheres, and oceans and its magnetic, electrical, and gravitational forces. Includes mineralogists, crystallographers, paleontologists, stratigraphers, geodesists, and seismologists. Analyze and interpret geological, geochemical, and geophysical information from sources such as survey data, well logs, bore holes, and aerial photos. Locate and estimate probable natural gas, oil, and mineral ore deposits and underground water resources, using aerial photographs, charts, or research and survey results. Plan and conduct geological, geochemical, and geophysical field studies and surveys, sample collection, or drilling and testing programs used to collect data for research or application. Analyze and interpret geological data, using computer software. Search for and review research articles or environmental, historical, and technical reports. Assess ground- and surface water movement to provide advice regarding issues such as waste management, route and site selection, and the restoration of contaminated sites. Prepare geological maps, cross-sectional diagrams, charts, and reports concerning mineral extraction, land use, and resource management, using results of field work and laboratory research. Investigate the composition, structure, and history of the Earth's crust through the collection, examination, measurement, and classification of soils, minerals, rocks, or fossil remains. Conduct geological and geophysical studies to provide information for use in regional development, site selection, and development of public works projects. Measure characteristics of the Earth, such as gravity and magnetic fields, using equipment such as seismographs, gravimeters, torsion balances, and magnetometers. Inspect construction projects to analyze engineering problems, applying geological knowledge and using test equipment and drilling machinery. Design geological mine maps, monitor mine structural integrity, or advise and monitor mining crews. Identify risks for natural disasters such as mudslides, earthquakes, and volcanic eruptions, providing advice on mitigation of potential damage.

2. Hydrologists

Personality Type: Investigative–Realistic

Earnings: $73,670
Growth: 18.3%
Annual Openings: 380

Most Common Education/Training Level:
Bachelor's or higher degree plus work experience

Research the distribution, circulation, and physical properties of underground and surface waters; study the form and intensity of precipitation and its rate of infiltration into the soil, its movement through the earth, and return to the ocean and atmosphere. Study and document quantities, distribution, disposition, and development of underground and surface waters. Prepare hydrogeologic evaluations of known or suspected hazardous waste sites and land treatment and feedlot facilities. Design and conduct scientific hydrogeological investigations to ensure that accurate and appropriate information is available for use in water resource management decisions. Collect and analyze water samples as part of field investigations or to validate data from automatic monitors. Apply research findings to help minimize the environmental impacts of pollution, waterborne diseases, erosion, and sedimentation. Measure and graph phenomena such as lake levels, stream flows, and changes in water volumes. Investigate complaints or conflicts related to the alteration of public waters, gathering information, recommending alternatives, informing participants of progress, and preparing draft orders.

3. Natural Sciences Managers

Personality Type: Enterprising–Investigative

Earnings: $114,560
Growth: 15.4%
Annual Openings: 2,010

Most Common Education/Training Level:
Master's degree

Plan, direct, or coordinate activities in such fields as life sciences, physical sciences, mathematics, and statistics and research and development in these fields. Confer with scientists, engineers, regulators, and others to plan and review projects and to provide technical assistance. Develop client relationships and communicate with clients to explain proposals, present research findings, establish specifications, or discuss project status. Plan and direct research, development, and production activities. Prepare project proposals. Design and coordinate successive phases of problem analysis, solution proposals, and testing. Review project activities and prepare and review research, testing, and operational reports. Hire, supervise, and evaluate engineers, technicians, researchers, and other staff. Determine scientific and technical goals within broad outlines provided by top management and make detailed plans to accomplish these goals. Develop and implement policies, standards, and procedures for the architectural, scientific, and technical work performed to ensure regulatory compliance and operations enhancement. Develop innovative technology and train staff for its implementation. Provide for stewardship of plant and animal resources and habitats, studying land use; monitoring animal populations; and providing shelter, resources, and medical treatment for animals. Conduct own research in field of expertise. Recruit personnel and oversee the development and maintenance of staff competence. Advise and assist in obtaining patents or meeting other legal requirements. Prepare and administer budget, approve and review expenditures, and prepare financial reports. Make presentations at professional meetings to further knowledge in the field.

Realistic

Job Specializations

Clinical Research Coordinators. Plan, direct, or coordinate clinical research projects. Direct the activities of workers engaged in clinical research projects to ensure compliance with protocols and overall clinical objectives. May evaluate and analyze clinical data. Solicit industry-sponsored trials through contacts and professional organizations. Review scientific literature, participate in continuing education activities, or attend conferences and seminars to maintain current knowledge of clinical studies affairs and issues. Register protocol patients with appropriate statistical centers as required. Prepare for or participate in quality assurance audits conducted by study sponsors, federal agencies, or specially designated review groups. Participate in preparation and management of research budgets and monetary disbursements. Perform specific protocol procedures such as interviewing subjects, taking vital signs, and performing electrocardiograms. Interpret protocols and advise treating physicians on appropriate dosage modifications or treatment calculations based on patient characteristics. Develop advertising and other informational materials to be used in subject recruitment. Contact industry representatives to ensure equipment and software specifications necessary for successful study completion. Confer with health-care professionals to determine the best recruitment practices for studies. Track enrollment status of subjects and document dropout information such as dropout causes and subject contact efforts. Review proposed study protocols to evaluate factors such as sample collection processes, data management plans, and potential subject risks. Record adverse event and side effect data and confer with investigators regarding the reporting of events to oversight agencies. Prepare study-related documentation such as protocol worksheets, procedural manuals, adverse event reports, institutional review board documents, and progress reports. Participate in the development of study protocols, including guidelines for administration or data collection procedures. Oversee subject enrollment to ensure that informed consent is properly obtained and documented. Order drugs or devices necessary for study completion.

Water Resource Specialists. Design or implement programs and strategies related to water resource issues, such as supply, quality, and regulatory compliance issues. Supervise teams of workers who capture water from wells and rivers. Review or evaluate designs for water detention facilities, storm drains, flood control facilities, or other hydraulic structures. Negotiate for water rights with communities or water facilities to meet water supply demands. Perform hydrologic, hydraulic, or water quality modeling. Compile water resource data, using geographic information systems (GIS) or global position systems (GPS) software. Compile and maintain documentation on the health of a body of water. Write proposals, project reports, informational brochures, or other documents on wastewater purification, water supply and demand, or other water resource subjects. Recommend new or revised policies, procedures, or regulations to support water resource or conservation goals. Provide technical expertise to assist communities in the development or implementation of stormwater monitoring or other water programs. Present water resource proposals to government, public interest groups, or community groups. Identify methods for distributing purified wastewater into rivers, streams, or oceans. Monitor water use, demand, or quality in a particular geographic area. Identify and characterize specific causes or sources of water pollution. Develop plans to protect watershed health or rehabilitate watersheds. Develop or implement standardized water monitoring and assessment methods. Conduct technical studies for water resources on topics such as pollutants and water treatment options. Conduct, or oversee the conduct of, investigations on matters such as water storage, wastewater discharge, pollutants, permits, or other compliance and regulatory issues. Conduct cost-benefit studies for watershed improvement projects or water management alternatives. Analyze stormwater systems to identify opportunities for water resource improvements.

Geophysics

Personality Type: Enterprising–Conventional

Useful Facts About the Major

Focuses on the scientific study of the physics of solids and its application to the study of the Earth and other planets.

Related CIP Program: 40.0603 Geophysics and Seismology

Specializations in the Major: Atmospheric physics, physical oceanography, seismology, volcanology, remote sensing, geomagnetism, paleomagnetism, environmental geophysics.

Typical Sequence of College Courses: English composition, calculus, introduction to computer science, general chemistry, general physics, introduction to geology, summer field geology, structural geology, mineralogy, remote sensing, exploration geophysics, physical oceanography, stratigraphy, igneous and metamorphic petrology.

Typical Sequence of High School Courses: English, algebra, geometry, trigonometry, chemistry, physics, pre-calculus, computer science, calculus.

Career Snapshot

Geophysics uses physical measurements and mathematical models to describe the structure, composition, and processes of the Earth and planets. Geophysicists study seismic waves and variations in gravitation and terrestrial magnetism, thus learning where petroleum and minerals are deposited, where (and sometimes even when) earthquakes and volcanic eruptions are likely to strike, and how to solve environmental problems such as

pollution. A bachelor's degree can lead to entry-level jobs, but a higher degree opens greater potential for advancement in research, as well as opportunities in college teaching.

Useful Averages for the Related Jobs

※ Annual Earnings: $90,000
※ Growth: 17.0%
※ Openings: 2,042
※ Self-Employed: 1.8%
※ Verbal Skill Rating: 60
※ Math Skill Rating: 71

Other Details About the Related Jobs

Career Clusters: 04 Business, Management, and Administration; 15 Science, Technology, Engineering, and Mathematics. **Career Pathways:** 04.2 Business, Financial Management, and Accounting; 04.4 Business Analysis; 15.2 Science and Mathematics.

Skills: Science, operations analysis, reading comprehension, mathematics, writing, systems evaluation, management of personnel resources, systems analysis. **Work Conditions:** Indoors; sitting; in a vehicle.

Related Jobs

1. Geoscientists, Except Hydrologists and Geographers

Personality Type: Investigative–Realistic

Earnings: $81,220
Growth: 17.5%
Annual Openings: 1,540

Most Common Education/Training Level:
Bachelor's or higher degree plus work experience

Study the composition, structure, and other physical aspects of Earth. May use knowledge of geology, physics, and mathematics in exploration for oil, gas, minerals, or underground water or in waste disposal, land reclamation, or other environmental problems. May study Earth's internal composition, atmospheres, and oceans and its magnetic, electrical, and gravitational forces. Includes mineralogists, crystallographers, paleontologists, stratigraphers, geodesists, and seismologists. Analyze and interpret geological, geochemical, and geophysical information from sources such as survey data, well logs, bore holes, and aerial photos. Locate and estimate probable natural gas, oil, and mineral ore deposits and underground water resources, using aerial photographs, charts, or research and survey results. Plan and conduct geological, geochemical, and geophysical field studies and surveys, sample collection, or drilling and testing programs used to collect data for research or application. Analyze and interpret geological data, using computer software. Search for and review research articles or environmental, historical, and technical reports. Assess ground- and surface water movement to provide advice regarding issues such as waste management, route and site selection, and the restoration of contaminated sites. Prepare geological maps, cross-sectional diagrams, charts, and reports concerning mineral extraction, land use, and resource management, using results of field work and laboratory research. Investigate the composition, structure, and history of the Earth's crust through the collection, examination, measurement, and classification of soils, minerals, rocks, or fossil remains. Conduct geological and geophysical studies to provide information for use in regional development, site selection, and development of public works projects. Measure characteristics of the Earth, such as gravity and magnetic fields, using equipment such as seismographs, gravimeters, torsion balances, and magnetometers. Inspect construction projects to analyze engineering problems, applying geological

knowledge and using test equipment and drilling machinery. Design geological mine maps, monitor mine structural integrity, or advise and monitor mining crews. Identify risks for natural disasters such as mudslides, earthquakes, and volcanic eruptions, providing advice on mitigation of potential damage.

2. Natural Sciences Managers

Personality Type: Enterprising–Investigative

Earnings: $114,560
Growth: 15.4%
Annual Openings: 2,010

Most Common Education/Training Level: Master's degree

Plan, direct, or coordinate activities in such fields as life sciences, physical sciences, mathematics, and statistics and research and development in these fields. Confer with scientists, engineers, regulators, and others to plan and review projects and to provide technical assistance. Develop client relationships and communicate with clients to explain proposals, present research findings, establish specifications, or discuss project status. Plan and direct research, development, and production activities. Prepare project proposals. Design and coordinate successive phases of problem analysis, solution proposals, and testing. Review project activities and prepare and review research, testing, and operational reports. Hire, supervise, and evaluate engineers, technicians, researchers, and other staff. Determine scientific and technical goals within broad outlines provided by top management and make detailed plans to accomplish these goals. Develop and implement policies, standards, and procedures for the architectural, scientific, and technical work performed to ensure regulatory compliance and operations enhancement. Develop innovative technology and train staff for its implementation. Provide for stewardship of plant and animal resources and habitats, studying land use; monitoring animal populations;

and providing shelter, resources, and medical treatment for animals. Conduct own research in field of expertise. Recruit personnel and oversee the development and maintenance of staff competence. Advise and assist in obtaining patents or meeting other legal requirements. Prepare and administer budget, approve and review expenditures, and prepare financial reports. Make presentations at professional meetings to further knowledge in the field.

Job Specializations

Clinical Research Coordinators. Plan, direct, or coordinate clinical research projects. Direct the activities of workers engaged in clinical research projects to ensure compliance with protocols and overall clinical objectives. May evaluate and analyze clinical data. Solicit industry-sponsored trials through contacts and professional organizations. Review scientific literature, participate in continuing education activities, or attend conferences and seminars to maintain current knowledge of clinical studies affairs and issues. Register protocol patients with appropriate statistical centers as required. Prepare for or participate in quality assurance audits conducted by study sponsors, federal agencies, or specially designated review groups. Participate in preparation and management of research budgets and monetary disbursements. Perform specific protocol procedures such as interviewing subjects, taking vital signs, and performing electrocardiograms. Interpret protocols and advise treating physicians on appropriate dosage modifications or treatment calculations based on patient characteristics. Develop advertising and other informational materials to be used in subject recruitment. Contact industry representatives to ensure equipment and software specifications necessary for successful study completion. Confer with health-care professionals to determine the best recruitment practices for studies. Track enrollment status of subjects and document

dropout information such as dropout causes and subject contact efforts. Review proposed study protocols to evaluate factors such as sample collection processes, data management plans, and potential subject risks. Record adverse event and side effect data and confer with investigators regarding the reporting of events to oversight agencies. Prepare study-related documentation such as protocol worksheets, procedural manuals, adverse event reports, institutional review board documents, and progress reports. Participate in the development of study protocols, including guidelines for administration or data collection procedures. Oversee subject enrollment to ensure that informed consent is properly obtained and documented. Order drugs or devices necessary for study completion.

Water Resource Specialists. Design or implement programs and strategies related to water resource issues, such as supply, quality, and regulatory compliance issues. Supervise teams of workers who capture water from wells and rivers. Review or evaluate designs for water detention facilities, storm drains, flood control facilities, or other hydraulic structures. Negotiate for water rights with communities or water facilities to meet water supply demands. Perform hydrologic, hydraulic, or water quality modeling. Compile water resource data, using geographic information systems (GIS) or global position systems (GPS) software. Compile and maintain documentation on the health of a body of water. Write proposals, project reports, informational brochures, or other documents on wastewater purification, water supply and demand, or other water resource subjects. Recommend new or revised policies, procedures, or regulations to support water resource or conservation goals. Provide technical expertise to assist communities in the development or implementation of stormwater monitoring or other water programs. Present water resource proposals to government, public interest groups, or community groups. Identify methods for distributing purified wastewater into rivers, streams, or oceans. Monitor water use, demand, or quality in a particular geographic area. Identify and characterize specific causes or sources of water pollution. Develop plans to protect watershed health or rehabilitate watersheds. Develop or implement standardized water monitoring and assessment methods. Conduct technical studies for water resources on topics such as pollutants and water treatment options. Conduct, or oversee the conduct of, investigations on matters such as water storage, wastewater discharge, pollutants, permits, or other compliance and regulatory issues. Conduct cost-benefit studies for watershed improvement projects or water management alternatives. Analyze stormwater systems to identify opportunities for water resource improvements.

Microbiology

Personality Type: Investigative–Realistic

Useful Facts About the Major

Focuses on the scientific study of unicellular organisms and colonies and subcellular genetic matter and their ecological interactions with human beings and other life.

Related CIP Programs: 26.0503 Medical Microbiology and Bacteriology; 26.0502 Microbiology, General; 26.0504 Virology

Specializations in the Major: Bacteria, fungi (mycology), algae, virology, immunology.

Typical Sequence of College Courses: English composition, calculus, introduction to computer science, general chemistry, general biology, organic chemistry, general physics, general microbiology, genetics, introduction to biochemistry, immunology, bacterial physiology, bacterial genetics.

Typical Sequence of High School Courses: English, biology, algebra, geometry, trigonometry, precalculus, chemistry, physics, computer science, calculus.

Career Snapshot

A bachelor's degree in microbiology or bacteriology may be an entry route to clinical laboratory work or to nonresearch work in industry or government. It also is good preparation for medical school. For a position in research or college teaching, a graduate degree is expected.

Useful Averages for the Related Jobs

- ✳ Annual Earnings: $83,000
- ✳ Growth: 21.6%
- ✳ Openings: 1,988
- ✳ Self-Employed: 1.8%
- ✳ Verbal Skill Rating: 70
- ✳ Math Skill Rating: 68

Other Details About the Related Jobs

Career Clusters: 04 Business, Management, and Administration; 08 Health Science; 15 Science, Technology, Engineering, and Mathematics. **Career Pathways:** 04.2 Business, Financial Management, and Accounting; 04.4 Business Analysis; 08.1 Therapeutic Services; 15.2 Science and Mathematics.

Skills: Science, operations analysis, mathematics, reading comprehension, active learning, management of personnel resources, systems evaluation, systems analysis. **Work Conditions:** Indoors; sitting; exposed to disease or infections; hazardous conditions; common protective or safety equipment; exposed to radiation; wear specialized protective or safety equipment.

Related Jobs

1. Medical Scientists, Except Epidemiologists

Personality Type:
Investigative–Realistic–Artistic

Earnings: $74,590
Growth: 40.3%
Annual Openings: 6,620

Most Common Education/Training Level:
Bachelor's or higher degree plus work experience

Conduct research dealing with the understanding of human diseases and the improvement of human health. Engage in clinical investigation or other research, production, technical writing, or related activities. Conduct research to develop methodologies, instrumentation, and procedures for medical application, analyzing data and presenting findings. Plan and direct studies to investigate human or animal disease, preventive methods, and treatments for disease. Follow strict safety procedures when handling toxic materials to avoid contamination. Evaluate effects of drugs, gases, pesticides, parasites, and microorganisms at various levels. Teach principles of medicine and medical and laboratory procedures to physicians, residents, students, and technicians. Prepare and analyze organ, tissue, and cell samples to identify toxicity, bacteria, or microorganisms or to study cell structure. Standardize drug dosages, methods of immunization, and procedures for manufacture of drugs and medicinal compounds. Investigate cause, progress, life cycle, or mode of transmission of diseases or parasites. Confer with health department, industry personnel, physicians, and others to develop health safety standards and public health improvement programs. Study animal and human health and physiological processes. Consult with and advise physicians, educators, researchers, and others regarding medical applications of physics, biology, and chemistry. Use equipment such as atomic absorption spectrometers, electron microscopes, flow cytometers, and chromatography systems.

2. Microbiologists

Personality Type: Investigative–Realistic

Earnings: $66,580
Growth: 12.2%
Annual Openings: 750

Most Common Education/Training Level:
Doctoral degree

Investigate the growth, structure, development, and other characteristics of microscopic organisms, such as bacteria, algae, or fungi. Includes medical microbiologists who study the relationship between organisms and disease or the effects of antibiotics on microorganisms. Investigate the relationship between organisms and disease, including the control of epidemics and the effects of antibiotics on microorganisms. Prepare technical reports and recommendations based upon research outcomes. Supervise biological technologists and technicians and other scientists. Provide laboratory services for health departments, for community environmental health programs, and for physicians needing information for diagnosis and treatment. Use a variety of specialized equipment such as electron microscopes, gas chromatographs, and high-pressure liquid chromatographs, electrophoresis units, thermocyclers, fluorescence-activated cell sorters, and phosphoimagers. Examine physiological, morphological, and cultural characteristics, using microscopes, to identify and classify microorganisms in human, water, and food specimens. Study growth, structure, development, and general characteristics of bacteria and other microorganisms to understand their relationships to human, plant, and animal health. Isolate and maintain cultures of bacteria or other microorganisms in prescribed or developed media, controlling moisture, aeration, temperature, and nutrition. Observe action of microorganisms upon living tissues of plants, higher animals, and other microorganisms and on dead organic matter. Study the structure and function of human, animal, and plant tissues, cells, pathogens, and toxins. Conduct chemical analyses of substances such as acids, alcohols, and enzymes. Monitor and perform tests on water, food, and the environment to detect harmful microorganisms or to obtain information about sources of pollution, contamination, or infection. Develop new products and procedures for sterilization, food and pharmaceutical supply preservation, or microbial contamination detection. Research use of bacteria and microorganisms to develop vitamins, antibiotics, amino acids, grain alcohol, sugars, and polymers.

3. Natural Sciences Managers

Personality Type: Enterprising–Investigative

Earnings: $114,560
Growth: 15.4%
Annual Openings: 2,010

Most Common Education/Training Level:
Bachelor's or higher degree plus work experience

Plan, direct, or coordinate activities in such fields as life sciences, physical sciences, mathematics, and statistics and research and development in these fields. Confer with scientists, engineers, regulators, and others to plan and review projects and to provide technical assistance. Develop client relationships and communicate with clients to explain proposals, present research findings, establish specifications, or discuss project status. Plan and direct research, development, and production activities. Prepare project proposals. Design and coordinate successive phases of problem analysis, solution proposals, and testing. Review project activities and prepare and review research, testing, and operational reports. Hire, supervise, and evaluate engineers, technicians, researchers, and other staff. Determine scientific and technical goals within broad outlines provided by top management and make detailed plans to accomplish these goals. Develop and implement policies, standards, and procedures for the architectural, scientific, and technical work performed to ensure regulatory compliance and operations enhancement. Develop innovative technology and train staff for its implementation. Provide for stewardship of plant and animal resources and habitats, studying land use; monitoring animal populations; and providing shelter, resources, and medical treatment for animals. Conduct own research in field of expertise. Recruit personnel and oversee the development and maintenance of staff competence. Advise and assist in obtaining patents or meeting other legal requirements. Prepare and administer budget, approve and review expenditures, and prepare financial reports. Make presentations at professional meetings to further knowledge in the field.

Job Specializations

Clinical Research Coordinators. Plan, direct, or coordinate clinical research projects. Direct the activities of workers engaged in clinical research projects to ensure compliance with protocols and overall clinical objectives. May evaluate and analyze clinical data. Solicit industry-sponsored trials through contacts and professional organizations. Review scientific literature, participate in continuing education activities, or attend conferences and seminars to maintain current knowledge of clinical studies affairs and issues. Register protocol patients with appropriate statistical centers as required. Prepare for or participate in quality assurance audits conducted by study sponsors, federal agencies, or specially designated review groups. Participate in preparation and management of research budgets and monetary disbursements. Perform specific protocol procedures such as interviewing subjects, taking vital signs, and performing electrocardiograms. Interpret protocols and advise treating physicians on appropriate dosage modifications or treatment calculations based on patient characteristics. Develop advertising and other informational materials to be used in subject recruitment. Contact industry representatives to ensure equipment and software specifications necessary for successful study completion. Confer with health-care professionals to determine the best recruitment practices for studies. Track enrollment status of subjects and document dropout information such as dropout causes and subject contact efforts. Review proposed study protocols to evaluate factors such as sample collection processes, data management plans, and potential subject risks. Record adverse event and side effect data and confer with investigators regarding the reporting of events to oversight agencies. Prepare study-related documentation such as protocol worksheets, procedural manuals, adverse event reports, institutional review board documents, and progress reports. Participate in the development of study protocols, including guidelines for administration or data collection procedures. Oversee subject enrollment to ensure that informed consent is properly obtained and documented. Order drugs or devices necessary for study completion.

Water Resource Specialists. Design or implement programs and strategies related to water resource issues, such as supply, quality, and regulatory compliance issues. Supervise teams of workers who capture water from wells and rivers. Review or evaluate designs for water detention facilities, storm drains, flood control facilities, or other hydraulic structures. Negotiate for water rights with communities or water facilities to meet water supply demands. Perform hydrologic, hydraulic, or water quality modeling. Compile water resource data, using geographic information systems (GIS) or global position systems (GPS) software. Compile and maintain documentation on the health of a body of water. Write proposals, project reports, informational brochures, or other documents on wastewater purification, water supply and demand, or other water resource subjects. Recommend new or revised policies, procedures, or regulations to support water resource or

conservation goals. Provide technical expertise to assist communities in the development or implementation of stormwater monitoring or other water programs. Present water resource proposals to government, public interest groups, or community groups. Identify methods for distributing purified wastewater into rivers, streams, or oceans. Monitor water use, demand, or quality in a particular geographic area. Identify and characterize specific causes or sources of water pollution. Develop plans to protect watershed health or rehabilitate watersheds. Develop or implement standardized water monitoring and assessment methods. Conduct technical studies for water resources on topics such as pollutants and water treatment options. Conduct, or oversee the conduct of, investigations on matters such as water storage, wastewater discharge, pollutants, permits, or other compliance and regulatory issues. Conduct cost-benefit studies for watershed improvement projects or water management alternatives. Analyze stormwater systems to identify opportunities for water resource improvements.

Oceanography

Personality Type: Investigative–Realistic

Useful Facts About the Major

Focuses on the scientific study of the ecology and behavior of microbes, plants, and animals inhabiting oceans, coastal waters, and saltwater wetlands and the chemical components, mechanisms, structure, and movement of ocean waters and their interaction with terrestrial and atmospheric phenomena.

Related CIP Programs: 26.1302 Marine Biology and Biological Oceanography; 40.0607 Oceanography, Chemical and Physical

Specializations in the Major: Ocean geology, ocean biology, ocean chemistry, ocean meteorology.

Typical Sequence of College Courses: English composition, introduction to computer science, calculus, differential equations, general chemistry, general physics, agricultural power and machines, physical oceanography, chemical oceanography, geological oceanography, biological oceanography, seminar (reporting on research).

Typical Sequence of High School Courses: English, algebra, geometry, trigonometry, chemistry, pre-calculus, physics, computer science, biology, calculus.

Career Snapshot

Oceans cover more of the earth than does dry land, yet many of the physical and biological characteristics of the oceans are poorly understood. Oceanographers use techniques of physical sciences to study the properties of ocean waters and how these affect coastal areas, climate, and weather. Those who specialize in ocean life work to improve the fishing industry, to protect the environment, and to understand the relationship between oceanic and terrestrial life forms. It is possible to get started in this field with a bachelor's degree; for advancement and many research jobs, however, a master's degree or Ph.D. is helpful or required.

Useful Averages for the Related Jobs

* Annual Earnings: $90,000
* Growth: 17.0%
* Openings: 2,085
* Self-Employed: 1.8%
* Verbal Skill Rating: 60
* Math Skill Rating: 71

Other Details About the Related Jobs

Career Clusters: 04 Business, Management, and Administration; 15 Science, Technology, Engineering, and Mathematics. **Career Pathways:** 04.2 Business, Financial Management, and Accounting; 04.4 Business Analysis; 15.2 Science and Mathematics.

Skills: Science, operations analysis, reading comprehension, mathematics, writing, systems evaluation, management of personnel resources, systems analysis. **Work Conditions:** Indoors; sitting; in a vehicle.

Related Jobs

1. Geoscientists, Except Hydrologists and Geographers

Personality Type: Investigative–Realistic

Earnings: $81,220
Growth: 17.5%
Annual Openings: 1,540

Most Common Education/Training Level: Bachelor's or higher degree plus work experience

Study the composition, structure, and other physical aspects of Earth. May use knowledge of geology, physics, and mathematics in exploration for oil, gas, minerals, or underground water or in waste disposal, land reclamation, or other environmental problems. May study Earth's internal composition, atmospheres, and oceans and its magnetic, electrical, and gravitational forces. Includes mineralogists, crystallographers, paleontologists, stratigraphers, geodesists, and seismologists. Analyze and interpret geological, geochemical, and geophysical information from sources such as survey data, well logs, bore holes, and aerial photos. Locate and estimate probable natural gas, oil, and mineral ore deposits and underground water resources, using aerial photographs, charts, or research and survey results. Plan and conduct geological, geochemical, and geophysical field studies and surveys, sample collection, or drilling and testing programs used to collect data for research or application. Analyze and interpret geological data, using computer software. Search for and review research articles or environmental, historical, and technical reports. Assess ground- and surface water movement to provide advice regarding issues such as waste management, route and site selection, and the restoration of contaminated sites. Prepare geological maps, cross-sectional diagrams, charts, and reports concerning mineral extraction, land use, and resource management, using results of fieldwork and laboratory research. Investigate the composition, structure, and history of the Earth's crust through the collection, examination, measurement, and classification of soils, minerals, rocks, or fossil remains. Conduct geological and geophysical studies to provide information for use in regional development, site selection, and development of public works projects. Measure characteristics of the Earth, such as gravity and magnetic fields, using equipment such as seismographs, gravimeters, torsion balances, and magnetometers. Inspect construction projects to analyze engineering problems, applying geological knowledge and using test equipment and drilling machinery. Design geological mine maps, monitor mine structural integrity, or advise and monitor mining crews. Identify risks for natural disasters such as mudslides, earthquakes, and volcanic eruptions, providing advice on mitigation of potential damage.

2. Hydrologists

Personality Type: Investigative–Realistic

Earnings: $73,670
Growth: 18.3%
Annual Openings: 380

Most Common Education/Training Level:
Bachelor's or higher degree plus work experience

Research the distribution, circulation, and physical properties of underground and surface waters; study the form and intensity of precipitation and its rate of infiltration into the soil, movement through the earth, and return to the ocean and atmosphere. Study and document quantities, distribution, disposition, and development of underground and surface waters. Prepare hydrogeologic evaluations of known or suspected hazardous waste sites and land treatment and feedlot facilities. Design and conduct scientific hydrogeological investigations to ensure that accurate and appropriate information is available for use in water resource management decisions. Collect and analyze water samples as part of field investigations or to validate data from automatic monitors. Apply research findings to help minimize the environmental impacts of pollution, waterborne diseases, erosion, and sedimentation. Measure and graph phenomena such as lake levels, stream flows, and changes in water volumes. Investigate complaints or conflicts related to the alteration of public waters, gathering information, recommending alternatives, informing participants of progress, and preparing draft orders.

3. Natural Sciences Managers

Personality Type: Enterprising–Investigative

Earnings: $114,560
Growth: 15.4%
Annual Openings: 2,010

Most Common Education/Training Level:
Master's degree

Plan, direct, or coordinate activities in such fields as life sciences, physical sciences, mathematics, and statistics and research and development in these fields. Confer with scientists, engineers, regulators, and others to plan and review projects and to provide technical assistance. Develop client relationships and communicate with clients to explain proposals, present research findings, establish specifications, or discuss project status. Plan and direct research, development, and production activities. Prepare project proposals. Design and coordinate successive phases of problem analysis, solution proposals, and testing. Review project activities and prepare and review research, testing, and operational reports. Hire, supervise, and evaluate engineers, technicians, researchers, and other staff. Determine scientific and technical goals within broad outlines provided by top management and make detailed plans to accomplish these goals. Develop and implement policies, standards, and procedures for the architectural, scientific, and technical work performed to ensure regulatory compliance and operations enhancement. Develop innovative technology and train staff for its implementation. Provide for stewardship of plant and animal resources and habitats, studying land use; monitoring animal populations; and providing shelter, resources, and medical treatment for animals. Conduct own research in field of expertise. Recruit personnel and oversee the development and maintenance of staff competence. Advise and assist in obtaining patents or meeting other legal requirements. Prepare and administer budget, approve and review expenditures, and prepare financial reports. Make presentations at professional meetings to further knowledge in the field.

Job Specializations

Clinical Research Coordinators. Plan, direct, or coordinate clinical research projects. Direct the activities of workers engaged in clinical research projects to ensure compliance with protocols and overall clinical objectives. May evaluate and analyze clinical data. Solicit industry-sponsored trials through contacts and professional organizations. Review scientific literature, participate in continuing education activities, or attend conferences and seminars to maintain current knowledge of clinical studies affairs and issues. Register protocol patients with appropriate statistical centers as required. Prepare for or participate in quality assurance audits conducted by study sponsors, federal agencies, or specially designated review groups. Participate in preparation and management of research budgets and monetary disbursements. Perform specific protocol procedures such as interviewing subjects, taking vital signs, and performing electrocardiograms. Interpret protocols and advise treating physicians on appropriate dosage modifications or treatment calculations based on patient characteristics. Develop advertising and other informational materials to be used in subject recruitment. Contact industry representatives to ensure equipment and software specifications necessary for successful study completion. Confer with health care professionals to determine the best recruitment practices for studies. Track enrollment status of subjects and document dropout information such as dropout causes and subject contact efforts. Review proposed study protocols to evaluate factors such as sample collection processes, data management plans, and potential subject risks. Record adverse event and side effect data and confer with investigators regarding the reporting of events to oversight agencies. Prepare study-related documentation such as protocol worksheets, procedural manuals, adverse event reports, institutional review board documents, and progress reports. Participate in the development of study protocols including guidelines for administration or data collection procedures. Oversee subject enrollment to ensure that informed consent is properly obtained and documented. Order drugs or devices necessary for study completion.

Water Resource Specialists. Design or implement programs and strategies related to water resource issues, such as supply, quality, and regulatory compliance issues. Supervise teams of workers who capture water from wells and rivers. Review or evaluate designs for water detention facilities, storm drains, flood control facilities, or other hydraulic structures. Negotiate for water rights with communities or water facilities to meet water supply demands. Perform hydrologic, hydraulic, or water quality modeling. Compile water resource data, using geographic information systems (GIS) or global position systems (GPS) software. Compile and maintain documentation on the health of a body of water. Write proposals, project reports, informational brochures, or other documents on wastewater purification, water supply and demand, or other water resource subjects. Recommend new or revised policies, procedures, or regulations to support water resource or conservation goals. Provide technical expertise to assist communities in the development or implementation of storm water monitoring or other water programs. Present water resource proposals to government, public interest groups, or community groups. Identify methods for distributing purified wastewater into rivers, streams, or oceans. Monitor water use, demand, or quality in a particular geographic area. Identify and characterize specific causes or sources of water pollution. Develop plans to protect watershed

health or rehabilitate watersheds. Develop or implement standardized water monitoring and assessment methods. Conduct technical studies for water resources on topics such as pollutants and water treatment options. Conduct, or oversee the conduct of, investigations on matters such as water storage, wastewater discharge, pollutants, permits, or other compliance and regulatory issues. Conduct cost-benefit studies for watershed improvement projects or water management alternatives. Analyze storm water systems to identify opportunities for water resource improvements.

Veterinary Medicine

See Investigative

Investigative Majors

Biochemistry

Personality Type:
Investigative–Artistic–Realistic

Useful Facts About the Major

Focuses on the scientific study of the chemistry of living systems, their fundamental chemical substances and reactions, and their chemical pathways and information transfer systems.

Related CIP Program: 26.0202 Biochemistry

Specializations in the Major: Research, forensic chemistry, pharmacological chemistry, recombinant DNA.

Typical Sequence of College Courses: English composition, calculus, introduction to computer science, general chemistry, general biology, organic chemistry, general physics, analytical chemistry, general microbiology, introduction to biochemistry, cell biology, molecular biology, physical chemistry, genetics.

Typical Sequence of High School Courses: English, algebra, trigonometry, biology, geometry, chemistry, physics, computer science, pre-calculus, calculus, calculus.

Career Snapshot

Biochemistry studies the fundamental chemical processes that support life. The recent growth of the pharmaceutical industry and of genetic engineering technology has fueled the demand for biochemistry majors, especially at the graduate level, but there will be a lot of competition for independent research positions that are supported by grants—as are many university jobs. Better opportunities are expected for those with bachelor's degrees who seek work in nonresearch jobs such as sales, marketing, and clinical laboratory testing.

Useful Averages for the Related Jobs

* Annual Earnings: $82,000
* Growth: 36.9%
* Openings: 3,498
* Self-Employed: 2.4%
* Verbal Skill Rating: 69
* Math Skill Rating: 70

Other Details About the Related Jobs

Career Clusters: 01 Agriculture, Food, and Natural Resources; 04 Business, Management, and Administration; 08 Health Science; 15 Science, Technology, Engineering, and Mathematics. **Career Pathways:** 01.2 Plant Systems; 04.2 Business, Financial Management, and Accounting; 04.4 Business Analysis; 08.1 Therapeutic Services; 15.2 Science and Mathematics.

Skills: Science, reading comprehension, mathematics, operations analysis, active learning, writing, programming, instructing. **Work Conditions:** Indoors; sitting; exposed to disease or infections; hazardous conditions; common protective or safety equipment; wear specialized protective or safety equipment; exposed to radiation.

Related Jobs

1. Biochemists and Biophysicists

Personality Type:
Investigative–Artistic–Realistic

Earnings: $82,390
Growth: 37.4%
Annual Openings: 1,620

Most Common Education/Training Level:
Doctoral degree

Study the chemical composition and physical principles of living cells and organisms and their electrical and mechanical energy and related phenomena. May conduct research in order to further understanding of the complex chemical combinations and reactions involved in metabolism, reproduction, growth, and heredity. May determine the effects of foods, drugs, serums, hormones, and other substances on tissues and vital processes of living organisms. Design and perform experiments with equipment such as lasers, accelerators, and mass spectrometers. Analyze brain functions, such as learning, thinking, and memory, and analyze the dynamics of seeing and hearing. Share research findings by writing scientific articles and by making presentations at scientific conferences. Develop and test new drugs and medications intended for commercial distribution. Develop methods to process, store, and use foods, drugs, and chemical compounds. Develop new methods to study the mechanisms of biological processes. Examine the molecular and chemical aspects of immune system functioning. Investigate the nature, composition, and expression of genes and research how genetic engineering can impact these processes. Determine the three-dimensional structure of biological macromolecules. Prepare reports and recommendations based upon research outcomes. Design and build laboratory equipment needed for special research projects. Isolate, analyze, and synthesize vitamins, hormones, allergens, minerals, and enzymes and determine their effects on body functions. Research cancer treatment, using radiation and nuclear particles. Research transformations of substances in cells, using atomic isotopes. Study how light is absorbed in processes such as photosynthesis or vision. Analyze foods to determine their nutritional values and the effects of cooking, canning, and processing on these values. Study spatial configurations of submicroscopic molecules such as proteins, using X-rays and electron microscopes. Teach and advise undergraduate and graduate students and supervise their research.

Investigate the transmission of electrical impulses along nerves and muscles. Research how characteristics of plants and animals are carried through successive generations. Investigate damage to cells and tissues caused by X-rays and nuclear particles.

2. Medical Scientists, Except Epidemiologists

Personality Type:
Investigative–Realistic–Artistic

Earnings: $74,590
Growth: 40.3%
Annual Openings: 6,620

Most Common Education/Training Level:
Bachelor's or higher degree plus work experience

Conduct research dealing with the understanding of human diseases and the improvement of human health. Engage in clinical investigation or other research, production, technical writing, or related activities. Conduct research to develop methodologies, instrumentation, and procedures for medical application, analyzing data and presenting findings. Plan and direct studies to investigate human or animal disease, preventive methods, and treatments for disease. Follow strict safety procedures when handling toxic materials to avoid contamination. Evaluate effects of drugs, gases, pesticides, parasites, and microorganisms at various levels. Teach principles of medicine and medical and laboratory procedures to physicians, residents, students, and technicians. Prepare and analyze organ, tissue, and cell samples to identify toxicity, bacteria, or microorganisms or to study cell structure. Standardize drug dosages, methods of immunization, and procedures for manufacture of drugs and medicinal compounds. Investigate cause, progress, life cycle, or mode of transmission of diseases or parasites. Confer with health department, industry personnel, physicians, and others to develop health safety standards and public health improvement programs. Study animal and human health and physiological processes. Consult with and advise physicians, educators, researchers, and others regarding medical applications of physics, biology, and chemistry. Use equipment such as atomic absorption spectrometers, electron microscopes, flow cytometers, and chromatography systems.

3. Natural Sciences Managers

Personality Type: Enterprising–Investigative

Earnings: $114,560
Growth: 15.4%
Annual Openings: 2,010

Most Common Education/Training Level:
Bachelor's or higher degree plus work experience

Plan, direct, or coordinate activities in such fields as life sciences, physical sciences, mathematics, and statistics and research and development in these fields. Confer with scientists, engineers, regulators, and others to plan and review projects and to provide technical assistance. Develop client relationships and communicate with clients to explain proposals, present research findings, establish specifications, or discuss project status. Plan and direct research, development, and production activities. Prepare project proposals. Design and coordinate successive phases of problem analysis, solution proposals, and testing. Review project activities and prepare and review research, testing, and operational reports. Hire, supervise, and evaluate engineers, technicians, researchers, and other staff. Determine scientific and technical goals within broad outlines provided by top management and make detailed plans to accomplish these goals. Develop and implement policies, standards, and procedures for the architectural, scientific, and technical work performed to ensure regulatory compliance and operations enhancement. Develop innovative technology and train staff for its implementation. Provide for stewardship of plant and animal resources and habitats, studying land use; monitoring animal populations; and providing shelter, resources, and medical treatment for animals. Conduct own research in field of expertise. Recruit personnel and oversee the development and maintenance of staff competence. Advise and assist in obtaining patents or meeting other legal requirements. Prepare and administer budget, approve and review expenditures, and prepare financial reports. Make presentations at professional meetings to further knowledge in the field.

Job Specializations

Clinical Research Coordinators. Plan, direct, or coordinate clinical research projects. Direct the activities of workers engaged in clinical research projects to ensure compliance with protocols and overall clinical objectives. May evaluate and analyze clinical data. Solicit industry-sponsored trials through contacts and professional organizations. Review scientific literature, participate in continuing education activities, or attend conferences and seminars to maintain current knowledge of clinical studies affairs and issues. Register protocol patients with appropriate statistical centers as required. Prepare for or participate in quality assurance audits conducted by study sponsors, federal agencies, or specially designated review groups. Participate in preparation and management of research budgets and monetary disbursements. Perform specific protocol procedures such as interviewing subjects, taking vital signs, and performing electrocardiograms. Interpret protocols and advise treating physicians on appropriate dosage modifications or treatment calculations based on patient characteristics. Develop advertising and other informational materials to be used in subject recruitment. Contact industry representatives to ensure equipment and software specifications necessary for successful study completion. Confer with health care professionals to determine the best recruitment practices for studies. Track enrollment status of subjects and document dropout information such as dropout causes and subject contact efforts. Review proposed study protocols to evaluate factors such as sample collection processes, data management plans, and potential subject risks. Record adverse event and side effect data and confer with investigators regarding the reporting of events to oversight agencies. Prepare study-related documentation such as protocol worksheets, procedural manuals, adverse event reports, institutional review board documents, and progress reports. Participate in the development of study protocols including guidelines for administration or data collection procedures. Oversee subject enrollment to ensure that informed consent is properly obtained and documented. Order drugs or devices necessary for study completion.

Water Resource Specialists. Design or implement programs and strategies related to water resource issues, such as supply, quality, and regulatory compliance issues. Supervise teams of workers who capture water from wells and rivers. Review or evaluate designs for water detention facilities, storm drains, flood control facilities, or other hydraulic structures. Negotiate for water rights with communities or water facilities to meet water supply demands. Perform hydrologic, hydraulic, or water quality modeling. Compile water resource data, using geographic information systems (GIS) or global position systems (GPS) software. Compile and maintain documentation on the health of a body of water. Write proposals, project reports, informational brochures, or other documents on wastewater purification, water supply and demand, or other water resource subjects. Recommend new or revised policies, procedures, or regulations to support water resource or conservation goals. Provide technical expertise to assist communities in the development or implementation of storm water monitoring or other water programs. Present water resource proposals to government, public interest groups, or community groups. Identify methods for distributing purified wastewater into rivers, streams, or oceans. Monitor water use, demand, or quality in a particular

geographic area. Identify and characterize specific causes or sources of water pollution. Develop plans to protect watershed health or rehabilitate watersheds. Develop or implement standardized water monitoring and assessment methods. Conduct technical studies for water resources on topics such as pollutants and water treatment options. Conduct, or oversee the conduct of, investigations on matters such as water storage, wastewater discharge, pollutants, permits, or other compliance and regulatory issues. Conduct cost-benefit studies for watershed improvement projects or water management alternatives. Analyze storm water systems to identify opportunities for water resource improvements.

Computer Engineering

Personality Type:
Investigative–Realistic–Conventional

Useful Facts About the Major

Prepares individuals to apply mathematical and scientific principles to the design, development, and operational evaluation of computer hardware and software systems and related equipment and facilities; and the analysis of specific problems of computer applications to various tasks.

Related CIP Programs: 14.0901 Computer Engineering, General; 14.0902 Computer Hardware Engineering; 14.0903 Computer Software Engineering

Specializations in the Major: Software/systems design, hardware design, systems analysis.

Typical Sequence of College Courses: English composition, technical writing, calculus, differential equations, general chemistry, introduction to computer science, general physics, introduction to engineering, introduction to electric circuits, engineering circuit analysis, numerical analysis, electrical networks, electronics, computer architecture, algorithms and data structures, digital system design, software engineering, operating systems, microcomputer systems, senior design project.

Typical Sequence of High School Courses: English, algebra, geometry, trigonometry, pre-calculus, calculus, chemistry, physics, computer science.

Career Snapshot

Computer engineers use their knowledge of scientific principles to design computers, networks of computers, and systems (such as telecommunications) that include computers. They need to understand both hardware and software, and they may build prototypes of new systems. The usual entry route is via a bachelor's degree. Opportunities for employment are good despite foreign competition, especially in nonmanufacturing jobs related to systems design. Some engineers go into management, and the computer industry provides many opportunities for creative and motivated engineers to become entrepreneurs.

Useful Averages for the Related Jobs

- ❋ Annual Earnings: $92,000
- ❋ Growth: 23.1%
- ❋ Openings: 10,109
- ❋ Self-Employed: 2.3%
- ❋ Verbal Skill Rating: 58
- ❋ Math Skill Rating: 69

Other Details About the Related Jobs

Career Clusters: 02 Architecture and Construction; 08 Health Science; 11 Information Technology; 13 Manufacturing; 15 Science, Technology, Engineering, and Mathematics. **Career Pathways:** 02.1 Design/Pre-Construction; 08.3 Health Informatics; 08.5 Biotechnology Research and Development; 11.1 Network Systems; 11.2 Information Support Services; 11.3 Interactive Media; 11.4 Programming and Software Development; 13.3 Maintenance, Installation, and Repair; 15.1 Engineering and Technology; 15.2 Science and Mathematics.

Skills: Programming, troubleshooting, technology design, operations analysis, science, systems evaluation, quality control analysis, systems analysis. **Work Conditions:** Indoors; sitting.

Related Jobs

1. Computer Hardware Engineers

Personality Type:
Investigative–Realistic–Conventional

Earnings: $98,820
Growth: 3.8%
Annual Openings: 2,350

Most Common Education/Training Level: Associate degree

Research, design, develop, and test computer or computer-related equipment for commercial, industrial, military, or scientific use. May supervise the manufacturing and installation of computer or computer-related equipment and components. Update knowledge and skills to keep up with rapid advancements in computer technology. Provide technical support to designers, marketing and sales departments, suppliers, engineers, and other team members throughout the product development and implementation process. Test and verify hardware and support peripherals to ensure that they meet specifications and requirements, analyzing and recording test data. Monitor functioning of equipment and make necessary modifications to ensure system operates in conformance with specifications. Analyze information to determine, recommend, and plan layout, including type of computers and peripheral equipment modifications. Build, test, and modify product prototypes, using working models or theoretical models constructed using computer simulation. Analyze user needs and recommend appropriate hardware. Direct technicians, engineering designers, or other technical support personnel as needed. Confer with engineering staff and consult specifications to evaluate interface between hardware and software and operational and performance requirements of overall system. Select hardware and material, assuring compliance with specifications and product requirements. Store, retrieve, and manipulate data for analysis of system capabilities and requirements. Write detailed functional specifications that document the hardware development process and support hardware introduction. Specify power supply requirements and configuration, drawing on system performance expectations and design specifications. Provide training and support to system designers and users. Assemble and modify existing pieces of equipment to meet special needs. Evaluate factors such as reporting formats required, cost constraints, and need for security restrictions to determine hardware configuration.

2. Computer Software Engineers, Applications

Personality Type:
Investigative–Realistic–Conventional

Earnings: $87,480
Growth: 34.0%
Annual Openings: 21,840

Most Common Education/Training Level: Associate degree

Develop, create, and modify general computer applications software or specialized utility programs. Analyze user needs and develop software solutions. Design software or customize software for client use with the aim of optimizing operational efficiency. May analyze and design databases within an application area, working individually or coordinating database

development as part of a team. Modify existing software to correct errors, allow it to adapt to new hardware, or to improve its performance. Develop and direct software system testing and validation procedures, programming, and documentation. Confer with systems analysts, engineers, programmers and others to design system and to obtain information on project limitations and capabilities, performance requirements and interfaces. Analyze user needs and software requirements to determine feasibility of design within time and cost constraints. Design, develop and modify software systems, using scientific analysis and mathematical models to predict and measure outcome and consequences of design. Store, retrieve, and manipulate data for analysis of system capabilities and requirements. Consult with customers about software system design and maintenance. Supervise the work of programmers, technologists and technicians and other engineering and scientific personnel. Coordinate software system installation and monitor equipment functioning to ensure specifications are met. Determine system performance standards. Obtain and evaluate information on factors such as reporting formats required, costs, and security needs to determine hardware configuration. Train users to use new or modified equipment. Specify power supply requirements and configuration. Recommend purchase of equipment to control dust, temperature, and humidity in area of system installation. Analyze information to determine, recommend, and plan computer specifications and layouts, and peripheral equipment modifications.

3. Computer Software Engineers, Systems Software

Personality Type:
Investigative–Conventional–Realistic

Earnings: $93,470
Growth: 30.4%
Annual Openings: 15,340

Investigative

Most Common Education/Training Level: Associate degree

Research, design, develop, and test operating-systems-level software, compilers, and network distribution software for medical, industrial, military, communications, aerospace, business, scientific, and general computing applications. Set operational specifications and formulate and analyze software requirements. Apply principles and techniques of computer science, engineering, and mathematical analysis. Modify existing software to correct errors, to adapt it to new hardware or to upgrade interfaces and improve performance. Advise customer about, or perform, maintenance of software system. Analyze information to determine, recommend and plan installation of a new system or modification of an existing system. Consult with engineering staff to evaluate interface between hardware and software, develop specifications and performance requirements and resolve customer problems. Direct software programming and development of documentation. Store, retrieve, and manipulate data for analysis of system capabilities and requirements. Consult with customers or other departments on project status, proposals and technical issues such as software system design and maintenance. Confer with data processing and project managers to obtain information on limitations and capabilities for data processing projects. Coordinate installation of software system. Prepare reports and correspondence concerning project specifications, activities and status. Develop and direct software system testing and validation procedures. Design and develop software systems, using scientific analysis and mathematical models to predict and measure outcome and consequences of design. Train users to use new or modified equipment. Supervise and assign work to programmers, designers, technologists and technicians and other engineering and scientific personnel. Monitor functioning of equipment to ensure system operates in conformance with specifications. Utilize microcontrollers

to develop control signals, implement control algorithms and measure process variables such as temperatures, pressures and positions. Evaluate factors such as reporting formats required, cost constraints, and need for security restrictions to determine hardware configuration. Recommend purchase of equipment to control dust, temperature, and humidity in area of system installation. Specify power supply requirements and configuration.

4. Computer Specialists, All Other

Personality Type:
Conventional–Investigative–Realistic

Earnings: $77,010
Growth: 13.1%
Annual Openings: 7,260

Most Common Education/Training Level:
Bachelor's degree

Solve problems and make plans involving the use of computers in the following fields: business intelligence, systems architecture, data warehousing, database architecture, document management, electronic commerce, geographic information systems, geospatial information, information technology project management, network design, software quality assurance, video game design, Web administration, and Web development. No task data available.

Job Specializations

Business Intelligence Analysts. Produce financial and market intelligence by querying data repositories and generating periodic reports. Devise methods for identifying data patterns and trends in available information sources. Provide technical support for existing reports, dashboards, or other tools. Maintain library of model documents, templates, or other reusable knowledge assets. Identify or monitor current and potential customers, using business intelligence tools. Create or review technical design documentation to ensure the accurate development of reporting solutions. Communicate with customers, competitors, suppliers, professional organizations, or others to stay abreast of industry or business trends. Maintain or update business intelligence tools, databases, dashboards, systems, or methods. Manage timely flow of business intelligence information to users. Identify and analyze industry or geographic trends with business strategy implications. Document specifications for business intelligence or information technology (IT) reports, dashboards, or other outputs. Disseminate information regarding tools, reports, or metadata enhancements. Create business intelligence tools or systems, including design of related databases, spreadsheets, or outputs. Conduct or coordinate tests to ensure that intelligence is consistent with defined needs. Collect business intelligence data from available industry reports, public information, field reports, or purchased sources. Analyze technology trends to identify markets for future product development or to improve sales of existing products. Analyze competitive market strategies through analysis of related product, market, or share trends. Synthesize current business intelligence or trend data to support recommendations for action. Generate standard or custom reports summarizing business, financial, or economic data for review by executives, managers, clients, and other stakeholders.

Computer Systems Engineers/Architects. Design and develop solutions to complex applications problems, system administration issues, or network concerns. Perform systems management and integration functions. Investigate system component suitability for specified purposes and make recommendations regarding component use. Identify system data, hardware, or software components required to meet user needs. Evaluate existing systems to determine effectiveness and suggest changes to meet organizational requirements. Evaluate current or emerging technologies to consider factors such as cost, portability, compatibility, or usability. Establish

functional or system standards to ensure operational requirements, quality requirements, and design constraints are addressed. Document design specifications, installation instructions, and other system-related information. Direct the analysis, development, and operation of complete computer systems. Direct the installation of operating systems, network or application software, or computer or network hardware. Develop system engineering, software engineering, system integration, or distributed system architectures. Develop or approve project plans, schedules, or budgets. Design and conduct hardware or software tests. Collaborate with engineers or software developers to select appropriate design solutions or ensure the compatibility of system components. Define and analyze objectives, scope, issues, or organizational impact of information systems. Provide guidelines for implementing secure systems to customers or installation teams. Provide technical guidance or support for the development or troubleshooting of systems. Provide advice on project costs, design concepts, or design changes. Communicate project information through presentations, technical reports or white papers. Perform security analyses of developed or packaged software components. Develop application-specific software. Monitor system operation to detect potential problems. Configure servers to meet functional specifications. Communicate with staff or clients to understand specific system requirements.

Data Warehousing Specialists. Design, model, or implement corporate data warehousing activities. Program and configure warehouses of database information and provide support to warehouse users. Test software systems or applications for software enhancements or new products. Review designs, codes, test plans, or documentation to ensure quality. Provide or coordinate troubleshooting support for data warehouses. Prepare functional or technical documentation for data warehouses. Write new programs or modify existing programs to meet customer requirements, using current programming languages and technologies. Verify the structure, accuracy, or quality of warehouse data. Select methods, techniques, or criteria for data warehousing evaluative procedures. Perform system analysis, data analysis or programming, using a variety of computer languages and procedures. Map data between source systems, data warehouses, and data marts. Implement business rules via stored procedures, middleware, or other technologies. Develop and implement data extraction procedures from other systems, such as administration, billing, or claims. Develop or maintain standards, such as organization, structure, or nomenclature, for the design of data warehouse elements, such as data architectures, models, tools, and databases. Design and implement warehouse database structures. Create supporting documentation, such as metadata and diagrams of entity relationships, business processes, and process flow. Create plans, test files, and scripts for data warehouse testing, ranging from unit to integration testing. Create or implement metadata processes and frameworks. Develop data warehouse process models, including sourcing, loading, transformation, and extraction. Design, implement, or operate comprehensive data warehouse systems to balance optimization of data access with batch loading and resource utilization factors, according to customer requirements.

Database Architects. Design strategies for enterprise database systems and set standards for operations, programming, and security. Design and construct large relational databases. Integrate new systems with existing warehouse structure and refine system performance and functionality. Test changes to database applications or systems. Provide technical support to junior staff or clients. Set up database clusters, backup, or recovery processes. Identify, evaluate and recommend hardware or software technologies to achieve desired database performance. Plan and install upgrades of database management system software to enhance database performance.

Monitor and report systems resource consumption trends to assure production systems meet availability requirements and hardware enhancements are scheduled appropriately. Identify and correct deviations from database development standards. Document and communicate database schemas, using accepted notations. Develop or maintain archived procedures, procedural codes, or queries for applications. Develop load-balancing processes to eliminate down time for backup processes. Develop data models for applications, metadata tables, views or related database structures. Design databases to support business applications, ensuring system scalability, security, performance and reliability. Design database applications, such as interfaces, data transfer mechanisms, global temporary tables, data partitions, and function-based indexes to enable efficient access of the generic database structure. Demonstrate database technical functionality, such as performance, security and reliability. Create and enforce database development standards. Collaborate with system architects, software architects, design analysts, and others to understand business or industry requirements. Develop database architectural strategies at the modeling, design and implementation stages to address business or industry requirements. Develop and document database architectures.

Document Management Specialists. Implement and administer enterprise-wide document management procedures for the capture, storage, retrieval, sharing, and destruction of electronic records and documents. Keep abreast of developments in document management by reviewing current literature, talking with colleagues, participating in educational programs, attending meetings or workshops, or participating in professional organizations or conferences. Monitor regulatory activity to maintain compliance with records and document management laws. Write, review, or execute plans for testing new or established document management systems. Search electronic sources, such as databases or repositories, or manual sources for information. Retrieve electronic assets from repository for distribution to users, collecting and returning to repository, if necessary. Propose recommendations for improving content management system capabilities. Prepare support documentation and training materials for end users of document management systems. Prepare and record changes to official documents and confirm changes with legal and compliance management staff. Exercise security surveillance over document processing, reproduction, distribution, storage, or archiving. Implement scanning or other automated data entry procedures, using imaging devices and document imaging software. Document technical functions and specifications for new or proposed content management systems. Develop, document, or maintain standards, best practices, or system usage procedures. Consult with end users regarding problems in accessing electronic content. Conduct needs assessments to identify document management requirements of departments or end users. Assist in the development of document or content classification taxonomies to facilitate information capture, search, and retrieval. Assist in the assessment, acquisition, or deployment of new electronic document management systems. Assist in determining document management policies to facilitate efficient, legal, and secure access to electronic content. Analyze, interpret, or disseminate system performance data.

Electronic Commerce Specialists. Market products on proprietary websites. Produce online advertising. Determine Web site content and design. Analyze customer preferences and online sales. Keep abreast of government regulations and emerging web technology to ensure regulatory compliance by reviewing current literature, talking with colleagues, participating in educational programs, attending meetings or workshops, or participating in professional conferences, workshops, or groups. Resolve product availability problems in collaboration with customer service staff. Implement online customer service processes to ensure positive and consistent user experiences. Identify, evaluate, or procure hardware or software for implementing online marketing campaigns. Identify methods for interfacing web application technologies with enterprise resource planning or other system software. Define product requirements based on market research analysis in collaboration with design and engineering staff. Assist in the evaluation and negotiation of contracts with vendors and online partners. Propose online or multiple-sales-channel campaigns to marketing executives. Assist in the development of online transactional and security policies. Prepare electronic commerce designs and prototypes, such as storyboards, mockups, and other content, using graphics design software. Participate in the development of online marketing strategy. Identify and develop commercial or technical specifications to promote transactional web site functionality, including usability, pricing, checkout, or data security. Develop transactional web applications, using web programming software and knowledge of programming languages, such as hypertext markup language (HTML) and extensible markup language (XML). Coordinate sales or other promotional strategies with merchandising, operations, or inventory control staff to ensure product catalogs are current and accurate. Conduct market research analysis to identify electronic commerce trends, market opportunities, or competitor performance. Conduct financial modeling for online marketing programs or website revenue forecasting.

Geographic Information Systems Technicians. Assist scientists, technologists, and related professionals in building, maintaining, modifying, and using geographic information systems (GIS) databases. May also perform some custom application development and provide user support. Recommend procedures and equipment or software upgrades to increase data accessibility or ease of use. Provide technical support to users or clients regarding the maintenance, development, or operation of Geographic Information Systems

(GIS) databases, equipment, or applications. Read current literature, talk with colleagues, continue education, or participate in professional organizations or conferences to keep abreast of developments in Geographic Information Systems (GIS) technology, equipment, or systems. Confer with users to analyze, configure, or troubleshoot applications. Select cartographic elements needed for effective presentation of information. Transfer or rescale information from original photographs onto maps or other photographs. Review existing or incoming data for currency, accuracy, usefulness, quality, or completeness of documentation. Interpret aerial or ortho photographs. Analyze Geographic Information Systems (GIS) data to identify spatial relationships or display results of analyses using maps, graphs, or tabular data. Perform geospatial data building, modeling, or analysis using advanced spatial analysis, data manipulation, or cartography software. Maintain or modify existing Geographic Information Systems (GIS) databases. Enter data into Geographic Information Systems (GIS) databases using techniques such as coordinate geometry, keyboard entry of tabular data, manual digitizing of maps, scanning or automatic conversion to vectors, and conversion of other sources of digital Design or prepare graphic representations of Geographic Information Systems (GIS) data using GIS hardware or software applications. Design or coordinate the development of integrated Geographic Information Systems (GIS) spatial or non-spatial databases.

Geospatial Information Scientists and Technologists. Research and develop geospatial technologies. May produce databases, perform applications programming, or coordinate projects. May specialize in areas such as agriculture, mining, health care, retail trade, urban planning or military intelligence. Produce data layers, maps, tables, or reports using spatial analysis procedures and Geographic Information Systems (GIS) technology, equipment, or systems. Coordinate the development or administration of

Geographic Information Systems (GIS) projects, including the development of technical priorities, client reporting and interface, or coordination and review of schedules and budgets. Provide technical expertise in Geographic Information Systems (GIS) technology to clients or users. Create, analyze, report, convert, or transfer data using specialized applications program software. Provide technical support for computer-based Geographic Information Systems (GIS) mapping software. Design, program, or model Geographic Information Systems (GIS) applications or procedures. Lead, train, or supervise technicians or related staff in the conduct of Geographic Information Systems (GIS) analytical procedures. Perform computer programming, data analysis, or software development for Geographic Information Systems (GIS) applications, including the maintenance of existing systems or research and development for future enhancements. Collect, compile, or integrate Geographic Information Systems (GIS) data such as remote sensing and cartographic data for inclusion in map manuscripts. Read current literature, talk with colleagues, continue education, or participate in professional organizations or conferences to keep abreast of developments in Geographic Information Systems (GIS) technology, equipment, or systems. Meet with clients to discuss topics such as technical specifications, customized solutions, and operational problems. Perform integrated and computerized Geographic Information Systems (GIS) analyses to address scientific problems. Create visual representations of geospatial data using complex procedures such as analytical modeling, three-dimensional renderings, and plot creation.

Information Technology Project Managers. Plan, initiate, and manage information technology (IT) projects. Lead and guide the work of technical staff. Serve as liaison between business and technical aspects of projects. Plan project stages and assess business implications for each stage. Monitor progress to assure deadlines, standards, and cost targets are met. Perform risk assessments to develop response strategies. Submit project deliverables, ensuring adherence to quality standards. Monitor the performance of project team members, providing and documenting performance feedback. Confer with project personnel to identify and resolve problems. Assess current or future customer needs and priorities through communicating directly with customers, conducting surveys, or other methods. Schedule and facilitate meetings related to information technology projects. Monitor or track project milestones and deliverables. Negotiate with project stakeholders or suppliers to obtain resources or materials. Initiate, review, or approve modifications to project plans. Identify, review, or select vendors or consultants to meet project needs. Establish and execute a project communication plan. Identify need for initial or supplemental project resources. Direct or coordinate activities of project personnel. Develop implementation plans that include analyses such as cost-benefit or return on investment (ROI). Coordinate recruitment or selection of project personnel. Develop and manage annual budgets for information technology projects. Assign duties, responsibilities, and spans of authority to project personnel. Prepare project status reports by collecting, analyzing, and summarizing information and trends. Manage project execution to ensure adherence to budget, schedule, and scope. Develop or update project plans for information technology projects including information such as project objectives, technologies, systems, information specifications, schedules, funding, and staffing. Develop and manage work breakdown structure (WBS) of information technology projects.

Network Designers. Determine user requirements and design specifications for computer networks. Plan and implement network upgrades. Communicate with customers, sales staff, or marketing staff to determine customer needs. Develop or recommend network security measures, such as firewalls, network security audits, or automated security probes. Develop network-related documentation. Prepare detailed network specifications, including diagrams, charts, equipment configurations, and recommended technologies. Supervise engineers and other staff in the design or implementation of network solutions. Develop conceptual, logical, or physical network designs. Evaluate network designs to determine whether customer requirements are met efficiently and effectively. Develop disaster recovery plans. Develop and implement solutions for network problems. Explain design specifications to integration or test engineers. Determine specific network hardware or software requirements, such as platforms, interfaces, bandwidths, or routine schemas. Coordinate network operations, maintenance, repairs, or upgrades. Prepare or monitor project schedules, budgets, or cost control systems. Coordinate installation of new equipment. Coordinate network or design activities with designers of associated networks. Estimate time and materials needed to complete projects. Participate in network technology upgrade or expansion projects, including installation of hardware and software and integration testing. Monitor and analyze network performance and data input/output reports to detect problems, identify inefficient use of computer resources, or perform capacity planning. Adjust network sizes to meet volume or capacity demands. Design, build, or operate equipment configuration prototypes, including network hardware, software, servers, or server operation systems. Prepare design presentations and proposals for staff or customers. Develop procedures to track, project, or report network availability, reliability, capacity, or utilization.

Software Quality Assurance Engineers and Testers. Develop and execute software test plans in order to identify software problems and their causes. Document test procedures to ensure replicability and compliance with standards. Perform initial debugging procedures by reviewing configuration files, logs, or code pieces to determine breakdown source. Participate in product design reviews to provide input on functional requirements, product designs, schedules, or potential problems. Monitor program performance to ensure efficient and problem-free operations. Investigate customer problems referred by technical support. Install, maintain, or use software testing programs. Install and configure re-creations of software production environments to allow testing of software performance. Identify, analyze, and document problems with program function, output, online screen, or content. Evaluate or recommend software for testing or bug tracking. Develop testing programs that address areas such as database impacts, software scenarios, regression testing, negative testing, error or bug retests, or usability. Monitor bug resolution efforts and track successes. Document software defects, using a bug tracking system, and report defects to software developers. Conduct software compatibility tests with programs, hardware, operating systems, or network environments. Create or maintain databases of known test defects. Design test plans, scenarios, scripts, or procedures. Design or develop automated testing tools. Develop or specify standards, methods, or procedures to determine product quality or release readiness. Identify program deviance from standards, and suggest modifications to ensure compliance. Test system modifications to prepare for implementation. Review software documentation to ensure technical accuracy, compliance, or completeness, or to mitigate risks. Provide technical support during software installation or configuration. Conduct historical analyses of test results. Coordinate user or third party testing. Collaborate with field staff or customers to evaluate or diagnose problems and recommend possible solutions.

Video Game Designers. Design core features of video games. Specify innovative game and role-play mechanics, storylines, and character biographies. Create and maintain design documentation. Guide and collaborate with production staff to produce games as designed. Review or evaluate competitive products, film, music, television, and other art forms to generate new game design ideas. Provide test specifications to quality assurance staff. Keep abreast of game design technology and techniques, industry trends, or audience interests, reactions, and needs by reviewing current literature, talking with colleagues, participating in educational programs, attending meetings or workshops, or participation in professional conferences, workshops, or groups. Create gameplay test plans for internal and external test groups. Provide feedback to designers and other colleagues regarding game design features. Balance and adjust gameplay experiences to ensure the critical and commercial success of the product. Write or supervise the writing of game text and dialogue. Solicit, obtain, and integrate feedback from design and technical staff into original game design. Provide feedback to production staff regarding technical game qualities or adherence to original design. Prepare two-dimensional concept layouts or three-dimensional mock-ups. Present new game design concepts to management and technical colleagues, including artists, animators, and programmers. Prepare and revise initial game sketches using two- and three-dimensional graphical design software. Oversee gameplay testing to ensure intended gaming experience and game adherence to original vision. Guide design discussions between development teams. Devise missions, challenges, or puzzles to be encountered in game play. Develop and maintain design level documentation, including mechanics, guidelines, and mission outlines. Determine supplementary virtual features, such as currency, item catalog, menu design, and audio direction. Create gameplay prototypes for presentation to creative and technical staff and management. Create and manage documentation, production schedules, prototyping goals, and communication plans in collaboration with production staff. Consult with multiple stakeholders to define requirements and implement online features.

Web Administrators. Manage Web environment design, deployment, development, and

maintenance activities. **Perform testing and quality assurance of Web sites and Web applications.** Back up or modify applications and related data to provide for disaster recovery. Determine sources of Web page or server problems, and take action to correct such problems. Review or update Web page content or links in a timely manner, using appropriate tools. Monitor systems for intrusions or denial of service attacks, and report security breaches to appropriate personnel. Implement Web site security measures, such as firewalls or message encryption. Administer Internet/intranet infrastructure, including components such as Web, file transfer protocol (FTP), news, and mail servers. Collaborate with development teams to discuss, analyze, or resolve usability issues. Test backup or recovery plans regularly and resolve any problems. Monitor Web developments through continuing education, reading, or participation in professional conferences, workshops, or groups. Implement updates, upgrades, and patches in a timely manner to limit loss of service. Identify or document backup or recovery plans. Collaborate with Web developers to create and operate internal and external Web sites, or to manage projects, such as e-marketing campaigns. Install or configure Web server software or hardware to ensure that directory structure is well-defined, logical, secure, and that files are named properly. Gather, analyze, or document user feedback to locate or resolve sources of problems. Develop Web site performance metrics. Identify or address interoperability requirements. Document installation or configuration procedures to allow maintenance and repetition. Identify, standardize, and communicate levels of access and security. Track, compile, and analyze Web site usage data. Test issues such as system integration, performance, and system security on a regular schedule or after any major program modifications. Recommend Web site improvements, and develop budgets to support recommendations. Inform Web site users of problems, problem resolutions, or application changes and updates.

Web Developers. Develop and design Web applications and Web sites. Create and specify architectural and technical parameters. Direct Web site content creation, enhancement, and maintenance. Document test plans, testing procedures, or test results. Design and implement web site security measures such as firewalls or message encryption. Renew domain name registrations. Respond to user email inquiries, or set up automated systems to send responses. Collaborate with management or users to develop e-commerce strategies and to integrate these strategies with web sites. Maintain understanding of current web technologies or programming practices through continuing education, reading, or participation in professional conferences, workshops, or groups. Communicate with network personnel or web site hosting agencies to address hardware or software issues affecting web sites. Develop and document style guidelines for web site content. Develop or implement procedures for ongoing web site revision. Write supporting code for web applications or web sites. Back up files from web sites to local directories for instant recovery in case of problems. Create searchable indices for web page content. Analyze user needs to determine technical requirements. Establish appropriate server directory trees. Design, build, or maintain web sites, using authoring or scripting languages, content creation tools, management tools, and digital media. Recommend and implement performance improvements. Perform or direct web site updates. Perform web site tests according to planned schedules, or after any web site or product revisions. Develop databases that support web applications and web sites. Monitor security system performance logs to identify problems and notify security specialists when problems occur. Identify problems uncovered by testing or customer feedback, and correct problems or refer problems to appropriate personnel for correction. Install and configure hypertext transfer protocol (HTTP) servers and associated operating systems. Register web sites with search engines to increase web site traffic.

Investigative

5. Engineering Managers

Personality Type:
Enterprising–Realistic–Investigative

Earnings: $117,000
Growth: 6.2%
Annual Openings: 4,870

Most Common Education/Training Level: Associate degree

Plan, direct, or coordinate activities or research and development in such fields as architecture and engineering. Confer with management, production, and marketing staff to discuss project specifications and procedures. Coordinate and direct projects, making detailed plans to accomplish goals and directing the integration of technical activities. Analyze technology, resource needs, and market demand, to plan and assess the feasibility of projects. Plan and direct the installation, testing, operation, maintenance, and repair of facilities and equipment. Direct, review, and approve product design and changes. Recruit employees, assign, direct, and evaluate their work, and oversee the development and maintenance of staff competence. Prepare budgets, bids, and contracts, and direct the negotiation of research contracts. Develop and implement policies, standards and procedures for the engineering and technical work performed in the department, service, laboratory or firm. Review and recommend or approve contracts and cost estimates. Perform administrative functions such as reviewing and writing reports, approving expenditures, enforcing rules, and making decisions about the purchase of materials or services. Present and explain proposals, reports, and findings to clients. Consult or negotiate with clients to prepare project specifications. Set scientific and technical goals within broad outlines provided by top management. Administer highway planning, construction, and maintenance. Direct the engineering of water control, treatment, and distribution projects. Plan, direct, and coordinate survey work with other staff activities, certifying survey work, and writing land legal descriptions. Confer with and report to officials and the public to provide information and solicit support for projects.

Job Specialization

Biofuels/Biodiesel Technology and Product Development Managers. Define, plan, or execute biofuel/biodiesel research programs that evaluate alternative feedstock and process technologies with near-term commercial potential. Develop lab scale models of industrial scale processes, such as fermentation. Develop computational tools or approaches to improve biofuels research and development activities. Develop carbohydrates arrays and associated methods for screening enzymes involved in biomass conversion. Provide technical or scientific guidance to technical staff in the conduct of biofuels research or development. Prepare, or oversee the preparation of, experimental plans for biofuels research or development. Prepare biofuels research and development reports for senior management or technical professionals. Perform protein functional analysis and engineering for processing of feedstock and creation of biofuels. Develop separation processes to recover biofuels. Develop methods to recover ethanol or other fuels from complex bioreactor liquid and gas streams. Develop methods to estimate the efficiency of biomass pretreatments. Design or execute solvent or product recovery experiments in laboratory or field settings. Design or conduct applied biodiesel or biofuels research projects on topics such as transport, thermodynamics, mixing, filtration, distillation, fermentation, extraction, and separation. Design chemical conversion processes, such as etherification, esterification, interesterification, transesterification, distillation, hydrogenation, oxidation or reduction of fats and oils, and vegetable oil refining. Conduct experiments on biomass or pretreatment technologies. Conduct experiments to test new or alternate feedstock fermentation processes.

Analyze data from biofuels studies, such as fluid dynamics, water treatments, or solvent extraction and recovery processes. Oversee biodiesel/biofuels prototyping or development projects. Propose new biofuels products, processes, technologies or applications based on findings from applied biofuels or biomass research projects.

Computer Science

Personality Type:
Investigative–Conventional–Realistic

Useful Facts About the Major

Focuses on computers, computing problems and solutions, and the design of computer systems and user interfaces from a scientific perspective.

Related CIP Programs: 11.0701 Computer Science; 11.0802 Data Modeling/Warehousing and Database Administration; 11.1003 Computer and Information Systems Security/Information Assurance; 11.1001 Network and System Administration/Administrator

Specializations in the Major: Business programming, scientific programming, database programming, systems programming, programming for the Internet, security and disaster recovery.

Typical Sequence of College Courses: English composition, calculus, introduction to economics, statistics for business and social sciences, introduction to computer science, programming in a language (e.g., C, Pascal, COBOL), algorithms and data structures, software engineering, operating systems, database systems, theory of computer languages, computer architecture, artificial intelligence.

Typical Sequence of High School Courses: English, algebra, geometry, trigonometry, pre-calculus, calculus, chemistry, physics, computer science.

Career Snapshot

Computer science teaches you not only specific languages, but the principles by which languages are created, the structures used to store data, and the logical structures by which programs solve problems. Job outlook is best for roles that are not easily outsourced to overseas workers, such as systems administration and information security.

Useful Averages for the Related Jobs

* Annual Earnings: $99,000
* Growth: 23.6%
* Openings: 7,023
* Self-Employed: 3.5%
* Verbal Skill Rating: 61
* Math Skill Rating: 66

Other Details About the Related Jobs

Career Clusters: 04 Business, Management, and Administration; 08 Health Science; 11 Information Technology; 13 Manufacturing; 15 Science, Technology, Engineering, and Mathematics. **Career Pathways:** 04.1 Management; 04.4 Business Analysis; 08.3 Health Informatics; 08.5 Biotechnology Research and Development; 11.1 Network Systems; 11.2 Information Support Services; 11.3 Interactive Media; 11.4 Programming and Software Development; 13.3 Maintenance, Installation, and Repair; 15.1 Engineering and Technology; 15.2 Science and Mathematics.

Skills: Programming, technology design, troubleshooting, systems evaluation, operations analysis, management of financial resources, systems analysis, equipment selection. **Work Conditions:** Indoors; sitting.

Investigative

Related Jobs

1. Computer and Information Scientists, Research

Personality Type:
Investigative–Realistic–Conventional

Earnings: $101,570
Growth: 24.2%
Annual Openings: 1,320

Most Common Education/Training Level: Associate degree

Conduct research into fundamental computer and information science as theorists, designers, or inventors. Solve or develop solutions to problems in the field of computer hardware and software. Evaluate project plans and proposals to assess feasibility issues. Analyze problems to develop solutions involving computer hardware and software. Conduct logical analyses of business, scientific, engineering, and other technical problems, formulating mathematical models of problems for solution by computers. Consult with users, management, vendors, and technicians to determine computing needs and system requirements. Participate in multidisciplinary projects in areas such as virtual reality, human-computer interaction, or robotics. Approve, prepare, monitor, and adjust operational budgets. Assign or schedule tasks in order to meet work priorities and goals. Develop and interpret organizational goals, policies, and procedures. Develop performance standards, and evaluate work in light of established standards. Direct daily operations of departments, coordinating project activities with other departments. Meet with managers, vendors, and others to solicit cooperation and resolve problems. Maintain network hardware and software, direct network security measures, and monitor networks to ensure availability to system users. Apply theoretical expertise and innovation to create or apply new technology, such as adapting principles for applying computers to new uses. Participate in staffing decisions and direct training of subordinates. Design computers and the software that runs them.

2. Computer and Information Systems Managers

Personality Type:
Enterprising–Conventional–Investigative

Earnings: $113,720
Growth: 16.9%
Annual Openings: 9,710

Most Common Education/Training Level:
Bachelor's degree

Plan, direct, or coordinate activities in such fields as electronic data processing, information systems, systems analysis, and computer programming. Manage backup, security, and user help systems. Consult with users, management, vendors, and technicians to assess computing needs and system requirements. Direct daily operations of department, analyzing workflow, establishing priorities, developing standards and setting deadlines. Assign and review the work of systems analysts, programmers, and other computer-related workers. Stay abreast of advances in technology. Develop computer information resources, providing for data security and control, strategic computing, and disaster recovery. Review and approve all systems charts and programs prior to their implementation. Evaluate the organization's technology use and needs and recommend improvements, such as hardware and software upgrades. Control operational budget and expenditures. Meet with department heads, managers, supervisors, vendors, and others, to solicit cooperation and resolve problems. Develop and interpret organizational goals, policies, and procedures. Recruit, hire, train and supervise staff, or participate in staffing decisions. Review project plans to plan and coordinate project activity. Evaluate data processing proposals to assess project feasibility and requirements. Prepare and review operational reports or project progress reports. Purchase necessary equipment.

3. Computer Software Engineers, Applications

Personality Type:
Investigative–Realistic–Conventional

Earnings: $87,480
Growth: 34.0%
Annual Openings: 21,840

Most Common Education/Training Level: Associate degree

Develop, create, and modify general computer applications software or specialized utility programs. Analyze user needs and develop software solutions. Design software or customize software for client use with the aim of optimizing operational efficiency. May analyze and design databases within an application area, working individually or coordinating database development as part of a team. Modify existing software to correct errors, allow it to adapt to new hardware, or to improve its performance. Develop and direct software system testing and validation procedures, programming, and documentation. Confer with systems analysts, engineers, programmers and others to design system and to obtain information on project limitations and capabilities, performance requirements and interfaces. Analyze user needs and software requirements to determine feasibility of design within time and cost constraints. Design, develop and modify software systems, using scientific analysis and mathematical models to predict and measure outcome and consequences of design. Store, retrieve, and manipulate data for analysis of system capabilities and requirements. Consult with customers about software system design and maintenance. Supervise the work of programmers, technologists and technicians and other engineering and scientific personnel. Coordinate software system installation and monitor equipment functioning to ensure specifications are met. Determine system performance standards. Obtain and evaluate information on factors such as reporting formats required, costs, and security needs to determine hardware configuration. Train users to use new or modified equipment. Specify power supply requirements and configuration. Recommend purchase of equipment to control dust, temperature, and humidity in area of system installation. Analyze information to determine, recommend, and plan computer specifications and layouts, and peripheral equipment modifications.

4. Computer Software Engineers, Systems Software

Personality Type:
Investigative–Conventional–Realistic

Earnings: $93,470
Growth: 30.4%
Annual Openings: 15,340

Most Common Education/Training Level: Associate degree

Research, design, develop, and test operating-systems-level software, compilers, and network distribution software for medical, industrial, military, communications, aerospace, business, scientific, and general computing applications. Set operational specifications and formulate and analyze software requirements. Apply principles and techniques of computer science, engineering, and mathematical analysis. Modify existing software to correct errors, to adapt it to new hardware or to upgrade interfaces and improve performance. Advise customer about, or perform, maintenance of software system. Analyze information to determine, recommend and plan installation of a new system or modification of an existing system. Consult with engineering staff to evaluate interface between hardware and software, develop specifications and performance requirements and resolve customer problems. Direct software programming and development of documentation. Store, retrieve, and manipulate data for analysis of system capabilities and requirements.

Investigative

Consult with customers or other departments on project status, proposals and technical issues such as software system design and maintenance. Confer with data processing and project managers to obtain information on limitations and capabilities for data processing projects. Coordinate installation of software system. Prepare reports and correspondence concerning project specifications, activities and status. Develop and direct software system testing and validation procedures. Design and develop software systems, using scientific analysis and mathematical models to predict and measure outcome and consequences of design. Train users to use new or modified equipment. Supervise and assign work to programmers, designers, technologists and technicians and other engineering and scientific personnel. Monitor functioning of equipment to ensure system operates in conformance with specifications. Utilize microcontrollers to develop control signals, implement control algorithms and measure process variables such as temperatures, pressures and positions. Evaluate factors such as reporting formats required, cost constraints, and need for security restrictions to determine hardware configuration. Recommend purchase of equipment to control dust, temperature, and humidity in area of system installation. Specify power supply requirements and configuration.

5. Computer Specialists, All Other

Personality Type:
Conventional–Investigative–Realistic

Earnings: $77,010
Growth: 13.1%
Annual Openings: 7,260

Most Common Education/Training Level:
Bachelor's degree

Solve problems and make plans involving the use of computers in the following fields: business intelligence, systems architecture, data warehousing, database architecture, document management, electronic commerce, geographic information systems, geospatial information, information technology project management, network design, software quality assurance, video game design, Web administration, and Web development. No task data available.

Job Specializations

Business Intelligence Analysts. Produce financial and market intelligence by querying data repositories and generating periodic reports. Devise methods for identifying data patterns and trends in available information sources. Provide technical support for existing reports, dashboards, or other tools. Maintain library of model documents, templates, or other reusable knowledge assets. Identify or monitor current and potential customers, using business intelligence tools. Create or review technical design documentation to ensure the accurate development of reporting solutions. Communicate with customers, competitors, suppliers, professional organizations, or others to stay abreast of industry or business trends. Maintain or update business intelligence tools, databases, dashboards, systems, or methods. Manage timely flow of business intelligence information to users. Identify and analyze industry or geographic trends with business strategy implications. Document specifications for business intelligence or information technology (IT) reports, dashboards, or other outputs. Disseminate information regarding tools, reports, or metadata enhancements. Create business intelligence tools or systems, including design of related databases, spreadsheets, or outputs. Conduct or coordinate tests to ensure that intelligence is consistent with defined needs. Collect business intelligence data from available industry reports, public information, field reports, or purchased sources. Analyze technology trends to identify markets for future product development or to improve sales of existing products. Analyze competitive market strategies through analysis of related product, market, or share trends. Synthesize current business intelligence or trend data to support recommendations for action. Generate standard or custom reports summarizing business, financial, or economic data for review by executives, managers, clients, and other stakeholders.

Computer Systems Engineers/Architects. Design and develop solutions to complex applications problems, system administration issues, or network concerns. Perform systems management and integration functions. Investigate system component suitability for specified purposes and make recommendations regarding component use. Identify system data, hardware, or software components required to meet user needs. Evaluate existing systems to determine effectiveness and suggest changes to meet organizational requirements. Evaluate current or emerging technologies to consider factors such as cost, portability, compatibility, or usability. Establish functional or system standards to ensure operational requirements, quality requirements, and design constraints are addressed. Document design specifications, installation instructions, and other system-related information. Direct the analysis, development, and operation of complete computer systems. Direct the installation of operating systems, network or application software, or computer or network hardware. Develop system engineering, software engineering, system integration, or distributed system architectures. Develop or approve project plans, schedules, or budgets. Design and conduct hardware or software tests. Collaborate with engineers or software developers to select appropriate design solutions or ensure the compatibility of system components. Define and analyze objectives, scope, issues, or organizational impact of information systems. Provide guidelines for implementing secure systems to customers or installation teams. Provide technical guidance or support for the development or troubleshooting of systems. Provide advice on project costs, design concepts, or design changes. Communicate project information through presentations, technical reports or white papers. Perform security analyses of developed or packaged software components. Develop application-specific software. Monitor system operation to detect potential problems. Configure servers to meet functional specifications. Communicate with staff or clients to understand specific system requirements.

Data Warehousing Specialists. Design, model, or implement corporate data warehousing activities. Program and configure warehouses of database information and provide support to warehouse users. Test software systems or applications for software enhancements or new products. Review designs, codes, test plans, or documentation to ensure quality. Provide or coordinate troubleshooting support for data warehouses. Prepare functional or technical documentation for data warehouses. Write new programs or modify existing programs to meet customer requirements, using current programming languages and technologies. Verify the structure, accuracy, or quality of warehouse data. Select methods, techniques, or criteria for data warehousing evaluative procedures. Perform system analysis, data analysis or programming, using a variety of computer languages and procedures. Map data between source systems, data warehouses, and data marts. Implement business rules via stored procedures, middleware, or other technologies. Develop and implement data extraction procedures from other systems, such as administration, billing, or claims. Develop or maintain standards, such as organization, structure, or nomenclature, for the design of data warehouse elements, such as data architectures, models, tools, and databases. Design and implement warehouse database structures. Create supporting documentation, such as metadata and diagrams of entity relationships, business processes, and process flow. Create plans, test files, and scripts for data warehouse testing, ranging from unit to integration testing. Create or implement metadata processes and frameworks. Develop data warehouse process models, including sourcing, loading, transformation, and extraction. Design, implement, or operate comprehensive data warehouse systems to balance optimization of data access with batch loading and resource utilization factors, according to customer requirements.

Database Architects. Design strategies for enterprise database systems and set standards for operations, programming, and security. Design and construct large relational databases. Integrate new systems with existing warehouse structure and refine system performance and functionality. Test changes to database applications or systems. Provide technical support to junior staff or clients. Set up database clusters, backup, or recovery processes. Identify, evaluate and recommend hardware or software technologies to achieve desired database performance. Plan and install upgrades of database management system software to enhance database performance. Monitor and report systems resource consumption trends to assure production systems meet availability requirements and hardware enhancements are scheduled appropriately. Identify and correct deviations from database development standards. Document and communicate database schemas, using accepted notations. Develop or maintain archived procedures, procedural codes, or queries for applications. Develop load-balancing processes to eliminate down time for backup processes. Develop data models for applications, metadata tables, views or related database structures. Design databases to support business applications, ensuring system scalability, security, performance and reliability. Design database applications, such as interfaces, data transfer mechanisms, global temporary tables, data partitions, and function-based indexes to enable efficient access of the generic database structure. Demonstrate database technical functionality, such as performance, security and reliability. Create and enforce database development standards. Collaborate with system architects, software architects, design analysts, and others to understand business or industry requirements.

Develop database architectural strategies at the modeling, design and implementation stages to address business or industry requirements. Develop and document database architectures.

Document Management Specialists. Implement and administer enterprise-wide document management procedures for the capture, storage, retrieval, sharing, and destruction of electronic records and documents. Keep abreast of developments in document management by reviewing current literature, talking with colleagues, participating in educational programs, attending meetings or workshops, or participating in professional organizations or conferences. Monitor regulatory activity to maintain compliance with records and document management laws. Write, review, or execute plans for testing new or established document management systems. Search electronic sources, such as databases or repositories, or manual sources for information. Retrieve electronic assets from repository for distribution to users, collecting and returning to repository, if necessary. Propose recommendations for improving content management system capabilities. Prepare support documentation and training materials for end users of document management systems. Prepare and record changes to official documents and confirm changes with legal and compliance management staff. Exercise security surveillance over document processing, reproduction, distribution, storage, or archiving. Implement scanning or other automated data entry procedures, using imaging devices and document imaging software. Document technical functions and specifications for new or proposed content management systems. Develop, document, or maintain standards, best practices, or system usage procedures. Consult with end users regarding problems in accessing electronic content. Conduct needs assessments to identify document management requirements of departments or end users. Assist in the development of document or content classification taxonomies to facilitate information capture, search, and retrieval. Assist in the assessment, acquisition, or deployment of new electronic document management systems. Assist in determining document management policies to facilitate efficient, legal, and secure access to electronic content. Analyze, interpret, or disseminate system performance data.

Electronic Commerce Specialists. Market products on proprietary Web sites. Produce online advertising. Determine Web site content and design. Analyze customer preferences and online sales. Keep abreast of government regulations and emerging web technology to ensure regulatory compliance by reviewing current literature, talking with colleagues, participating in educational programs, attending meetings or workshops, or participation in professional conferences, workshops, or groups. Resolve product availability problems in collaboration with customer service staff. Implement online customer service processes to ensure positive and consistent user experiences. Identify, evaluate, or procure hardware or software for implementing online marketing campaigns. Identify methods for interfacing web application technologies with enterprise resource planning or other system software. Define product requirements based on market research analysis in collaboration with design and engineering staff. Assist in the evaluation and negotiation of contracts with vendors and online partners. Propose online or multiple-sales-channel campaigns to marketing executives. Assist in the development of online transactional and security policies. Prepare electronic commerce designs and prototypes, such as storyboards, mockups, and other content, using graphics design software. Participate in the development of online marketing strategy. Identify and develop commercial or technical specifications to promote transactional web site functionality, including usability, pricing, checkout, or data security. Develop transactional web applications, using web programming software and knowledge of programming languages, such as hypertext markup language (HTML) and extensible markup language (XML).

Coordinate sales or other promotional strategies with merchandising, operations, or inventory control staff to ensure product catalogs are current and accurate. Conduct market research analysis to identify electronic commerce trends, market opportunities, or competitor performance. Conduct financial modeling for online marketing programs or website revenue forecasting.

Geographic Information Systems Technicians. Assist scientists, technologists, and related professionals in building, maintaining, modifying, and using geographic information systems (GIS) databases. May also perform some custom application development and provide user support. Recommend procedures and equipment or software upgrades to increase data accessibility or ease of use. Provide technical support to users or clients regarding the maintenance, development, or operation of Geographic Information Systems (GIS) databases, equipment, or applications. Read current literature, talk with colleagues, continue education, or participate in professional organizations or conferences to keep abreast of developments in Geographic Information Systems (GIS) technology, equipment, or systems. Confer with users to analyze, configure, or troubleshoot applications. Select cartographic elements needed for effective presentation of information. Transfer or rescale information from original photographs onto maps or other photographs. Review existing or incoming data for currency, accuracy, usefulness, quality, or completeness of documentation. Interpret aerial or ortho photographs. Analyze Geographic Information Systems (GIS) data to identify spatial relationships or display results of analyses using maps, graphs, or tabular data. Perform geospatial data building, modeling, or analysis using advanced spatial analysis, data manipulation, or cartography software. Maintain or modify existing Geographic Information Systems (GIS) databases. Enter data into Geographic Information Systems (GIS) databases using techniques such as coordinate geometry, keyboard entry of tabular data, manual digitizing of maps, scanning or automatic conversion to vectors, and conversion of other sources of digital Design or prepare graphic representations of Geographic Information Systems (GIS) data using GIS hardware or software applications. Design or coordinate the development of integrated Geographic Information Systems (GIS) spatial or non-spatial databases.

Geospatial Information Scientists and Technologists. Research and develop geospatial technologies. May produce databases, perform applications programming, or coordinate projects. May specialize in areas such as agriculture, mining, health care, retail trade, urban planning or military intelligence. Produce data layers, maps, tables, or reports using spatial analysis procedures and Geographic Information Systems (GIS) technology, equipment, or systems. Coordinate the development or administration of Geographic Information Systems (GIS) projects, including the development of technical priorities, client reporting and interface, or coordination and review of schedules and budgets. Provide technical expertise in Geographic Information Systems (GIS) technology to clients or users. Create, analyze, report, convert, or transfer data using specialized applications program software. Provide technical support for computer-based Geographic Information Systems (GIS) mapping software. Design, program, or model Geographic Information Systems (GIS) applications or procedures. Lead, train, or supervise technicians or related staff in the conduct of Geographic Information Systems (GIS) analytical procedures. Perform computer programming, data analysis, or software development for Geographic Information Systems (GIS) applications, including the maintenance of existing systems or research and development for future enhancements. Collect, compile, or integrate Geographic Information Systems (GIS) data such as remote sensing and cartographic data for inclusion in map manuscripts. Read current literature, talk with colleagues, continue education, or participate in professional organizations or conferences to keep abreast of developments in Geographic Information Systems (GIS) technology, equipment, or systems. Meet with clients to discuss topics such as technical specifications, customized solutions, and operational problems. Perform integrated and computerized Geographic Information Systems (GIS) analyses to address scientific problems. Create visual representations of geospatial data using complex procedures such as analytical modeling, three-dimensional renderings, and plot creation.

Information Technology Project Managers. Plan, initiate, and manage information technology (IT) projects. Lead and guide the work of technical staff. Serve as liaison between business and technical aspects of projects. Plan project stages and assess business implications for each stage. Monitor progress to assure deadlines, standards, and cost targets are met. Perform risk assessments to develop response strategies. Submit project deliverables, ensuring adherence to quality standards. Monitor the performance of project team members, providing and documenting performance feedback. Confer with project personnel to identify and resolve problems. Assess current or future customer needs and priorities through communicating directly with customers, conducting surveys, or other methods. Schedule and facilitate meetings related to information technology projects. Monitor or track project milestones and deliverables. Negotiate with project stakeholders or suppliers to obtain resources or materials. Initiate, review, or approve modifications to project plans. Identify, review, or select vendors or consultants to meet project needs. Establish and execute a project communication plan. Identify need for initial or supplemental project resources. Direct or coordinate activities of project personnel. Develop implementation plans that include analyses such as cost-benefit or return on investment (ROI). Coordinate recruitment or selection of project personnel. Develop and manage annual budgets for information technology projects. Assign duties, responsibilities, and spans of authority to project personnel. Prepare project status reports by collecting, analyzing, and summarizing information and trends. Manage project execution to ensure adherence to budget, schedule, and scope. Develop or update project plans for information technology projects including information such as project objectives, technologies, systems, information specifications, schedules, funding, and staffing. Develop and manage work breakdown structure (WBS) of information technology projects.

Network Designers. Determine user requirements and design specifications for computer networks. Plan and implement network upgrades. Communicate with customers, sales staff, or marketing staff to determine customer needs. Develop or recommend network security measures, such as firewalls, network security audits, or automated security probes. Develop network-related documentation. Prepare detailed network specifications, including diagrams, charts, equipment configurations, and recommended technologies. Supervise engineers and other staff in the design or implementation of network solutions. Develop conceptual, logical, or physical network designs. Evaluate network designs to determine whether customer requirements are met efficiently and effectively. Develop disaster recovery plans. Develop and implement solutions for network problems. Explain design specifications to integration or test engineers. Determine specific network hardware or software requirements, such as platforms, interfaces, bandwidths, or routine schemas. Coordinate network operations, maintenance, repairs, or upgrades. Prepare or monitor project schedules, budgets, or cost control systems. Coordinate installation of new equipment. Coordinate network or design activities with designers of associated networks. Estimate time and materials needed to complete projects. Participate in network technology upgrade or expansion projects, including installation of hardware and software and integration testing. Monitor and analyze

network performance and data input/output reports to detect problems, identify inefficient use of computer resources, or perform capacity planning. Adjust network sizes to meet volume or capacity demands. Design, build, or operate equipment configuration prototypes, including network hardware, software, servers, or server operation systems. Prepare design presentations and proposals for staff or customers. Develop procedures to track, project, or report network availability, reliability, capacity, or utilization.

Software Quality Assurance Engineers and Testers. Develop and execute software test plans in order to identify software problems and their causes. Document test procedures to ensure replicability and compliance with standards. Perform initial debugging procedures by reviewing configuration files, logs, or code pieces to determine breakdown source. Participate in product design reviews to provide input on functional requirements, product designs, schedules, or potential problems. Monitor program performance to ensure efficient and problem-free operations. Investigate customer problems referred by technical support. Install, maintain, or use software testing programs. Install and configure re-creations of software production environments to allow testing of software performance. Identify, analyze, and document problems with program function, output, online screen, or content. Evaluate or recommend software for testing or bug tracking. Develop testing programs that address areas such as database impacts, software scenarios, regression testing, negative testing, error or bug retests, or usability. Monitor bug resolution efforts and track successes. Document software defects, using a bug tracking system, and report defects to software developers. Conduct software compatibility tests with programs, hardware, operating systems, or network environments. Create or maintain databases of known test defects. Design test plans, scenarios, scripts, or procedures. Design or develop automated testing tools. Develop or specify standards, methods, or procedures to determine product quality or release readiness. Identify program deviance from standards, and suggest modifications to ensure compliance. Test system modifications to prepare for implementation. Review software documentation to ensure technical accuracy, compliance, or completeness, or to mitigate risks. Provide technical support during software installation or configuration. Conduct historical analyses of test results. Coordinate user or third party testing. Collaborate with field staff or customers to evaluate or diagnose problems and recommend possible solutions.

Video Game Designers. Design core features of video games. Specify innovative game and role-play mechanics, storylines, and character biographies. Create and maintain design documentation. Guide and collaborate with production staff to produce games as designed. Review or evaluate competitive products, film, music, television, and other art forms to generate new game design ideas. Provide test specifications to quality assurance staff. Keep abreast of game design technology and techniques, industry trends, or audience interests, reactions, and needs by reviewing current literature, talking with colleagues, participating in educational programs, attending meetings or workshops, or participation in professional conferences, workshops, or groups. Create gameplay test plans for internal and external test groups. Provide feedback to designers and other colleagues regarding game design features. Balance and adjust gameplay experiences to ensure the critical and commercial success of the product. Write or supervise the writing of game text and dialogue. Solicit, obtain, and integrate feedback from design and technical staff into original game design. Provide feedback to production staff regarding technical game qualities or adherence to original design. Prepare two-dimensional concept layouts or three-dimensional mock-ups. Present new game design concepts to management and technical colleagues, including artists, animators, and programmers. Prepare and revise initial game sketches

using two- and three-dimensional graphical design software. Oversee gameplay testing to ensure intended gaming experience and game adherence to original vision. Guide design discussions between development teams. Devise missions, challenges, or puzzles to be encountered in game play. Develop and maintain design level documentation, including mechanics, guidelines, and mission outlines. Determine supplementary virtual features, such as currency, item catalog, menu design, and audio direction. Create gameplay prototypes for presentation to creative and technical staff and management. Create and manage documentation, production schedules, prototyping goals, and communication plans in collaboration with production staff. Consult with multiple stakeholders to define requirements and implement online features.

Web Administrators. Manage Web environment design, deployment, development, and maintenance activities. Perform testing and quality assurance of websites and Web applications. Back up or modify applications and related data to provide for disaster recovery. Determine sources of Web page or server problems, and take action to correct such problems. Review or update Web page content or links in a timely manner, using appropriate tools. Monitor systems for intrusions or denial of service attacks, and report security breaches to appropriate personnel. Implement Web site security measures, such as firewalls or message encryption. Administer Internet/intranet infrastructure, including components such as Web, file transfer protocol (FTP), news, and mail servers. Collaborate with development teams to discuss, analyze, or resolve usability issues. Test backup or recovery plans regularly and resolve any problems. Monitor Web developments through continuing education, reading, or participation in professional conferences, workshops, or groups. Implement updates, upgrades, and patches in a timely manner to limit loss of service. Identify or document backup or recovery plans. Collaborate with Web developers to create and operate internal and external websites or to manage projects, such as e-marketing campaigns. Install or configure Web server software or hardware to ensure that directory structure is well-defined, logical, secure, and that files are named properly. Gather, analyze, or document user feedback to locate or resolve sources of problems. Develop Web site performance metrics. Identify or address interoperability requirements. Document installation or configuration procedures to allow maintenance and repetition. Identify, standardize, and communicate levels of access and security. Track, compile, and analyze website usage data. Test issues such as system integration, performance, and system security on a regular schedule or after any major program modifications. Recommend Web site improvements, and develop budgets to support recommendations. Inform Web site users of problems, problem resolutions, or application changes and updates.

Web Developers. Develop and design Web applications and websites. Create and specify architectural and technical parameters. Direct Web site content creation, enhancement, and maintenance. Document test plans, testing procedures, or test results. Design and implement web site security measures such as firewalls or message encryption. Renew domain name registrations. Respond to user email inquiries, or set up automated systems to send responses. Collaborate with management or users to develop e-commerce strategies and to integrate these strategies with web sites. Maintain understanding of current web technologies or programming practices through continuing education, reading, or participation in professional conferences, workshops, or groups. Communicate with network personnel or web site hosting agencies to address hardware or software issues affecting web sites. Develop and document style guidelines for web site content. Develop or implement procedures for ongoing web site revision. Write supporting code for Web applications or websites. Back up files from web sites to local directories for instant recovery in case of problems. Create searchable

indices for web page content. Analyze user needs to determine technical requirements. Establish appropriate server directory trees. Design, build, or maintain web sites, using authoring or scripting languages, content creation tools, management tools, and digital media. Recommend and implement performance improvements. Perform or direct web site updates. Perform web site tests according to planned schedules, or after any web site or product revisions. Develop databases that support Web applications and websites. Monitor security system performance logs to identify problems and notify security specialists when problems occur. Identify problems uncovered by testing or customer feedback, and correct problems or refer problems to appropriate personnel for correction. Install and configure hypertext transfer protocol (HTTP) servers and associated operating systems. Register websites with search engines to increase web site traffic.

6. Database Administrators

Personality Type: Conventional–Investigative

Earnings: $71,550
Growth: 20.3%
Annual Openings: 4,440

Most Common Education/Training Level: Associate degree

Coordinate changes to computer databases; test and implement the databases, applying knowledge of database management systems. May plan, coordinate, and implement security measures to safeguard computer databases. Develop standards and guidelines to guide the use and acquisition of software and to protect vulnerable information. Modify existing databases and database management systems or direct programmers and analysts to make changes. Test programs or databases, correct errors and make necessary modifications. Plan, coordinate, and implement security measures to safeguard information in computer files against accidental or unauthorized damage, modification or disclosure. Approve, schedule, plan, and supervise the installation and testing of new products and improvements to computer systems such as the installation of new databases. Train users and answer questions. Establish and calculate optimum values for database parameters, using manuals and calculator. Specify users and user access levels for each segment of database. Develop data model describing data elements and how they are used, following procedures and using pen, template or computer software. Develop methods for integrating different products so they work properly together such as customizing commercial databases to fit specific needs. Review project requests describing database user needs to estimate time and cost required to accomplish project. Review procedures in database management system manuals for making changes to database. Work as part of a project team to coordinate database development and determine project scope and limitations. Select and enter codes to monitor database performance and to create production database. Identify and evaluate industry trends in database systems to serve as a source of information and advice for upper management. Write and code logical and physical database descriptions and specify identifiers of database to management system or direct others in coding descriptions. Review workflow charts developed by programmer analyst to understand tasks computer will perform, such as updating records. Revise company definition of data as defined in data dictionary.

7. Network and Computer Systems Administrators

Personality Type:
Investigative–Conventional–Realistic

Earnings: $67,710
Growth: 23.2%
Annual Openings: 13,550

Most Common Education/Training Level:
Bachelor's or higher degree plus work experience

Install, configure, and support organizations' local area networks (LANs), wide area networks (WANs), and Internet systems or segments of network systems. Maintain network hardware and software. Monitor networks to ensure network availability to all system users and perform necessary maintenance to support network availability. May supervise other network support and client server specialists and plan, coordinate, and implement network security measures. Diagnose hardware and software problems, and replace defective components. Perform data backups and disaster recovery operations. Maintain and administer computer networks and related computing environments including computer hardware, systems software, applications software, and all configurations. Plan, coordinate, and implement network security measures to protect data, software, and hardware. Operate master consoles to monitor the performance of computer systems and networks, and to coordinate computer network access and use. Perform routine network startup and shutdown procedures, and maintain control records. Design, configure, and test computer hardware, networking software and operating system software. Recommend changes to improve systems and network configurations, and determine hardware or software requirements related to such changes. Confer with network users about how to solve existing system problems. Monitor network performance to determine whether adjustments need to be made, and to determine where changes will need to be made in the future. Train people in computer system use. Load computer tapes and disks, and install software and printer paper or forms. Gather data pertaining to customer needs, and use the information to identify, predict, interpret, and evaluate system and network requirements. Analyze equipment performance records to determine the need for repair or replacement. Maintain logs related to network functions, as well as maintenance and repair records. Research new technology, and implement it or recommend its implementation. Maintain an inventory of parts for emergency repairs. Coordinate with vendors and with company personnel to facilitate purchases.

Job Specialization

Computer Security Specialists. Plan, coordinate, and implement security measures for information systems to regulate access to computer data files and prevent unauthorized modification, destruction, or disclosure of information. Encrypt data transmissions and erect firewalls to conceal confidential information as it is being transmitted and to keep out tainted digital transfers. Develop plans to safeguard computer files against accidental or unauthorized modification, destruction, or disclosure and to meet emergency data processing needs. Review violations of computer security procedures and discuss procedures with violators to ensure violations are not repeated. Monitor use of data files and regulate access to safeguard information in computer files. Monitor current reports of computer viruses to determine when to update virus protection systems. Modify computer security files to incorporate new software, correct errors, or change individual access status. Perform risk assessments and execute tests of data processing system to ensure functioning of data processing activities and security measures. Train users and promote security awareness to ensure system security and to improve server and network efficiency. Confer with users to discuss issues such as computer data access needs, security violations, and programming changes. Coordinate implementation of computer system plan with establishment personnel and outside vendors. Document computer security and emergency measures policies, procedures, and tests. Maintain permanent fleet cryptologic and carry-on direct support systems required in special land, sea surface and subsurface operations.

8. Network Systems and Data Communications Analysts

Personality Type: Investigative–Conventional

Earnings: $73,250
Growth: 53.4%
Annual Openings: 20,830

Most Common Education/Training Level: Associate degree

Analyze, design, test, and evaluate network systems, such as local area networks (LAN); wide area networks (WAN); and Internet, intranet, and other data communications systems. Perform network modeling, analysis, and planning. Research and recommend network and data communications hardware and software. Includes telecommunications specialists who deal with the interfacing of computer and communications equipment. May supervise computer programmers. Maintain needed files by adding and deleting files on the network server and backing up files to guarantee their safety in the event of problems with the network. Test and evaluate hardware and software to determine efficiency, reliability, and compatibility with existing system, and make purchase recommendations. Design and implement systems, network configurations, and network architecture, including hardware and software technology, site locations, and integration of technologies. Assist users to diagnose and solve data communication problems. Monitor system performance and provide security measures, troubleshooting and maintenance as needed. Work with other engineers, systems analysts, programmers, technicians, scientists and top-level managers in the design, testing and evaluation of systems. Identify areas of operation that need upgraded equipment such as modems, fiber optic cables, and telephone wires. Consult customers, visit workplaces or conduct surveys to determine present and future user needs. Train users in use of equipment. Maintain the peripherals,

Investigative

such as printers, that are connected to the network. Visit vendors, attend conferences or training and study technical journals to keep up with changes in technology. Set up user accounts, regulating and monitoring file access to ensure confidentiality and proper use. Adapt and modify existing software to meet specific needs. Read technical manuals and brochures to determine which equipment meets establishment requirements. Develop and write procedures for installation, use, and troubleshooting of communications hardware and software.

Job Specialization

Telecommunications Specialists. Design or configure voice and data communications systems, supervise installation, and arrange for post-installation service and maintenance. Keep abreast of changes in industry practices and emerging telecommunications technology by reviewing current literature, talking with colleagues, participating in educational programs, attending meetings or workshops, or participation in professional conferences, workshops, or groups. Estimate costs for system or component implementation and operation. Develop, maintain, or implement telecommunications disaster recovery plans to ensure business continuity. Test and evaluate hardware and software to determine efficiency, reliability, or compatibility with existing systems. Supervise maintenance of telecommunications equipment. Review and evaluate requests from engineers, managers, and technicians for system modifications. Provide user support by diagnosing network and device problems and implementing technical or procedural solutions. Prepare system activity and performance reports. Prepare purchase requisitions for computer hardware and software, networking and telecommunications equipment, test equipment, cabling, or tools. Use computer-aided design (CAD) software to prepare or evaluate network diagrams, floor plans, or site configurations for existing facilities, renovations, or new systems. Order or

maintain inventory of telecommunications equipment, including telephone sets, headsets, cellular phones, switches, trunks, printed circuit boards, network routers, and cabling. Monitor and analyze system performance, such as network traffic, security, and capacity. Manage user access to systems and equipment through account management and password administration. Instruct in use of voice and data communications systems, such as voicemail and videoconferencing systems. Inspect sites to determine physical configuration, such as device locations and conduit pathways. Implement system renovation projects in collaboration with technical staff, engineering consultants, installers, and vendors. Implement or perform preventive maintenance, backup, or recovery procedures.

Dentistry

Personality Type: Investigative–Realistic–Social

Useful Facts About the Major

Prepares individuals for the independent professional practice of dentistry/dental medicine, encompassing the evaluation, diagnosis, prevention, and treatment of diseases, disorders, and conditions of the oral cavity, maxillofacial area, and adjacent structures and their impact on the human body and health.

Related CIP Program: 51.0401 Dentistry (DDS, DMD)

Specializations in the Major: Oral and maxillofacial surgery, periodontics, endodontics, orthodontics, public health dentistry, oral pathology.

Typical Sequence of College Courses: English composition, introduction to psychology, college algebra, introduction to business management, introduction to sociology, oral communication, general chemistry, general biology, organic chemistry, nutrition, introduction to accounting, introduction to biochemistry, dental morphology and function, occlusion, dental materials, ethics in health care, head and neck anatomy, oral radiology, assessment and treatment planning, dental anesthesia, pharmacology, prosthodontics (fixed/removable, partial/complete), community dentistry programs, endodontics, oral pathology, pediatric dentistry, dental emergency diagnosis and treatment, chronic orofacial pain, oral implantology, professional practice management, clinical experience in dentistry.

Typical Sequence of High School Courses: English, algebra, geometry, trigonometry, biology, computer science, public speaking, chemistry, foreign language, physics, pre-calculus.

Career Snapshot

Dentists generally get at least eight years of education beyond high school. Those who want to teach or do research usually must get additional education. Besides academic ability, students of dentistry need good eye-hand coordination and communication skills. Although it seems unlikely that a vaccine against decay germs will be developed anytime soon, tooth sealants and fluoridation have reduced the incidence of tooth decay among young people, which means that dentistry's emphasis has shifted to prevention and maintenance. Note that as long as you take the courses that dentistry schools require for admissions, you have quite a lot of choice about your undergraduate major.

Useful Averages for the Related Jobs

- ❋ Annual Earnings: $142,000
- ❋ Growth: 15.3%
- ❋ Openings: 5,180
- ❋ Self-Employed: 28.0%
- ❋ Verbal Skill Rating: 60
- ❋ Math Skill Rating: 44

Other Details About the Related Jobs

Career Cluster: 08 Health Science. **Career Pathway:** 08.1 Therapeutic Services.

Skills: Science, management of financial resources, management of material resources, active learning, reading comprehension, operation and control, judgment and decision making, complex problem solving. **Work Conditions:** Indoors; sitting; exposed to disease or infections; common protective or safety equipment; exposed to radiation; close to co-workers; using hands; bending or twisting the body; making repetitive motions; cramped work space, awkward positions.

Related Jobs

Dentists, General

Personality Type: Investigative–Realistic–Social

Earnings: $142,090
Growth: 15.3%
Annual Openings: 5,180

Most Common Education/Training Level: First professional degree

Diagnose and treat diseases, injuries, and malformations of teeth and gums and related oral structures. May treat diseases of nerve, pulp, and other dental tissues affecting vitality of teeth. Use masks, gloves and safety glasses to protect themselves and their patients from infectious diseases. Administer anesthetics to limit the amount of pain experienced by patients during procedures. Examine teeth, gums, and related tissues, using dental instruments, X-rays, and other diagnostic equipment, to evaluate dental health, diagnose diseases or abnormalities, and plan appropriate treatments. Formulate plan of treatment for patient's teeth and mouth tissue. Use air turbine and hand instruments, dental appliances and surgical implements. Advise and instruct patients

Investigative

regarding preventive dental care, the causes and treatment of dental problems, and oral health care services. Design, make, and fit prosthodontic appliances such as space maintainers, bridges, and dentures, or write fabrication instructions or prescriptions for denturists and dental technicians. Fill pulp chamber and canal with endodontic materials. Write prescriptions for antibiotics and other medications.

Economics

Personality Type:
Investigative–Enterprising–Conventional

Useful Facts About the Major

Focuses on the systematic study of the production, conservation, and allocation of resources in conditions of scarcity, together with the organizational frameworks related to these processes.

Related CIP Program: 45.0601 Economics, General

Specializations in the Major: Economic theory, applied economics, econometrics.

Typical Sequence of College Courses: English composition, introduction to psychology, introduction to sociology, American government, foreign language, statistics, calculus, introduction to economics, statistics for business and social sciences, introduction to computer science, microeconomic theory, macroeconomic theory, mathematical methods in economics, econometrics.

Typical Sequence of High School Courses: Algebra, English, foreign language, social science, trigonometry, pre-calculus.

Career Snapshot

Economics is most basically the study of human needs and how they are satisfied. Therefore, it looks at how goods and services are produced, distributed, and consumed; how markets for these goods and services are created and behave; and how the actions of individuals, businesses, and governments affect these markets. Graduates of economics programs may work for business, government, or universities. With teacher training, some may find jobs in secondary schools, where economics is becoming a popular course. The best job opportunities should be in the private sector for those with graduate degrees.

Useful Averages for the Related Jobs

- ❋ Annual Earnings: $65,000
- ❋ Growth: 24.1%
- ❋ Openings: 4,081
- ❋ Self-Employed: 7.0%
- ❋ Verbal Skill Rating: 71
- ❋ Math Skill Rating: 64

Other Details About the Related Jobs

Career Clusters: 01 Agriculture, Food, and Natural Resources; 04 Business, Management, and Administration; 14 Marketing, Sales, and Service; 15 Science, Technology, Engineering, and Mathematics. **Career Pathways:** 01.2 Plant Systems; 01.5 Natural Resources Systems; 04.1 Management; 14.5 Marketing Information Management and Research; 15.2 Science and Mathematics.

Skills: Systems analysis, programming, operations analysis, systems evaluation, mathematics, reading comprehension, writing, science. **Work Conditions:** Indoors; sitting.

Related Jobs

1. Economists
Personality Type:
Investigative–Conventional–Enterprising

Earnings: $86,930
Growth: 5.8%
Annual Openings: 500

Most Common Education/Training Level:
Master's degree

Conduct research, prepare reports, or formulate plans to aid in solution of economic problems arising from production and distribution of goods and services. May collect and process economic and statistical data, using econometric and sampling techniques. Study economic and statistical data in area of specialization, such as finance, labor, or agriculture. Provide advice and consultation on economic relationships to businesses, public and private agencies, and other employers. Compile, analyze, and report data to explain economic phenomena and forecast market trends, applying mathematical models and statistical techniques. Formulate recommendations, policies, or plans to solve economic problems or to interpret markets. Develop economic guidelines and standards and prepare points of view used in forecasting trends and formulating economic policy. Testify at regulatory or legislative hearings concerning the estimated effects of changes in legislation or public policy and present recommendations based on cost-benefit analyses. Supervise research projects and students' study projects. Forecast production and consumption of renewable resources and supply, consumption, and depletion of non-renewable resources. Teach theories, principles, and methods of economics.

Job Specialization

Environmental Economists. Assess and quantify the benefits of environmental alternatives, such as use of renewable energy resources. Prepare and deliver presentations to communicate economic and environmental study results, to present policy recommendations, or to raise awareness of environmental consequences. Monitor or analyze market and environmental trends. Interpret indicators to ascertain the overall health of an environment. Identify and recommend environmentally friendly business practices. Demonstrate or promote the economic benefits of sound environmental regulations. Write technical documents or academic articles to communicate study results or economic forecasts. Write social, legal, or economic impact statements to inform decision-makers for natural resource policies, standards, or programs. Write research proposals and grant applications to obtain private or public funding for environmental and economic studies. Examine the exhaustibility of natural resources or the long-term costs of environmental rehabilitation. Develop systems for collecting, analyzing, and interpreting environmental and economic data. Develop programs or policy recommendations to achieve economic and environmental sustainability. Develop environmental research project plans, including information on budgets, goals, deliverables, timelines, and resource requirements. Develop economic models, forecasts, or scenarios to predict future economic and environmental outcomes. Collect and analyze data to compare the environmental implications of economic policy or practice alternatives. Assess the environmental costs and benefits of various economic activities, policies, or regulations. Assess the economic costs and benefits of environmental events or activities. Perform complex, dynamic, and integrated mathematical modeling of ecological, environmental, or economic systems. Conduct research to study the relationships among environmental problems and patterns of economic production and consumption.

2. Market Research Analysts

Personality Type:
Investigative–Enterprising–Conventional

Earnings: $61,580
Growth: 28.1%
Annual Openings: 13,730

Most Common Education/Training Level:
Master's degree

Research market conditions in local, regional, or national areas to determine potential sales of a product or service. May gather information on competitors, prices, sales, and methods of marketing and distribution. May use survey results to create a marketing campaign based on regional preferences and buying habits. Prepare reports of findings, illustrating data graphically and translating complex findings into written text. Seek and provide information to help companies determine their position in the marketplace. Gather data on competitors and analyze their prices, sales, and method of marketing and distribution. Collect and analyze data on customer demographics, preferences, needs, and buying habits to identify potential markets and factors affecting product demand. Devise and evaluate methods and procedures for collecting data, such as surveys, opinion polls, or questionnaires, or arrange to obtain existing data. Monitor industry statistics and follow trends in trade literature. Measure and assess customer and employee satisfaction. Measure the effectiveness of marketing, advertising, and communications programs and strategies. Forecast and track marketing and sales trends, analyzing collected data. Attend staff conferences to provide management with information and proposals concerning the promotion, distribution, design, and pricing of company products or services. Conduct research on consumer opinions and marketing strategies, collaborating with marketing professionals, statisticians, pollsters, and other professionals. Develop and implement procedures for identifying advertising needs. Direct trained survey interviewers.

3. Survey Researchers

Personality Type:
Investigative–Conventional–Enterprising

Earnings: $35,380
Growth: 30.4%
Annual Openings: 1,340

Most Common Education/Training Level:
Bachelor's degree

Design or conduct surveys. May supervise interviewers who conduct the survey in person or over the telephone. May present survey results to client. Prepare and present summaries and analyses of survey data, including tables, graphs, and fact sheets that describe survey techniques and results. Consult with clients in order to identify survey needs and any specific requirements, such as special samples. Analyze data from surveys, old records, and/or case studies, using statistical software programs. Review, classify, and record survey data in preparation for computer analysis. Conduct research in order to gather information about survey topics. Conduct surveys and collect data, using methods such as interviews, questionnaires, focus groups, market analysis surveys, public opinion polls, literature reviews, and file reviews. Collaborate with other researchers in the planning, implementation, and evaluation of surveys. Direct and review the work of staff members, including survey support staff and interviewers who gather survey data. Monitor and evaluate survey progress and performance, using sample disposition reports and response rate calculations. Produce documentation of the questionnaire development process, data collection methods, sampling designs, and decisions related to sample statistical weighting. Determine and specify details of survey projects, including sources of information, procedures to be used, and the design of survey instruments and materials. Support, plan, and coordinate operations for single or multiple surveys. Direct updates and changes in survey implementation and methods. Hire and train recruiters and data collectors. Write training manuals to be used by survey interviewers.

Environmental Science

Personality Type:
Investigative–Realistic–Conventional

Useful Facts About the Major

Focuses on the application of biological, chemical, and physical principles to the study of the physical environment and the solution of environmental problems, including subjects such as abating or controlling environmental pollution and degradation; the interaction between human society and the natural environment; and natural resources management.

Related CIP Programs: 03.0104 Environmental Science; 03.0103 Environmental Studies

Specializations in the Major: Land resources, natural history, environmental technology, environmental policy, environmental education.

Typical Sequence of College Courses: English composition, college algebra, general biology, general chemistry, organic chemistry, oral communication, statistics, introduction to computer science, introduction to geology, ecology, introduction to environmental science, natural resource management and water quality, microbiology, introduction to economics, introduction to ground water/hydrology, regional planning and environmental protection, environmental impact assessment, environmental economics, environmental law, environmental chemistry.

Typical Sequence of High School Courses: Biology, chemistry, algebra, geometry, trigonometry, computer science, English, public speaking, geography.

Career Snapshot

Environmental science (or studies) is a multidisciplinary subject that involves a number of sciences such as biology, geology, and chemistry, as well as social sciences such as economics and geography. It also touches on urban/regional planning and on law and public policy. Those with a bachelor's degree may work for an environmental consulting business or a government planning agency, or may go on to get a graduate or professional degree in one of these related fields.

Useful Averages for the Related Jobs

* Annual Earnings: $59,000
* Growth: 28.0%
* Openings: 5,470
* Self-Employed: 2.3%
* Verbal Skill Rating: 70
* Math Skill Rating: 70

Other Details About the Related Jobs

Career Clusters: 01 Agriculture, Food, and Natural Resources; 13 Manufacturing; 16 Transportation, Distribution, and Logistics. **Career Pathways:** 01.5 Natural Resources Systems; 13.2 Manufacturing Production Process Development; 16.6 Health, Safety, and Environmental Management.

Skills: Science, programming, mathematics, reading comprehension, operations analysis, writing, systems analysis, complex problem solving. **Work Conditions:** In a vehicle; more often outdoors than indoors; sitting; high places; noisy; very hot or cold.

Investigative

Related Jobs

1. Environmental Science and Protection Technicians, Including Health

Personality Type:
Investigative–Realistic–Conventional

Earnings: $40,790
Growth: 28.9%
Annual Openings: 2,520

Most Common Education/Training Level: Associate degree

Perform laboratory and field tests to monitor the environment and investigate sources of pollution, including those that affect health. Under direction of environmental scientists or specialists, may collect samples of gases, soil, water, and other materials for testing and take corrective actions as assigned. Collect samples of gases, soils, water, industrial wastewater, and asbestos products to conduct tests on pollutant levels and identify sources of pollution. Record test data and prepare reports, summaries, and charts that interpret test results. Develop and implement programs for monitoring of environmental pollution and radiation. Discuss test results and analyses with customers. Set up equipment or stations to monitor and collect pollutants from sites such as smokestacks, manufacturing plants, or mechanical equipment. Maintain files, such as hazardous waste databases, chemical usage data, personnel exposure information, and diagrams showing equipment locations. Develop testing procedures or direct activities of workers in laboratory. Prepare samples or photomicrographs for testing and analysis. Calibrate microscopes and test instruments. Examine and analyze material for presence and concentration of contaminants such as asbestos, using variety of microscopes. Calculate amount of pollutant in samples or compute air pollution or gas flow in industrial processes, using chemical and mathematical formulas. Make recommendations to control or eliminate unsafe conditions at workplaces or public facilities. Weigh, analyze, and measure collected sample particles such as lead, coal dust, or rock to determine concentration of pollutants. Provide information and technical and program assistance to government representatives, employers, and the general public on the issues of public health, environmental protection, or workplace safety. Conduct standardized tests to ensure materials and supplies used throughout power supply systems meet processing and safety specifications. Perform statistical analysis of environmental data. Respond to and investigate hazardous conditions or spills or outbreaks of disease or food poisoning, collecting samples for analysis.

2. Environmental Scientists and Specialists, Including Health

Personality Type:
Investigative–Realistic–Conventional

Earnings: $61,010
Growth: 27.9%
Annual Openings: 4,840

Most Common Education/Training Level: Master's degree

Conduct research or perform investigation for the purpose of identifying, abating, or eliminating sources of pollutants or hazards that affect either the environment or the health of the population. Using knowledge of various scientific disciplines, may collect, synthesize, study, report, and take action based on data derived from measurements or observations of air, food, soil, water, and other sources. Collect, synthesize, analyze, manage, and report environmental data such as pollution emission measurements, atmospheric monitoring measurements, meteorological and mineralogical information, and soil or water samples. Analyze data to determine validity, quality, and scientific significance, and to interpret correlations between human activities and environmental effects. Communicate scientific and technical information to the public, organizations, or internal audiences through oral briefings, written documents, workshops, conferences, training sessions, or public hearings. Provide scientific and technical guidance, support, coordination, and oversight to governmental agencies, environmental programs, industry, or the public. Process and review environmental permits, licenses, and related materials. Review and implement environmental technical standards, guidelines, policies, and formal regulations that meet all appropriate requirements. Prepare charts or graphs from data samples, providing summary information on the environmental relevance of the data. Determine data collection methods to be employed in research projects and surveys. Investigate and report on accidents affecting the environment. Research sources of pollution to determine their effects on the environment and to develop theories or methods of pollution abatement or control. Provide advice on proper standards and regulations or the development of policies, strategies, and codes of practice for environmental management. Monitor effects of pollution and land degradation, and recommend means of prevention or control. Supervise or train students, environmental technologists, technicians, or other related staff. Evaluate violations or problems discovered during inspections to determine appropriate regulatory actions or to provide advice on the development and prosecution of regulatory cases. Conduct environmental audits and inspections, and investigations of violations.

Job Specializations

Climate Change Analysts. Research and analyze policy developments related to climate change. Make climate-related recommendations for actions such as legislation, awareness campaigns, or fundraising approaches. Write reports or academic papers to communicate findings of climate-related studies. Promote initiatives to mitigate climate change with government or environmental groups. Present climate-related information at public interest, governmental, or other meetings. Present and defend proposals for climate change research projects. Prepare grant applications to obtain funding for programs related to climate change, environmental management, or sustainability. Gather and review climate-related studies from government agencies, research laboratories, and other organizations. Develop, or contribute to the development of, educational or outreach programs on the environment or climate change. Review existing policies or legislation to identify environmental impacts. Provide analytical support for policy briefs related to renewable energy, energy efficiency, or climate change. Prepare study reports, memoranda, briefs, testimonies, or other written materials to inform government or environmental groups on environmental issues such as climate change. Make legislative recommendations related to climate change or environmental management, based on climate change policies, principles, programs, practices, and processes. Research policies, practices, or procedures for climate or environmental management. Propose new or modified policies involving use of traditional and alternative fuels, transportation of goods, and other factors relating to climate and climate change. Analyze and distill climate-related research findings to inform legislators, regulatory agencies, or other stakeholders.

Environmental Restoration Planners. Collaborate with field and biology staff to oversee the implementation of restoration projects and to develop new products. Process and synthesize complex scientific data into practical strategies for restoration, monitoring or management. Notify regulatory or permitting agencies of deviations from implemented remediation plans. Develop environmental restoration project schedules and budgets. Develop and communicate recommendations for landowners to maintain or restore environmental conditions. Create diagrams to communicate environmental remediation planning using geographic information systems (GIS), computer-

Investigative

aided design (CAD), or other mapping or diagramming software. Apply for permits required for the implementation of environmental remediation projects. Review existing environmental remediation designs. Supervise and provide technical guidance, training, or assistance to employees working in the field to restore habitats. Provide technical direction on environmental planning to energy engineers, biologists, geologists, or other professionals working to develop restoration plans or strategies. Plan or supervise environmental studies to achieve compliance with environmental regulations in construction, modification, operation, acquisition, or divestiture of facilities such as power plants. Inspect active remediation sites to ensure compliance with environmental or safety policies, standards, or regulations. Plan environmental restoration projects, using biological databases, environmental strategies, and planning software. Identify short- and long-term impacts of environmental remediation activities. Identify environmental mitigation alternatives, ensuring compliance with applicable standards, laws, or regulations. Create environmental models or simulations, using geographic information system (GIS) data and knowledge of particular ecosystems or ecological regions. Conduct feasibility and cost-benefit studies for environmental remediation projects. Conduct environmental impact studies to examine the ecological effects of pollutants, disease, human activities, nature, and climate change.

Industrial Ecologists. Study or investigate industrial production and natural ecosystems to achieve high production, sustainable resources, and environmental safety or protection. May apply principles and activities of natural ecosystems to develop models for industrial systems. Write ecological reports and other technical documents for publication in the research literature or in industrial or government reports. Recommend methods to protect the environment or minimize environmental damage. Investigate accidents affecting the environment to assess ecological

impact. Investigate the adaptability of various animal and plant species to changed environmental conditions. Review industrial practices, such as the methods and materials used in construction or production, to identify potential liabilities and environmental hazards. Research sources of pollution to determine environmental impact or to develop methods of pollution abatement or control. Provide industrial managers with technical materials on environmental issues, regulatory guidelines, or compliance actions. Plan or conduct studies of the ecological implications of historic or projected changes in industrial processes or development. Plan or conduct field research on topics such as industrial production, industrial ecology, population ecology, and environmental production or sustainability. Monitor the environmental impact of development activities, pollution, or land degradation. Model alternative energy investment scenarios to compare economic and environmental costs and benefits. Identify or develop strategies or methods to minimize the environmental impact of industrial production processes. Investigate the impact of changed land management or land use practices on ecosystems. Develop or test protocols to monitor ecosystem components and ecological processes. Create complex and dynamic mathematical models of population, community, or ecological systems. Conduct scientific protection, mitigation, or restoration projects to prevent resource damage, maintain the integrity of critical habitats, and minimize the impact of human activities. Carry out environmental assessments in accordance with applicable standards, regulations, or laws.

Medicine

Personality Type: Investigative–Social–Realistic

Useful Facts About the Major

Prepares individuals for the independent professional practice of medicine (or osteopathic medicine), involving the prevention, diagnosis, and treatment of illnesses, injuries, and other disorders of the human body.

Related CIP Programs: 51.1901 Osteopathic Medicine/Osteopathy (DO); 51.1201 Medicine (MD)

Specializations in the Major: Internal medicine, pediatrics, family medicine, emergency medicine, obstetrics/gynecology, surgery, radiology, psychiatry.

Typical Sequence of College Courses: English composition, introduction to psychology, college algebra, calculus, introduction to sociology, oral communication, general chemistry, general biology, introduction to computer science, organic chemistry, human anatomy and physiology, general microbiology, genetics, introduction to biochemistry, pathology, pharmacology, abnormal psychology, medical interviewing techniques, patient examination and evaluation, clinical laboratory procedures, ethics in health care, clinical experience in internal medicine, clinical experience in emergency medicine, clinical experience in obstetrics/gynecology, clinical experience in family medicine, clinical experience in psychiatry, clinical experience in surgery, clinical experience in pediatrics, clinical experience in geriatrics.

Typical Sequence of High School Courses: English, algebra, geometry, trigonometry, pre-calculus, biology, computer science, public speaking, chemistry, foreign language, physics.

Career Snapshot

Medicine requires long years of education—four years of college, four years of medical school, and three to eight years of internship and residency, depending on the specialty. Entrance to medical school is highly competitive. Although "pre-med" is often referred to as a major, many students meet the entry requirements for medical school while majoring in a nonscientific subject. This may be

helpful to demonstrate that you are a well-rounded person and to prepare you for another career in case you are not admitted to medical school. Today, physicians are more likely than in the past to work as salaried employees of group practices or HMOs. Good opportunities are expected in rural and low-income areas. Job prospects will also be especially good for physicians in specialties that afflict the rapidly growing elderly population. Examples of such specialties are cardiology and radiology, because the risks for heart disease and cancer increase as people age.

Useful Averages for the Related Jobs

* Annual Earnings: $164,000
* Growth: 21.8%
* Openings: 26,050
* Self-Employed: 11.7%
* Verbal Skill Rating: 66
* Math Skill Rating: 52

Other Details About the Related Jobs

Career Clusters: 08 Health Science; 10 Human Services; 15 Science, Technology, Engineering, and Mathematics. **Career Pathways:** 08.1 Therapeutic Services; 08.2 Diagnostics Services; 10.2 Counseling and Mental Health Services; 15.2 Science and Mathematics.

Skills: Science, reading comprehension, social perceptiveness, operations analysis, active learning, instructing, service orientation, judgment and decision making. **Work Conditions:** Indoors; exposed to disease or infections; close to co-workers; common protective or safety equipment; exposed to radiation; cramped work space, awkward positions; wear specialized protective or safety equipment.

Investigative

Related Jobs

Physicians and Surgeons

Personality Type: Investigative–Social–Realistic

Earnings: $164,430
Growth: 21.8%
Annual Openings: 26,050

Most Common Education/Training Level: First professional degree

Job Specializations

Allergists and Immunologists. Diagnose, treat, and help prevent allergic diseases and disease processes affecting the immune system. Present research findings at national meetings or in peer-reviewed journals. Engage in self-directed learning and continuing education activities. Document patients' medical histories. Conduct laboratory or clinical research on allergy or immunology topics. Provide allergy or immunology consultation or education to physicians or other health care providers. Prescribe medication such as antihistamines, antibiotics, and nasal, oral, topical, or inhaled glucocorticosteroids. Conduct physical examinations of patients. Order or perform diagnostic tests such as skin pricks and intradermal, patch, or delayed hypersensitivity tests. Educate patients about diagnoses, prognoses, or treatments. Interpret diagnostic test results to make appropriate differential diagnoses. Develop individualized treatment plans for patients, considering patient preferences, clinical data, or the risks and benefits of therapies. Coordinate the care of patients with other health care professionals or support staff. Assess the risks and benefits of therapies for allergic and immunologic disorders. Provide therapies, such as allergen immunotherapy and immunoglobin therapy, to treat immune conditions. Perform allergen provocation tests such as nasal, conjunctival, bronchial, oral, food, and medication challenges. Diagnose or treat allergic or immunologic conditions.

Anesthesiologists. Administer anesthetics during surgery or other medical procedures. Administer anesthetic or sedation during medical procedures, using local, intravenous, spinal, or caudal methods. Monitor patient before, during, and after anesthesia and counteract adverse reactions or complications. Provide and maintain life support and airway management and help prepare patients for emergency surgery. Record type and amount of anesthesia and patient condition throughout procedure. Examine patient; obtain medical history; and use diagnostic tests to determine risk during surgical, obstetrical, and other medical procedures. Position patient on operating table to maximize patient comfort and surgical accessibility. Decide when patients have recovered or stabilized enough to be sent to another room or ward or to be sent home following outpatient surgery. Coordinate administration of anesthetics with surgeons during operation. Confer with other medical professionals to determine type and method of anesthetic or sedation to render patient insensible to pain. Coordinate and direct work of nurses, medical technicians, and other health-care providers. Order laboratory tests, X-rays, and other diagnostic procedures. Diagnose illnesses, using examinations, tests, and reports. Manage anesthesiological services, coordinating them with other medical activities and formulating plans and procedures. Provide medical care and consultation in many settings, prescribing medication and treatment and referring patients for surgery. Inform students and staff of types and methods of anesthesia administration, signs of complications, and emergency methods to counteract reactions. Schedule and maintain use of surgical suite, including operating, wash-up, and waiting rooms and anesthetic and sterilizing equipment. Instruct individuals and groups on ways to preserve health and prevent disease. Conduct medical research to aid in controlling and curing disease, to investigate new medications, and to develop and test new medical techniques.

Dermatologists. Diagnose, treat, and help prevent diseases or other conditions of the skin. Refer patients to other specialists, as needed. Record patients' health histories. Provide dermatologic consultation to other health professionals. Provide liposuction treatment to patients. Read current literature, talk with colleagues, and participate in professional organizations or conferences to keep abreast of developments in dermatology. Instruct interns or residents in diagnosis and treatment of dermatological diseases. Evaluate patients to determine eligibility for cosmetic procedures such as liposuction, laser resurfacing, and microdermabrasion. Conduct or order diagnostic tests such as chest radiographs (X-rays), microbiologic tests, and endocrinologic tests. Recommend diagnostic tests based on patients' histories and physical examination findings. Conduct clinical or basic research. Provide therapies such as intralesional steroids, chemical peels, and comodo removal to treat age spots, sun damage, rough skin, discolored skin, or oily skin. Provide dermabrasion or laser abrasion to treat atrophic scars, elevated scars, or other skin conditions. Prescribe hormonal agents or topical treatments such as contraceptives, spironolactone, antiandrogens, oral corticosteroids, retinoids, benzoyl peroxide, and antibiotics. Perform skin surgery to improve appearance, make early diagnoses, or control diseases such as skin cancer. Perform incisional biopsies to diagnose melanoma. Diagnose and treat pigmented lesions such as common acquired nevi, congenital nevi, dysplastic nevi, Spitz nevi, blue nevi, and melanoma. Counsel patients on topics such as the need for annual dermatologic screenings, sun protection, skin cancer awareness, or skin and lymph node self-examinations. Conduct complete skin examinations. Diagnose and treat skin conditions such as acne, dandruff, athlete's foot, moles, psoriasis, and skin cancer.

Family and General Practitioners. Diagnose, treat, and help prevent diseases and injuries that commonly occur in the general population. Prescribe or administer treatment, therapy, medication, vaccination, and other specialized medical care to treat or prevent illness, disease, or injury. Order, perform, and interpret tests and analyze records, reports, and examination information to diagnose patients' condition. Monitor the patients' conditions and progress and re-evaluate treatments as necessary. Explain procedures and discuss test results or prescribed treatments with patients. Collect, record, and maintain patient information, such as medical history, reports, and examination results. Advise patients and community members concerning diet, activity, hygiene, and disease prevention. Refer patients to medical specialists or other practitioners when necessary. Direct and coordinate activities of nurses, students, assistants, specialists, therapists, and other medical staff. Coordinate work with nurses, social workers, rehabilitation therapists, pharmacists, psychologists, and other health-care providers. Deliver babies. Operate on patients to remove, repair, or improve functioning of diseased or injured body parts and systems. Plan, implement, or administer health programs or standards in hospital, business, or community for information, prevention, or treatment of injury or illness. Prepare reports for government or management of birth, death, and disease statistics; workforce evaluations; or medical status of individuals. Conduct research to study anatomy and develop or test medications, treatments, or procedures to prevent or control disease or injury.

Hospitalists. Provide inpatient care predominantly in settings such as medical wards, acute care units, intensive care units, rehabilitation centers, or emergency rooms. Manage and coordinate patient care throughout treatment. Refer patients to medical specialists, social services or other professionals as appropriate. Participate in continuing education activities to maintain or enhance knowledge and skills. Direct, coordinate, or supervise the patient care activities of nursing or support staff. Write patient discharge summaries and send them to primary care physicians. Direct

Investigative

the operations of short stay or specialty units. Train or supervise medical students, residents, or other health professionals. Prescribe medications or treatment regimens to hospital inpatients. Order or interpret the results of tests such as laboratory tests and radiographs (X-rays). Attend inpatient consultations in areas of specialty. Conduct discharge planning and discharge patients. Diagnose, treat, or provide continuous care to hospital inpatients. Admit patients for hospital stays.

Internists, General. Diagnose and provide nonsurgical treatment of diseases and injuries of internal organ systems. Provide care mainly for adults who have a wide range of problems associated with the internal organs. Treat internal disorders, such as hypertension; heart disease; diabetes; and problems of the lung, brain, kidney, and gastrointestinal tract. Analyze records, reports, test results, or examination information to diagnose medical condition of patient. Prescribe or administer medication, therapy, and other specialized medical care to treat or prevent illness, disease, or injury. Provide and manage long-term, comprehensive medical care, including diagnosis and nonsurgical treatment of diseases, for adult patients in an office or hospital. Manage and treat common health problems, such as infections, influenza and pneumonia, as well as serious, chronic, and complex illnesses, in adolescents, adults, and the elderly. Monitor patients' conditions and progress and re-evaluate treatments as necessary. Collect, record, and maintain patient information, such as medical history, reports, and examination results. Make diagnoses when different illnesses occur together or in situations where the diagnosis may be obscure. Explain procedures and discuss test results or prescribed treatments with patients. Advise patients and community members concerning diet, activity, hygiene, and disease prevention. Refer patient to medical specialist or other practitioner when necessary. Immunize patients to protect them from preventable diseases. Advise surgeon of a patient's risk status and recommend appropriate

intervention to minimize risk. Direct and coordinate activities of nurses, students, assistants, specialists, therapists, and other medical staff. Provide consulting services to other doctors caring for patients with special or difficult problems. Operate on patients to remove, repair, or improve functioning of diseased or injured body parts and systems. Plan, implement, or administer health programs in hospitals, businesses, or communities for prevention and treatment of injuries or illnesses.

Neurologists. Diagnose, treat, and help prevent diseases and disorders of the nervous system. Participate in neuroscience research activities. Provide training to medical students or staff members. Participate in continuing education activities to maintain and expand competence. Supervise medical technicians in the performance of neurological diagnostic or therapeutic activities. Counsel patients or others on the background of neurological disorders including risk factors, or genetic or environmental concerns. Interpret the results of neuroimaging studies such as Magnetic Resonance Imaging (MRI), Single Photon Emission Computed Tomography (SPECT), and Positron Emission Tomography (PET) scans. Refer patients to other health care practitioners as necessary. Advise other physicians on the treatment of neurological problems. Prescribe or administer medications, such as anti-epileptic drugs, and monitor patients for behavioral and cognitive side effects. Prescribe or administer treatments such as transcranial magnetic stimulation, vagus nerve stimulation, and deep brain stimulation. Prepare, maintain, or review records that include patients' histories, neurological examination findings, treatment plans, or outcomes. Perform specialized treatments in areas such as sleep disorders, neuroimmunology, neuro-oncology, behavioral neurology, and neurogenetics. Order or interpret results of laboratory analyses of patients' blood or cerebrospinal fluid. Order supportive care services such as physical therapy, specialized nursing care, and social services. Interview patients to obtain information such as complaints, symptoms, medical histories, and family histories. Inform patients or families of neurological diagnoses and prognoses, or benefits, risks and costs of various treatment plans. Diagnose neurological conditions based on interpretation of examination findings, histories, or test results. Develop treatment plans based on diagnoses and on evaluation of factors such as age and general health, or procedural risks and costs.

Nuclear Medicine Physicians. Diagnose and treat diseases, using radioactive materials and techniques. May monitor radionuclide preparation, administration, and disposition. Teach nuclear medicine, diagnostic radiology, or other specialties at graduate educational level. Schedule examinations and staff activities. Provide advice on the selection of nuclear medicine supplies or equipment. Monitor cleanup of radioactive spills to ensure that proper procedures are followed and that decontamination activities are conducted. Monitor handling of radioactive materials to ensure that established procedures are followed. Formulate plans and procedures for nuclear medicine departments. Direct the safe management and disposal of radioactive substances. Establish and enforce radiation protection standards for patients and staff. Advise other physicians of the clinical indications, limitations, assessments, or risks of diagnostic and therapeutic applications of radioactive materials. Review procedure requests and patients' medical histories to determine applicability of procedures and radioisotopes to be used.

Obstetricians and Gynecologists. Diagnose, treat, and help prevent diseases of women, especially those affecting the reproductive system and the process of childbirth. Care for and treat women during prenatal, natal, and post-natal periods. Explain procedures and discuss test results or prescribed treatments with patients. Treat diseases of female organs. Monitor patients' condition and progress and re-evaluate treatments as necessary. Perform cesarean sections or other surgical

procedures as needed to preserve patients' health and deliver babies safely. Prescribe or administer therapy, medication, and other specialized medical care to treat or prevent illness, disease, or injury. Analyze records, reports, test results, or examination information to diagnose medical condition of patient. Collect, record, and maintain patient information, such as medical histories, reports, and examination results. Advise patients and community members concerning diet, activity, hygiene, and disease prevention. Refer patient to medical specialist or other practitioner when necessary. Consult with, or provide consulting services to, other physicians. Direct and coordinate activities of nurses, students, assistants, specialists, therapists, and other medical staff. Plan, implement, or administer health programs in hospitals, businesses, or communities for prevention and treatment of injuries or illnesses. Prepare government and organizational reports on birth, death, and disease statistics; workforce evaluations; or the medical status of individuals. Conduct research to develop or test medications, treatments, or procedures to prevent or control disease or injury.

Ophthalmologists. Diagnose, treat, and help prevent diseases and injuries of the eyes and related structures. Provide ophthalmic consultation to other medical professionals. Refer patients for more specialized treatments when conditions exceed the experience, expertise, or scope of practice of practitioner. Instruct interns, residents, or others in ophthalmologic procedures and techniques. Develop or implement plans and procedures for ophthalmologic services. Educate patients about maintenance and promotion of healthy vision. Conduct clinical or laboratory-based research in ophthalmology. Collaborate with multidisciplinary teams of health professionals to provide optimal patient care. Provide or direct the provision of postoperative care. Document or evaluate patients' medical histories. Prescribe corrective lenses such as glasses and contact lenses. Prescribe or administer topical or systemic medications to treat ophthalmic

Investigative

conditions and to manage pain. Perform, order, or interpret the results of diagnostic or clinical tests. Develop treatment plans based on patients' histories and goals, the nature and severity of disorders, and treatment risks and benefits. Perform laser surgeries to alter, remove, reshape, or replace ocular tissue. Perform ophthalmic surgeries such as cataract, glaucoma, refractive, corneal, vitro-retinal, eye muscle, and oculoplastic surgeries. Prescribe ophthalmologic treatments or therapies such as chemotherapy, cryotherapy, and low vision therapy. Perform comprehensive examinations of the visual system to determine the nature or extent of ocular disorders. Diagnose or treat injuries, disorders, or diseases of the eye and eye structures including the cornea, sclera, conjunctiva, or eyelids.

Pathologists. Diagnose presence and stage of diseases, using laboratory techniques and patient specimens. Study the nature, cause, and development of diseases. May perform autopsies. Testify in depositions or trials as an expert witness. Review cases by analyzing autopsies, laboratory findings, or case investigation reports. Manage medical laboratories. Read current literature, talk with colleagues, or participate in professional organizations or conferences to keep abreast of developments in pathology. Develop or adopt new tests or instruments to improve diagnosis of diseases. Educate physicians, students, and other personnel in medical laboratory professions such as medical technology, cytotechnology, and histotechnology. Conduct research and present scientific findings. Perform autopsies to determine causes of deaths. Plan and supervise the work of the pathology staff, residents or visiting pathologists. Obtain specimens by performing procedures such as biopsies and fine need aspirations (FNAs) of superficial nodules. Identify the etiology, pathogenesis, morphological change, and clinical significance of diseases. Diagnose infections, such as Hepatitis B and Acquired Immune Deficiency Syndrome (AIDS), by conducting tests to detect the antibodies that patients' immune systems make

to fight such infections. Conduct genetic analyses of deoxyribonucleic acid (DNA) or chromosomes to diagnose small biopsies and cell samples. Write pathology reports summarizing analyses, results, and conclusions. Analyze and interpret results from tests such as microbial or parasite tests, urine analyses, hormonal assays, fine needle aspirations (FNAs), and polymerase chain reactions (PCRs). Communicate pathologic findings to surgeons or other physicians. Consult with physicians about ordering and interpreting tests or providing treatments. Examine microscopic samples to identify diseases or other abnormalities. Diagnose diseases or study medical conditions using techniques such as gross pathology, histology, cytology, cytopathology, clinical chemistry, immunology, flow cytometry, and molecular biology.

Pediatricians, General. Diagnose, treat, and help prevent children's diseases and injuries. Examine patients or order, perform, and interpret diagnostic tests to obtain information on medical condition and determine diagnosis. Examine children regularly to assess their growth and development. Prescribe or administer treatment, therapy, medication, vaccination, and other specialized medical care to treat or prevent illness, disease, or injury in infants and children. Collect, record, and maintain patient information, such as medical history, reports, and examination results. Advise patients, parents or guardians, and community members concerning diet, activity, hygiene, and disease prevention. Treat children who have minor illnesses, acute and chronic health problems, and growth and development concerns. Explain procedures and discuss test results or prescribed treatments with patients and parents or guardians. Monitor patients' condition and progress and re-evaluate treatments as necessary. Plan and execute medical care programs to aid in the mental and physical growth and development of children and adolescents. Refer patient to medical specialist or other practitioner when necessary. Direct and coordinate activities of nurses, students, assistants, specialists, therapists, and other medical staff. Provide consulting services to other physicians. Plan, implement, or administer health programs or standards in hospital, business, or community for information, prevention, or treatment of injury or illness. Operate on patients to remove, repair, or improve functioning of diseased or injured body parts and systems. Conduct research to study anatomy and develop or test medications, treatments, or procedures to prevent or control disease or injury. Prepare reports for government or management of birth, death, and disease statistics; workforce evaluations; or medical status of individuals.

Physical Medicine and Rehabilitation Physicians. Diagnose and treat disorders requiring physiotherapy to provide physical, mental, and occupational rehabilitation. Instruct interns and residents in the diagnosis and treatment of temporary or permanent physically disabling conditions. Conduct physical tests such as functional capacity evaluations to determine injured workers' capabilities to perform the physical demands of their jobs. Assess characteristics of patients' pain such as intensity, location, and duration using standardized clinical measures. Monitor effectiveness of pain management interventions such as medication and spinal injections. Examine patients to assess mobility, strength, communication, or cognition. Document examination results, treatment plans, and patients' outcomes. Diagnose or treat performance-related conditions such as sports injuries or repetitive motion injuries. Develop comprehensive plans for immediate and long-term rehabilitation including therapeutic exercise; speech and occupational therapy; counseling; cognitive retraining; patient, family or caregiver education; or community reintegration. Prescribe physical therapy to relax the muscles and improve strength. Coordinate physical medicine and rehabilitation services with other medical activities. Consult or coordinate with other rehabilitative professionals including physical and occupational therapists,

rehabilitation nurses, speech pathologists, neuropsychologists, behavioral psychologists, social workers, or medical technicians. Perform electrodiagnosis including electromyography, nerve conduction studies, or somatosensory evoked potentials of neuromuscular disorders or damage. Prescribe therapy services, such as electrotherapy, ultrasonography, heat or cold therapy, hydrotherapy, debridement, short-wave or microwave diathermy, and infrared or ultraviolet radiation, to enhance rehabilitation. Prescribe orthotic and prosthetic applications and adaptive equipment, such as wheelchairs, bracing, and communication devices, to maximize patient function and self-sufficiency.

Preventive Medicine Physicians. Apply knowledge of general preventive medicine and public health issues to promote health care to groups or individuals and aid in the prevention or reduction of risk of disease, injury, disability, or death. May practice population-based medicine or diagnose and treat patients in the context of clinical health promotion and disease prevention. Teach or train medical staff regarding preventive medicine issues. Document or review comprehensive patients' histories with an emphasis on occupation or environmental risks. Prepare preventive health reports including problem descriptions, analyses, alternative solutions, and recommendations. Supervise or coordinate the work of physicians, nurses, statisticians, or other professional staff members. Deliver presentations to lay or professional audiences. Evaluate the effectiveness of prescribed risk reduction measures or other interventions. Identify groups at risk for specific preventable diseases or injuries. Design or use surveillance tools, such as screening, lab reports, and vital records, to identify health risks. Direct public health education programs dealing with topics such as preventable diseases, injuries, nutrition, food service sanitation, water supply safety, sewage and waste disposal, insect control, and immunizations.

Investigative

Psychiatrists. Diagnose, treat, and help prevent disorders of the mind. Prescribe, direct, and administer psychotherapeutic treatments or medications to treat mental, emotional, or behavioral disorders. Analyze and evaluate patient data and test findings to diagnose nature and extent of mental disorders. Collaborate with physicians, psychologists, social workers, psychiatric nurses, or other professionals to discuss treatment plans and progress. Gather and maintain patient information and records, including social and medical histories obtained from patients, relatives, and other professionals. Design individualized care plans, using a variety of treatments. Counsel outpatients and other patients during office visits. Examine or conduct laboratory or diagnostic tests on patients to provide information on general physical conditions and mental disorders. Advise and inform guardians, relatives, and significant others of patients' conditions and treatments. Teach, take continuing education classes, attend conferences and seminars, and conduct research and publish findings to increase understanding of mental, emotional, and behavioral states and disorders. Review and evaluate treatment procedures and outcomes of other psychiatrists and medical professionals. Prepare and submit case reports and summaries to government and mental health agencies. Serve on committees to promote and maintain community mental health services and delivery systems.

Radiologists. Examine and diagnose disorders and diseases, using X-rays and radioactive materials. May treat patients. Implement protocols in areas such as drugs, resuscitation, emergencies, power failures, and infection control. Treat malignant internal or external growths by exposure to radiation from radiographs (X-rays), high energy sources, or natural or synthetic radioisotopes. Serve as an offsite teleradiologist for facilities that do not have on-site radiologists. Provide advice on types or quantities of radiology equipment needed to maintain facilities. Participate in research projects involving radiology. Participate in quality improvement activities including discussions of areas where risk of error is high. Supervise and teach residents or medical students. Schedule examinations and assign radiologic personnel. Participate in continuing education activities to maintain and develop expertise. Develop treatment plans for radiology patients. Establish or enforce standards for protection of patients or personnel. Administer radiopaque substances by injection, orally, or as enemas to render internal structures and organs visible on X-ray films or fluoroscopic screens. Administer or maintain conscious sedation during and after procedures. Review or transmit images and information using picture archiving or communications systems. Interpret images using computer-aided detection or diagnosis systems. Recognize or treat complications during and after procedures, including blood pressure problems, pain, oversedation, or bleeding. Prepare comprehensive interpretive reports of findings. Obtain patients' histories from electronic records, patient interviews, dictated reports, or by communicating with referring clinicians. Conduct physical examinations to inform decisions about appropriate procedures. Confer with medical professionals regarding image-based diagnoses. Instruct radiologic staff in desired techniques, positions, or projections.

Sports Medicine Physicians. Diagnose, treat, and help prevent injuries that occur during sporting events, athletic training, and physical activities. Select and prepare medical equipment or medications to be taken to athletic competition sites. Provide coaches and therapists with assistance in selecting and fitting protective equipment. Advise against injured athletes returning to games or competition if resuming activity could lead to further injury. Observe and evaluate athletes' mental well-being. Participate in continuing education activities to improve and maintain knowledge and skills. Develop and prescribe exercise programs such as off-season conditioning regimens. Advise athletes on how substances, such as herbal remedies, could affect drug testing results.

Conduct research in the prevention or treatment of injuries or medical conditions related to sports and exercise. Advise athletes, trainers, or coaches to alter or cease sports practices that are potentially harmful. Attend games and competitions to provide evaluation and treatment of activity-related injuries or medical conditions. Record athletes' medical histories and perform physical examinations. Supervise the rehabilitation of injured athletes. Refer athletes for specialized consultation, physical therapy, or diagnostic testing. Record athletes' medical care information and maintain medical records. Inform coaches, trainers, or other interested parties regarding the medical conditions of athletes. Provide education and counseling on illness and injury prevention. Prescribe orthotics, prosthetics, and adaptive equipment. Prescribe medications for the treatment of athletic-related injuries. Order and interpret the results of laboratory tests and diagnostic imaging procedures. Inform athletes about nutrition, hydration, dietary supplements, or uses and possible consequences of medication. Evaluate and manage chronic pain conditions. Examine and evaluate athletes prior to participation in sports activities to determine level of physical fitness or predisposition to injuries.

Surgeons. Treat diseases, injuries, and deformities by invasive methods, such as manual manipulation, or by using instruments and appliances. Analyze patient's medical history, medication allergies, physical condition, and examination results to verify operation's necessity and to determine best procedure. Operate on patients to correct deformities, repair injuries, prevent and treat diseases, or improve or restore patients' functions. Follow established surgical techniques during the operation. Prescribe preoperative and postoperative treatments and procedures, such as sedatives, diets, antibiotics, and preparation and treatment of the patient's operative area. Examine patient to provide information on medical condition and surgical risk. Diagnose bodily disorders and orthopedic conditions and provide treatments, such as

medicines and surgeries, in clinics, hospital wards, and operating rooms. Direct and coordinate activities of nurses, assistants, specialists, residents, and other medical staff. Provide consultation and surgical assistance to other physicians and surgeons. Refer patient to medical specialist or other practitioners when necessary. Examine instruments, equipment, and operating room to ensure sterility. Prepare case histories. Manage surgery services, including planning, scheduling and coordination, determination of procedures, and procurement of supplies and equipment. Conduct research to develop and test surgical techniques that can improve operating procedures and outcomes.

Urologists. Diagnose, treat, and help prevent benign and malignant medical and surgical disorders of the genitourinary system and the renal glands. Teach or train medical and clinical staff. Document or review patients' histories. Provide urology consultation to physicians or other health care professionals. Refer patients to specialists when condition exceeds experience, expertise, or scope of practice. Direct the work of nurses, residents, or other staff to provide patient care. Treat urologic disorders using alternatives to traditional surgery such as extracorporeal shock wave lithotripsy, laparoscopy, and laser techniques. Treat lower urinary tract dysfunctions using equipment such as diathermy machines, catheters, cystoscopes, and radium emanation tubes. Prescribe or administer antibiotics, antiseptics, or compresses to treat infection or injury. Prescribe medications to treat patients with erectile dysfunction (ED), infertility, or ejaculation problems. Perform abdominal, pelvic, or retroperitoneal surgeries. Perform brachytherapy, cryotherapy, high intensity focused ultrasound (HIFU), or photodynamic therapy to treat prostate or other cancers. Order and interpret the results of diagnostic tests, such as prostate specific antigen (PSA) screening, to detect prostate cancer. Examine patients using equipment, such as radiograph (X-ray) machines and fluoroscopes, to determine the nature and extent of disorder or

Investigative

injury. Diagnose or treat diseases or disorders of genitourinary organs and tracts including erectile dysfunction (ED), infertility, incontinence, bladder cancer, prostate cancer, urethral stones, or premature ejaculation.

Optometry

Personality Type: Investigative–Social–Realistic

Useful Facts About the Major

Prepares individuals for the independent professional practice of optometry and focuses on the principles and techniques for examining, diagnosing, and treating conditions of the visual system.

Related CIP Program: 51.1701 Optometry (OD)

Specializations in the Major: Contact lenses, low vision.

Typical Sequence of College Courses: English composition, introduction to psychology, calculus, introduction to sociology, oral communication, general chemistry, general biology, organic chemistry, general microbiology, introduction to biochemistry, microbiology for optometry, geometric, physical and visual optics, ocular health assessment, neuroanatomy, ocular anatomy and physiology, pathology, theory and methods of refraction, general and ocular pharmacology, optical and motor aspects of vision, ophthalmic optics, environmental and occupational vision, assessment of oculomotor system, strabismus and vision therapy, visual information processing and perception, ocular disease, contact lenses, pediatric and developmental vision, ethics in health care, professional practice management, low vision and geriatric vision, clinical experience in optometry.

Typical Sequence of High School Courses: English, algebra, geometry, trigonometry, pre-calculus, biology, computer science, public speaking, chemistry, calculus, physics, foreign language.

Career Snapshot

Optometrists measure patients' visual ability and prescribe visual aids such as glasses and contact lenses. They may evaluate patients' suitability for laser surgery and/or provide post-operative care, but they do not perform surgery. The usual educational preparation is at least three years of college, followed by a four-year program of optometry school. The job outlook is good because the aging population will need increased attention to vision. The best opportunities probably will be at retail vision centers and outpatient clinics.

Useful Averages for the Related Jobs

- ❋ Annual Earnings: $96,000
- ❋ Growth: 24.4%
- ❋ Openings: 2,010
- ❋ Self-Employed: 24.6%
- ❋ Verbal Skill Rating: 57
- ❋ Math Skill Rating: 64

Other Details About the Related Jobs

Career Cluster: 08 Health Science. **Career Pathway:** 08.1 Therapeutic Services.

Skills: Science, reading comprehension, management of financial resources, operations analysis, quality control analysis, management of material resources, operation and control, service orientation. **Work Conditions:** Indoors; sitting; exposed to disease or infections; close to co-workers; using hands.

Related Jobs

Optometrists

Personality Type: Investigative–Social–Realistic

Earnings: $96,140
Growth: 24.4%
Annual Openings: 2,010

Most Common Education/Training Level: First professional degree

Diagnose, manage, and treat conditions and diseases of the human eye and visual system. Examine eyes and visual systems, diagnose problems or impairments, prescribe corrective lenses, and provide treatment. May prescribe therapeutic drugs to treat specific eye conditions. Examine eyes, using observation, instruments, and pharmaceutical agents, to determine visual acuity and perception, focus, and coordination and to diagnose diseases and other abnormalities such as glaucoma or color blindness. Prescribe medications to treat eye diseases if state laws permit. Analyze test results and develop treatment plans. Prescribe, supply, fit, and adjust eyeglasses, contact lenses, and other vision aids. Educate and counsel patients on contact lens care, visual hygiene, lighting arrangements, and safety factors. Remove foreign bodies from eyes. Consult with and refer patients to ophthalmologist or other health care practitioners if additional medical treatment is determined necessary. Provide patients undergoing eye surgeries such as cataract and laser vision correction, with pre- and post-operative care. Prescribe therapeutic procedures to correct or conserve vision. Provide vision therapy and low vision rehabilitation.

Pharmacy

Personality Type:
Investigative–Conventional–Social

Useful Facts About the Major

Prepares individuals for the independent or employed practice of preparing and dispensing drugs and medications in consultation with prescribing physicians ad other health care professionals, and for managing pharmacy practices and counseling patients.

Related CIP Program: 51.2001 Pharmacy (PharmD [USA], PharmD or BS/BPharm [Canada])

Specializations in the Major: Pharmaceutical chemistry, pharmacology, pharmacy administration.

Typical Sequence of College Courses: English composition, introduction to psychology, calculus, introduction to sociology, oral communication, general chemistry, general biology, organic chemistry, introduction to biochemistry, human anatomy and physiology, pharmaceutical calculations, pharmacology, pharmaceutics, microbiology and immunology, patient assessment and education, medicinal chemistry, therapeutics, pharmacy law and ethics, pharmacokinetics, electrical inspection.

Typical Sequence of High School Courses: English, algebra, geometry, trigonometry, biology, computer science, public speaking, chemistry, calculus, physics, foreign language.

Career Snapshot

Pharmacists dispense medications as prescribed by physicians and other health practitioners and give advice to patients about how to use medications. Pharmacists must be knowledgeable about the chemical and physical properties of drugs, how they behave in the body, and how they may interact with other drugs and substances. Schools of pharmacy take about four years to complete and usually require at least one or two years of prior college work. Some pharmacists go on to additional graduate training to prepare for research, administration, or college teaching. Some find work in sales for pharmaceutical companies or in marketing research for managed care organizations. The job outlook for pharmacists is expected to be good, thanks to the aging of the population, combined with the shift of medical care from the scalpel to the pill.

Useful Averages for the Related Jobs

- ❋ Annual Earnings: $109,000
- ❋ Growth: 17.0%
- ❋ Openings: 10,580
- ❋ Self-Employed: 0.6%
- ❋ Verbal Skill Rating: 69
- ❋ Math Skill Rating: 65

Other Details About the Related Jobs

Career Cluster: 08 Health Science. **Career Pathways:** 08.1 Therapeutic Services; 08.5 Biotechnology Research and Development.

Skills: Science, operations analysis, reading comprehension, management of material resources, active listening, writing, instructing, management of financial resources. **Work Conditions:** Indoors; standing; exposed to disease or infections; using hands; making repetitive motions; close to co-workers; walking and running.

Related Jobs

Pharmacists

Personality Type:
Investigative–Conventional–Social

Earnings: $109,180
Growth: 17.0%
Annual Openings: 10,580

Most Common Education/Training Level: First professional degree

Compound and dispense medications, following prescriptions issued by physicians, dentists, or other authorized medical practitioners. Review prescriptions to assure accuracy, to ascertain the needed ingredients, and to evaluate their suitability. Provide information and advice regarding drug interactions, side effects, dosage and proper medication storage. Assess the identity, strength and purity of medications. Maintain records, such as pharmacy files, patient profiles, charge system files, inventories, control records for radioactive nuclei, and registries of poisons, narcotics, and controlled drugs. Compound and dispense medications as prescribed by doctors and dentists, by calculating, weighing, measuring, and mixing ingredients, or oversee these activities. Plan, implement, and maintain procedures for mixing, packaging, and labeling pharmaceuticals, according to policy and legal requirements, to ensure quality, security, and proper disposal. Teach pharmacy students serving as interns in preparation for their graduation or licensure. Advise customers on the selection of medication brands, medical equipment and health-care supplies. Provide specialized services to help patients manage conditions such as diabetes, asthma, smoking cessation, or high blood pressure. Collaborate with other health care professionals to plan, monitor, review, and evaluate the quality and effectiveness of drugs and drug regimens, providing advice on drug applications and characteristics. Analyze prescribing trends to monitor patient compliance and to prevent excessive usage or harmful interactions. Manage pharmacy operations, hiring and supervising staff, performing administrative duties, and buying and selling non-pharmaceutical merchandise. Order and purchase pharmaceutical supplies, medical supplies, and drugs, maintaining stock and storing and handling it properly. Offer health promotion and prevention activities, for example, training people to use devices such as blood pressure or diabetes monitors. Refer patients to other health professionals and agencies when appropriate.

Veterinary Medicine

Personality Type: Investigative–Realistic

Useful Facts About the Major

Prepares individuals for the independent professional practice of veterinary medicine, involving the diagnosis, treatment, and health care management of animals and animal populations and the prevention and management of diseases that may be transmitted to humans.

Related CIP Program: 51.2401 Veterinary Medicine (DVM)

Specializations in the Major: Companion animals, large animals (horses, cattle), public health, research.

Typical Sequence of College Courses: English composition, introduction to psychology, college algebra, calculus, introduction to sociology, oral communication, general chemistry, general biology, introduction to computer science, organic chemistry, human anatomy and physiology, general microbiology, genetics, introduction to biochemistry, veterinary gross anatomy, neuroanatomy, veterinary histology and cell biology, veterinary radiology, animal nutrition and nutritional diseases, neuroanatomy, pathology, veterinary microbiology, pharmacology, veterinary ophthalmology, public health, veterinary surgery, reproduction, veterinary toxicology, clinical veterinary experience.

Typical Sequence of High School Courses: English, algebra, geometry, trigonometry, biology, computer science, public speaking, chemistry, foreign language, physics, pre-calculus.

Career Snapshot

Veterinarians care for the health of animals—from dogs and cats to horses and cattle to exotic zoo animals—protect humans from diseases carried by animals, and conduct basic research on animal health. Most of them work in private practices. Some inspect animals or animal products for government agencies. Most students who enter the four-year veterinary school program have already completed a bachelor's degree that includes math and science coursework. Competition for entry to veterinary school is keen, but the job outlook is expected to be good.

Useful Averages for the Related Jobs

* Annual Earnings: $81,000
* Growth: 32.9%
* Openings: 3,020
* Self-Employed: 6.9%
* Verbal Skill Rating: 57
* Math Skill Rating: 59

Other Details About the Related Jobs

Career Clusters: 01 Agriculture, Food, and Natural Resources; 08 Health Science. **Career Pathways:** 01.3 Animal Systems; 08.1 Therapeutic Services.

Skills: Science, operations analysis, reading comprehension, active learning, instructing, service orientation, writing, judgment and decision making. **Work Conditions:** Indoors; standing; exposed to disease or infections; exposed to radiation; wear specialized protective or safety equipment; minor burns, cuts, bites, or stings; close to co-workers; contaminants; hazardous conditions.

Related Jobs

Veterinarians

Personality Type: Investigative–Realistic

Earnings: $80,510
Growth: 33.0%
Annual Openings: 3,020

Investigative

Most Common Education/Training Level: First professional degree

Diagnose and treat diseases and dysfunctions of animals. May engage in a particular function, such as research and development, consultation, administration, technical writing, sale or production of commercial products, or rendering of technical services to commercial firms or other organizations. Includes veterinarians who inspect livestock. Treat sick or injured animals by prescribing medication, setting bones, dressing wounds, or performing surgery. Examine animals to detect and determine the nature of diseases or injuries. Provide care to a wide range of animals or specialize in a particular species, such as horses or exotic birds. Inoculate animals against various diseases such as rabies and distemper. Advise animal owners regarding sanitary measures, feeding, general care, medical conditions, and treatment options. Operate diagnostic equipment such as radiographic and ultrasound equipment, and interpret the resulting images. Educate the public about diseases that can be spread from animals to humans. Collect body tissue, feces, blood, urine, or other body fluids for examination and analysis. Attend lectures, conferences, and continuing education courses. Euthanize animals. Train and supervise workers who handle and care for animals. Conduct postmortem studies and analyses to determine the causes of animals' deaths. Specialize in a particular type of treatment such as dentistry, pathology, nutrition, surgery, microbiology, or internal medicine. Direct the overall operations of animal hospitals, clinics, or mobile services to farms. Drive mobile clinic vans to farms so that health problems can be treated or prevented. Establish and conduct quarantine and testing procedures that prevent the spread of diseases to other animals or to humans, and that comply with applicable government regulations. Plan and execute animal nutrition and reproduction programs. Determine the effects of drug therapies, antibiotics, or new surgical techniques by testing them on animals. Perform administrative and business management tasks such as scheduling appointments, accepting payments from clients, budgeting, and maintaining business records. Inspect and test horses, sheep, poultry, and other animals to detect the presence of communicable diseases. Research diseases to which animals could be susceptible.

Artistic Majors

Architecture

Personality Type:
Artistic–Investigative–Enterprising

Useful Facts About the Major

Prepares individuals for the independent professional practice of architecture and for conducting research in various aspects of the field.

Related CIP Program: 04.0201 Architecture (BArch, BA/BS, MArch, MA/MS, PhD)

Specializations in the Major: Design, history, theory and criticism, urban studies, architectural engineering.

Typical Sequence of College Courses: English composition, basic drawing, art history: Renaissance to modern, calculus, introduction to computer science, general physics, history of architecture, structures, building science, visual analysis of architecture, architectural graphics, architectural design, architectural computer graphics, site analysis, introduction to urban planning.

Typical Sequence of High School Courses: English, algebra, geometry, trigonometry, pre-calculus, calculus, physics, computer science, art.

Career Snapshot

Architects design buildings and the spaces between them. They must have a combination of artistic, technical, and business skills. In order to be licensed, they must obtain a professional degree in architecture (sometimes a five-year bachelor's degree, sometimes a master's degree after a bachelor's in another field); work as an intern, typically for three years; and pass a licensing exam. About one-third are self-employed, and most architectural firms are quite small. Computer skills can be a big advantage for new graduates. Best internship opportunities will be for those who have interned while still in school. Demand for architectural services depends on the amount of building construction and therefore varies with economic ups and downs and by geographic region. Job competition is expected to be keen.

Useful Averages for the Related Jobs

- ❋ Annual Earnings: $86,000
- ❋ Growth: 13.8%
- ❋ Openings: 5,898
- ❋ Self-Employed: 16.1%
- ❋ Verbal Skill Rating: 58
- ❋ Math Skill Rating: 60

Other Details About the Related Jobs

Career Clusters: 02 Architecture and Construction; 11 Information Technology; 15 Science, Technology, Engineering, and Mathematics. **Career Pathways:** 02.1 Design/Pre-Construction; 11.4 Programming and Software Development; 15.1 Engineering and Technology; 15.2 Science and Mathematics.

Skills: Operations analysis, management of financial resources, management of material resources, mathematics, science, judgment and decision making, complex problem solving, quality control analysis. **Work Conditions:** More often indoors than outdoors; in a vehicle; sitting; high places; climbing ladders, scaffolds, or poles.

Artistic

Related Jobs

1. Architects, Except Landscape and Naval

Personality Type: Artistic–Investigative

Earnings: $72,700
Growth: 16.2%
Annual Openings: 4,680

Most Common Education/Training Level:
Bachelor's or higher degree plus work experience

Plan and design structures such as private residences, office buildings, theaters, factories, and other structural property. Consult with client to determine functional and spatial requirements of structure. Prepare scale drawings. Plan layout of project. Prepare information regarding design, structure specifications, materials, color, equipment, estimated costs, or construction time. Prepare contract documents for building contractors. Integrate engineering element into unified design. Direct activities of workers engaged in preparing drawings and specification documents. Conduct periodic on-site observation of work during construction to monitor compliance with plans. Seek new work opportunities through marketing, writing proposals, or giving presentations. Administer construction contracts. Represent client in obtaining bids and awarding construction contracts. Prepare operating and maintenance manuals, studies, and reports.

2. Engineering Managers

Personality Type:
Enterprising–Realistic–Investigative

Earnings: $117,000
Growth: 6.2%
Annual Openings: 4,870

Most Common Education/Training Level:
Bachelor's or higher degree plus work experience

Plan, direct, or coordinate activities or research and development in such fields as architecture and engineering. Confer with management, production, and marketing staff to discuss project specifications and procedures. Coordinate and direct projects, making detailed plans to accomplish goals and directing the integration of technical activities. Analyze technology, resource needs, and market demand, to plan and assess the feasibility of projects. Plan and direct the installation, testing, operation, maintenance, and repair of facilities and equipment. Direct, review, and approve product design and changes. Recruit employees, assign, direct, and evaluate their work, and oversee the development and maintenance of staff competence. Prepare budgets, bids, and contracts, and direct the negotiation of research contracts. Develop and implement policies, standards and procedures for the engineering and technical work performed in the department, service, laboratory or firm. Review and recommend or approve contracts and cost estimates. Perform administrative functions such as reviewing and writing reports, approving expenditures, enforcing rules, and making decisions about the purchase of materials or services. Present and explain proposals, reports, and findings to clients. Consult or negotiate with clients to prepare project specifications. Set scientific and technical goals within broad outlines provided by top management. Administer highway planning, construction, and maintenance. Direct the engineering of water control, treatment, and distribution projects. Plan, direct, and coordinate survey work with other staff activities, certifying survey work, and writing land legal descriptions. Confer with and report to officials and the public to provide information and solicit support for projects.

Job Specialization

Biofuels/Biodiesel Technology and Product Development Managers. Define, plan, or execute

biofuel/biodiesel research programs that evaluate alternative feedstock and process technologies with near-term commercial potential. Develop lab scale models of industrial scale processes, such as fermentation. Develop computational tools or approaches to improve biofuels research and development activities. Develop carbohydrates arrays and associated methods for screening enzymes involved in biomass conversion. Provide technical or scientific guidance to technical staff in the conduct of biofuels research or development. Prepare, or oversee the preparation of, experimental plans for biofuels research or development. Prepare biofuels research and development reports for senior management or technical professionals. Perform protein functional analysis and engineering for processing of feedstock and creation of biofuels. Develop separation processes to recover biofuels. Develop methods to recover ethanol or other fuels from complex bioreactor liquid and gas streams. Develop methods to estimate the efficiency of biomass pretreatments. Design or execute solvent or product recovery experiments in laboratory or field settings. Design or conduct applied biodiesel or biofuels research projects on topics such as transport, thermodynamics, mixing, filtration, distillation, fermentation, extraction, and separation. Design chemical conversion processes, such as etherification, esterification, interesterification, transesterification, distillation, hydrogenation, oxidation or reduction of fats and oils, and vegetable oil refining. Conduct experiments on biomass or pretreatment technologies. Conduct experiments to test new or alternate feedstock fermentation processes. Analyze data from biofuels studies, such as fluid dynamics, water treatments, or solvent extraction and recovery processes. Oversee biodiesel/biofuels prototyping or development projects. Propose new biofuels products, processes, technologies or applications based on findings from applied biofuels or biomass research projects.

Chinese

Personality Type: Artistic–Social

Useful Facts About the Major

Focuses on the Chinese language and its associated dialects and literature.

Related CIP Program: 16.0301 Chinese Language and Literature

Specializations in the Major: Literature, translation, history and culture, language education.

Typical Sequence of College Courses: Chinese language, conversation, composition, linguistics, Chinese literature, East Asian literature, East Asian studies, grammar, phonetics.

Typical Sequence of High School Courses: English, public speaking, foreign language, history, literature, social science.

Career Snapshot

Because Chinese is spoken by more people than any other language, and China now has the world's second-biggest economy, there is a growing need for Americans with knowledge of the Chinese language and culture. A bachelor's degree in Chinese, perhaps with additional education in business or law, may lead to an Asia-centered career in business or government. A graduate degree is good preparation for translation or college teaching.

Useful Averages for the Related Jobs

- ❋ Annual Earnings: $41,000
- ❋ Growth: 22.2%
- ❋ Openings: 2,340
- ❋ Self-Employed: 26.1%
- ❋ Verbal Skill Rating: 71
- ❋ Math Skill Rating: 31

Artistic

Other Details About the Related Jobs

Career Clusters: 05 Education and Training; 10 Human Services. **Career Pathways:** 05.3 Teaching/Training; 10.5 Consumer Services Career.

Skills: Writing, reading comprehension, active listening, speaking, social perceptiveness, service orientation, learning strategies, monitoring. **Work Conditions:** Indoors; sitting; close to co-workers; exposed to disease or infections; exposed to radiation; making repetitive motions.

Related Jobs

Interpreters and Translators

Personality Type: Artistic–Social

Earnings: $40,860
Growth: 22.2%
Annual Openings: 2,340

Most Common Education/Training Level: Long-term on-the-job training

Translate or interpret written, oral, or sign language text into another language for others. Follow ethical codes that protect the confidentiality of information. Identify and resolve conflicts related to the meanings of words, concepts, practices, or behaviors. Proofread, edit, and revise translated materials. Translate messages simultaneously or consecutively into specified languages orally or by using hand signs, maintaining message content, context, and style as much as possible. Check translations of technical terms and terminology to ensure that they are accurate and remain consistent throughout translation revisions. Read written materials such as legal documents, scientific works, or news reports and rewrite material into specified languages. Refer to reference materials such as dictionaries, lexicons, encyclopedias, and computerized terminology banks as needed to ensure translation accuracy. Compile terminology and information to be used in translations, including technical terms such as those for legal or medical material. Adapt translations to students' cognitive and grade levels, collaborating with educational team members as necessary. Listen to speakers' statements to determine meanings and to prepare translations, using electronic listening systems as necessary. Check original texts or confer with authors to ensure that translations retain the content, meaning, and feeling of the original material. Compile information about the content and context of information to be translated, as well as details of the groups for whom translation or interpretation is being performed. Discuss translation requirements with clients and determine any fees to be charged for services provided. Adapt software and accompanying technical documents to another language and culture. Educate students, parents, staff, and teachers about the roles and functions of educational interpreters. Train and supervise other translators/interpreters. Travel with or guide tourists who speak another language.

Classics

Personality Type: Artistic–Social

Useful Facts About the Major

Focuses on the literary culture of the ancient Graeco-Roman world, as well as the Greek and Latin languages and literatures and their development prior to the fall of the Roman Empire.

Related CIP Programs: 16.1203 Latin Language and Literature; 16.1202 Ancient/Classical Greek Language and Literature; 16.1200 Classics and Classical Languages, Literatures, and Linguistics, General

Specializations in the Major: Classical literature/mythology, classical civilization, classical linguistics, greek, latin, archeology.

Typical Sequence of College Courses: Latin, Greek, grammar, linguistics, literature of the

Roman Empire, literature in ancient Greek, history of the ancient world.

Typical Sequence of High School Courses: English, public speaking, foreign language, history, literature, social science.

Career Snapshot

The classical languages—Latin and Greek—may be dead, but students who study them often end up in very lively careers. The mental discipline and critical-thinking skills learned in the classics can be first-rate preparation for law school and medical school, and business recruiters report that classics graduates have an exceptional breadth of view. The demand for Latin teachers in secondary schools is strong. A classics major is also a good first step to graduate training in archeology, history, or theology.

Useful Averages for the Related Jobs

- ❈ Annual Earnings: $41,000
- ❈ Growth: 22.4%
- ❈ Openings: 2,452
- ❈ Self-Employed: 25.4%
- ❈ Verbal Skill Rating: 71
- ❈ Math Skill Rating: 32

Other Details About the Related Jobs

Career Clusters: 05 Education and Training; 10 Human Services; 15 Science, Technology, Engineering, and Mathematics. **Career Pathways:** 05.3 Teaching/Training; 10.5 Consumer Services Career; 15.2 Science and Mathematics.

Skills: Writing, reading comprehension, active listening, speaking, social perceptiveness, service orientation, learning strategies, active learning. **Work**

Conditions: Indoors; sitting; close to co-workers; exposed to disease or infections.

Related Jobs

1. Anthropologists and Archeologists

Personality Type: Investigative–Artistic

Earnings: $53,460
Growth: 28.1%
Annual Openings: 450

Most Common Education/Training Level: Master's degree

Study the origin, development, and behavior of humans. May study the way of life, language, or physical characteristics of existing people in various parts of the world. May engage in systematic recovery and examination of material evidence, such as tools or pottery remaining from past human cultures, to determine the history, customs, and living habits of earlier civilizations. No task data available.

Job Specializations

Anthropologists. Research, evaluate, and establish public policy concerning the origins of humans; their physical, social, linguistic, and cultural development; and their behavior, as well as the cultures, organizations, and institutions they have created. Collect information and make judgments through observation, interviews, and the review of documents. Plan and direct research to characterize and compare the economic, demographic, health-care, social, political, linguistic, and religious institutions of distinct cultural groups, communities, and organizations. Write about and present research findings for a variety of specialized and general audiences. Advise government agencies, private organizations, and communities regarding proposed programs, plans, and policies and their potential impacts on cultural

Artistic

institutions, organizations, and communities. Identify culturally specific beliefs and practices affecting health status and access to services for distinct populations and communities in collaboration with medical and public health officials. Build and use text-based database management systems to support the analysis of detailed first-hand observational records, or "field notes." Develop intervention procedures, utilizing techniques such as individual and focus group interviews, consultations, and participant observation of social interaction. Construct and test data collection methods. Explain the origins and physical, social, or cultural development of humans, including physical attributes, cultural traditions, beliefs, languages, resource management practices, and settlement patterns. Conduct participatory action research in communities and organizations to assess how work is done and to design work systems, technologies, and environments. Train others in the application of ethnographic research methods to solve problems in organizational effectiveness, communications, technology development, policy-making, and program planning. Formulate general rules that describe and predict the development and behavior of cultures and social institutions.

Archeologists. Conduct research to reconstruct record of past human life and culture from human remains, artifacts, architectural features, and structures recovered through excavation, underwater recovery, or other means of discovery. Write, present, and publish reports that record site history, methodology, and artifact analysis results, along with recommendations for conserving and interpreting findings. Compare findings from one site with archeological data from other sites to find similarities or differences. Research, survey, or assess sites of past societies and cultures in search of answers to specific research questions. Study objects and structures recovered by excavation to identify, date, and authenticate them and to interpret their significance. Develop and test theories concerning the origin and development

of past cultures. Consult site reports, existing artifacts, and topographic maps to identify archeological sites. Create a grid of each site and draw and update maps of unit profiles, stratum surfaces, features, and findings. Record the exact locations and conditions of artifacts uncovered in diggings or surveys, using drawings and photographs as necessary. Assess archeological sites for resource management, development, or conservation purposes and recommend methods for site protection. Describe artifacts' physical properties or attributes, such as the materials from which artifacts are made and their size, shape, function, and decoration. Teach archeology at colleges and universities. Collect artifacts made of stone, bone, metal, and other materials, placing them in bags and marking them to show where they were found. Create artifact typologies to organize and make sense of past material cultures. Lead field training sites and train field staff, students, and volunteers in excavation methods. Clean, restore, and preserve artifacts.

2. Interpreters and Translators

Personality Type: Artistic–Social

Earnings: $40,860
Growth: 22.2%
Annual Openings: 2,340

Most Common Education/Training Level: Master's degree

Translate or interpret written, oral, or sign language text into another language for others. Follow ethical codes that protect the confidentiality of information. Identify and resolve conflicts related to the meanings of words, concepts, practices, or behaviors. Proofread, edit, and revise translated materials. Translate messages simultaneously or consecutively into specified languages orally or by using hand signs, maintaining message content, context, and style as much as possible. Check translations of technical terms and terminology to ensure that they are accurate and remain consistent throughout translation revisions. Read written materials such as legal documents, scientific works, or news reports and rewrite material into specified languages. Refer to reference materials such as dictionaries, lexicons, encyclopedias, and computerized terminology banks as needed to ensure translation accuracy. Compile terminology and information to be used in translations, including technical terms such as those for legal or medical material. Adapt translations to students' cognitive and grade levels, collaborating with educational team members as necessary. Listen to speakers' statements to determine meanings and to prepare translations, using electronic listening systems as necessary. Check original texts or confer with authors to ensure that translations retain the content, meaning, and feeling of the original material. Compile information about the content and context of information to be translated, as well as details of the groups for whom translation or interpretation is being performed. Discuss translation requirements with clients and determine any fees to be charged for services provided. Adapt software and accompanying technical documents to another language and culture. Educate students, parents, staff, and teachers about the roles and functions of educational interpreters. Train and supervise other translators/interpreters. Travel with or guide tourists who speak another language.

French

Personality Type: Artistic–Social

Useful Facts About the Major

Focuses on the French language and related dialects and creoles.

Related CIP Program: 16.0901 French Language and Literature

Specializations in the Major: Literature, translation, history and culture, language education.

Typical Sequence of College Courses: French language, conversation, composition, linguistics, French literature, French history and civilization, European history and civilization, grammar, phonetics.

Typical Sequence of High School Courses: English, public speaking, French, history, literature, social science.

Career Snapshot

French is a native tongue on several continents and in parts of the United States, and it has a rich cultural heritage associated with the arts and literature. French majors may go into careers in international business, travel, or teaching. Teaching at the secondary level requires education courses and, in many districts, a master's; college teaching requires a graduate degree.

Useful Averages for the Related Jobs

- ❋ Annual Earnings: $41,000
- ❋ Growth: 22.2%
- ❋ Openings: 2,340
- ❋ Self-Employed: 26.1%
- ❋ Verbal Skill Rating: 71
- ❋ Math Skill Rating: 31

Other Details About the Related Jobs

Career Clusters: 05 Education and Training; 10 Human Services. **Career Pathways:** 05.3 Teaching/Training; 10.5 Consumer Services Career.

Skills: Writing, reading comprehension, active listening, speaking, social perceptiveness, service orientation, learning strategies, monitoring. **Work Conditions:** Indoors; sitting; close to co-workers; exposed to disease or infections; exposed to radiation; making repetitive motions.

Artistic

Related Jobs

Interpreters and Translators

Personality Type: Artistic–Social

Earnings: $40,860
Growth: 22.2%
Annual Openings: 2,340

Most Common Education/Training Level:
Long-term on-the-job training

Translate or interpret written, oral, or sign language text into another language for others. Follow ethical codes that protect the confidentiality of information. Identify and resolve conflicts related to the meanings of words, concepts, practices, or behaviors. Proofread, edit, and revise translated materials. Translate messages simultaneously or consecutively into specified languages orally or by using hand signs, maintaining message content, context, and style as much as possible. Check translations of technical terms and terminology to ensure that they are accurate and remain consistent throughout translation revisions. Read written materials such as legal documents, scientific works, or news reports and rewrite material into specified languages. Refer to reference materials such as dictionaries, lexicons, encyclopedias, and computerized terminology banks as needed to ensure translation accuracy. Compile terminology and information to be used in translations, including technical terms such as those for legal or medical material. Adapt translations to students' cognitive and grade levels, collaborating with educational team members as necessary. Listen to speakers' statements to determine meanings and to prepare translations, using electronic listening systems as necessary. Check original texts or confer with authors to ensure that translations retain the content, meaning, and feeling of the original material. Compile information about the content and context of information to be translated, as well as details of the groups for whom translation or interpretation is being performed. Discuss translation requirements with clients and determine any fees to be charged for services provided. Adapt software and accompanying technical documents to another language and culture. Educate students, parents, staff, and teachers about the roles and functions of educational interpreters. Train and supervise other translators/interpreters. Travel with or guide tourists who speak another language.

German

Personality Type: Artistic–Social

Useful Facts About the Major

Focuses on the German language and related dialects as used in Austria, Germany, Switzerland, neighboring European countries containing German-speaking minorities, and elsewhere.

Related CIP Program: 16.0501 German Language and Literature

Specializations in the Major: Literature, translation, history and culture, language education.

Typical Sequence of College Courses: German language, conversation, composition, linguistics, German literature, German history and civilization, European history and civilization, grammar, phonetics.

Typical Sequence of High School Courses: English, public speaking, German, history, literature, social science.

Career Snapshot

Germany is the dominant economic force in Europe and an important center of culture. A degree in German can open many doors in international business, travel, and law. Many employers are looking for graduates with an understanding of a second language and culture. Those with a graduate degree in German may go into translation or college teaching. With coursework in education, high school teaching is an option; many districts require a master's.

Useful Averages for the Related Jobs

- ❋ Annual Earnings: $41,000
- ❋ Growth: 22.2%
- ❋ Openings: 2,340
- ❋ Self-Employed: 26.1%
- ❋ Verbal Skill Rating: 71
- ❋ Math Skill Rating: 31

Other Details About the Related Jobs

Career Clusters: 05 Education and Training; 10 Human Services. **Career Pathways:** 05.3 Teaching/Training; 10.5 Consumer Services Career.

Skills: Writing, reading comprehension, active listening, speaking, social perceptiveness, service orientation, learning strategies, monitoring. **Work Conditions:** Indoors; sitting; close to co-workers; exposed to disease or infections; exposed to radiation; making repetitive motions.

Related Jobs

Interpreters and Translators

Personality Type: Artistic–Social

Earnings: $40,860
Growth: 22.2%
Annual Openings: 2,340

Most Common Education/Training Level: Long-term on-the-job training

Translate or interpret written, oral, or sign language text into another language for others. Follow ethical codes that protect the confidentiality of information. Identify and resolve conflicts related to the meanings of words, concepts, practices, or behaviors. Proofread, edit, and revise translated materials. Translate messages simultaneously or consecutively into specified languages orally or by using hand signs, maintaining message content, context, and style as much as possible. Check translations of technical terms and terminology to ensure that they are accurate and remain consistent throughout translation revisions. Read written materials such as legal documents, scientific works, or news reports and rewrite material into specified languages. Refer to reference materials such as dictionaries, lexicons, encyclopedias, and computerized terminology banks as needed to ensure translation accuracy. Compile terminology and information to be used in translations, including technical terms such as those for legal or medical material. Adapt translations to students' cognitive and grade levels, collaborating with educational team members as necessary. Listen to speakers' statements to determine meanings and to prepare translations, using electronic listening systems as necessary. Check original texts or confer with authors to ensure that translations retain the content, meaning, and feeling of the original material. Compile information about the content and context of information to be translated, as well as details of the groups for whom translation or interpretation is being performed. Discuss translation requirements with clients and determine any fees to be charged for services provided. Adapt software and accompanying technical documents to another language and culture. Educate students, parents, staff, and teachers about the roles and functions of educational interpreters. Train and supervise other translators/interpreters. Travel with or guide tourists who speak another language.

Graphic Design, Commercial Art, and Illustration

Personality Type: Artistic–Realistic–Enterprising

Artistic

Useful Facts About the Major

Prepares individuals to use artistic techniques to effectively communicate ideas and information to business and consumer audiences via illustrations and other forms of digital or printed media, documents, images, graphics, sound, and multimedia products on the World Wide Web.

Related CIP Programs: 50.0410 Illustration; 50.0411 Game and Interactive Media Design; 11.0801 Web Page, Digital/Multimedia, and Information Resources Design; 50.0402 Commercial and Advertising Art

Specializations in the Major: Illustration, letterform, typography, cartooning, Web page design.

Typical Sequence of College Courses: English composition, college algebra, basic drawing, oral communication, art history: prehistoric to Renaissance, art history: Renaissance to modern, art history: Renaissance to modern, introduction to graphic design, visual thinking and problem solving, presentation graphics, history of graphic design, letterform, two-dimensional design, three-dimensional design, visual communication, typography, computer applications in graphic design, senior design project.

Typical Sequence of High School Courses: Algebra, geometry, trigonometry, pre-calculus, English, public speaking, art, computer science, mechanical drawing, photography.

Career Snapshot

Many consumer goods, such as books, magazines, and Web pages, consist primarily of graphic elements: illustrations and text. Other goods, such as cereal boxes, use graphic elements conspicuously. Graphic design teaches you how to represent ideas graphically and give maximum visual appeal to text and pictures. The program involves considerable studio time, and an important goal is creating a good portfolio of work. Graduates with an associate or bachelor's degree work for publishers and design firms. Some freelance. Competition is expected to be keen; opportunities will be best for those with a bachelor's degree and experience with Web page design or animation.

Useful Averages for the Related Jobs

- ❋ Annual Earnings: $46,000
- ❋ Growth: 12.0%
- ❋ Openings: 13,796
- ❋ Self-Employed: 25.7%
- ❋ Verbal Skill Rating: 59
- ❋ Math Skill Rating: 37

Other Details About the Related Jobs

Career Clusters: 01 Agriculture, Food, and Natural Resources; 03 Arts, Audio/Video Technology, and Communications; 08 Health Science; 11 Information Technology; 15 Science, Technology, Engineering, and Mathematics. **Career Pathways:** 01.7 Agribusiness Systems; 03.1 Audio and Video Technology and Film; 03.2 Printing Technology; 03.3 Visual Arts; 03.4 Performing Arts; 08.3 Health Informatics; 08.5 Biotechnology Research and Development; 11.1 Network Systems; 11.2 Information Support Services; 11.3 Interactive Media; 11.4 Programming and Software Development; 15.1 Engineering and Technology; 15.2 Science and Mathematics.

Skills: Operations analysis, technology design, negotiation, management of financial resources, time management, complex problem solving. **Work Conditions:** Indoors; sitting; making repetitive motions; using hands.

Related Jobs

1. Commercial and Industrial Designers

Personality Type: Artistic–Enterprising–Realistic

Earnings: $58,060
Growth: 9.0%
Annual Openings: 1,760

Most Common Education/Training Level: Associate degree

Develop and design manufactured products, such as cars, home appliances, and children's toys. Combine artistic talent with research on product use, marketing, and materials to create the most functional and appealing product design. Prepare sketches of ideas, detailed drawings, illustrations, artwork, or blueprints, using drafting instruments, paints and brushes, or computer-aided design equipment. Direct and coordinate the fabrication of models or samples and the drafting of working drawings and specification sheets from sketches. Modify and refine designs, using working models, to conform with customer specifications, production limitations, or changes in design trends. Coordinate the look and function of product lines. Confer with engineering, marketing, production, or sales departments, or with customers, to establish and evaluate design concepts for manufactured products. Present designs and reports to customers or design committees for approval, and discuss need for modification. Evaluate feasibility of design ideas, based on factors such as appearance, safety, function, serviceability, budget, production costs/methods, and market characteristics.

2. Computer Programmers

Personality Type: Investigative–Conventional

Earnings: $70,940
Growth: –2.9%
Annual Openings: 8,030

Most Common Education/Training Level: Bachelor's degree

Convert project specifications and statements of problems and procedures to detailed logical flow charts for coding into computer language. Develop and write computer programs to store, locate, and retrieve specific documents, data, and information. May program Web sites. Correct errors by making appropriate changes and rechecking the program to ensure that the desired results are produced. Conduct trial runs of programs and software applications to be sure they will produce the desired information and that the instructions are correct. Write, update, and maintain computer programs or software packages to handle specific jobs such as tracking inventory, storing or retrieving data, or controlling other equipment. Write, analyze, review, and rewrite programs, using workflow chart and diagram, and applying knowledge of computer capabilities, subject matter, and symbolic logic. Perform or direct revision, repair, or expansion of existing programs to increase operating efficiency or adapt to new requirements. Consult with managerial, engineering, and technical personnel to clarify program intent, identify problems, and suggest changes. Perform systems analysis and programming tasks to maintain and control the use of computer systems software as a systems programmer. Compile and write documentation of program development and subsequent revisions, inserting comments in the coded instructions so others can understand the program. Prepare detailed workflow charts and diagrams that describe input, output, and logical operation, and convert them into a series of instructions coded in a computer language. Consult with and assist computer operators or system analysts to define and resolve problems in running computer programs. Investigate whether networks, workstations, the central processing unit of the system, or peripheral equipment are responding to a program's instructions. Assign, coordinate, and

Artistic

review work and activities of programming personnel. Write or contribute to instructions or manuals to guide end users. Train subordinates in programming and program coding. Collaborate with computer manufacturers and other users to develop new programming methods.

3. Computer Specialists, All Other

Personality Type:
Conventional–Investigative–Realistic

Earnings: $77,010
Growth: 13.1%
Annual Openings: 7,260

Most Common Education/Training Level:
Bachelor's degree

Solve problems and make plans involving the use of computers in the following fields: business intelligence, systems architecture, data warehousing, database architecture, document management, electronic commerce, geographic information systems, geospatial information, information technology project management, network design, software quality assurance, video game design, Web administration, and Web development. No task data available.

Job Specializations

Business Intelligence Analysts. Produce financial and market intelligence by querying data repositories and generating periodic reports. Devise methods for identifying data patterns and trends in available information sources. Provide technical support for existing reports, dashboards, or other tools. Maintain library of model documents, templates, or other reusable knowledge assets. Identify or monitor current and potential customers, using business intelligence tools. Create or review technical design documentation to ensure the accurate development of reporting solutions. Communicate with customers, competitors, suppliers, professional organizations, or others to stay abreast of industry or business trends. Maintain or update business intelligence tools, databases, dashboards, systems, or methods. Manage timely flow of business intelligence information to users. Identify and analyze industry or geographic trends with business strategy implications. Document specifications for business intelligence or information technology (IT) reports, dashboards, or other outputs. Disseminate information regarding tools, reports, or metadata enhancements. Create business intelligence tools or systems, including design of related databases, spreadsheets, or outputs. Conduct or coordinate tests to ensure that intelligence is consistent with defined needs. Collect business intelligence data from available industry reports, public information, field reports, or purchased sources. Analyze technology trends to identify markets for future product development or to improve sales of existing products. Analyze competitive market strategies through analysis of related product, market, or share trends. Synthesize current business intelligence or trend data to support recommendations for action. Generate standard or custom reports summarizing business, financial, or economic data for review by executives, managers, clients, and other stakeholders.

Computer Systems Engineers/Architects. Design and develop solutions to complex applications problems, system administration issues, or network concerns. Perform systems management and integration functions. Investigate system component suitability for specified purposes and make recommendations regarding component use. Identify system data, hardware, or software components required to meet user needs. Evaluate existing systems to determine effectiveness and suggest changes to meet organizational requirements. Evaluate current or emerging technologies to consider factors such as cost, portability, compatibility, or usability. Establish functional or system standards to ensure operational requirements, quality requirements, and design constraints are addressed. Document design specifications, installation instructions, and other system-related information. Direct the analysis, development, and operation of complete computer systems. Direct the installation of operating systems, network or application software, or computer or network hardware. Develop system engineering, software engineering, system integration, or distributed system architectures. Develop or approve project plans, schedules, or budgets. Design and conduct hardware or software tests. Collaborate with engineers or software developers to select appropriate design solutions or ensure the compatibility of system components. Define and analyze objectives, scope, issues, or organizational impact of information systems. Provide guidelines for implementing secure systems to customers or installation teams. Provide technical guidance or support for the development or troubleshooting of systems. Provide advice on project costs, design concepts, or design changes. Communicate project information through presentations, technical reports or white papers. Perform security analyses of developed or packaged software components. Develop application-specific software. Monitor system operation to detect potential problems. Configure servers to meet functional specifications. Communicate with staff or clients to understand specific system requirements.

Data Warehousing Specialists. Design, model, or implement corporate data warehousing activities. Program and configure warehouses of database information and provide support to warehouse users. Test software systems or applications for software enhancements or new products. Review designs, codes, test plans, or documentation to ensure quality. Provide or coordinate troubleshooting support for data warehouses. Prepare functional or technical documentation for data warehouses. Write new programs or modify existing programs to meet customer requirements, using current programming languages and technologies. Verify the structure, accuracy, or quality of warehouse data. Select methods, techniques, or

criteria for data warehousing evaluative procedures. Perform system analysis, data analysis or programming, using a variety of computer languages and procedures. Map data between source systems, data warehouses, and data marts. Implement business rules via stored procedures, middleware, or other technologies. Develop and implement data extraction procedures from other systems, such as administration, billing, or claims. Develop or maintain standards, such as organization, structure, or nomenclature, for the design of data warehouse elements, such as data architectures, models, tools, and databases. Design and implement warehouse database structures. Create supporting documentation, such as metadata and diagrams of entity relationships, business processes, and process flow. Create plans, test files, and scripts for data warehouse testing, ranging from unit to integration testing. Create or implement metadata processes and frameworks. Develop data warehouse process models, including sourcing, loading, transformation, and extraction. Design, implement, or operate comprehensive data warehouse systems to balance optimization of data access with batch loading and resource utilization factors, according to customer requirements.

Database Architects. Design strategies for enterprise database systems and set standards for operations, programming, and security. Design and construct large relational databases. Integrate new systems with existing warehouse structure and refine system performance and functionality. Test changes to database applications or systems. Provide technical support to junior staff or clients. Set up database clusters, backup, or recovery processes. Identify, evaluate and recommend hardware or software technologies to achieve desired database performance. Plan and install upgrades of database management system software to enhance database performance. Monitor and report systems resource consumption trends to assure production systems meet availability requirements and hardware enhancements are

Artistic

scheduled appropriately. Identify and correct deviations from database development standards. Document and communicate database schemas, using accepted notations. Develop or maintain archived procedures, procedural codes, or queries for applications. Develop load-balancing processes to eliminate down time for backup processes. Develop data models for applications, metadata tables, views or related database structures. Design databases to support business applications, ensuring system scalability, security, performance and reliability. Design database applications, such as interfaces, data transfer mechanisms, global temporary tables, data partitions, and function-based indexes to enable efficient access of the generic database structure. Demonstrate database technical functionality, such as performance, security and reliability. Create and enforce database development standards. Collaborate with system architects, software architects, design analysts, and others to understand business or industry requirements. Develop database architectural strategies at the modeling, design and implementation stages to address business or industry requirements. Develop and document database architectures.

Document Management Specialists. Implement and administer enterprise-wide document management procedures for the capture, storage, retrieval, sharing, and destruction of electronic records and documents. Keep abreast of developments in document management by reviewing current literature, talking with colleagues, participating in educational programs, attending meetings or workshops, or participating in professional organizations or conferences. Monitor regulatory activity to maintain compliance with records and document management laws. Write, review, or execute plans for testing new or established document management systems. Search electronic sources, such as databases or repositories, or manual sources for information. Retrieve electronic assets from repository for distribution to users, collecting and returning to repository, if necessary.

Propose recommendations for improving content management system capabilities. Prepare support documentation and training materials for end users of document management systems. Prepare and record changes to official documents and confirm changes with legal and compliance management staff. Exercise security surveillance over document processing, reproduction, distribution, storage, or archiving. Implement scanning or other automated data entry procedures, using imaging devices and document imaging software. Document technical functions and specifications for new or proposed content management systems. Develop, document, or maintain standards, best practices, or system usage procedures. Consult with end users regarding problems in accessing electronic content. Conduct needs assessments to identify document management requirements of departments or end users. Assist in the development of document or content classification taxonomies to facilitate information capture, search, and retrieval. Assist in the assessment, acquisition, or deployment of new electronic document management systems. Assist in determining document management policies to facilitate efficient, legal, and secure access to electronic content. Analyze, interpret, or disseminate system performance data.

Electronic Commerce Specialists. Market products on proprietary Web sites. Produce online advertising. Determine Web site content and design. Analyze customer preferences and online sales. Keep abreast of government regulations and emerging web technology to ensure regulatory compliance by reviewing current literature, talking with colleagues, participating in educational programs, attending meetings or workshops, or participation in professional conferences, workshops, or groups. Resolve product availability problems in collaboration with customer service staff. Implement online customer service processes to ensure positive and consistent user experiences. Identify, evaluate, or procure hardware or software for implementing online marketing campaigns. Identify methods for interfacing web application technologies with enterprise resource planning or other system software. Define product requirements based on market research analysis in collaboration with design and engineering staff. Assist in the evaluation and negotiation of contracts with vendors and online partners. Propose online or multiple-sales-channel campaigns to marketing executives. Assist in the development of online transactional and security policies. Prepare electronic commerce designs and prototypes, such as storyboards, mockups, and other content, using graphics design software. Participate in the development of online marketing strategy. Identify and develop commercial or technical specifications to promote transactional web site functionality, including usability, pricing, checkout, or data security. Develop transactional web applications, using web programming software and knowledge of programming languages, such as hypertext markup language (HTML) and extensible markup language (XML). Coordinate sales or other promotional strategies with merchandising, operations, or inventory control staff to ensure product catalogs are current and accurate. Conduct market research analysis to identify electronic commerce trends, market opportunities, or competitor performance. Conduct financial modeling for online marketing programs or website revenue forecasting.

Geographic Information Systems Technicians. Assist scientists, technologists, and related professionals in building, maintaining, modifying, and using geographic information systems (GIS) databases. May also perform some custom application development and provide user support. Recommend procedures and equipment or software upgrades to increase data accessibility or ease of use. Provide technical support to users or clients regarding the maintenance, development, or operation of Geographic Information Systems (GIS) databases, equipment, or applications. Read current literature, talk with colleagues, continue education, or participate in professional organizations or conferences to keep abreast of developments in Geographic Information Systems (GIS) technology, equipment, or systems. Confer with users to analyze, configure, or troubleshoot applications. Select cartographic elements needed for effective presentation of information. Transfer or rescale information from original photographs onto maps or other photographs. Review existing or incoming data for currency, accuracy, usefulness, quality, or completeness of documentation. Interpret aerial or ortho photographs. Analyze Geographic Information Systems (GIS) data to identify spatial relationships or display results of analyses using maps, graphs, or tabular data. Perform geospatial data building, modeling, or analysis using advanced spatial analysis, data manipulation, or cartography software. Maintain or modify existing Geographic Information Systems (GIS) databases. Enter data into Geographic Information Systems (GIS) databases using techniques such as coordinate geometry, keyboard entry of tabular data, manual digitizing of maps, scanning or automatic conversion to vectors, and conversion of other sources of digital Design or prepare graphic representations of Geographic Information Systems (GIS) data using GIS hardware or software applications. Design or coordinate the development of integrated Geographic Information Systems (GIS) spatial or non-spatial databases.

Geospatial Information Scientists and Technologists. Research and develop geospatial technologies. May produce databases, perform applications programming, or coordinate projects. May specialize in areas such as agriculture, mining, health care, retail trade, urban planning or military intelligence. Produce data layers, maps, tables, or reports using spatial analysis procedures and Geographic Information Systems (GIS) technology, equipment, or systems. Coordinate the development or administration of Geographic Information Systems (GIS) projects, including the development of technical priorities, client reporting and interface, or coordination and

Artistic

review of schedules and budgets. Provide technical expertise in Geographic Information Systems (GIS) technology to clients or users. Create, analyze, report, convert, or transfer data using specialized applications program software. Provide technical support for computer-based Geographic Information Systems (GIS) mapping software. Design, program, or model Geographic Information Systems (GIS) applications or procedures. Lead, train, or supervise technicians or related staff in the conduct of Geographic Information Systems (GIS) analytical procedures. Perform computer programming, data analysis, or software development for Geographic Information Systems (GIS) applications, including the maintenance of existing systems or research and development for future enhancements. Collect, compile, or integrate Geographic Information Systems (GIS) data such as remote sensing and cartographic data for inclusion in map manuscripts. Read current literature, talk with colleagues, continue education, or participate in professional organizations or conferences to keep abreast of developments in Geographic Information Systems (GIS) technology, equipment, or systems. Meet with clients to discuss topics such as technical specifications, customized solutions, and operational problems. Perform integrated and computerized Geographic Information Systems (GIS) analyses to address scientific problems. Create visual representations of geospatial data using complex procedures such as analytical modeling, three-dimensional renderings, and plot creation.

Information Technology Project Managers. Plan, initiate, and manage information technology (IT) projects. Lead and guide the work of technical staff. Serve as liaison between business and technical aspects of projects. Plan project stages and assess business implications for each stage. Monitor progress to assure deadlines, standards, and cost targets are met. Perform risk assessments to develop response strategies. Submit project deliverables, ensuring adherence to quality standards. Monitor the performance of project team members, providing and documenting performance feedback. Confer with project personnel to identify and resolve problems. Assess current or future customer needs and priorities through communicating directly with customers, conducting surveys, or other methods. Schedule and facilitate meetings related to information technology projects. Monitor or track project milestones and deliverables. Negotiate with project stakeholders or suppliers to obtain resources or materials. Initiate, review, or approve modifications to project plans. Identify, review, or select vendors or consultants to meet project needs. Establish and execute a project communication plan. Identify need for initial or supplemental project resources. Direct or coordinate activities of project personnel. Develop implementation plans that include analyses such as cost-benefit or return on investment (ROI). Coordinate recruitment or selection of project personnel. Develop and manage annual budgets for information technology projects. Assign duties, responsibilities, and spans of authority to project personnel. Prepare project status reports by collecting, analyzing, and summarizing information and trends. Manage project execution to ensure adherence to budget, schedule, and scope. Develop or update project plans for information technology projects including information such as project objectives, technologies, systems, information specifications, schedules, funding, and staffing. Develop and manage work breakdown structure (WBS) of information technology projects.

Network Designers. Determine user requirements and design specifications for computer networks. Plan and implement network upgrades. Communicate with customers, sales staff, or marketing staff to determine customer needs. Develop or recommend network security measures, such as firewalls, network security audits, or automated security probes. Develop network-related documentation. Prepare detailed network specifications, including diagrams, charts, equipment configurations, and recommended technologies.

Supervise engineers and other staff in the design or implementation of network solutions. Develop conceptual, logical, or physical network designs. Evaluate network designs to determine whether customer requirements are met efficiently and effectively. Develop disaster recovery plans. Develop and implement solutions for network problems. Explain design specifications to integration or test engineers. Determine specific network hardware or software requirements, such as platforms, interfaces, bandwidths, or routine schemas. Coordinate network operations, maintenance, repairs, or upgrades. Prepare or monitor project schedules, budgets, or cost control systems. Coordinate installation of new equipment. Coordinate network or design activities with designers of associated networks. Estimate time and materials needed to complete projects. Participate in network technology upgrade or expansion projects, including installation of hardware and software and integration testing. Monitor and analyze network performance and data input/output reports to detect problems, identify inefficient use of computer resources, or perform capacity planning. Adjust network sizes to meet volume or capacity demands. Design, build, or operate equipment configuration prototypes, including network hardware, software, servers, or server operation systems. Prepare design presentations and proposals for staff or customers. Develop procedures to track, project, or report network availability, reliability, capacity, or utilization.

Software Quality Assurance Engineers and Testers. Develop and execute software test plans in order to identify software problems and their causes. Document test procedures to ensure replicability and compliance with standards. Perform initial debugging procedures by reviewing configuration files, logs, or code pieces to determine breakdown source. Participate in product design reviews to provide input on functional requirements, product designs, schedules, or potential problems. Monitor program performance to ensure efficient

and problem-free operations. Investigate customer problems referred by technical support. Install, maintain, or use software testing programs. Install and configure recreations of software production environments to allow testing of software performance. Identify, analyze, and document problems with program function, output, online screen, or content. Evaluate or recommend software for testing or bug tracking. Develop testing programs that address areas such as database impacts, software scenarios, regression testing, negative testing, error or bug retests, or usability. Monitor bug resolution efforts and track successes. Document software defects, using a bug tracking system, and report defects to software developers. Conduct software compatibility tests with programs, hardware, operating systems, or network environments. Create or maintain databases of known test defects. Design test plans, scenarios, scripts, or procedures. Design or develop automated testing tools. Develop or specify standards, methods, or procedures to determine product quality or release readiness. Identify program deviance from standards, and suggest modifications to ensure compliance. Test system modifications to prepare for implementation. Review software documentation to ensure technical accuracy, compliance, or completeness, or to mitigate risks. Provide technical support during software installation or configuration. Conduct historical analyses of test results. Coordinate user or third party testing. Collaborate with field staff or customers to evaluate or diagnose problems and recommend possible solutions.

Video Game Designers. Design core features of video games. Specify innovative game and role-play mechanics, storylines, and character biographies. Create and maintain design documentation. Guide and collaborate with production staff to produce games as designed. Review or evaluate competitive products, film, music, television, and other art forms to generate new game design ideas. Provide test specifications to quality assurance staff. Keep abreast of game design

Artistic

technology and techniques, industry trends, or audience interests, reactions, and needs by reviewing current literature, talking with colleagues, participating in educational programs, attending meetings or workshops, or participation in professional conferences, workshops, or groups. Create gameplay test plans for internal and external test groups. Provide feedback to designers and other colleagues regarding game design features. Balance and adjust gameplay experiences to ensure the critical and commercial success of the product. Write or supervise the writing of game text and dialogue. Solicit, obtain, and integrate feedback from design and technical staff into original game design. Provide feedback to production staff regarding technical game qualities or adherence to original design. Prepare two-dimensional concept layouts or three-dimensional mock-ups. Present new game design concepts to management and technical colleagues, including artists, animators, and programmers. Prepare and revise initial game sketches using two- and three-dimensional graphical design software. Oversee gameplay testing to ensure intended gaming experience and game adherence to original vision. Guide design discussions between development teams. Devise missions, challenges, or puzzles to be encountered in game play. Develop and maintain design level documentation, including mechanics, guidelines, and mission outlines. Determine supplementary virtual features, such as currency, item catalog, menu design, and audio direction. Create gameplay prototypes for presentation to creative and technical staff and management. Create and manage documentation, production schedules, prototyping goals, and communication plans in collaboration with production staff. Consult with multiple stakeholders to define requirements and implement online features.

Web Administrators. Manage Web environment design, deployment, development, and maintenance activities. Perform testing and quality assurance of Web sites and Web applications. Back up or modify applications and related data

to provide for disaster recovery. Determine sources of Web page or server problems, and take action to correct such problems. Review or update Web page content or links in a timely manner, using appropriate tools. Monitor systems for intrusions or denial of service attacks, and report security breaches to appropriate personnel. Implement Web site security measures, such as firewalls or message encryption. Administer Internet/intranet infrastructure, including components such as Web, file transfer protocol (FTP), news, and mail servers. Collaborate with development teams to discuss, analyze, or resolve usability issues. Test backup or recovery plans regularly and resolve any problems. Monitor Web developments through continuing education, reading, or participation in professional conferences, workshops, or groups. Implement updates, upgrades, and patches in a timely manner to limit loss of service. Identify or document backup or recovery plans. Collaborate with Web developers to create and operate internal and external Web sites, or to manage projects, such as e-marketing campaigns. Install or configure Web server software or hardware to ensure that directory structure is well-defined, logical, secure, and that files are named properly. Gather, analyze, or document user feedback to locate or resolve sources of problems. Develop Web site performance metrics. Identify or address interoperability requirements. Document installation or configuration procedures to allow maintenance and repetition. Identify, standardize, and communicate levels of access and security. Track, compile, and analyze Web site usage data. Test issues such as system integration, performance, and system security on a regular schedule or after any major program modifications. Recommend Web site improvements, and develop budgets to support recommendations. Inform Web site users of problems, problem resolutions, or application changes and updates.

Web Developers. Develop and design Web applications and Web sites. Create and specify architectural and technical parameters. Direct

Web site content creation, enhancement, and maintenance. Document test plans, testing procedures, or test results. Design and implement web site security measures such as firewalls or message encryption. Renew domain name registrations. Respond to user email inquiries, or set up automated systems to send responses. Collaborate with management or users to develop e-commerce strategies and to integrate these strategies with web sites. Maintain understanding of current web technologies or programming practices through continuing education, reading, or participation in professional conferences, workshops, or groups. Communicate with network personnel or web site hosting agencies to address hardware or software issues affecting web sites. Develop and document style guidelines for web site content. Develop or implement procedures for ongoing web site revision. Write supporting code for web applications or web sites. Back up files from web sites to local directories for instant recovery in case of problems. Create searchable indices for web page content. Analyze user needs to determine technical requirements. Establish appropriate server directory trees. Design, build, or maintain web sites, using authoring or scripting languages, content creation tools, management tools, and digital media. Recommend and implement performance improvements. Perform or direct web site updates. Perform web site tests according to planned schedules, or after any web site or product revisions. Develop databases that support web applications and web sites. Monitor security system performance logs to identify problems and notify security specialists when problems occur. Identify problems uncovered by testing or customer feedback, and correct problems or refer problems to appropriate personnel for correction. Install and configure hypertext transfer protocol (HTTP) servers and associated operating systems. Register web sites with search engines to increase web site traffic.

4. Graphic Designers

Personality Type: Artistic–Enterprising–Realistic

Earnings: $43,180
Growth: 12.9%
Annual Openings: 12,480

Most Common Education/Training Level: Associate degree

Design or create graphics to meet specific commercial or promotional needs such as packaging, displays, or logos. May use a variety of media to achieve artistic or decorative effects. Create designs, concepts, and sample layouts based on knowledge of layout principles and esthetic design concepts. Determine size and arrangement of illustrative material and copy; and select style and size of type. Confer with clients to discuss and determine layout designs. Develop graphics and layouts for product illustrations, company logos, and Internet Web sites. Review final layouts and suggest improvements as needed. Prepare illustrations or rough sketches of material, discussing them with clients or supervisors and making necessary changes. Use computer software to generate new images. Key information into computer equipment to create layouts for client or supervisor. Maintain archive of images, photos, or previous work products. Prepare notes and instructions for workers who assemble and prepare final layouts for printing. Draw and print charts, graphs, illustrations, and other artwork, using computer. Study illustrations and photographs to plan presentations of materials, products, or services. Research new software or design concepts. Mark up, paste, and assemble final layouts to prepare layouts for printer. Produce still and animated graphics for on-air and taped portions of television news broadcasts, using electronic video equipment. Photograph layouts, using cameras, to make layout prints for supervisors or clients. Develop negatives and prints to produce layout photographs, using negative and print developing equipment and tools.

Artistic

5. Multi-Media Artists and Animators

Personality Type: Artistic–Investigative

Earnings: $58,250
Growth: 14.1%
Annual Openings: 2,890

Most Common Education/Training Level: Associate degree

Create special effects, animation, or other visual images, using film, video, computers, or other electronic tools and media, for use in products or creations such as computer games, movies, music videos, and commercials. Design complex graphics and animation, using independent judgment, creativity, and computer equipment. Create two-dimensional and three-dimensional images depicting objects in motion or illustrating a process, using computer animation or modeling programs. Make objects or characters appear lifelike by manipulating light, color, texture, shadow, and transparency, or manipulating static images to give the illusion of motion. Apply story development, directing, cinematography, and editing to animation to create storyboards that show the flow of the animation and map out key scenes and characters. Create basic designs, drawings, and illustrations for product labels, cartons, direct mail, or television. Develop briefings, brochures, multimedia presentations, web pages, promotional products, technical illustrations, and computer artwork for use in products, technical manuals, literature, newsletters and slide shows.

6. Set and Exhibit Designers

Personality Type: Artistic–Realistic

Earnings: $45,400
Growth: 16.6%
Annual Openings: 510

Most Common Education/Training Level: Associate degree

Design special exhibits and movie, television, and theater sets. May study scripts, confer with directors, and conduct research to determine appropriate architectural styles. Examine objects to be included in exhibits to plan where and how to display them. Acquire, or arrange for acquisition of, specimens or graphics required to complete exhibits. Prepare rough drafts and scale working drawings of sets, including floor plans, scenery, and properties to be constructed. Confer with clients and staff to gather information about exhibit space, proposed themes and content, timelines, budgets, materials, and promotion requirements. Estimate set- or exhibit-related costs, including materials, construction, and rental of props or locations. Develop set designs based on evaluation of scripts, budgets, research information, and available locations. Direct and coordinate construction, erection, or decoration activities to ensure that sets or exhibits meet design, budget, and schedule requirements. Inspect installed exhibits for conformance to specifications and satisfactory operation of special effects components. Plan for location-specific issues such as space limitations, traffic flow patterns, and safety concerns. Submit plans for approval and adapt plans to serve intended purposes or to conform to budget or fabrication restrictions. Prepare preliminary renderings of proposed exhibits, including detailed construction, layout, and material specifications and diagrams relating to aspects such as special effects and lighting. Select and purchase lumber and hardware necessary for set construction. Collaborate with those in charge of lighting and sound so that those production aspects can be coordinated with set designs or exhibit layouts. Research architectural and stylistic elements appropriate to the time period to be depicted, consulting experts for information as necessary. Design and produce displays and materials that can be used to decorate windows, interior displays, or event locations such as streets and fairgrounds. Coordinate the removal of sets, props, and exhibits after productions or events are complete.

Interior Design

Personality Type: Artistic–Enterprising

Useful Facts About the Major

Prepares individuals to apply artistic principles and techniques to the professional planning, designing, equipping, and furnishing residential and commercial interior spaces.

Related CIP Program: 50.0408 Interior Design

Specializations in the Major: Residential design, kitchens, bathrooms, public spaces, restoration, acoustics, computer-aided design.

Typical Sequence of College Courses: Basic drawing, history of architecture, introduction to interior design, interior materials, history of interiors, presentation graphics, computer-aided design, color and design, lighting design, interior design studio, construction codes and material rating, senior design project.

Typical Sequence of High School Courses: English, algebra, literature, history, geometry, art, physics, trigonometry, pre-calculus, computer science.

Career Snapshot

Interior designers plan how to shape and decorate the interiors of all kinds of buildings, including homes and commercial structures. They may design new interiors or renovate existing places. They respond to their clients' needs and budgets by developing designs based on traditional forms, innovative uses of layout and materials, sound principles of engineering, and safety codes. A bachelor's degree in the field is not universally required, but it contributes to your qualifications for licensure (in some states) and for membership in a professional association. It also gives you an edge over self-taught competitors, which can be important in this very competitive field.

Useful Averages for the Related Jobs

❈ Annual Earnings: $46,000
❈ Growth: 19.4%
❈ Openings: 3,590
❈ Self-Employed: 26.7%
❈ Verbal Skill Rating: 62
❈ Math Skill Rating: 49

Other Details About the Related Jobs

Career Clusters: 02 Architecture and Construction; 03 Arts, Audio/Video Technology, and Communications; 13 Manufacturing; 14 Marketing, Sales, and Service. **Career Pathways:** 02.1 Design/Pre-Construction; 03.3 Visual Arts; 13.3 Maintenance, Installation, and Repair; 14.2 Professional Sales and Marketing.

Skills: Management of financial resources, operations analysis, management of material resources, negotiation, persuasion, service orientation, coordination, mathematics. **Work Conditions:** Indoors; sitting; in a vehicle.

Related Jobs

Interior Designers

Personality Type: Artistic–Enterprising

Earnings: $46,180
Growth: 19.4%
Annual Openings: 3,590

Most Common Education/Training Level: Associate degree

Plan, design, and furnish interiors of residential, commercial, or industrial buildings.

Artistic

Formulate design that is practical, aesthetic, and conducive to intended purposes, such as raising productivity, selling merchandise, or improving lifestyle. May specialize in a particular field, style, or phase of interior design. Confer with client to determine factors affecting planning interior environments, such as budget, architectural preferences, and purpose and function. Advise client on interior design factors such as space planning, layout and utilization of furnishings or equipment, and color coordination. Coordinate with other professionals, such as contractors, architects, engineers, and plumbers, to ensure job success. Review and detail shop drawings for construction plans. Estimate material requirements and costs, and present design to client for approval. Subcontract fabrication, installation, and arrangement of carpeting, fixtures, accessories, draperies, paint and wall coverings, art work, furniture, and related items. Formulate environmental plan to be practical, esthetic, and conducive to intended purposes, such as raising productivity or selling merchandise. Select or design, and purchase furnishings, art works, and accessories. Render design ideas in form of paste-ups or drawings. Use computer-aided drafting (CAD) and related software to produce construction documents. Plan and design interior environments for boats, planes, buses, trains, and other enclosed spaces.

Japanese

Personality Type: Artistic–Social

Useful Facts About the Major

Focuses on the Japanese language.

Related CIP Program: 16.0302 Japanese Language and Literature

Specializations in the Major: Literature, translation, history and culture, language education.

Typical Sequence of College Courses: Japanese language, conversation, composition, linguistics, Japanese literature, East Asian literature, East Asian studies, grammar, phonetics.

Typical Sequence of High School Courses: English, public speaking, foreign language, history, literature, social science.

Career Snapshot

Japan is a major trading partner of the United States, but comparatively few English speakers have mastered the Japanese language. This means that a major in Japanese can be a valuable entry route to careers in international business, travel, and law. A graduate degree in Japanese is good preparation for college teaching or translation.

Useful Averages for the Related Jobs

* Annual Earnings: $41,000
* Growth: 22.2%
* Openings: 2,340
* Self-Employed: 26.1%
* Verbal Skill Rating: 71
* Math Skill Rating: 31

Other Details About the Related Jobs

Career Clusters: 05 Education and Training; 10 Human Services. **Career Pathways:** 05.3 Teaching/Training; 10.5 Consumer Services Career.

Skills: Writing, reading comprehension, active listening, speaking, social perceptiveness, service orientation, learning strategies, monitoring. **Work Conditions:** Indoors; sitting; close to co-workers; exposed to disease or infections; exposed to radiation; making repetitive motions.

Related Jobs

Interpreters and Translators

Personality Type: Artistic–Social

Earnings: $40,860
Growth: 22.2%
Annual Openings: 2,340

Most Common Education/Training Level:
Long-term on-the-job training

Translate or interpret written, oral, or sign language text into another language for others. Follow ethical codes that protect the confidentiality of information. Identify and resolve conflicts related to the meanings of words, concepts, practices, or behaviors. Proofread, edit, and revise translated materials. Translate messages simultaneously or consecutively into specified languages orally or by using hand signs, maintaining message content, context, and style as much as possible. Check translations of technical terms and terminology to ensure that they are accurate and remain consistent throughout translation revisions. Read written materials such as legal documents, scientific works, or news reports and rewrite material into specified languages. Refer to reference materials such as dictionaries, lexicons, encyclopedias, and computerized terminology banks as needed to ensure translation accuracy. Compile terminology and information to be used in translations, including technical terms such as those for legal or medical material. Adapt translations to students' cognitive and grade levels, collaborating with educational team members as necessary. Listen to speakers' statements to determine meanings and to prepare translations, using electronic listening systems as necessary. Check original texts or confer with authors to ensure that translations retain the content, meaning, and feeling of the original material. Compile information about the content and context of information to be translated, as well as details of the groups for whom translation or interpretation is being performed. Discuss translation requirements with clients and determine any fees to be charged for services provided. Adapt software and accompanying technical documents to another language and culture. Educate students, parents, staff, and teachers about the roles and functions of educational interpreters. Train and supervise other translators/interpreters. Travel with or guide tourists who speak another language.

Modern Foreign Language

Personality Type:
Enterprising–Realistic–Conventional

Useful Facts About the Major

Focuses on a language being used in the modern world and includes related dialects, the cultural and historical contexts, and applications to business, science/technology, and other settings.

Related CIP Programs: 16.0704 Bengali Language and Literature; 16.0301 Chinese Language and Literature; 16.1301 Celtic Languages, Literatures, and Linguistics; 16.1101 Arabic Language and Literature; 16.1401 Australian/Oceanic/Pacific Languages, Literatures, and Linguistics; 16.0406 Czech Language and Literature; 16.0405 Bulgarian Language and Literature; 16.0901 French Language and Literature; 16.1403 Burmese Language and Literature; 16.0503 Danish Language and Literature; 16.0401 Baltic Languages, Literatures, and Linguistics; 16.0300 East Asian Languages, Literatures, and Linguistics, General; 16.0907 Catalan Language and Literature; 16.0501 German Language and Literature; others ; 16.1001 American Indian/Native American Languages, Literatures, and Linguistics; 16.0404 Albanian Language and Literature; 16.0201 African Languages, Literatures, and Linguistics; 16.0504 Dutch/Flemish Language and Literature

Specializations in the Major: Literature, translation, history and culture, language education, regional studies.

Artistic

Typical Sequence of College Courses: Foreign language, conversation, composition, linguistics, foreign literature and culture, grammar, phonetics, history of a world region.

Typical Sequence of High School Courses: English, public speaking, foreign language, history, social science.

Career Snapshot

The most popular foreign language majors—Chinese, French, German, Japanese, Russian, and Spanish—are described elsewhere in this book. But many colleges offer majors in other modern languages, such as Arabic, Hebrew, Hindi, Portuguese, Swahili, Swedish, or Turkish, to name just a few. As global trade continues to increase, a degree in a foreign language can lead to many job opportunities in international business, travel, security, and law. Many employers are looking for graduates with an understanding of a second language and culture. Translation or college teaching are options for those with a graduate degree in a foreign language.

Useful Averages for the Related Jobs

* Annual Earnings: $41,000
* Growth: 22.2%
* Openings: 2,340
* Self-Employed: 26.1%
* Verbal Skill Rating: 71
* Math Skill Rating: 31

Other Details About the Related Jobs

Career Clusters: 05 Education and Training; 10 Human Services. **Career Pathways:** 05.3 Teaching/Training; 10.5 Consumer Services Career.

Skills: Writing, reading comprehension, active listening, speaking, social perceptiveness, service orientation, learning strategies, monitoring. **Work Conditions:** Indoors; sitting; close to co-workers; exposed to disease or infections; exposed to radiation; making repetitive motions.

Related Jobs

Interpreters and Translators

Personality Type: Artistic–Social

Earnings: $40,860
Growth: 22.2%
Annual Openings: 2,340

Most Common Education/Training Level: Long-term on-the-job training

Translate or interpret written, oral, or sign language text into another language for others. Follow ethical codes that protect the confidentiality of information. Identify and resolve conflicts related to the meanings of words, concepts, practices, or behaviors. Proofread, edit, and revise translated materials. Translate messages simultaneously or consecutively into specified languages orally or by using hand signs, maintaining message content, context, and style as much as possible. Check translations of technical terms and terminology to ensure that they are accurate and remain consistent throughout translation revisions. Read written materials such as legal documents, scientific works, or news reports and rewrite material into specified languages. Refer to reference materials such as dictionaries, lexicons, encyclopedias, and computerized terminology banks as needed to ensure translation accuracy. Compile terminology and information to be used in translations, including technical terms such as those for legal or medical material. Adapt translations to students' cognitive and grade levels, collaborating with educational team members as necessary. Listen to speakers' statements to determine meanings and to prepare translations, using electronic listening systems as necessary. Check original texts or confer with authors to ensure that translations retain the content, meaning, and feeling of the original material. Compile information about the content and context of information to be translated, as well as details of the groups for whom translation or interpretation is being performed. Discuss translation requirements with clients and determine any fees to be charged for services provided. Adapt software and accompanying technical documents to another language and culture. Educate students, parents, staff, and teachers about the roles and functions of educational interpreters. Train and supervise other translators/interpreters. Travel with or guide tourists who speak another language.

Russian

Personality Type: Artistic–Social

Useful Facts About the Major

Focuses on the Russian language.

Related CIP Program: 16.0402 Russian Language and Literature

Specializations in the Major: Literature, translation, history and culture, language education.

Typical Sequence of College Courses: Russian language, conversation, composition, linguistics, Russian literature, Russian history and civilization, European history and civilization, grammar, phonetics.

Typical Sequence of High School Courses: English, public speaking, foreign language, history, literature, social science.

Career Snapshot

Despite the breakup of the Soviet Union, Russian is still an important world language that not many Americans know. As business and governmental ties with Russia continue to increase as it opens to free trade, a degree in Russian can lead to careers in international business, travel, and law. College teaching and translation are options for those with a graduate degree in Russian.

Useful Averages for the Related Jobs

* Annual Earnings: $41,000
* Growth: 22.2%
* Openings: 2,340
* Self-Employed: 26.1%
* Verbal Skill Rating: 71
* Math Skill Rating: 31

Other Details About the Related Jobs

Career Clusters: 05 Education and Training; 10 Human Services. **Career Pathways:** 05.3 Teaching/Training; 10.5 Consumer Services Career.

Skills: Writing, reading comprehension, active listening, speaking, social perceptiveness, service orientation, learning strategies, monitoring. **Work Conditions:** Indoors; sitting; close to co-workers; exposed to disease or infections; exposed to radiation; making repetitive motions.

Related Jobs

Interpreters and Translators

Personality Type: Artistic–Social

Earnings: $40,860
Growth: 22.2%
Annual Openings: 2,340

Most Common Education/Training Level: Long-term on-the-job training

Translate or interpret written, oral, or sign language text into another language for others.

Artistic

Follow ethical codes that protect the confidentiality of information. Identify and resolve conflicts related to the meanings of words, concepts, practices, or behaviors. Proofread, edit, and revise translated materials. Translate messages simultaneously or consecutively into specified languages orally or by using hand signs, maintaining message content, context, and style as much as possible. Check translations of technical terms and terminology to ensure that they are accurate and remain consistent throughout translation revisions. Read written materials such as legal documents, scientific works, or news reports and rewrite material into specified languages. Refer to reference materials such as dictionaries, lexicons, encyclopedias, and computerized terminology banks as needed to ensure translation accuracy. Compile terminology and information to be used in translations, including technical terms such as those for legal or medical material. Adapt translations to students' cognitive and grade levels, collaborating with educational team members as necessary. Listen to speakers' statements to determine meanings and to prepare translations, using electronic listening systems as necessary. Check original texts or confer with authors to ensure that translations retain the content, meaning, and feeling of the original material. Compile information about the content and context of information to be translated, as well as details of the groups for whom translation or interpretation is being performed. Discuss translation requirements with clients and determine any fees to be charged for services provided. Adapt software and accompanying technical documents to another language and culture. Educate students, parents, staff, and teachers about the roles and functions of educational interpreters. Train and supervise other translators/interpreters. Travel with or guide tourists who speak another language.

Spanish

Personality Type: Artistic–Social

Useful Facts About the Major

Focuses on the Spanish language and related dialects.

Related CIP Program: 16.0905 Spanish Language and Literature

Specializations in the Major: Literature, translation, history and culture, language education.

Typical Sequence of College Courses: Spanish language, conversation, composition, linguistics, Spanish literature, Spanish-American literature, Spanish history and civilization, European history and civilization, grammar, phonetics.

Typical Sequence of High School Courses: English, public speaking, Spanish, history, literature, social science.

Career Snapshot

Spanish has become the second language in the United States, as well as maintaining its importance as a world language, especially in the Western Hemisphere. A degree in Spanish can be useful preparation (perhaps with an additional degree) for many careers in business, travel, and public service, and not just with an international orientation. High school teaching usually requires a master's degree for security and advancement.

Useful Averages for the Related Jobs

- ❋ Annual Earnings: $41,000
- ❋ Growth: 22.2%
- ❋ Openings: 2,340
- ❋ Self-Employed: 26.1%
- ❋ Verbal Skill Rating: 71
- ❋ Math Skill Rating: 31

Other Details About the Related Jobs

Career Clusters: 05 Education and Training; 10 Human Services. **Career Pathways:** 05.3 Teaching/Training; 10.5 Consumer Services Career.

Skills: Writing, reading comprehension, active listening, speaking, social perceptiveness, service orientation, learning strategies, monitoring. **Work Conditions:** Indoors; sitting; close to co-workers; exposed to disease or infections; exposed to radiation; making repetitive motions.

Related Jobs

Interpreters and Translators

Personality Type: Artistic–Social

Earnings: $40,860
Growth: 22.2%
Annual Openings: 2,340

Most Common Education/Training Level:
Long-term on-the-job training

Translate or interpret written, oral, or sign language text into another language for others. Follow ethical codes that protect the confidentiality of information. Identify and resolve conflicts related to the meanings of words, concepts, practices, or behaviors. Proofread, edit, and revise translated materials. Translate messages simultaneously or consecutively into specified languages orally or by using hand signs, maintaining message content, context, and style as much as possible. Check translations of technical terms and terminology to ensure that they are accurate and remain consistent throughout translation revisions. Read written materials such as legal documents, scientific works, or news reports and rewrite material into specified languages. Refer to reference materials such as dictionaries, lexicons, encyclopedias, and computerized terminology banks as needed to ensure translation accuracy. Compile terminology and information to be used in translations, including technical terms such as those for legal or medical material. Adapt translations to students' cognitive and grade levels, collaborating with educational team members as necessary. Listen to speakers' statements to determine meanings and to prepare translations, using electronic listening systems as necessary. Check original texts or confer with authors to ensure that translations retain the content, meaning, and feeling of the original material. Compile information about the content and context of information to be translated, as well as details of the groups for whom translation or interpretation is being performed. Discuss translation requirements with clients and determine any fees to be charged for services provided. Adapt software and accompanying technical documents to another language and culture. Educate students, parents, staff, and teachers about the roles and functions of educational interpreters. Train and supervise other translators/interpreters. Travel with or guide tourists who speak another language.

Artistic

Social Majors

African-American Studies

Personality Type: Social–Investigative–Artistic

Useful Facts About the Major

Focuses on the history, sociology, politics, culture, and economics of the North American peoples descended from the African diaspora; focusing on the United States, Canada, and the Caribbean, but also including reference to Latin American elements of the diaspora.

Related CIP Program: 05.0201 African-American/Black Studies

Specializations in the Major: History and culture, behavioral and social inquiry, literature, language, and the arts.

Typical Sequence of College Courses: English composition, foreign language, American history, introduction to African American studies, African American literature, African American history, African Diaspora studies, research methods in African American studies, seminar (reporting on research).

Typical Sequence of High School Courses: English, algebra, foreign language, history, literature, public speaking, social science.

Career Snapshot

African-American studies draws on a number of disciplines, including history, sociology, literature, linguistics, and political science. Usually you can shape the program to emphasize whichever appeals most to you. Graduates frequently pursue higher degrees as a means of establishing a career in a field such as college teaching or the law.

Useful Averages for the Related Jobs

- Annual Earnings: $65,000
- Growth: 15.1%
- Openings: Roughly 200
- Self-Employed: No data available
- Verbal Skill Rating: 84
- Math Skill Rating: 39

Other Details About the Related Jobs

Career Clusters: 05 Education and Training; 10 Human Service. **Career Pathways:** 05.3 Teaching/Training; 10.2 Counseling and Mental Health Services.

Skills: Science, writing, operations analysis, learning strategies, speaking, reading comprehension, active learning, active listening. **Work Conditions:** Indoors; sitting; exposed to disease or infections.

Related Jobs

Area, Ethnic, and Cultural Studies Teachers, Postsecondary

Personality Type: Social–Investigative–Artistic

Earnings: $65,030
Growth: 15.1%
Annual Openings: 200

Most Common Education/Training Level: Doctoral degree

Teach courses pertaining to the culture and development of an area (e.g., Latin America), an ethnic group, or any other group (e.g., women's studies, urban affairs). Keep abreast of developments in their field by reading current literature, talking with colleagues, and participating in professional conferences. Conduct research in a particular field of knowledge and publish findings in professional journals, books, and/or electronic media. Evaluate and grade students' classwork, assignments, and papers. Prepare course materials such as syllabi, homework assignments, and handouts. Prepare and deliver lectures to undergraduate and/or graduate students on topics such as race and ethnic relations, gender studies, and cross-cultural perspectives. Initiate, facilitate, and moderate classroom discussions. Compile, administer, and grade examinations or assign this work to others. Maintain regularly scheduled office hours in order to advise and assist students. Plan, evaluate, and revise curricula, course content, and course materials and methods of instruction. Maintain student attendance records, grades, and other required records. Advise students on academic and vocational curricula and on career issues. Supervise undergraduate and/or graduate teaching, internship, and research work. Select and obtain materials and supplies such as textbooks. Collaborate with colleagues to address teaching and research issues. Serve on academic or administrative committees that deal with institutional policies, departmental matters, and academic issues. Compile bibliographies of specialized materials for outside reading assignments. Write grant proposals to procure external research funding. Participate in campus and community events. Participate in student recruitment, registration, and placement activities. Act as advisers to student organizations. Incorporate experiential/site visit components into courses. Perform administrative duties such as serving as department head. Provide professional consulting services to government and/or industry.

American Studies

Personality Type: Social–Investigative–Artistic

Useful Facts About the Major

Focuses on the history, society, politics, culture, and economics of the United States and its Pre-Columbian and colonial predecessors, including the flow of immigrants from other societies.

Related CIP Program: 05.0102 American/United States Studies/Civilization

Specializations in the Major: History and political science, literature, language, and the arts, popular culture.

Typical Sequence of College Courses: English composition, American history, American government, American literature, American popular culture, seminar (reporting on research).

Typical Sequence of High School Courses: English, algebra, foreign language, history, literature, public speaking, social science.

Career Snapshot

American studies is an interdisciplinary major that allows you to concentrate on the aspect of American culture that is of greatest interest to you—for example, history, the arts, or social and ethnic groups. Many, perhaps most, graduates use this major as a springboard to postgraduate or professional training that prepares for a career in college teaching, business, law, the arts, politics, or some other field.

Useful Averages for the Related Jobs

* Annual Earnings: $65,000
* Growth: 15.1%
* Openings: Roughly 200
* Self-Employed: No data available
* Verbal Skill Rating: 84
* Math Skill Rating: 39

Social

Other Details About the Related Jobs

Career Clusters: 05 Education and Training; 10 Human Service. **Career Pathways:** 05.3 Teaching/Training; 10.2 Counseling and Mental Health Services.

Skills: Science, writing, operations analysis, learning strategies, speaking, reading comprehension, active learning, active listening. **Work Conditions:** Indoors; sitting; exposed to disease or infections.

Related Jobs

Area, Ethnic, and Cultural Studies Teachers, Postsecondary

Personality Type: Social–Investigative–Artistic

Earnings: $65,030
Growth: 15.1%
Annual Openings: 200

Most Common Education/Training Level: Doctoral degree

Teach courses pertaining to the culture and development of an area (e.g., Latin America), an ethnic group, or any other group (e.g., women's studies, urban affairs). Keep abreast of developments in their field by reading current literature, talking with colleagues, and participating in professional conferences. Conduct research in a particular field of knowledge and publish findings in professional journals, books, and/or electronic media. Evaluate and grade students' classwork, assignments, and papers. Prepare course materials such as syllabi, homework assignments, and handouts. Prepare and deliver lectures to undergraduate and/or graduate students on topics such as race and ethnic relations, gender studies, and cross-cultural perspectives. Initiate, facilitate, and moderate classroom discussions. Compile, administer, and grade examinations or assign this work to others.

Maintain regularly scheduled office hours in order to advise and assist students. Plan, evaluate, and revise curricula, course content, and course materials and methods of instruction. Maintain student attendance records, grades, and other required records. Advise students on academic and vocational curricula and on career issues. Supervise undergraduate and/or graduate teaching, internship, and research work. Select and obtain materials and supplies such as textbooks. Collaborate with colleagues to address teaching and research issues. Serve on academic or administrative committees that deal with institutional policies, departmental matters, and academic issues. Compile bibliographies of specialized materials for outside reading assignments. Write grant proposals to procure external research funding. Participate in campus and community events. Participate in student recruitment, registration, and placement activities. Act as advisers to student organizations. Incorporate experiential/site visit components into courses. Perform administrative duties such as serving as department head. Provide professional consulting services to government and/or industry.

Area Studies

Personality Type: Social–Investigative–Artistic

Useful Facts About the Major

Focuses on the history, society, politics, culture, and economics of one or more of the peoples within a geographic region and the subcultures within modern and historical countries and societies.

Related CIP Programs: 05.0103 Asian Studies/ Civilization; 05.0122 Regional Studies (U.S., Canadian, Foreign); 05.0101 African Studies; 05.0102 American/United States Studies/Civilization; 05.0115 Canadian Studies; 05.0105 Russian, Central European, East European and Eurasian Studies; 05.0104 East Asian Studies; 05.0106 European Studies/Civilization; 05.0107 Latin American

Studies; others ; 05.0109 Pacific Area/Pacific Rim Studies; 05.0110 Russian Studies; 05.0112 South Asian Studies; 05.0113 Southeast Asian Studies; 05.0114 Western European Studies; 05.0108 Near and Middle Eastern Studies

Specializations in the Major: History and culture, economics and trade, political science, language and literature.

Typical Sequence of College Courses: English composition, foreign language, foreign literature and culture, comparative governments, introduction to economics, international economics, seminar (reporting on research).

Typical Sequence of High School Courses: English, foreign language, history, literature, social science, algebra.

Career Snapshot

Certain very popular area studies—African-American studies, American studies, and women's studies—are described elsewhere in this book. But many colleges offer other area studies majors, usually defined in terms of a region of the world: East Asian studies, European studies, Latin American studies, and so on. These are interdisciplinary majors that may involve some combination of linguistics, literature, history, sociology, political science, economic development, or other disciplines. Usually you can emphasize whichever aspects interest you most. Graduates of area studies may go into a business or government career where knowledge of a foreign culture is an advantage. Many get higher degrees to prepare for a career in law or college teaching.

Useful Averages for the Related Jobs

❀ Annual Earnings: $65,000

❀ Growth: 15.1%

❀ Openings: Roughly 200

❀ Self-Employed: No data available

❀ Verbal Skill Rating: 84

❀ Math Skill Rating: 39

Other Details About the Related Jobs

Career Clusters: 05 Education and Training; 10 Human Service. **Career Pathways:** 05.3 Teaching/Training; 10.2 Counseling and Mental Health Services.

Skills: Science, writing, operations analysis, learning strategies, speaking, reading comprehension, active learning, active listening. **Work Conditions:** Indoors; sitting; exposed to disease or infections.

Related Jobs

Area, Ethnic, and Cultural Studies Teachers, Postsecondary

Personality Type: Social–Investigative–Artistic

Earnings: $65,030
Growth: 15.1%
Annual Openings: 200

Most Common Education/Training Level: Doctoral degree

Teach courses pertaining to the culture and development of an area (e.g., Latin America), an ethnic group, or any other group (e.g., women's studies, urban affairs). Keep abreast of developments in their field by reading current literature, talking with colleagues, and participating in professional conferences. Conduct research in a

Social

particular field of knowledge and publish findings in professional journals, books, and/or electronic media. Evaluate and grade students' classwork, assignments, and papers. Prepare course materials such as syllabi, homework assignments, and handouts. Prepare and deliver lectures to undergraduate and/or graduate students on topics such as race and ethnic relations, gender studies, and cross-cultural perspectives. Initiate, facilitate, and moderate classroom discussions. Compile, administer, and grade examinations or assign this work to others. Maintain regularly scheduled office hours in order to advise and assist students. Plan, evaluate, and revise curricula, course content, and course materials and methods of instruction. Maintain student attendance records, grades, and other required records. Advise students on academic and vocational curricula and on career issues. Supervise undergraduate and/or graduate teaching, internship, and research work. Select and obtain materials and supplies such as textbooks. Collaborate with colleagues to address teaching and research issues. Serve on academic or administrative committees that deal with institutional policies, departmental matters, and academic issues. Compile bibliographies of specialized materials for outside reading assignments. Write grant proposals to procure external research funding. Participate in campus and community events. Participate in student recruitment, registration, and placement activities. Act as advisers to student organizations. Incorporate experiential/site visit components into courses. Perform administrative duties such as serving as department head. Provide professional consulting services to government and/or industry.

Chiropractic

Personality Type: Social–Investigative–Realistic

Useful Facts About the Major

Prepares individuals for the independent professional practice of chiropractic, a health-care and healing system based on the application of noninvasive treatments and spinal adjustments to alleviate health problems caused by vertebral misalignments affecting bodily function as derived from the philosophy of Daniel Palmer.

Related CIP Program: 51.0101 Chiropractic (DC)

Specializations in the Major: Sports medicine, orthopedics, diagnostic imaging.

Typical Sequence of College Courses: English composition, introduction to psychology, college algebra, calculus, introduction to sociology, oral communication, general chemistry, general biology, introduction to computer science, organic chemistry, human anatomy and physiology, general microbiology, genetics, introduction to biochemistry, veterinary gross anatomy, spinal anatomy, histology, biomechanics, physical diagnosis, neuroanatomy, neurophysiology, radiographic anatomy, emergency care, nutrition, neuromusculoskeletal diagnosis and treatment, chiropractic manipulative therapeutics, pathology, public health, patient examination and evaluation, pharmacology, minor surgery, clinical experience in obstetrics/gynecology, clinical experience in pediatrics, clinical experience in geriatrics, mental health, ethics in health care, professional practice management.

Typical Sequence of High School Courses: English, algebra, geometry, trigonometry, biology, computer science, public speaking, chemistry, foreign language, physics, pre-calculus.

Career Snapshot

Chiropractors are health practitioners who specialize in health problems associated with the muscular, nervous, and skeletal systems, especially the spine. They learn a variety of specialized diagnostic and treatment techniques but also tend to emphasize the patient's overall health and wellness, recommending changes in diet and lifestyle that can help the body's own healing powers. The educational program includes not only theory and laboratory work, but also a lot of supervised clinical work with patients. With the aging of the population and increased acceptance of chiropractic medicine, job opportunities for graduates are expected to be good, especially for those who enter a multidisciplined practice.

Useful Averages for the Related Jobs

- ❋ Annual Earnings: $68,000
- ❋ Growth: 19.5%
- ❋ Openings: 1,820
- ❋ Self-Employed: 44.5%
- ❋ Verbal Skill Rating: 63
- ❋ Math Skill Rating: 43

Other Details About the Related Jobs

Career Cluster: 08 Health Science. **Career Pathway:** 08.1 Therapeutic Services.

Skills: Science, service orientation, management of financial resources, operations analysis, writing, reading comprehension, systems evaluation, time management. **Work Conditions:** Indoors; exposed to disease or infections; exposed to radiation; close to co-workers; standing; bending or twisting the body.

Related Jobs

Chiropractors

Personality Type: Social–Investigative–Realistic

Earnings: $67,650
Growth: 19.5%
Annual Openings: 1,820

Most Common Education/Training Level: First professional degree

Adjust spinal column and other articulations of the body to correct abnormalities of the human body believed to be caused by interference with the nervous system. Examine patients to determine nature and extent of disorders. Manipulate spines or other involved areas. May utilize supplementary measures such as exercise, rest, water, light, heat, and nutritional therapy. Diagnose health problems by reviewing patients' health and medical histories; questioning, observing, and examining patients; and interpreting X-rays. Maintain accurate case histories of patients. Evaluate the functioning of the neuromuscularskeletal system and the spine, using systems of chiropractic diagnosis. Perform a series of manual adjustments to spines, or other articulations of the body, to correct musculoskeletal systems. Obtain and record patients' medical histories. Advise patients about recommended courses of treatment. Consult with and refer patients to appropriate health practitioners when necessary. Analyze X-rays to locate the sources of patients' difficulties and to rule out fractures or diseases as sources of problems. Counsel patients about nutrition, exercise, sleeping habits, stress management, and other matters. Arrange for diagnostic X-rays to be taken. Suggest and apply the use of supports such as straps, tapes, bandages, and braces if necessary.

Communications Studies/ Speech

Personality Type: Social–Artistic–Enterprising

Useful Facts About the Major

Focuses on the scientific, humanistic, and critical study of human communication in a variety of formats, media, and contexts.

Related CIP Program: 09.0101 Speech Communication and Rhetoric

Specializations in the Major: Speech/rhetoric, business communications.

Social

Typical Sequence of College Courses: Public speaking, introduction to psychology, English composition, communications theory, introduction to mass communication, argumentation and critical thinking, interpersonal communication, rhetorical tradition and techniques.

Typical Sequence of High School Courses: English, public speaking, foreign language, applied communications, social science.

Career Snapshot

This major is sometimes offered in the same department as mass communications or theater, but it is not designed to teach a technical skill such as television production or acting. Instead, it teaches how effective communication depends on a combination of verbal and nonverbal elements. Students work in various media and learn how to strike a balance between covering the subject matter, appealing to the listener or reader, and projecting the intended image of the speaker or writer. Graduates of communication and speech programs may go on to careers in sales, public relations, law, or teaching.

Useful Averages for the Related Jobs

- ❋ Annual Earnings: $52,000
- ❋ Growth: 23.3%
- ❋ Openings: 14,170
- ❋ Self-Employed: 8.0%
- ❋ Verbal Skill Rating: 74
- ❋ Math Skill Rating: 44

Other Details About the Related Jobs

Career Clusters: 03 Arts, Audio/Video Technology, and Communications; 04 Business, Management, and Administration; 08 Health Science; 10

Human Services. **Career Pathways:** 03.4 Performing Arts; 03.5 Journalism and Broadcasting; 04.1 Management; 04.5 Marketing; 08.3 Health Informatics; 10.5 Consumer Services Career.

Skills: Operations analysis, writing, social perceptiveness, negotiation, speaking, persuasion, systems evaluation, time management. **Work Conditions:** Indoors; sitting; in a vehicle.

Related Jobs

1. Public Address System and Other Announcers

Personality Type: Social–Enterprising–Artistic

Earnings: $27,210
Growth: 8.2%
Annual Openings: 450

Most Common Education/Training Level: Bachelor's degree

Make announcements over loudspeaker at sporting or other public events. May act as master of ceremonies or disc jockey at weddings, parties, clubs, or other gathering places. Greet attendees and serve as masters of ceremonies at banquets, store openings, and other events. Preview any music intended to be broadcast over the public address system. Inform patrons of coming events at a specific venue. Meet with event directors to review schedules and exchange information about details, such as national anthem performers and starting lineups. Announce programs and player substitutions or other changes to patrons. Read prepared scripts describing acts or tricks presented during performances. Improvise commentary on items of interest, such as background and history of an event or past records of participants. Instruct and calm crowds during emergencies. Learn to pronounce the names of players, coaches, institutional personnel, officials, and other individuals involved in an event. Study the layout of an event venue in order to be able to give accurate directions in the event of an emergency. Review and announce crowd control procedures before the beginning of each event. Provide running commentaries of event activities, such as play-by-play descriptions or explanations of official decisions. Organize team information, such as statistics and tournament records, to ensure accessibility for use during events. Furnish information concerning plays to scoreboard operators.

2. Public Relations Specialists

Personality Type: Enterprising–Artistic–Social

Earnings: $51,960
Growth: 24.0%
Annual Openings: 13,130

Most Common Education/Training Level:
Bachelor's degree

Engage in promoting or creating goodwill for individuals, groups, or organizations by writing or selecting favorable publicity material and releasing it through various communications media. May prepare and arrange displays and make speeches. Respond to requests for information from the media or designate another appropriate spokesperson or information source. Study the objectives, promotional policies and needs of organizations to develop public relations strategies that will influence public opinion or promote ideas, products and services. Plan and direct development and communication of informational programs to maintain favorable public and stockholder perceptions of an organization's accomplishments and agenda. Establish and maintain cooperative relationships with representatives of community, consumer, employee, and public interest groups. Prepare or edit organizational publications for internal and external audiences, including employee newsletters and stockholders' reports. Coach client representatives in effective communication with the public and with employees. Confer with production and support personnel to produce or coordinate production of advertisements and promotions.

Confer with other managers to identify trends and key group interests and concerns or to provide advice on business decisions. Arrange public appearances, lectures, contests, or exhibits for clients to increase product and service awareness and to promote goodwill. Consult with advertising agencies or staff to arrange promotional campaigns in all types of media for products, organizations, or individuals. Purchase advertising space and time as required to promote client's product or agenda. Prepare and deliver speeches to further public relations objectives. Plan and conduct market and public opinion research to test products or determine potential for product success, communicating results to client or management.

3. Technical Writers

Personality Type:
Artistic–Investigative–Conventional

Earnings: $62,730
Growth: 18.2%
Annual Openings: 1,680

Most Common Education/Training Level:
Bachelor's degree

Write technical materials, such as equipment manuals, appendices, or operating and maintenance instructions. May assist in layout work. Organize material and complete writing assignment according to set standards regarding order, clarity, conciseness, style, and terminology. Maintain records and files of work and revisions. Edit, standardize, or make changes to material prepared by other writers or establishment personnel. Confer with customer representatives, vendors, plant executives, or publisher to establish technical specifications and to determine subject material to be developed for publication. Review published materials and recommend revisions or changes in scope, format, content, and methods of reproduction and binding. Select photographs, drawings, sketches, diagrams, and charts to illustrate material. Study drawings, specifications, mockups, and

Social

product samples to integrate and delineate technology, operating procedure, and production sequence and detail. Interview production and engineering personnel and read journals and other material to become familiar with product technologies and production methods. Observe production, developmental, and experimental activities to determine operating procedure and detail. Arrange for typing, duplication, and distribution of material. Assist in laying out material for publication. Analyze developments in specific field to determine need for revisions in previously published materials and development of new material. Review manufacturer's and trade catalogs, drawings, and other data relative to operation, maintenance, and service of equipment. Draw sketches to illustrate specified materials or assembly sequence.

4. Writers and Authors

Personality Type:
Artistic–Enterprising–Investigative

Earnings: $53,900
Growth: 14.8%
Annual Openings: 5,420

Most Common Education/Training Level:
Bachelor's degree

Originate and prepare written material, such as scripts, stories, advertisements, and other material. No task data available.

Job Specializations

Copy Writers. Write advertising copy for use by publication or broadcast media to promote sale of goods and services. Write to customers in their terms and on their level so that the advertiser's sales message is more readily received. Discuss with the client the product, advertising themes and methods, and any changes that should be made in advertising copy. Write advertising copy for use by publication, broadcast or internet media to promote the sale of goods and services. Present drafts and ideas to clients. Vary language and tone of messages based on product and medium. Consult with sales, media and marketing representatives to obtain information on product or service and discuss style and length of advertising copy. Edit or rewrite existing copy as necessary, and submit copy for approval by supervisor. Develop advertising campaigns for a wide range of clients, working with an advertising agency's creative director and art director to determine the best way to present advertising information. Write articles, bulletins, sales letters, speeches, and other related informative, marketing and promotional material. Conduct research and interviews to determine which of a product's selling features should be promoted. Invent names for products and write the slogans that appear on packaging, brochures and other promotional material. Review advertising trends, consumer surveys, and other data regarding marketing of goods and services to determine the best way to promote products.

Poets, Lyricists, and Creative Writers. Create original written works, such as scripts, essays, prose, poetry, or song lyrics, for publication or performance. Revise written material to meet personal standards and to satisfy needs of clients, publishers, directors, or producers. Choose subject matter and suitable form to express personal feelings and experiences or ideas, or to narrate stories or events. Plan project arrangements or outlines, and organize material accordingly. Prepare works in appropriate format for publication, and send them to publishers or producers. Follow appropriate procedures to get copyrights for completed work. Write fiction or nonfiction prose such as short stories, novels, biographies, articles, descriptive or critical analyses, and essays. Develop factors such as themes, plots, characterizations, psychological analyses, historical environments, action, and dialogue, to create material. Confer with clients, editors, publishers, or producers to discuss changes or revisions to written material. Conduct research to obtain factual information and authentic detail, using sources such as newspaper accounts, diaries, and interviews. Write narrative, dramatic, lyric, or other types of poetry for publication. Attend book launches and publicity events, or conduct public readings. Write words to fit musical compositions, including lyrics for operas, musical plays, and choral works. Adapt text to accommodate musical requirements of composers and singers. Teach writing classes. Write humorous material for publication, or for performances such as comedy routines, gags, and comedy shows. Collaborate with other writers on specific projects.

Elementary Education

Personality Type: Social–Artistic–Conventional

Useful Facts About the Major

Prepares individuals to teach students in the elementary grades, which may include kindergarten through grade eight, depending on the school system or state regulations.

Related CIP Program: 13.1202 Elementary Education and Teaching

Specializations in the Major: Art education, music education, science education, mathematics education, reading, bilingual education.

Typical Sequence of College Courses: Introduction to psychology, English composition, oral communication, history and philosophy of education, human growth and development, teaching methods, educational alternatives for exceptional students, educational psychology, reading assessment and teaching, mathematics education, art education, physical education, social studies education, health education, science education, language arts and literature, student teaching.

Typical Sequence of High School Courses: English, algebra, geometry, trigonometry, science, foreign language, public speaking.

Career Snapshot

In elementary education, it is usually possible to specialize in a particular subject, such as reading or science, or to get a general background. Everyone in this field needs to learn general principles of how young people develop physically and mentally, as well as the teaching and classroom-management techniques that work best with children of this age. A bachelor's degree is often sufficient to enter this career, but in many school districts it is expected that you will continue your education as far as a master's degree. Enrollments in elementary schools are expected to decline for some time, but there will be job growth in Sunbelt communities and many openings to replace teachers who retire.

Useful Averages for the Related Jobs

* Annual Earnings: $51,000
* Growth: 15.8%
* Openings: 59,650
* Self-Employed: 0.0%
* Verbal Skill Rating: 64
* Math Skill Rating: 53

Other Details About the Related Jobs

Career Cluster: 05 Education and Training. **Career Pathway:** 05.3 Teaching/Training.

Skills: Learning strategies, social perceptiveness, systems evaluation, monitoring, service orientation, writing, systems analysis, instructing. **Work Conditions:** More often indoors than outdoors; standing; close to co-workers; exposed to disease or infections; walking and running; noisy; kneeling, crouching, stooping, or crawling.

Social

Related Jobs

Elementary School Teachers, Except Special Education

Personality Type: Social–Artistic–Conventional

Earnings: $50,510
Growth: 15.8%
Annual Openings: 59,650

Most Common Education/Training Level: Bachelor's degree

Teach pupils in public or private schools at the elementary level basic academic, social, and other formative skills. Establish and enforce rules for behavior and procedures for maintaining order among the students for whom they are responsible. Observe and evaluate students' performance, behavior, social development, and physical health. Prepare materials and classrooms for class activities. Adapt teaching methods and instructional materials to meet students' varying needs and interests. Plan and conduct activities for a balanced program of instruction, demonstration, and work time that provides students with opportunities to observe, question, and investigate. Instruct students individually and in groups, using various teaching methods such as lectures, discussions, and demonstrations. Establish clear objectives for all lessons, units, and projects and communicate those objectives to students. Assign and grade class work and homework. Read books to entire classes or small groups. Prepare, administer, and grade tests and assignments to evaluate students' progress.

Graduate Study for College Teaching

Personality Type: Social–Investigative

Useful Facts About the Major

No data available; a large number of CIP programs may be studied at the graduate level.

Related CIP Programs: No data available; a large number of CIP programs may be studied at the graduate level.

Specializations in the Major: Any of the subjects that are taught in postsecondary institutions: agricultural sciences; anthropology and archeology; architecture; area, ethnic, and cultural studies; art, drama, and music; atmospheric, earth, marine, and space sciences; biological science; business; chemistry; communications; computer science; criminal justice and law enforcement; economics; education; engineering; English language and literature; environmental science; foreign language and literature; forestry and conservation science; geography; graduate teaching assistants; health specialties; history; home economics; law; library science; mathematical science; nursing instructors and; philosophy and religion; physics; political science; psychology; recreation and fitness studies; social sciences; social work; sociology; vocational education; others.

Typical Sequence of College Courses: Courses appropriate for a bachelor's program in an undergraduate major, followed by graduate courses in a related major, including seminars (where research is presented to the class) and research methods and concluding with an original research project and a dissertation describing it.

Typical Sequence of High School Courses: English, algebra, geometry, trigonometry, biology, chemistry, computer science, public speaking. Also advanced courses in science, social science, or humanities.

Career Snapshot

Focuses on an academic subject at an advanced level to prepare students to teach courses in a postsecondary institution such as a college, university, professional school, or adult school.

Useful Averages for the Related Jobs

❋ Annual Earnings: $63,000
❋ Growth: 15.1%
❋ Openings: 55,290
❋ Self-Employed: 0.2%
❋ Verbal Skill Rating: 80
❋ Math Skill Rating: 60

Other Details About the Related Jobs

Career Clusters: 01 Agriculture, Food, and Natural Resources; 02 Architecture and Construction; 03 Arts, Audio/Video Technology, and Communications; 04 Business, Management, and Administration; 05 Education and Training; 06 Finance; 07 Government and Public Administration; 08 Health Science; 10 Human Services; 11 Information Technology; 12 Law, Public Safety, Corrections, and Security; 14 Marketing, Sales, and Service; 15 Science, Technology, Engineering, and Mathematics. **Career Pathways:** 01.1 Food Products and Processing Systems; 01.2 Plant Systems; 01.3 Animal Systems; 01.4 Power Structure and Technical Systems; 01.5 Natural Resources Systems; 01.7 Agribusiness Systems; 02.1 Design/Pre-Construction; 03.1 Audio and Video Technology and Film; 03.2 Printing Technology; 03.3 Visual Arts; 03.4 Performing Arts; 03.5 Journalism and Broadcasting; 04.1 Management; 04.2 Business, Financial Management, and Accounting; 04.3 Human Resources; 04.5 Marketing; 05.1 Administration and Administrative Support; 05.2 Professional Support Services; 05.3 Teaching/Training; 06.1 Financial and Investment Planning; 06.4 Insurance Services; 07.1 Governance; 07.4 Planning; 08.1 Therapeutic Services; 08.2 Diagnostics Services; 08.3 Health Informatics; 08.4 Support Services; 08.5 Biotechnology Research and Development; 10.1 Early Childhood Development and Services; 10.2 Counseling and Mental Health Services; 10.3 Family and Community Services; 10.5 Consumer Services Career; 11.1 Network Systems; 11.2 Information Support Services; 11.4 Programming and Software Development; 12.1 Correction Services; 12.3 Security and Protective Services; 12.4 Law Enforcement Services; 12.5 Legal Services; 14.1 Management and Entrepreneurship; 14.5 Marketing Information Management and Research; 15.1 Engineering and Technology; 15.2 Science and Mathematics.

Skills: Writing, instructing, learning strategies, science, speaking, reading comprehension, active learning, operations analysis. **Work Conditions:** No data available.

Related Jobs

Postsecondary Teachers

Personality Type: Social–Investigative

Earnings: $62,700
Growth: 15.1%
Annual Openings: 55,290

Most Common Education/Training Level: Doctoral degree

Teach courses in a college, university, or adult-eduation setting. Prepare course materials such as syllabi, homework assignments, and handouts. Evaluate and grade students' classwork, laboratory work, assignments, and papers. Keep abreast of developments in their field by reading current literature, talking with colleagues, and participating in professional conferences. Initiate, facilitate, and moderate classroom discussions. Conduct research in a particular field of knowledge and publish findings in professional journals, books, and/or electronic media. Supervise undergraduate and/or graduate teaching, internship, and research work. Compile, administer, and grade examinations or assign this work to others. Advise students on academic and vocational curricula and

Social

on career issues. Plan, evaluate, and revise curricula, course content, and course materials and methods of instruction. Maintain student attendance records, grades, and other required records. Write grant proposals to procure external research funding. Collaborate with colleagues to address teaching and research issues. Maintain regularly scheduled office hours in order to advise and assist students. Participate in student recruitment, registration, and placement activities. Select and obtain materials and supplies such as textbooks and laboratory equipment. Act as advisers to student organizations. Participate in campus and community events. Serve on academic or administrative committees that deal with institutional policies, departmental matters, and academic issues. Provide professional consulting services to government and/or industry. Perform administrative duties such as serving as department head. Compile bibliographies of specialized materials for outside reading assignments.

Job Specializations

Agricultural Sciences Teachers, Postsecondary. Teach courses in the agricultural sciences, including agronomy, dairy sciences, fisheries management, horticultural sciences, poultry sciences, range management, and agricultural soil conservation. Prepare and deliver lectures to undergraduate and/or graduate students on topics such as crop production, plant genetics, and soil chemistry. Supervise laboratory sessions and fieldwork and coordinate laboratory operations.

Anthropology and Archeology Teachers, Postsecondary. Teach courses in anthropology or archeology. Prepare and deliver lectures to undergraduate and graduate students on topics such as research methods, urban anthropology, and language and culture.

Architecture Teachers, Postsecondary. Teach courses in architecture and architectural design, such as architectural environmental design, interior architecture/design, and landscape architecture. Prepare and deliver lectures to undergraduate and/or graduate students on topics such as architectural design methods, aesthetics and design, and structures and materials.

Area, Ethnic, and Cultural Studies Teachers, Postsecondary. Teach courses pertaining to the culture and development of an area (e.g., Latin America), an ethnic group, or any other group (e.g., women's studies, urban affairs). Prepare and deliver lectures to undergraduate and/or graduate students on topics such as race and ethnic relations, gender studies, and cross-cultural perspectives.

Art, Drama, and Music Teachers, Postsecondary. Teach courses in drama; music; and the arts, including fine and applied art, such as painting and sculpture, or design and crafts. Explain and demonstrate artistic techniques. Prepare and deliver lectures to undergraduate or graduate students on topics such as acting techniques, fundamentals of music, and art history. Organize performance groups and direct their rehearsals.

Atmospheric, Earth, Marine, and Space Sciences Teachers, Postsecondary. Teach courses in the physical sciences, except chemistry and physics. Prepare and deliver lectures to undergraduate and/or graduate students on topics such as structural geology, micrometeorology, and atmospheric thermodynamics.

Biological Science Teachers, Postsecondary. Teach courses in biological sciences. Prepare and deliver lectures to undergraduate and/or graduate students on topics such as molecular biology, marine biology, and botany.

Business Teachers, Postsecondary. Teach courses in business administration and management, such as accounting, finance, human resources, labor relations, marketing, and operations research. Prepare and deliver lectures to undergraduate and/or graduate students on topics such as financial accounting, principles of marketing, and operations management.

Chemistry Teachers, Postsecondary. Teach courses pertaining to the chemical and physical properties and compositional changes of substances. Work may include instruction in the methods of qualitative and quantitative chemical analysis. Includes both teachers primarily engaged in teaching and those who do a combination of both teaching and research. Prepare and deliver lectures to undergraduate and/or graduate students on topics such as organic chemistry, analytical chemistry, and chemical separation. Supervise students' laboratory work.

Communications Teachers, Postsecondary. Teach courses in communications, such as organizational communications, public relations, radio/television broadcasting, and journalism. Prepare and deliver lectures to undergraduate or graduate students on topics such as public speaking, media criticism, and oral traditions.

Computer Science Teachers, Postsecondary. Teach courses in computer science. May specialize in a field of computer science, such as the design and function of computers or operations and research analysis. Prepare and deliver lectures to undergraduate and/or graduate students on topics such as programming, data structures, and software design.

Criminal Justice and Law Enforcement Teachers, Postsecondary. Teach courses in criminal justice, corrections, and law enforcement administration. Prepare and deliver lectures to undergraduate or graduate students on topics such as criminal law, defensive policing, and investigation techniques.

Economics Teachers, Postsecondary. Teach courses in economics. Prepare and deliver lectures to undergraduate and/or graduate students on topics such as econometrics, price theory, and macroeconomics.

Education Teachers, Postsecondary. Teach courses pertaining to education, such as counseling, curriculum, guidance, instruction, teacher education, and teaching English as a second language. Prepare and deliver lectures to undergraduate and/or graduate students on topics such as children's literature, learning and development, and reading instruction.

Engineering Teachers, Postsecondary. Teach courses pertaining to the application of physical laws and principles of engineering for the development of machines, materials, instruments, processes, and services. Includes teachers of subjects such as chemical, civil, electrical, industrial, mechanical, mineral, and petroleum engineering. Includes both teachers primarily engaged in teaching and those who do a combination of both teaching and research. Prepare and deliver lectures to undergraduate and/or graduate students on topics such as mechanics, hydraulics, and robotics.

English Language and Literature Teachers, Postsecondary. Teach courses in English language and literature, including linguistics and comparative literature. Prepare and deliver lectures to undergraduate and graduate students on topics such as poetry, novel structure, and translation and adaptation.

Environmental Science Teachers, Postsecondary. Teach courses in environmental science. Prepare and deliver lectures to undergraduate and/or graduate students on topics such as hazardous waste management, industrial safety, and environmental toxicology.

Foreign Language and Literature Teachers, Postsecondary. Teach courses in foreign (i.e., other than English) languages and literature. Prepare and deliver lectures to undergraduate and graduate students on topics such as how to speak

Social

and write a foreign language and the cultural aspects of areas where a particular language is used.

Forestry and Conservation Science Teachers, Postsecondary. Teach courses in environmental and conservation science. Prepare and deliver lectures to undergraduate and/or graduate students on topics such as forest resource policy, forest pathology, and mapping. Evaluate and grade students' classwork, assignments, and papers.

Geography Teachers, Postsecondary. Teach courses in geography. Prepare and deliver lectures to undergraduate and/or graduate students on topics such as urbanization, environmental systems, and cultural geography. Maintain geographic information systems laboratories, performing duties such as updating software. Perform spatial analysis and modeling, using geographic information system techniques.

Graduate Teaching Assistants. Assist department chairperson, faculty members, or other professional staff members in colleges or universities by performing teaching or teaching-related duties such as teaching lower-level courses, developing teaching materials, preparing and giving examinations, and grading examinations or papers. Graduate assistants must be enrolled in graduate school programs. Lead discussion sections, tutorials, and laboratory sections. Evaluate and grade examinations, assignments, and papers, and record grades. Return assignments to students in accordance with established deadlines. Schedule and maintain regular office hours to meet with students. Inform students of the procedures for completing and submitting class work such as lab reports. Prepare and proctor examinations. Notify instructors of errors or problems with assignments. Meet with supervisors to discuss students' grades, and to complete required grade-related paperwork. Copy and distribute classroom materials. Demonstrate use of laboratory equipment, and enforce laboratory rules. Teach undergraduate-level courses. Complete laboratory

projects prior to assigning them to students so that any needed modifications can be made. Develop teaching materials such as syllabi, visual aids, answer keys, supplementary notes, and course websites. Provide assistance to faculty members or staff with laboratory or field research. Arrange for supervisors to conduct teaching observations; meet with supervisors to receive feedback about teaching performance. Attend lectures given by the instructor whom they are assisting. Order or obtain materials needed for classes. Provide instructors with assistance in the use of audiovisual equipment. Assist faculty members or staff with student conferences.

Health Specialties Teachers, Postsecondary. Teach courses in health specialties, such as veterinary medicine, dentistry, pharmacy, therapy, laboratory technology, and public health. Prepare and deliver lectures to undergraduate or graduate students on topics such as public health, stress management, and worksite health promotion.

History Teachers, Postsecondary. Teach courses in human history and historiography. Prepare and deliver lectures to undergraduate and/or graduate students on topics such as ancient history, postwar civilizations, and the history of third-world countries.

Home Economics Teachers, Postsecondary. Teach courses in child care, family relations, finance, nutrition, and related subjects as pertaining to home management. Prepare and deliver lectures to undergraduate or graduate students on topics such as food science, nutrition, and child care.

Law Teachers, Postsecondary. Teach courses in law. Prepare and deliver lectures to undergraduate or graduate students on topics such as civil procedure, contracts, and torts. Assign cases for students to hear and try.

Library Science Teachers, Postsecondary. Teach courses in library science. Prepare and deliver lectures to undergraduate or graduate students on topics such as collection development, archival methods, and indexing and abstracting.

Mathematical Science Teachers, Postsecondary. Teach courses pertaining to mathematical concepts, statistics, and actuarial science and to the application of original and standardized mathematical techniques in solving specific problems and situations. Prepare and deliver lectures to undergraduate and/or graduate students on topics such as linear algebra, differential equations, and discrete mathematics.

Nursing Instructors and Teachers, Postsecondary. Demonstrate and teach patient care in classroom and clinical units to nursing students. Includes both teachers primarily engaged in teaching and those who do a combination of both teaching and research. Prepare and deliver lectures to undergraduate or graduate students on topics such as pharmacology, mental health nursing, and community health-care practices. Assess clinical education needs and patient and client teaching needs, utilizing a variety of methods.

Philosophy and Religion Teachers, Postsecondary. Teach courses in philosophy, religion, and theology. Prepare and deliver lectures to undergraduate and graduate students on topics such as ethics, logic, and contemporary religious thought.

Physics Teachers, Postsecondary. Teach courses pertaining to the laws of matter and energy. Includes both teachers primarily engaged in teaching and those who do a combination of both teaching and research. Prepare and deliver lectures to undergraduate and/or graduate students on topics such as quantum mechanics, particle physics, and optics.

Political Science Teachers, Postsecondary. Teach courses in political science, international affairs, and international relations. Prepare and deliver lectures to undergraduate or graduate students on topics such as classical political

thought, international relations, and democracy and citizenship.

Psychology Teachers, Postsecondary. Teach courses in psychology, such as child, clinical, and developmental psychology and psychological counseling. Prepare and deliver lectures to undergraduate and/or graduate students on topics such as abnormal psychology, cognitive processes, and work motivation.

Recreation and Fitness Studies Teachers, Postsecondary. Teach courses pertaining to recreation, leisure, and fitness studies, including exercise physiology and facilities management. Prepare and deliver lectures to undergraduate and graduate students on topics such as anatomy, therapeutic recreation, and conditioning theory.

Social Work Teachers, Postsecondary. Teach courses in social work. Prepare and deliver lectures to undergraduate or graduate students on topics such as family behavior, child and adolescent mental health, and social intervention evaluation.

Sociology Teachers, Postsecondary. Teach courses in sociology. Prepare and deliver lectures to undergraduate and graduate students on topics such as race and ethnic relations, measurement and data collection, and workplace social relations.

Vocational Education Teachers, Postsecondary. Teach or instruct vocational or occupational subjects at the postsecondary level (but at less than the baccalaureate) to students who have graduated or left high school. Includes correspondence school instructors; industrial, commercial, and government training instructors; and adult education teachers and instructors who prepare persons to operate industrial machinery and equipment and transportation and communications equipment. Teaching may take place in public or private schools whose primary business is education or in a school associated with an organization whose primary business is other than education. Supervise and

Social

monitor students' use of tools and equipment. Observe and evaluate students' work to determine progress, provide feedback, and make suggestions for improvement. Present lectures and conduct discussions to increase students' knowledge and competence, using visual aids such as graphs, charts, videotapes, and slides. Administer oral, written, or performance tests to measure progress and to evaluate training effectiveness. Prepare reports and maintain records such as student grades, attendance rolls, and training activity details. Supervise independent or group projects, field placements, laboratory work, or other training. Determine training needs of students or workers. Provide individualized instruction and tutorial or remedial instruction. Conduct on-the-job training, classes, or training sessions to teach and demonstrate principles, techniques, procedures, and methods of designated subjects. Develop curricula and plan course content and methods of instruction. Integrate academic and vocational curricula so that students can obtain a variety of skills. Arrange for lectures by experts in designated fields.

Humanities

Personality Type: Social–Artistic

Useful Facts About the Major

Focuses on combined studies and research in the humanities subjects as distinguished from the social and physical sciences, emphasizing languages, literatures, art, music, philosophy and religion.

Related CIP Program: 24.0103 Humanities/Humanistic Studies

Specializations in the Major: Language, literature, the arts, history, religion, peace and justice studies, philosophy.

Typical Sequence of College Courses: Foreign language, major thinkers and issues in philosophy, literature, art and culture, European history and civilization, writing, seminar (reporting on research).

Typical Sequence of High School Courses: English, algebra, foreign language, history, literature, public speaking, social science.

Career Snapshot

Humanities (sometimes called liberal arts) is an interdisciplinary major that covers a wide range of the arts and other nonscientific modes of thought, such as history, philosophy, religious studies, and language. Graduates of this major usually have strong skills for communicating and critical thinking, and they often advance further in the business world than those who hold more business-focused degrees. Some pursue careers in teaching, media, or the arts. Others get professional degrees in the law or medicine.

Useful Averages for the Related Jobs

- ❋ Annual Earnings: $65,000
- ❋ Growth: 15.1%
- ❋ Openings: Roughly 200
- ❋ Self-Employed: No data available
- ❋ Verbal Skill Rating: 83
- ❋ Math Skill Rating: 47

Other Details About the Related Jobs

Career Clusters: 03 Arts, Audio/Video Technology, and Communications; 04 Business, Management, and Administration; 05 Education and Training; 07 Government and Public Administration; 08 Health Science; 10 Human Services; 12 Law, Public Safety, Corrections, and Security; 15 Science, Technology, Engineering, and Mathematics. **Career Pathways:** 05.3 Teaching/Training; 10.2 Counseling and Mental Health Services.

Skills: Instructing, learning strategies, writing, reading comprehension, speaking, active listening, operations analysis, active learning. **Work Conditions:** Indoors; sitting; close to co-workers.

Related Jobs

Postsecondary Teachers

Personality Type: Social–Investigative

Earnings: $62,700
Growth: 15.1%
Annual Openings: 55,290

Most Common Education/Training Level: Doctoral degree

Teach courses in a college, university, or adult-eduation setting. Prepare course materials such as syllabi, homework assignments, and handouts. Evaluate and grade students' classwork, laboratory work, assignments, and papers. Keep abreast of developments in their field by reading current literature, talking with colleagues, and participating in professional conferences. Initiate, facilitate, and moderate classroom discussions. Conduct research in a particular field of knowledge and publish findings in professional journals, books, and/or electronic media. Supervise undergraduate and/or graduate teaching, internship, and research work. Compile, administer, and grade examinations or assign this work to others. Advise students on academic and vocational curricula and on career issues. Plan, evaluate, and revise curricula, course content, and course materials and methods of instruction. Maintain student attendance records, grades, and other required records. Write grant proposals to procure external research funding. Collaborate with colleagues to address teaching and research issues. Maintain regularly scheduled office hours in order to advise and assist students. Participate in student recruitment, registration, and placement activities. Select and obtain materials and supplies such as textbooks and laboratory equipment. Act as advisers to student organizations. Participate in campus and community events. Serve on academic or administrative committees that deal with institutional policies, departmental matters, and academic issues. Provide professional consulting services to government and/or industry. Perform administrative duties such as serving as department head. Compile bibliographies of specialized materials for outside reading assignments.

Job Specializations

Anthropology and Archeology Teachers, Postsecondary. Teach courses in anthropology or archeology. Prepare and deliver lectures to undergraduate and graduate students on topics such as research methods, urban anthropology, and language and culture.

Area, Ethnic, and Cultural Studies Teachers, Postsecondary. Teach courses pertaining to the culture and development of an area (e.g., Latin America), an ethnic group, or any other group (e.g., women's studies, urban affairs). Prepare and deliver lectures to undergraduate and/or graduate students on topics such as race and ethnic relations, gender studies, and cross-cultural perspectives.

Art, Drama, and Music Teachers, Postsecondary. Teach courses in drama; music; and the arts, including fine and applied art, such as painting and sculpture, or design and crafts. Explain and demonstrate artistic techniques. Prepare and deliver lectures to undergraduate or graduate students on topics such as acting techniques, fundamentals of music, and art history. Organize performance groups and direct their rehearsals.

Communications Teachers, Postsecondary. Teach courses in communications, such as organizational communications, public relations, radio/television broadcasting, and journalism. Prepare and deliver lectures to undergraduate or graduate students on topics such as public

Social

speaking, media criticism, and oral traditions.

Economics Teachers, Postsecondary. Teach courses in economics. Prepare and deliver lectures to undergraduate and/or graduate students on topics such as econometrics, price theory, and macroeconomics.

Education Teachers, Postsecondary. Teach courses pertaining to education, such as counseling, curriculum, guidance, instruction, teacher education, and teaching English as a second language. Prepare and deliver lectures to undergraduate and/or graduate students on topics such as children's literature, learning and development, and reading instruction.

English Language and Literature Teachers, Postsecondary. Teach courses in English language and literature, including linguistics and comparative literature. Prepare and deliver lectures to undergraduate and graduate students on topics such as poetry, novel structure, and translation and adaptation.

Foreign Language and Literature Teachers, Postsecondary. Teach courses in foreign (i.e., other than English) languages and literature. Prepare and deliver lectures to undergraduate and graduate students on topics such as how to speak and write a foreign language and the cultural aspects of areas where a particular language is used.

Geography Teachers, Postsecondary. Teach courses in geography. Prepare and deliver lectures to undergraduate and/or graduate students on topics such as urbanization, environmental systems, and cultural geography. Maintain geographic information systems laboratories, performing duties such as updating software. Perform spatial analysis and modeling, using geographic information system techniques.

Graduate Teaching Assistants. Assist department chairperson, faculty members, or other professional staff members in colleges or universities by performing teaching or teaching-related duties such as teaching lower-level courses, developing teaching materials, preparing and giving examinations, and grading examinations or papers. Graduate assistants must be enrolled in graduate school programs. Lead discussion sections, tutorials, and laboratory sections. Evaluate and grade examinations, assignments, and papers, and record grades. Return assignments to students in accordance with established deadlines. Schedule and maintain regular office hours to meet with students. Inform students of the procedures for completing and submitting class work such as lab reports. Prepare and proctor examinations. Notify instructors of errors or problems with assignments. Meet with supervisors to discuss students' grades, and to complete required grade-related paperwork. Copy and distribute classroom materials. Demonstrate use of laboratory equipment, and enforce laboratory rules. Teach undergraduate-level courses. Complete laboratory projects prior to assigning them to students so that any needed modifications can be made. Develop teaching materials such as syllabi, visual aids, answer keys, supplementary notes, and course websites. Provide assistance to faculty members or staff with laboratory or field research. Arrange for supervisors to conduct teaching observations; meet with supervisors to receive feedback about teaching performance. Attend lectures given by the instructor whom they are assisting. Order or obtain materials needed for classes. Provide instructors with assistance in the use of audiovisual equipment. Assist faculty members or staff with student conferences.

History Teachers, Postsecondary. Teach courses in human history and historiography. Prepare and deliver lectures to undergraduate and/or graduate students on topics such as ancient history, postwar civilizations, and the history of third-world countries.

Library Science Teachers, Postsecondary. Teach courses in library science. Prepare and deliver lectures to undergraduate or graduate students on topics such as collection development, archival methods, and indexing and abstracting.

Philosophy and Religion Teachers, Postsecondary. Teach courses in philosophy, religion, and theology. Prepare and deliver lectures to undergraduate and graduate students on topics such as ethics, logic, and contemporary religious thought.

Political Science Teachers, Postsecondary. Teach courses in political science, international affairs, and international relations. Prepare and deliver lectures to undergraduate or graduate students on topics such as classical political thought, international relations, and democracy and citizenship.

Psychology Teachers, Postsecondary. Teach courses in psychology, such as child, clinical, and developmental psychology and psychological counseling. Prepare and deliver lectures to undergraduate and/or graduate students on topics such as abnormal psychology, cognitive processes, and work motivation.

Sociology Teachers, Postsecondary. Teach courses in sociology. Prepare and deliver lectures to undergraduate and graduate students on topics such as race and ethnic relations, measurement and data collection, and workplace social relations.

Nursing (R.N. Training)

Personality Type: Social–Investigative

Useful Facts About the Major

Prepares individuals in the knowledge, techniques and procedures for promoting health and providing care for sick, disabled, infirm, or other individuals or groups.

Related CIP Program: 51.3801 Registered Nursing/Registered Nurse Training

Specializations in the Major: Community health nursing, pediatric nursing, mental health nursing, nursing administration.

Typical Sequence of College Courses: English composition, introduction to psychology, college algebra, introduction to sociology, oral communication, general chemistry, general biology, human anatomy and physiology, general microbiology, ethics in health care, patient examination and evaluation, pharmacology, reproductive health nursing, pediatric nursing, adult health nursing, mental health nursing, nursing leadership and management, community health nursing, clinical nursing experience.

Typical Sequence of High School Courses: English, algebra, geometry, trigonometry, biology, computer science, public speaking, chemistry, foreign language.

Career Snapshot

The study of nursing includes a combination of classroom and clinical work. Students learn what science tells us about the origins and treatment of disease, how to care effectively for the physical and emotional needs of sick and injured people, and how to teach people to maintain health. Nurses work in a variety of health care settings, including physicians' offices, patients' homes, schools and companies, and in desk jobs for HMOs. The employment outlook is excellent in all specialties.

Useful Averages for the Related Jobs

- ❀ Annual Earnings: $64,000
- ❀ Growth: 22.2%
- ❀ Openings: 103,900
- ❀ Self-Employed: 0.6%
- ❀ Verbal Skill Rating: 66
- ❀ Math Skill Rating: 52

Social

Other Details About the Related Jobs

Career Cluster: 08 Health Science. **Career Pathway:** 08.1 Therapeutic Services.

Skills: Science, social perceptiveness, service orientation, learning strategies, systems evaluation, active learning, monitoring, instructing. **Work Conditions:** Indoors; standing; exposed to disease or infections; exposed to radiation; close to co-workers; common protective or safety equipment; wear specialized protective or safety equipment; walking and running; cramped work space, awkward positions.

Related Jobs

Registered Nurses

Personality Type:
Social–Investigative–Conventional

Earnings: $63,750
Growth: 22.2%
Annual Openings: 103,900

Most Common Education/Training Level: Associate degree

Assess patient health problems and needs, develop and implement nursing care plans, and maintain medical records. Administer nursing care to ill, injured, convalescent, or disabled patients. May advise patients on health maintenance and disease prevention or provide case management. Licensing or registration required. Includes advance practice nurses such as nurse practitioners, clinical nurse specialists, certified nurse midwives, and certified registered nurse anesthetists. Advanced practice nursing is practiced by RNs who have specialized formal, post-basic education and who function in highly autonomous and specialized roles. Monitor, record, and report symptoms and changes in patients' conditions. Maintain accurate, detailed reports and records. Record patients'

medical information and vital signs. Order, interpret, and evaluate diagnostic tests to identify and assess patients' conditions. Modify patient treatment plans as indicated by patients' responses and conditions. Direct and supervise less skilled nursing or health-care personnel or supervise particular units. Consult and coordinate with health-care team members to assess, plan, implement, and evaluate patient care plans. Monitor all aspects of patient care, including diet and physical activity. Instruct individuals, families, and other groups on topics such as health education, disease prevention, and childbirth and develop health improvement programs. Prepare patients for, and assist with, examinations and treatments. Assess the needs of individuals, families, or communities, including assessment of individuals' home or work environments to identify potential health or safety problems. Provide health care, first aid, immunizations, and assistance in convalescence and rehabilitation in locations such as schools, hospitals, and industry. Prepare rooms, sterile instruments, equipment, and supplies and ensure that stock of supplies is maintained. Inform physicians of patients' conditions during anesthesia. Administer local, inhalation, intravenous, and other anesthetics. Perform physical examinations, make tentative diagnoses, and treat patients en route to hospitals or at disaster site triage centers. Observe nurses and visit patients to ensure proper nursing care. Conduct specified laboratory tests. Direct and coordinate infection control programs, advising and consulting with specified personnel about necessary precautions. Prescribe or recommend drugs; medical devices; or other forms of treatment such as physical therapy, inhalation therapy, or related therapeutic procedures.

Job Specializations

Acute Care Nurses. Provide advanced nursing care for patients with acute conditions such as heart attacks, respiratory distress syndrome, or

shock. May care for pre- and post-operative patients or perform advanced, invasive diagnostic or therapeutic procedures. Perform emergency medical procedures, such as basic cardiac life support (BLS), advanced cardiac life support (ACLS), and other condition stabilizing interventions. Document data related to patients' care including assessment results, interventions, medications, patient responses, or treatment changes. Manage patients' pain relief and sedation by providing pharmacologic and non-pharmacologic interventions, monitoring patients' responses, and changing care plans accordingly. Administer blood and blood product transfusions or intravenous infusions, monitoring patients for adverse reactions. Order, perform, or interpret the results of diagnostic tests and screening procedures based on assessment results, differential diagnoses, and knowledge about age, gender and health status of clients. Assess urgent and emergent health conditions using both physiologically and technologically derived data. Interpret information obtained from electrocardiograms (EKGs) or radiographs (X-rays). Set up, operate, or monitor invasive equipment and devices such as colostomy or tracheotomy equipment, mechanical ventilators, catheters, gastrointestinal tubes, and central lines. Diagnose acute or chronic conditions that could result in rapid physiological deterioration or life-threatening instability. Discuss illnesses and treatments with patients and family members. Collaborate with members of multidisciplinary health care teams to plan, manage, or assess patient treatments. Obtain specimens or samples for laboratory work. Collaborate with patients to plan for future health care needs or to coordinate transitions and referrals. Assist patients in organizing their health care system activities. Analyze the indications, contraindications, risk complications, and cost-benefit tradeoffs of therapeutic interventions.

Advanced Practice Psychiatric Nurses. Provide advanced nursing care for patients with psychiatric disorders. May provide psychotherapy under the direction of a psychiatrist. Teach classes in mental health topics such as stress reduction. Participate in activities aimed at professional growth and development including conferences or continuing education activities. Direct or provide home health services. Monitor the use and status of medical and pharmaceutical supplies. Develop practice protocols for mental health problems based on review and evaluation of published research. Develop, implement, or evaluate programs such as outreach activities, community mental health programs, and crisis situation response activities. Write prescriptions for psychotropic medications as allowed by state regulations and collaborative practice agreements. Refer patients requiring more specialized or complex treatment to psychiatrists, primary care physicians, or other medical specialists. Participate in treatment team conferences regarding diagnosis or treatment of difficult cases.

Critical Care Nurses. Provide advanced nursing care for patients in critical or coronary care units. Assess patients' pain levels and sedation requirements. Monitor patients for changes in status and indications of conditions such as sepsis or shock and institute appropriate interventions. Set up and monitor medical equipment and devices such as cardiac monitors, mechanical ventilators and alarms, oxygen delivery devices, transducers, and pressure lines. Administer medications intravenously, by injection, orally, through gastric tubes, or by other methods. Evaluate patients' vital signs and laboratory data to determine emergency intervention needs. Prioritize nursing care for assigned critically ill patients based on assessment data and identified needs. Document patients' medical histories and assessment findings. Conduct pulmonary assessments to identify abnormal respiratory patterns or breathing sounds that indicate problems. Advocate for patients' and families' needs, or provide emotional support for patients and their families. Administer blood and blood products, monitoring patients for signs and

Social

symptoms related to transfusion reactions. Monitor patients' fluid intake and output to detect emerging problems such as fluid and electrolyte imbalances. Compile and analyze data obtained from monitoring or diagnostic tests. Document patients' treatment plans, interventions, outcomes, or plan revisions. Collaborate with other health care professionals to develop and revise treatment plans based on identified needs and assessment data. Assess patients' psychosocial status and needs including areas such as sleep patterns, anxiety, grief, anger, and support systems. Perform approved therapeutic or diagnostic procedures based upon patients' clinical status. Identify patients who are at risk of complications due to nutritional status. Collect specimens for laboratory tests. Identify patients' age-specific needs and alter care plans as necessary to meet those needs. Coordinate patient care conferences.

Occupational Therapy

Personality Type: Social–Investigative

Useful Facts About the Major

Prepares individuals to assist patients limited by physical, cognitive, psychosocial, mental, developmental, and learning disabilities, as well as adverse environmental conditions, to maximize their independence and maintain optimum health through a planned mix of acquired skills, performance motivation, environmental adaptations, assistive technologies, and physical agents.

Related CIP Program: 51.2306 Occupational Therapy/Therapist

Specializations in the Major: Pediatric OT, geriatric OT, prosthetics.

Typical Sequence of College Courses: English composition, statistics for business and social sciences, general chemistry, general biology, human

anatomy and physiology, introduction to psychology, human growth and development, introduction to computer science, abnormal psychology, fundamentals of medical science, neuroscience for therapy, occupational therapy for developmental problems, occupational therapy for physiological diagnoses, occupational therapy for psychosocial diagnoses, administration of occupational therapy services, research methods in occupational therapy, methods of facilitating therapeutic adaptation, occupational therapy fieldwork experience, seminar (reporting on research).

Typical Sequence of High School Courses: English, algebra, geometry, trigonometry, chemistry, physics, biology, foreign language, computer science.

Career Snapshot

Occupational therapists help people cope with disabilities and lead more productive and enjoyable lives. Some therapists enter the field with a bachelor's degree in occupational therapy; others get a master's after a bachelor's in another field. They learn about the nature of various kinds of disabilities—developmental, emotional, and so on—and how to help people overcome them or compensate for them in their daily lives. The long-range outlook for jobs is considered quite good, although in the short run it may be affected by cutbacks in Medicare coverage of therapies.

Useful Averages for the Related Jobs

- ❋ Annual Earnings: $70,000
- ❋ Growth: 25.6%
- ❋ Openings: 4,580
- ❋ Self-Employed: 7.0%
- ❋ Verbal Skill Rating: 56
- ❋ Math Skill Rating: 34

Other Details About the Related Jobs

Career Cluster: 08 Health Science. **Career Pathway:** 08.1 Therapeutic Services.

Skills: Service orientation, learning strategies, writing, social perceptiveness, instructing, negotiation, active listening, technology design. **Work Conditions:** More often indoors than outdoors; in a vehicle; exposed to disease or infections; close to co-workers; keeping or regaining balance; walking and running.

Related Jobs

Occupational Therapists

Personality Type: Social–Investigative

Earnings: $69,630
Growth: 25.6%
Annual Openings: 4,580

Most Common Education/Training Level: Master's degree

Assess, plan, organize, and participate in rehabilitative programs that help restore vocational, homemaking, and daily living skills, as well as general independence, to disabled persons. Plan, organize, and conduct occupational therapy programs in hospital, institutional, or community settings to help rehabilitate those impaired because of illness, injury, or psychological or developmental problems. Test and evaluate patients' physical and mental abilities and analyze medical data to determine realistic rehabilitation goals for patients. Select activities that will help individuals learn work and life-management skills within limits of their mental and physical capabilities. Evaluate patients' progress and prepare reports that detail progress. Complete and maintain necessary records. Train caregivers to provide for the needs of patients during and after therapies. Recommend changes in patients' work or living environments, consistent with their needs and capabilities. Develop and participate in health promotion programs, group activities, or discussions to promote client health, facilitate social adjustment, alleviate stress, and prevent physical or mental disability. Consult with rehabilitation team to select activity programs and coordinate occupational therapy with other therapeutic activities. Plan and implement programs and social activities to help patients learn work and school skills and adjust to handicaps. Design and create, or requisition, special supplies and equipment such as splints, braces and computer-aided adaptive equipment. Conduct research in occupational therapy. Provide training and supervision in therapy techniques and objectives for students and nurses and other medical staff. Help clients improve decision making, abstract reasoning, memory, sequencing, coordination, and perceptual skills, using computer programs. Advise on health risks in the workplace and on health-related transition to retirement. Lay out materials such as puzzles, scissors, and eating utensils for use in therapy, and clean and repair these tools after therapy sessions. Provide patients with assistance in locating and holding jobs.

Job Specialization

Low Vision Therapists, Orientation and Mobility Specialists, and Vision Rehabilitation Therapists. Provide therapy to patients with visual impairments to improve their functioning in daily life activities. May train patients in activities such as computer use, communication skills, or home management skills. Teach cane skills including cane use with a guide, diagonal techniques, and two-point touches. Refer clients to services, such as eye care, health care, rehabilitation, and counseling, to enhance visual and life functioning or when condition exceeds scope of practice. Provide consultation, support, or education to groups such as parents and teachers. Participate in professional development activities such

Social

as reading literature, continuing education, attending conferences, and collaborating with colleagues. Obtain, distribute, or maintain low vision devices. Design instructional programs to improve communication using devices such as slates and styluses, braillers, keyboards, adaptive handwriting devices, talking book machines, digital books, and optical character readers (OCRs). Collaborate with specialists, such as rehabilitation counselors, speech pathologists, and occupational therapists, to provide client solutions.

Physical Education

Personality Type: Social–Enterprising

Useful Facts About the Major

Prepares individuals to teach physical education programs and/or to coach sports at various educational levels.

Related CIP Program: 13.1314 Physical Education Teaching and Coaching

Specializations in the Major: Sports activities, coaching, recreation, health education.

Typical Sequence of College Courses: Introduction to psychology, English composition, oral communication, history and philosophy of education, human growth and development, introduction to special education, history and philosophy of physical education, first aid and CPR, methods of teaching physical education, human anatomy and physiology, kinesiology, special needs in physical education, psychomotor development, organization and administration of physical ed, evaluation in physical education, methods of teaching dance, methods of teaching sports activities, methods of teaching aerobics and weight training, swimming and water safety, student teaching.

Typical Sequence of High School Courses: English, algebra, geometry, trigonometry, science, foreign language, public speaking.

Career Snapshot

This major covers not only educational techniques, but also the workings of the human body. Thanks to a national concern for fitness and health, physical education graduates are finding employment not only as teachers, but also as instructors and athletic directors in health and sports clubs. Most jobs are still to be found in elementary and secondary schools, where a bachelor's degree is often sufficient for entry, but a master's may be required for advancement to a more secure and better-paid position. Some graduates may go on to get a master's in athletic training and work for a college or professional sports team.

Useful Averages for the Related Jobs

- ✱ Annual Earnings: $44,000
- ✱ Growth: 16.0%
- ✱ Openings: 23,020
- ✱ Self-Employed: 6.4%
- ✱ Verbal Skill Rating: 64
- ✱ Math Skill Rating: 51

Other Details About the Related Jobs

Career Cluster: 05 Education and Training. **Career Pathways:** 05.1 Administration and Administrative Support; 05.3 Teaching/Training.

Skills: Learning strategies, systems evaluation, management of personnel resources, instructing, monitoring, social perceptiveness, negotiation, management of material resources. **Work Conditions:** Indoors; standing; close to co-workers; exposed to disease or infections.

Related Jobs

1. Coaches and Scouts

Personality Type: Social–Realistic–Enterprising

Earnings: $28,380
Growth: 24.8%
Annual Openings: 9,920

Most Common Education/Training Level:
Long-term on-the-job training

Instruct or coach groups or individuals in the fundamentals of sports. Demonstrate techniques and methods of participation. May evaluate athletes' strengths and weaknesses as possible recruits or to improve the athletes' technique to prepare them for competition. Plan, organize, and conduct practice sessions. Provide training direction, encouragement, and motivation to prepare athletes for games, competitive events, or tours. Identify and recruit potential athletes, arranging and offering incentives such as athletic scholarships. Plan strategies and choose team members for individual games or sports seasons. Plan and direct physical conditioning programs that will enable athletes to achieve maximum performance. Adjust coaching techniques based on the strengths and weaknesses of athletes. File scouting reports that detail player assessments, provide recommendations on athlete recruitment, and identify locations and individuals to be targeted for future recruitment efforts. Keep records of athlete, team, and opposing team performance. Instruct individuals or groups in sports rules, game strategies, and performance principles such as specific ways of moving the body, hands, and feet in order to achieve desired results. Analyze the strengths and weaknesses of opposing teams to develop game strategies. Evaluate athletes' skills and review performance records to determine their fitness and potential in a particular area of athletics. Keep abreast of changing rules, techniques, technologies, and philosophies relevant to their sport. Monitor athletes' use of equipment to ensure safe and proper use. Explain and enforce safety rules and regulations. Develop and arrange competition schedules and programs. Serve as organizer, leader, instructor, or referee for outdoor and indoor games such as volleyball, football, and soccer. Explain and demonstrate the use of sports and training equipment, such as trampolines or weights. Perform activities that support a team or a specific sport, such as meeting with media representatives and appearing at fundraising events. Arrange and conduct sports-related activities such as training camps, skill-improvement courses, clinics, or pre-season try-outs.

2. Middle School Teachers, Except Special and Vocational Education

Personality Type: Social–Artistic

Earnings: $50,770
Growth: 15.3%
Annual Openings: 25,110

Most Common Education/Training Level:
Bachelor's degree

Teach students in public or private schools in one or more subjects at the middle, intermediate, or junior high level, which falls between elementary and senior high school as defined by applicable state laws and regulations. Establish and enforce rules for behavior and procedures for maintaining order among students. Adapt teaching methods and instructional materials to meet students' varying needs and interests. Instruct through lectures, discussions, and demonstrations in one or more subjects, such as English, mathematics, or social studies. Prepare, administer, and grade tests and assignments to evaluate students' progress. Establish clear objectives for all lessons, units, and projects, and communicate these objectives to students. Plan and conduct activities for a balanced program of instruction, demonstration, and work time that provides students with opportunities to observe, question, and investigate. Maintain accurate, complete, and correct student

Social

records as required by laws, district policies, and administrative regulations. Observe and evaluate students' performance, behavior, social development, and physical health. Prepare materials and classrooms for class activities.

3. Secondary School Teachers, Except Special and Vocational Education

Personality Type: Social–Artistic–Enterprising

Earnings: $52,200
Growth: 8.9%
Annual Openings: 41,240

Most Common Education/Training Level: Bachelor's degree

Instruct students in secondary public or private schools in one or more subjects at the secondary level, such as English, mathematics, or social studies. May be designated according to subject matter specialty, such as typing instructors, commercial teachers, or English teachers. Establish and enforce rules for behavior and procedures for maintaining order among students. Instruct through lectures, discussions, and demonstrations in one or more subjects, such as English, mathematics, or social studies. Establish clear objectives for all lessons, units, and projects and communicate those objectives to students. Prepare, administer, and grade tests and assignments to evaluate students' progress. Prepare materials and classrooms for class activities. Adapt teaching methods and instructional materials to meet students' varying needs and interests. Maintain accurate and complete student records as required by laws, district policies, and administrative regulations. Assign and grade class work and homework. Observe and evaluate students' performance, behavior, social development, and physical health. Enforce all administration policies and rules governing students.

Physical Therapy

Personality Type: Social–Investigative–Realistic

Useful Facts About the Major

Prepares individuals to alleviate physical and functional impairments and limitations caused by injury or disease through the design and implementation of therapeutic interventions to promote fitness and health.

Related CIP Program: 51.2308 Physical Therapy/Therapist Training

Specializations in the Major: Orthopedics, sports medicine, geriatric physical therapy, neurological physical therapy, physical therapy education.

Typical Sequence of College Courses: English composition, statistics for business and social sciences, general chemistry, general biology, human anatomy and physiology, introduction to psychology, human growth and development, introduction to computer science, abnormal psychology, fundamentals of medical science, neuroanatomy, neuroscience for therapy, cardiopulmonary system, musculoskeletal system, clinical orthopedics, clinical applications of neurophysiology, therapeutic exercise techniques, physical and electrical agents in physical therapy, medical considerations in physical therapy, psychomotor development throughout the lifespan, psychosocial aspects of physical disability, research in physical therapy practice, research in physical therapy practice.

Typical Sequence of High School Courses: English, algebra, geometry, trigonometry, chemistry, physics, biology, foreign language, computer science.

Career Snapshot

Physical therapists help people overcome pain and limited movement caused by disease or injury, and help them avoid further disabilities. They review patients' medical records and the prescriptions of physicians, evaluate patients' mobility, then guide patients through appropriate exercise routines and apply therapeutic agents such as heat and electrical stimulation. They need to be knowledgeable about many disabling conditions and therapeutic techniques. The master's program is becoming the standard requirement for entry into this field. Entry to master's programs is extremely competitive. The short-term job outlook has been hurt by cutbacks in Medicare coverage of therapy; however, the long-term outlook is expected to be good.

Useful Averages for the Related Jobs

❀ Annual Earnings: $74,000
❀ Growth: 30.3%
❀ Openings: 7,860
❀ Self-Employed: 8.0%
❀ Verbal Skill Rating: 59
❀ Math Skill Rating: 39

Other Details About the Related Jobs

Career Cluster: 08 Health Science. **Career Pathway:** 08.3 Health Informatics.

Skills: Science, operations analysis, service orientation, instructing, persuasion, time management, social perceptiveness, reading comprehension. **Work Conditions:** Indoors; standing; exposed to disease or infections; close to co-workers; keeping or regaining balance; walking and running; kneeling, crouching, stooping, or crawling; cramped work space, awkward positions.

Related Jobs

Physical Therapists

Personality Type: Social–Investigative–Realistic

Earnings: $74,480
Growth: 30.3%
Annual Openings: 7,860

Most Common Education/Training Level: Master's degree

Assess, plan, organize, and participate in rehabilitative programs that improve mobility, relieve pain, increase strength, and decrease or prevent deformity of patients suffering from disease or injury. Perform and document initial exams, evaluating data to identify problems and determine diagnoses prior to interventions. Plan, prepare, and carry out individually designed programs of physical treatment to maintain, improve, or restore physical functioning; alleviate pain; and prevent physical dysfunction in patients. Record prognoses, treatments, responses, and progresses in patients' charts or enter information into computers. Identify and document goals, anticipated progresses, and plans for reevaluation. Evaluate effects of treatments at various stages and adjust treatments to achieve maximum benefits. Administer manual exercises, massages, or traction to help relieve pain, increase patient strength, or decrease or prevent deformity or crippling. Test and measure patients' strength, motor development and function, sensory perception, functional capacity, and respiratory and circulatory efficiency and record data. Instruct patients and families in treatment procedures to be continued at home. Confer with patients, medical practitioners, and appropriate others to plan, implement, and assess intervention programs. Review physicians' referrals and patients' medical records to help determine diagnoses and physical therapy treatments required. Obtain patients' informed consent to proposed interventions. Discharge patients from physical therapy when goals or projected outcomes have been attained and provide for appropriate follow-up care or referrals. Provide information to patients about proposed interventions, material risks, and expected benefits and any reasonable alternatives.

Social

Inform patients when diagnoses reveal findings outside the scope of physical therapy to treat and refer to appropriate practitioners. Direct, supervise, assess, and communicate with supportive personnel. Provide educational information about physical therapy and physical therapists, injury prevention, ergonomics, and ways to promote health. Refer clients to community resources and services.

Physician Assisting

Personality Type: Social–Investigative–Realistic

Useful Facts About the Major

Prepares individuals to practice medicine, including diagnoses and treatment therapies, under the supervision of a physician.

Related CIP Program: 51.0912 Physician Assistant Training

Specializations in the Major: Internal medicine, pediatrics, family medicine, emergency medicine.

Typical Sequence of College Courses: English composition, college algebra, general chemistry, general biology, introduction to psychology, human growth and development, general microbiology, human physiology, human anatomy, pharmacology, medical interviewing techniques, patient examination and evaluation, clinical laboratory procedures, ethics in health care, clinical experience in internal medicine, clinical experience in emergency medicine, clinical experience in obstetrics/gynecology, clinical experience in family medicine, clinical experience in psychiatry, clinical experience in surgery, clinical experience in pediatrics, clinical experience in geriatrics.

Typical Sequence of High School Courses: English, algebra, geometry, trigonometry, pre-calculus, biology, computer science, public speaking, chemistry, foreign language.

Career Snapshot

Physician assistants work under the supervision of physicians, but in some cases they provide care in settings where a physician may be present only a couple of days per week. They perform many of the diagnostic, therapeutic, and preventative functions that we are used to associating with physicians. The typical educational program results in a bachelor's degree. It often takes only two years to complete, but entrants usually must have at least two years of prior college and often must have work experience in the field of health care. Employment opportunities are expected to be good.

Useful Averages for the Related Jobs

- Annual Earnings: $84,000
- Growth: 39.0%
- Openings: 4,280
- Self-Employed: 1.4%
- Verbal Skill Rating: 64
- Math Skill Rating: 52

Other Details About the Related Jobs

Career Cluster: 08 Health Science. **Career Pathway:** 08.2 Diagnostics Services.

Skills: Science, instructing, service orientation, judgment and decision making, social perceptiveness, reading comprehension, operations analysis, systems evaluation. **Work Conditions:** Indoors; standing; exposed to disease or infections; exposed to radiation; close to co-workers; wear specialized protective or safety equipment; common protective or safety equipment.

Related Jobs

Physician Assistants

Personality Type: Investigative–Social–Realistic

Earnings: $84,420
Growth: 39.0%
Annual Openings: 4,280

Most Common Education/Training Level:
Master's degree

Under the supervision of physicians, provide health-care services typically performed by a physician. Conduct complete physicals, provide treatment, and counsel patients. May, in some cases, prescribe medication. Must graduate from an accredited educational program for physician assistants. Examine patients to obtain information about their physical conditions. Obtain, compile, and record patient medical data, including health history, progress notes, and results of physical examinations. Interpret diagnostic test results for deviations from normal. Make tentative diagnoses and decisions about management and treatment of patients. Prescribe therapy or medication with physician approval. Administer or order diagnostic tests, such as X-ray, electrocardiogram, and laboratory tests. Instruct and counsel patients about prescribed therapeutic regimens, normal growth and development, family planning, emotional problems of daily living, and health maintenance. Perform therapeutic procedures such as injections, immunizations, suturing and wound care, and infection management. Provide physicians with assistance during surgery or complicated medical procedures. Visit and observe patients on hospital rounds or house calls, updating charts, ordering therapy, and reporting back to physicians. Supervise and coordinate activities of technicians and technical assistants. Order medical and laboratory supplies and equipment.

Job Specialization

Anesthesiologist Assistants. Assist anesthesiologists in the administration of anesthesia for surgical and non-surgical procedures. Monitor patient status and provide patient care during surgical treatment. Verify availability of operating room supplies, medications, and gases. Provide clinical instruction, supervision or training to staff in areas such as anesthesia practices. Collect samples or specimens for diagnostic testing. Participate in seminars, workshops, or other professional activities to keep abreast of developments in anesthesiology. Collect and document patients' pre-anesthetic health histories. Provide airway management interventions including tracheal intubation, fiber optics, or ventilary support. Respond to emergency situations by providing cardiopulmonary resuscitation (CPR), basic cardiac life support (BLS), advanced cardiac life support (ACLS), or pediatric advanced life support (PALS). Monitor and document patients' progress during post-anesthesia period. Pretest and calibrate anesthesia delivery systems and monitors. Assist anesthesiologists in monitoring of patients including electrocardiogram (EKG), direct arterial pressure, central venous pressure, arterial blood gas, hematocrit, or routine measurement of temperature, respiration, blood pressure and heart rate. Assist in the provision of advanced life support techniques including those procedures using high frequency ventilation or intra-arterial cardiovascular assistance devices. Assist anesthesiologists in performing anesthetic procedures such as epidural and spinal injections. Assist in the application of monitoring techniques such as pulmonary artery catheterization, electroencephalographic spectral analysis, echocardiography, and evoked potentials. Administer blood, blood products, or supportive fluids. Control anesthesia levels during procedures. Administer anesthetic, adjuvant, or accessory drugs under the direction of an anesthesiologist.

Social

Speech-Language Pathology and Audiology

Personality Type: Social–Investigative–Artistic

Useful Facts About the Major

Prepares individuals as audiologists and speech-language pathologists.

Related CIP Program: 51.0204 Audiology/ Audiologist and Speech-Language Pathology/ Pathologist

Specializations in the Major: Speech-language pathology, audiology.

Typical Sequence of College Courses: General biology, English composition, general physics, introduction to psychology, human growth and development, statistics, introduction to sociology, introduction to speech, language and hearing, phonetics, anatomy of the speech and hearing mechanism, linguistics, psychoacoustics, neuroscience, auditory anatomy and physiology, stuttering and other fluency disorders, voice disorders, hearing problems, psycholinguistics and speech perception, diagnostic procedures in audiology, aural rehabilitation, research methods in speech pathology and audiology, student teaching.

Typical Sequence of High School Courses: English, algebra, geometry, trigonometry, biology, chemistry, physics, computer science, public speaking, social science, pre-calculus.

Career Snapshot

Speech-language pathologists and audiologists help people with a variety of communication disorders. About half of speech-language pathologists work in schools, most of the rest for health care facilities. Among audiologists, about half work in health care settings, with a smaller number in schools. A master's degree is the standard entry route for speech-language pathologists. For audiologists, a master's still suffices in many states, but a doctoral degree is expected to become the standard. It is possible to complete the requirements for entering both kinds of graduate program within a variety of undergraduate majors. Because of the aging of the population and an emphasis on early diagnosis, job opportunities are expected to be excellent for speech-language pathologists, though less certain for audiologists. Knowledge of a second language is an advantage.

Useful Averages for the Related Jobs

- ❋ Annual Earnings: $65,000
- ❋ Growth: 18.7%
- ❋ Openings: 4,525
- ❋ Self-Employed: 8.8%
- ❋ Verbal Skill Rating: 90
- ❋ Math Skill Rating: 49

Other Details About the Related Jobs

Career Cluster: 08 Health Science. **Career Pathway:** 08.1 Therapeutic Services.

Skills: Science, learning strategies, social perceptiveness, writing, monitoring, active learning, systems evaluation, technology design. **Work Conditions:** Indoors; sitting; exposed to disease or infections; close to co-workers; noisy; exposed to radiation.

Related Jobs

1. Audiologists

Personality Type: Investigative–Social

Earnings: $63,230
Growth: 25.0%
Annual Openings: 580

Most Common Education/Training Level:
Master's degree

Assess and treat persons with hearing and related disorders. May fit hearing aids and provide auditory training. May perform research related to hearing problems. Examine and clean patients' ear canals. Educate and supervise audiology students and health care personnel. Develop and supervise hearing screening programs. Counsel and instruct patients and their families in techniques to improve hearing and communication related to hearing loss. Evaluate hearing and balance disorders to determine diagnoses and courses of treatment. Program and monitor cochlear implants to fit the needs of patients. Participate in conferences or training to update or share knowledge of new hearing or balance disorder treatment methods or technologies. Conduct or direct research on hearing or balance topics and report findings to help in the development of procedures, technology, or treatments. Plan and conduct treatment programs for patients' hearing or balance problems, consulting with educators, physicians, nurses, psychologists, speech-language pathologists, and other health care personnel as necessary.

2. Speech-Language Pathologists

Personality Type: Social–Investigative–Artistic

Earnings: $65,090
Growth: 18.5%
Annual Openings: 4,380

Most Common Education/Training Level: First professional degree

Assess and treat persons with speech, language, voice, and fluency disorders. May select alternative communication systems and teach their use. May perform research related to speech and language problems. Monitor patients' progress and adjust treatments accordingly. Evaluate hearing or speech and language test results, barium swallow results, and medical or background information to diagnose and plan treatment for speech, language, fluency, voice, and swallowing disorders. Administer hearing or speech and language evaluations, tests, or examinations to patients to collect information on type and degree of impairments, using written and oral tests and special instruments. Write reports and maintain proper documentation of information, such as client Medicaid and billing records and caseload activities, including the initial evaluation, treatment, progress, and discharge of clients. Develop and implement treatment plans for problems such as stuttering, delayed language, swallowing disorders, and inappropriate pitch or harsh voice problems, based on own assessments and recommendations of physicians, psychologists, or social workers. Develop individual or group activities and programs in schools to deal with behavior, speech, language, or swallowing problems. Participate in and write reports for meetings regarding patients' progress, such as individualized educational planning (IEP) meetings, in-service meetings, or intervention assistance team meetings. Complete administrative responsibilities, such as coordinating paperwork, scheduling case management activities, or writing lesson plans. Educate patients and family members about various topics, such as communication techniques and strategies to cope with or to avoid personal misunderstandings. Instruct clients in techniques for more effective communication, including sign language, lip reading, and voice improvement. Teach clients to control or strengthen tongue, jaw, face muscles, and breathing mechanisms. Develop speech exercise programs to reduce disabilities. Communicate with non-speaking students, using sign language or computer technology.

Women's Studies

Personality Type: Social–Investigative–Artistic

Social

Useful Facts About the Major

Focuses on the history, sociology, politics, culture, and economics of women, and the development of modern feminism in relation to the roles played by women in different periods and locations in North America and the world.

Related CIP Program: 05.0207 Women's Studies

Specializations in the Major: Women's issues in art and culture, women's political issues, history of feminism, feminist theory.

Typical Sequence of College Courses: English composition, foreign language, American history, introduction to women's studies, women of color, theories of feminism, historical and philosophical origins of feminism, feminism from a global perspective, seminar (reporting on research).

Typical Sequence of High School Courses: English, algebra, foreign language, history, literature, public speaking, social science.

Career Snapshot

Women's studies is an interdisciplinary major that looks at the experience of women from the perspectives of history, literature, psychology, and sociology, among others. Graduates of this major may go into business fields where understanding of women's issues can be helpful—for example, advertising or human resources management. With further education, they may also find careers in fields where they can affect the lives of women, such as social work, law, public health, or public administration.

Useful Averages for the Related Jobs

- Annual Earnings: $65,000
- Growth: 15.1%
- Openings: Roughly 200
- Self-Employed: No data available
- Verbal Skill Rating: 84
- Math Skill Rating: 39

Other Details About the Related Jobs

Career Clusters: 05 Education and Training; 10 Human Service. **Career Pathways:** 05.3 Teaching/Training; 10.2 Counseling and Mental Health Services.

Skills: Science, writing, operations analysis, learning strategies, speaking, reading comprehension, active learning, active listening. **Work Conditions:** Indoors; sitting; exposed to disease or infections.

Related Jobs

Area, Ethnic, and Cultural Studies Teachers, Postsecondary

Personality Type: Social–Investigative–Artistic

Earnings: $65,030
Growth: 15.1%
Annual Openings: 200

Most Common Education/Training Level: Doctoral degree

Teach courses pertaining to the culture and development of an area (e.g., Latin America), an ethnic group, or any other group (e.g., women's studies, urban affairs). Keep abreast of developments in their field by reading current literature, talking with colleagues, and participating in professional conferences. Conduct research in a particular field of knowledge and publish findings in professional journals, books, and/or electronic media. Evaluate and grade students' classwork, assignments, and papers. Prepare course materials such as syllabi, homework assignments, and handouts. Prepare and deliver lectures to undergraduate and/or graduate students on topics such as race and ethnic relations, gender studies, and cross-cultural perspectives. Initiate, facilitate, and moderate classroom discussions. Compile, administer, and grade examinations or assign this work to others. Maintain regularly scheduled office hours in order to advise and assist students. Plan, evaluate, and revise curricula, course content, and course materials and methods of instruction. Maintain student attendance records, grades, and other required records. Advise students on academic and vocational curricula and on career issues. Supervise undergraduate and/or graduate teaching, internship, and research work. Select and obtain materials and supplies such as textbooks. Collaborate with colleagues to address teaching and research issues. Serve on academic or administrative committees that deal with institutional policies, departmental matters, and academic issues. Compile bibliographies of specialized materials for outside reading assignments. Write grant proposals to procure external research funding. Participate in campus and community events. Participate in student recruitment, registration, and placement activities. Act as advisers to student organizations. Incorporate experiential/site visit components into courses. Perform administrative duties such as serving as department head. Provide professional consulting services to government and/or industry.

Social

Enterprising Majors

Bioengineering

Personality Type:
Enterprising–Investigative–Realistic

Useful Facts About the Major

Prepares individuals to apply mathematical and scientific principles to the design, development, and operational evaluation of biomedical and health systems and products such as integrated biomedical systems, instrumentation, medical information systems, artificial organs and prostheses, and health management and care delivery systems.

Related CIP Program: 14.0501 Bioengineering and Biomedical Engineering

Specializations in the Major: Biomedical engineering, molecular bioengineering, computational bioengineering, engineered biomaterials, medical imaging, biomechanics, prosthetics and artificial organs, controlled drug delivery.

Typical Sequence of College Courses: English composition, technical writing, calculus, differential equations, general chemistry, introduction to computer science, general physics, introduction to electric circuits, general biology, mechanics, introduction to bioengineering, bioinstrumentation, biomaterials, biomechanics, business information processing.

Typical Sequence of High School Courses: English, algebra, geometry, trigonometry, pre-calculus, calculus, chemistry, biology, physics, computer science.

Career Snapshot

Bioengineering uses engineering principles of analysis and design to solve problems in medicine and biology. It finds ways to improve health care, agriculture, and industrial processes. Graduates with a bachelor's may work in industry, but increasing competition is making an advanced degree more important, and it is needed to prepare for a career in research or college teaching. Some graduates go on to medical school. This is one of the fastest-moving fields in engineering, so people in this field need to learn continuously to keep up with new technologies.

Useful Averages for the Related Jobs

* Annual Earnings: $108,000
* Growth: 23.2%
* Openings: 2,708
* Self-Employed: 1.3%
* Verbal Skill Rating: 65
* Math Skill Rating: 77

Other Details About the Related Jobs

Career Clusters: 02 Architecture and Construction; 11 Information Technology; 15 Science, Technology, Engineering, and Mathematics. **Career Pathways:** 02.1 Design/Pre-Construction; 11.4 Programming and Software Development; 15.1 Engineering and Technology; 15.2 Science and Mathematics.

Skills: Operations analysis, science, management of financial resources, mathematics, management of material resources, systems evaluation, technology design, systems analysis. **Work Conditions:** Indoors; sitting; exposed to radiation; hazardous conditions.

Related Jobs

1. Biomedical Engineers

Personality Type: Investigative–Realistic

Earnings: $78,860
Growth: 72.0%
Annual Openings: 1,490

Most Common Education/Training Level: Bachelor's or higher degree plus work experience

Apply knowledge of engineering, biology, and biomechanical principles to the design, development, and evaluation of biological and health systems and products, such as artificial organs, prostheses, instrumentation, medical information systems, and health management and care delivery systems. Evaluate the safety, efficiency, and effectiveness of biomedical equipment. Advise and assist in the application of instrumentation in clinical environments. Research new materials to be used for products, such as implanted artificial organs. Design and develop medical diagnostic and clinical instrumentation, equipment, and procedures, using the principles of engineering and biobehavioral sciences. Conduct research, along with life scientists, chemists, and medical scientists, on the engineering aspects of the biological systems of humans and animals. Teach biomedical engineering or disseminate knowledge about field through writing or consulting. Design and deliver technology to assist people with disabilities. Analyze new medical procedures to forecast likely outcomes. Develop new applications for energy sources, such as using nuclear power for biomedical implants. Install, adjust, maintain, repair, or provide technical support for biomedical equipment.

2. Engineering Managers

Personality Type:
Enterprising–Realistic–Investigative

Earnings: $117,000
Growth: 6.2%
Annual Openings: 4,870

Most Common Education/Training Level: Bachelor's degree

Plan, direct, or coordinate activities or research and development in such fields as architecture and engineering. Confer with management, production, and marketing staff to discuss project specifications and procedures. Coordinate and direct projects, making detailed plans to accomplish goals and directing the integration of technical activities. Analyze technology, resource needs, and market demand, to plan and assess the feasibility of projects. Plan and direct the installation, testing, operation, maintenance, and repair of facilities and equipment. Direct, review, and approve product design and changes. Recruit employees, assign, direct, and evaluate their work, and oversee the development and maintenance of staff competence. Prepare budgets, bids, and contracts, and direct the negotiation of research contracts. Develop and implement policies, standards and procedures for the engineering and technical work performed in the department, service, laboratory or firm. Review and recommend or approve contracts and cost estimates. Perform administrative functions such as reviewing and writing reports, approving expenditures, enforcing rules, and making decisions about the purchase of materials or services. Present and explain proposals, reports, and findings to clients. Consult or negotiate with clients to prepare project specifications. Set scientific and technical goals within broad outlines provided by top management. Administer highway planning, construction, and maintenance. Direct the engineering of water control, treatment, and distribution projects. Plan, direct, and coordinate survey work with other staff activities, certifying survey work, and writing land legal descriptions. Confer with and report to officials and the public to provide information and solicit support for projects.

Job Specialization

Biofuels/Biodiesel Technology and Product Development Managers. Define, plan, or execute biofuel/biodiesel research programs that

Enterprising

evaluate alternative feedstock and process technologies with near-term commercial potential. Develop lab scale models of industrial scale processes, such as fermentation. Develop computational tools or approaches to improve biofuels research and development activities. Develop carbohydrates arrays and associated methods for screening enzymes involved in biomass conversion. Provide technical or scientific guidance to technical staff in the conduct of biofuels research or development. Prepare, or oversee the preparation of, experimental plans for biofuels research or development. Prepare biofuels research and development reports for senior management or technical professionals. Perform protein functional analysis and engineering for processing of feedstock and creation of biofuels. Develop separation processes to recover biofuels. Develop methods to recover ethanol or other fuels from complex bioreactor liquid and gas streams. Develop methods to estimate the efficiency of biomass pretreatments. Design or execute solvent or product recovery experiments in laboratory or field settings. Design or conduct applied biodiesel or biofuels research projects on topics such as transport, thermodynamics, mixing, filtration, distillation, fermentation, extraction, and separation. Design chemical conversion processes, such as etherification, esterification, interesterification, transesterification, distillation, hydrogenation, oxidation or reduction of fats and oils, and vegetable oil refining. Conduct experiments on biomass or pretreatment technologies. Conduct experiments to test new or alternate feedstock fermentation processes. Analyze data from biofuels studies, such as fluid dynamics, water treatments, or solvent extraction and recovery processes. Oversee biodiesel/biofuels prototyping or development projects. Propose new biofuels products, processes, technologies or applications based on findings from applied biofuels or biomass research projects.

Biology

Personality Type: Enterprising–Investigative

Useful Facts About the Major

Focuses on the scientific study of plants, animals, microbial organisms, and habitats and ecosystem relations of living things.

Related CIP Program: 26.0101 Biology/Biological Sciences, General

Specializations in the Major: Botany, zoology, biochemistry, genetics, cell biology, microbiology, ecology.

Typical Sequence of College Courses: English composition, calculus, introduction to computer science, general chemistry, statistics, general biology, organic chemistry, genetics, general physics, cell biology, introduction to biochemistry, general microbiology, ecology, organisms and populations, animal anatomy and physiology, plant anatomy.

Typical Sequence of High School Courses: Algebra, English, biology, geometry, trigonometry, chemistry, physics, pre-calculus, computer science, calculus.

Career Snapshot

Although it is often possible to study a specialization—such as botany, zoology, or biochemistry—many colleges offer a major in the general field of biology. With a bachelor's degree in biology, one may work as a technician or entry-level researcher in a medical, pharmaceutical, or governmental regulatory setting, or as a sales representative in a technical field such as pharmaceuticals. Such job opportunities are expected to be good. Teaching biology in high school or middle school almost always requires additional coursework (perhaps a master's) in teaching theory and methods, plus supervised classroom experience. A large number of biology majors go on to pursue graduate or professional degrees and thus prepare for careers as researchers, college teachers, physicians, dentists, and veterinarians.

Useful Averages for the Related Jobs

* Annual Earnings: $115,000
* Growth: 15.5%
* Openings: 2,010
* Self-Employed: 0.0%
* Verbal Skill Rating: 58
* Math Skill Rating: 65

Other Details About the Related Jobs

Career Clusters: 04 Business, Management, and Administration; 15 Science, Technology, Engineering, and Mathematics. **Career Pathways:** 04.2 Business, Financial Management, and Accounting; 04.4 Business Analysis; 15.2 Science and Mathematics.

Skills: Science, operations analysis, management of financial resources, technology design, management of personnel resources, mathematics, time management, reading comprehension. **Work Conditions:** Indoors; sitting; hazardous conditions; exposed to disease or infections.

Related Jobs

Natural Sciences Managers

Personality Type: Enterprising–Investigative

Earnings: $114,560
Growth: 15.4%
Annual Openings: 2,010

Most Common Education/Training Level:
Bachelor's or higher degree plus work experience

Plan, direct, or coordinate activities in such fields as life sciences, physical sciences, mathematics, and statistics and research and development in these fields. Confer with scientists, engineers, regulators, and others to plan and review projects and to provide technical assistance. Develop client relationships and communicate with clients to explain proposals, present research findings, establish specifications, or discuss project status. Plan and direct research, development, and production activities. Prepare project proposals. Design and coordinate successive phases of problem analysis, solution proposals, and testing. Review project activities and prepare and review research, testing, and operational reports. Hire, supervise, and evaluate engineers, technicians, researchers, and other staff. Determine scientific and technical goals within broad outlines provided by top management and make detailed plans to accomplish these goals. Develop and implement policies, standards, and procedures for the architectural, scientific, and technical work performed to ensure regulatory compliance and operations enhancement. Develop innovative technology and train staff for its implementation. Provide for stewardship of plant and animal resources and habitats, studying land use; monitoring animal populations; and providing shelter, resources, and medical treatment for animals. Conduct own research in field of expertise. Recruit personnel and oversee the development and maintenance of staff competence. Advise and assist in obtaining patents or meeting other legal requirements. Prepare and administer budget, approve and review expenditures, and prepare financial reports. Make presentations at professional meetings to further knowledge in the field.

Job Specializations

Clinical Research Coordinators. Plan, direct, or coordinate clinical research projects. Direct

Enterprising

the activities of workers engaged in clinical research projects to ensure compliance with protocols and overall clinical objectives. May evaluate and analyze clinical data. Solicit industry-sponsored trials through contacts and professional organizations. Review scientific literature, participate in continuing education activities, or attend conferences and seminars to maintain current knowledge of clinical studies affairs and issues. Register protocol patients with appropriate statistical centers as required. Prepare for or participate in quality assurance audits conducted by study sponsors, federal agencies, or specially designated review groups. Participate in preparation and management of research budgets and monetary disbursements. Perform specific protocol procedures such as interviewing subjects, taking vital signs, and performing electrocardiograms. Interpret protocols and advise treating physicians on appropriate dosage modifications or treatment calculations based on patient characteristics. Develop advertising and other informational materials to be used in subject recruitment. Contact industry representatives to ensure equipment and software specifications necessary for successful study completion. Confer with health care professionals to determine the best recruitment practices for studies. Track enrollment status of subjects and document dropout information such as dropout causes and subject contact efforts. Review proposed study protocols to evaluate factors such as sample collection processes, data management plans, and potential subject risks. Record adverse event and side effect data and confer with investigators regarding the reporting of events to oversight agencies. Prepare study-related documentation such as protocol worksheets, procedural manuals, adverse event reports, institutional review board documents, and progress reports. Participate in the development of study protocols including guidelines for administration or data collection procedures. Oversee subject enrollment to ensure that informed consent is properly obtained and documented. Order drugs or devices necessary for study completion.

Water Resource Specialists. Design or implement programs and strategies related to water resource issues, such as supply, quality, and regulatory compliance issues. Supervise teams of workers who capture water from wells and rivers. Review or evaluate designs for water detention facilities, storm drains, flood control facilities, or other hydraulic structures. Negotiate for water rights with communities or water facilities to meet water supply demands. Perform hydrologic, hydraulic, or water quality modeling. Compile water resource data, using geographic information systems (GIS) or global position systems (GPS) software. Compile and maintain documentation on the health of a body of water. Write proposals, project reports, informational brochures, or other documents on wastewater purification, water supply and demand, or other water resource subjects. Recommend new or revised policies, procedures, or regulations to support water resource or conservation goals. Provide technical expertise to assist communities in the development or implementation of storm water monitoring or other water programs. Present water resource proposals to government, public interest groups, or community groups. Identify methods for distributing purified wastewater into rivers, streams, or oceans. Monitor water use, demand, or quality in a particular geographic area. Identify and characterize specific causes or sources of water pollution. Develop plans to protect watershed health or rehabilitate watersheds. Develop or implement standardized water monitoring and assessment methods. Conduct technical studies for water resources on topics such as pollutants and water treatment options. Conduct, or oversee the conduct of, investigations on matters such as water storage, wastewater discharge, pollutants, permits, or other compliance and regulatory issues. Conduct cost-benefit studies for watershed improvement projects or water management alternatives.

Analyze storm water systems to identify opportunities for water resource improvements.

Botany

Personality Type: Enterprising–Investigative

Useful Facts About the Major

Focuses on the scientific study of plants, related microbial organisms, and plant habitats and ecosystem relations.

Related CIP Program: 26.0301 Botany/Plant Biology

Specializations in the Major: Forestry, plant genetics, phytopathology (plant disease).

Typical Sequence of College Courses: English composition, calculus, introduction to computer science, general chemistry, statistics, general biology, organic chemistry, genetics, general physics, cell biology, introduction to biochemistry, general microbiology, taxonomy of flowering plants, ecology, plant anatomy, plant physiology.

Typical Sequence of High School Courses: English, algebra, biology, geometry, trigonometry, chemistry, physics, pre-calculus, computer science, calculus.

Career Snapshot

Botany is the science of plants. Since all of our food resources and the very air we breathe ultimately depend on the growth of plants, botany is a vital field of knowledge. A bachelor's degree in this field prepares you for some nonresearch jobs in industry, agriculture, forestry, and environmental protection. Best opportunities are in agricultural research, where a graduate degree is expected.

Useful Averages for the Related Jobs

❋ Annual Earnings: $115,000
❋ Growth: 15.5%
❋ Openings: 2,010
❋ Self-Employed: 0.0%
❋ Verbal Skill Rating: 58
❋ Math Skill Rating: 65

Other Details About the Related Jobs

Career Clusters: 04 Business, Management, and Administration; 15 Science, Technology, Engineering, and Mathematics. **Career Pathways:** 04.2 Business, Financial Management, and Accounting; 04.4 Business Analysis; 15.2 Science and Mathematics.

Skills: Science, operations analysis, management of financial resources, technology design, management of personnel resources, mathematics, time management, reading comprehension. **Work Conditions:** Indoors; sitting; hazardous conditions; exposed to disease or infections.

Related Jobs

Natural Sciences Managers

Personality Type: Enterprising–Investigative

Earnings: $114,560
Growth: 15.4%
Annual Openings: 2,010

Most Common Education/Training Level: Bachelor's or higher degree plus work experience

Plan, direct, or coordinate activities in such fields as life sciences, physical sciences, mathematics,

Enterprising

and statistics and research and development in these fields. Confer with scientists, engineers, regulators, and others to plan and review projects and to provide technical assistance. Develop client relationships and communicate with clients to explain proposals, present research findings, establish specifications, or discuss project status. Plan and direct research, development, and production activities. Prepare project proposals. Design and coordinate successive phases of problem analysis, solution proposals, and testing. Review project activities and prepare and review research, testing, and operational reports. Hire, supervise, and evaluate engineers, technicians, researchers, and other staff. Determine scientific and technical goals within broad outlines provided by top management and make detailed plans to accomplish these goals. Develop and implement policies, standards, and procedures for the architectural, scientific, and technical work performed to ensure regulatory compliance and operations enhancement. Develop innovative technology and train staff for its implementation. Provide for stewardship of plant and animal resources and habitats, studying land use; monitoring animal populations; and providing shelter, resources, and medical treatment for animals. Conduct own research in field of expertise. Recruit personnel and oversee the development and maintenance of staff competence. Advise and assist in obtaining patents or meeting other legal requirements. Prepare and administer budget, approve and review expenditures, and prepare financial reports. Make presentations at professional meetings to further knowledge in the field.

Job Specializations

Clinical Research Coordinators. Plan, direct, or coordinate clinical research projects. Direct the activities of workers engaged in clinical research projects to ensure compliance with protocols and overall clinical objectives. May evaluate and analyze clinical data. Solicit industry-sponsored trials through contacts and professional organizations. Review scientific literature, participate in continuing education activities, or attend conferences and seminars to maintain current knowledge of clinical studies affairs and issues. Register protocol patients with appropriate statistical centers as required. Prepare for or participate in quality assurance audits conducted by study sponsors, federal agencies, or specially designated review groups. Participate in preparation and management of research budgets and monetary disbursements. Perform specific protocol procedures such as interviewing subjects, taking vital signs, and performing electrocardiograms. Interpret protocols and advise treating physicians on appropriate dosage modifications or treatment calculations based on patient characteristics. Develop advertising and other informational materials to be used in subject recruitment. Contact industry representatives to ensure equipment and software specifications necessary for successful study completion. Confer with health care professionals to determine the best recruitment practices for studies. Track enrollment status of subjects and document dropout information such as dropout causes and subject contact efforts. Review proposed study protocols to evaluate factors such as sample collection processes, data management plans, and potential subject risks. Record adverse event and side effect data and confer with investigators regarding the reporting of events to oversight agencies. Prepare study-related documentation such as protocol worksheets, procedural manuals, adverse event reports, institutional review board documents, and progress reports. Participate in the development of study protocols including guidelines for administration or data collection procedures. Oversee subject enrollment to ensure that informed consent is properly obtained and documented. Order drugs or devices necessary for study completion.

Water Resource Specialists. Design or implement programs and strategies related to water resource issues, such as supply, quality, and

regulatory compliance issues. Supervise teams of workers who capture water from wells and rivers. Review or evaluate designs for water detention facilities, storm drains, flood control facilities, or other hydraulic structures. Negotiate for water rights with communities or water facilities to meet water supply demands. Perform hydrologic, hydraulic, or water quality modeling. Compile water resource data, using geographic information systems (GIS) or global position systems (GPS) software. Compile and maintain documentation on the health of a body of water. Write proposals, project reports, informational brochures, or other documents on wastewater purification, water supply and demand, or other water resource subjects. Recommend new or revised policies, procedures, or regulations to support water resource or conservation goals. Provide technical expertise to assist communities in the development or implementation of storm water monitoring or other water programs. Present water resource proposals to government, public interest groups, or community groups. Identify methods for distributing purified wastewater into rivers, streams, or oceans. Monitor water use, demand, or quality in a particular geographic area. Identify and characterize specific causes or sources of water pollution. Develop plans to protect watershed health or rehabilitate watersheds. Develop or implement standardized water monitoring and assessment methods. Conduct technical studies for water resources on topics such as pollutants and water treatment options. Conduct, or oversee the conduct of, investigations on matters such as water storage, wastewater discharge, pollutants, permits, or other compliance and regulatory issues. Conduct cost-benefit studies for watershed improvement projects or water management alternatives. Analyze storm water systems to identify opportunities for water resource improvements.

Business Management

Personality Type: Enterprising–Conventional

Useful Facts About the Major

Prepares individuals to plan, organize, direct, and control the functions and processes of a firm or organization.

Related CIP Program: 52.0201 Business Administration and Management, General

Specializations in the Major: Marketing, management, operations, international business.

Typical Sequence of College Courses: English composition, business writing, introduction to psychology, principles of microeconomics, principles of macroeconomics, calculus for business and social sciences, statistics for business and social sciences, introduction to management information systems, introduction to accounting, legal environment of business, principles of management and organization, operations management, strategic management, business finance, introduction to marketing, organizational behavior, human resource management, international management, organizational theory.

Typical Sequence of High School Courses: English, algebra, geometry, trigonometry, science, foreign language, computer science, public speaking.

Career Snapshot

Students of business management learn about the principles of economics, the legal and social environment in which business operates, and quantitative methods for measuring and projecting business activity. Graduates may enter the business world directly or pursue a master's degree. Some get a bachelor's degree in a nonbusiness field and enter a master's of business administration program after getting some entry-level work experience.

Enterprising

Useful Averages for the Related Jobs

- ❀ Annual Earnings: $116,000
- ❀ Growth: 2.1%
- ❀ Openings: 28,909
- ❀ Self-Employed: 12.4%
- ❀ Verbal Skill Rating: 58
- ❀ Math Skill Rating: 61

Other Details About the Related Jobs

Career Clusters: 02 Architecture and Construction; 04 Business, Management, and Administration; 07 Government and Public Administration; 10 Human Services; 13 Manufacturing; 14 Marketing, Sales, and Service; 15 Science, Technology, Engineering, and Mathematics; 16 Transportation, Distribution, and Logistics. **Career Pathways:** 02.2 Construction; 04.1 Management; 07.1 Governance; 07.3 Foreign Service; 07.6 Regulation; 07.7 Public Management and Administration; 10.3 Family and Community Services; 10.5 Consumer Services Career; 13.1 Production; 14.1 Management and Entrepreneurship; 14.4 Marketing Communications and Promotion; 15.1 Engineering and Technology; 16.1 Transportation Operations; 16.2 Logistics, Planning, and Management Services.

Skills: Management of financial resources, management of material resources, operations analysis, management of personnel resources, systems analysis, systems evaluation, persuasion, negotiation. **Work Conditions:** Indoors; sitting; in a vehicle.

Related Jobs

1. Administrative Services Managers

Personality Type: Enterprising–Conventional

Earnings: $75,520
Growth: 12.5%
Annual Openings: 8,660

Most Common Education/Training Level: Bachelor's degree

Plan, direct, or coordinate supportive services of an organization, such as recordkeeping, mail distribution, telephone operator/receptionist, and other office support services. May oversee facilities planning and maintenance and custodial operations. Direct or coordinate the supportive services department of a business, agency, or organization. Prepare and review operational reports and schedules to ensure accuracy and efficiency. Set goals and deadlines for the department. Acquire, distribute and store supplies. Analyze internal processes and recommend and implement procedural or policy changes to improve operations, such as supply changes or the disposal of records. Plan, administer and control budgets for contracts, equipment and supplies. Monitor the facility to ensure that it remains safe, secure, and well-maintained. Hire and terminate clerical and administrative personnel. Oversee the maintenance and repair of machinery, equipment, and electrical and mechanical systems. Oversee construction and renovation projects to improve efficiency and to ensure that facilities meet environmental, health, and security standards, and comply with government regulations. Conduct classes to teach procedures to staff. Participate in architectural and engineering planning and design, including space and installation management. Manage leasing of facility space. Dispose of, or oversee the disposal of, surplus or unclaimed property.

2. Chief Executives

Personality Type: Enterprising–Conventional

Earnings: $160,720
Growth: –1.4%
Annual Openings: 11,250

Most Common Education/Training Level:
Bachelor's or higher degree plus work experience

Determine and formulate policies and provide the overall direction of companies or private and public sector organizations within the guidelines set up by a board of directors or similar governing body. Plan, direct, or coordinate operational activities at the highest level of management with the help of subordinate executives and staff managers. Direct and coordinate an organization's financial and budget activities in order to fund operations, maximize investments, and increase efficiency. Confer with board members, organization officials, and staff members to discuss issues, coordinate activities, and resolve problems. Analyze operations to evaluate performance of a company and its staff in meeting objectives and to determine areas of potential cost reduction, program improvement, or policy change. Direct, plan, and implement policies, objectives, and activities of organizations or businesses in order to ensure continuing operations, to maximize returns on investments, and to increase productivity. Prepare budgets for approval, including those for funding and implementation of programs. Direct and coordinate activities of businesses or departments concerned with production, pricing, sales, and/or distribution of products. Negotiate or approve contracts and agreements with suppliers, distributors, federal and state agencies, and other organizational entities. Review reports submitted by staff members in order to recommend approval or to suggest changes. Appoint department heads or managers and assign or delegate responsibilities to them. Direct human resources activities, including the approval of human resource plans and activities, the selection of directors and other high-level staff, and establishment and organization of major departments. Preside over or serve on boards of directors, management committees, or other governing boards. Prepare and present reports concerning activities, expenses, budgets, government statutes and rulings, and other items affecting businesses or

program services. Establish departmental responsibilities and coordinate functions among departments and sites. Implement corrective action plans to solve organizational or departmental problems.

Job Specialization

Chief Sustainability Officers. Communicate and coordinate with management, shareholders, customers, and employees to address sustainability issues. Enact or oversee a corporate sustainability strategy. Identify educational, training, or other development opportunities for sustainability employees or volunteers. Identify and evaluate pilot projects or programs to enhance the sustainability research agenda. Conduct sustainability- or environment-related risk assessments. Create and maintain sustainability program documents, such as schedules and budgets. Write project proposals, grant applications, or other documents to pursue funding for environmental initiatives. Supervise employees or volunteers working on sustainability projects. Write and distribute financial or environmental impact reports. Review sustainability program objectives, progress, or status to ensure compliance with policies, standards, regulations, or laws. Formulate or implement sustainability campaign or marketing strategies. Research environmental sustainability issues, concerns, or stakeholder interests. Evaluate and approve proposals for sustainability projects, considering factors such as cost effectiveness, technical feasibility, and integration with other initiatives. Develop sustainability reports, presentations, or proposals for supplier, employee, academia, media, government, public interest, or other groups. Develop, or oversee the development of, sustainability evaluation or monitoring systems. Develop, or oversee the development of, marketing or outreach media for sustainability projects or events. Develop methodologies to assess the viability or success of sustainability initiatives. Monitor and evaluate effectiveness of sustainability programs.

Enterprising

Direct sustainability program operations to ensure compliance with environmental or governmental regulations. Develop or execute strategies to address issues such as energy use, resource conservation, recycling, pollution reduction, waste elimination, transportation, education, and building design.

3. Construction Managers

Personality Type:
Enterprising–Realistic–Conventional

Earnings: $82,330
Growth: 17.2%
Annual Openings: 13,770

Most Common Education/Training Level:
Bachelor's degree

Plan, direct, coordinate, or budget, usually through subordinate supervisory personnel, activities concerned with the construction and maintenance of structures, facilities, and systems. Participate in the conceptual development of a construction project and oversee its organization, scheduling, and implementation. Confer with supervisory personnel, owners, contractors, and design professionals to discuss and resolve matters such as work procedures, complaints, and construction problems. Plan, organize, and direct activities concerned with the construction and maintenance of structures, facilities, and systems. Schedule the project in logical steps and budget time required to meet deadlines. Determine labor requirements and dispatch workers to construction sites. Inspect and review projects to monitor compliance with building and safety codes, and other regulations. Interpret and explain plans and contract terms to administrative staff, workers, and clients, representing the owner or developer. Prepare contracts and negotiate revisions, changes and additions to contractual agreements with architects, consultants, clients, suppliers and subcontractors. Obtain all necessary permits and licenses. Direct and supervise workers. Study job specifications to

determine appropriate construction methods. Select, contract, and oversee workers who complete specific pieces of the project, such as painting or plumbing. Requisition supplies and materials to complete construction projects. Prepare and submit budget estimates and progress and cost tracking reports. Take actions to deal with the results of delays, bad weather, or emergencies at construction site. Develop and implement quality control programs. Investigate damage, accidents, or delays at construction sites, to ensure that proper procedures are being carried out. Evaluate construction methods and determine cost-effectiveness of plans, using computers. Direct acquisition of land for construction projects.

4. Cost Estimators

Personality Type: Conventional–Enterprising

Earnings: $57,300
Growth: 25.3%
Annual Openings: 10,360

Most Common Education/Training Level:
Bachelor's degree

Prepare cost estimates for product manufacturing, construction projects, or services to aid management in bidding on or determining prices of products or services. May specialize according to particular service performed or type of product manufactured. Analyze blueprints and other documentation to prepare time, cost, materials, and labor estimates. Assess cost effectiveness of products, projects or services, tracking actual costs relative to bids as the project develops. Consult with clients, vendors, personnel in other departments or construction foremen to discuss and formulate estimates and resolve issues. Confer with engineers, architects, owners, contractors and subcontractors on changes and adjustments to cost estimates. Prepare estimates used by management for purposes such as planning, organizing, and scheduling work. Prepare estimates for use in selecting vendors or subcontractors. Review material and labor requirements to decide whether it is more cost-effective to produce or purchase components. Prepare cost and expenditure statements and other necessary documentation at regular intervals for the duration of the project. Prepare and maintain a directory of suppliers, contractors and subcontractors. Set up cost monitoring and reporting systems and procedures. Establish and maintain tendering process, and conduct negotiations. Conduct special studies to develop and establish standard hour and related cost data or to effect cost reduction. Visit site and record information about access, drainage and topography, and availability of services such as water and electricity.

5. General and Operations Managers

Personality Type:
Enterprising–Conventional–Social

Earnings: $92,650
Growth: –0.1%
Annual Openings: 50,220

Most Common Education/Training Level:
Work experience in a related occupation

Plan, direct, or coordinate the operations of companies or public- and private-sector organizations. Duties and responsibilities include formulating policies, managing daily operations, and planning the use of materials and human resources, but are too diverse and general in nature to be classified in any one functional area of management or administration, such as personnel, purchasing, or administrative services. Includes owners and managers who head small business establishments whose duties are primarily managerial. Direct and coordinate activities of businesses or departments concerned with the production, pricing, sales, or distribution of products. Manage staff, preparing work schedules and assigning specific duties. Review financial statements, sales and activity reports, and other performance data to measure productivity and goal achievement and to determine areas needing

cost reduction and program improvement. Establish and implement departmental policies, goals, objectives, and procedures, conferring with board members, organization officials, and staff members as necessary. Determine staffing requirements, and interview, hire and train new employees, or oversee those personnel processes. Monitor businesses and agencies to ensure that they efficiently and effectively provide needed services while staying within budgetary limits. Oversee activities directly related to making products or providing services. Direct and coordinate organization's financial and budget activities to fund operations, maximize investments, and increase efficiency. Determine goods and services to be sold, and set prices and credit terms, based on forecasts of customer demand. Manage the movement of goods into and out of production facilities. Locate, select, and procure merchandise for resale, representing management in purchase negotiations. Perform sales floor work such as greeting and assisting customers, stocking shelves, and taking inventory. Develop and implement product marketing strategies including advertising campaigns and sales promotions. Plan and direct activities such as sales promotions, coordinating with other department heads as required. Direct non-merchandising departments of businesses, such as advertising and purchasing. Recommend locations for new facilities or oversee the remodeling of current facilities. Plan store layouts, and design displays.

6. Industrial Production Managers

Personality Type: Enterprising–Conventional

Earnings: $85,080
Growth: –7.6%
Annual Openings: 5,470

Most Common Education/Training Level:
Work experience in a related occupation

Plan, direct, or coordinate the work activities and resources necessary for manufacturing products in accordance with specifications

for cost, quality, and quantity. Direct and co-ordinate production, processing, distribution, and marketing activities of industrial organization. Review processing schedules and production orders to make decisions concerning inventory requirements, staffing requirements, work procedures, and duty assignments, considering budgetary limitations and time constraints. Review operations and confer with technical or administrative staff to resolve production or processing problems. Develop and implement production tracking and quality control systems, analyzing reports on production, quality control, maintenance, and other aspects of operations to detect problems. Hire, train, evaluate, and discharge staff, and resolve personnel grievances. Set and monitor product standards, examining samples of raw products or directing testing during processing, to ensure finished products are of prescribed quality. Prepare and maintain production reports and personnel records. Coordinate and recommend procedures for maintenance or modification of facilities and equipment, including the replacement of machines. Initiate and coordinate inventory and cost control programs. Institute employee suggestion or involvement programs. Maintain current knowledge of the quality control field, relying on current literature pertaining to materials use, technological advances, and statistical studies. Review plans and confer with research and support staff to develop new products and processes. Develop budgets and approve expenditures for supplies, materials, and human resources, ensuring that materials, labor, and equipment are used efficiently to meet production targets. Negotiate prices of materials with suppliers.

Job Specializations

Biofuels Production Managers. Manage operations at biofuel power-generation facilities. Collect and process information on plant performance, diagnose problems, and design corrective procedures. Provide training to subordinate or new employees to improve biofuels plant safety or increase the production of biofuels. Provide direction to employees to ensure compliance with biofuels plant safety, environmental, or operational standards and regulations. Monitor transportation and storage of flammable or other potentially dangerous feedstocks or products to ensure adherence to safety guidelines. Draw samples of biofuels products or secondary by-products for quality control testing. Confer with technical and supervisory personnel to report or resolve conditions affecting biofuels plant safety, operational efficiency, and product quality. Supervise production employees in the manufacturing of biofuels, such as biodiesel or ethanol. Shut down and re-start biofuels plant or equipment in emergency situations or for equipment maintenance, repairs, or replacements. Review logs, datasheets, or reports to ensure adequate production levels or to identify abnormalities with biofuels production equipment or processes. Prepare and manage biofuels plant or unit budgets. Monitor meters, flow gauges, or other real-time data to ensure proper operation of biofuels production equipment, implementing corrective measures as needed. Conduct cost, material, and efficiency studies for biofuels production plants or operations. Approve proposals for the acquisition, replacement, or repair of biofuels processing equipment or the implementation of new production processes. Adjust temperature, pressure, vacuum, level, flow rate, or transfer of biofuels to maintain processes at required levels. Manage operations at biofuels power generation facilities, including production, shipping, maintenance, or quality assurance activities.

Biomass Production Managers. Manage operations at biomass power-generation facilities. Direct work activities at plant, including supervision of operations and maintenance staff. Test, maintain, or repair electrical power distribution machinery or equipment, using hand tools, power tools, and testing devices. Manage parts and supply inventories for biomass plants. Monitor and operate communications systems, such as mobile radios. Compile and record operational data on forms or in log books. Adjust equipment controls to generate specified amounts of electrical power. Supervise operations or maintenance employees in the production of power from biomass such as wood, coal, paper sludge, or other waste or refuse. Shut down and restart biomass power plants or equipment in emergency situations or for equipment maintenance, repairs, or replacements. Review logs, datasheets, or reports to ensure adequate production levels and safe production environments or to identify abnormalities with power production equipment or processes. Review biomass operations performance specifications to ensure compliance with regulatory requirements. Prepare reports on biomass plant operations, status, maintenance, and other information. Prepare and manage biomass plant budgets. Plan and schedule plant activities such as wood, waste, or refuse fuel deliveries, ash removal, and regular maintenance. Operate controls to start, stop, or regulate biomass-fueled generators, generator units, boilers, engines, or auxiliary systems. Inspect biomass gasification processes, equipment, and facilities for ways to maximize capacity and minimize operating costs. Evaluate power production or demand trends to identify opportunities for improved operations. Supervise biomass plant or substation operations, maintenance, repair, or testing activities. Monitor the operating status of biomass plants by observing control system parameters, distributed control systems, switchboard gauges, dials, or other indicators. Conduct field inspections of biomass plants, stations, or substations to ensure normal and safe operating conditions.

Geothermal Production Managers. Manage operations at geothermal power generation facilities. Maintain and monitor geothermal plant equipment for efficient and safe plant operations. Conduct well field site assessments. Select and implement corrosion control or mitigation

systems for geothermal plants. Communicate geothermal plant conditions to employees. Troubleshoot and make minor repairs to geothermal plant instrumentation or electrical systems. Record, review or maintain daily logs, reports, maintenance, and other records associated with geothermal operations. Prepare environmental permit applications or compliance reports. Obtain permits for constructing, upgrading, or operating geothermal power plants. Perform or direct the performance of preventative maintenance on geothermal plant equipment. Negotiate interconnection agreements with other utilities. Monitor geothermal operations, using programmable logic controllers. Identify opportunities to improve plant electrical equipment, controls, or process control methodologies. Identify and evaluate equipment, procedural, or conditional inefficiencies involving geothermal plant systems. Develop operating plans and schedules for geothermal operations. Develop or manage budgets for geothermal operations. Supervise employees in geothermal power plants or well fields. Oversee geothermal plant operations, maintenance, and repairs to ensure compliance with applicable standards or regulations. Inspect geothermal plant or injection well fields to verify proper equipment operations.

Hydroelectric Production Managers. Manage operations at hydroelectric power-generation facilities. Maintain and monitor hydroelectric plant equipment for efficient and safe plant operations. Develop or implement policy evaluation procedures for hydroelectric generation activities. Provide technical direction in the erection and commissioning of hydroelectric equipment and supporting electrical or mechanical systems. Develop and implement projects to improve efficiency, economy, or effectiveness of hydroelectric plant operations. Supervise hydropower plant equipment installations, upgrades, or maintenance. Respond to problems related to ratepayers, water users, power users, government agencies, educational institutions, and other private and public power

Enterprising

resource interests. Plan or manage hydroelectric plant upgrades. Plan and coordinate hydroelectric production operations to meet customer requirements. Perform or direct preventive or corrective containment and cleanup to protect the environment. Operate energized high- and low-voltage hydroelectric power transmission system substations according to procedures and safety requirements. Negotiate power generation contracts with other public or private utilities. Maintain records of hydroelectric facility operations, maintenance, or repairs. Monitor or inspect hydroelectric equipment, such as hydro-turbines, generators, and control systems. Inspect hydroelectric facilities, including switchyards, control houses, or relay houses, for normal operation and adherence to safety standards. Identify and communicate power system emergencies. Develop or review budgets, annual plans, power contracts, power rates, standing operating procedures, power reviews, or engineering studies. Create and enforce hydrostation voltage schedules. Check hydroelectric operations for compliance with prescribed operating limits, such as loads, voltages, temperatures, lines, and equipment. Supervise or monitor hydroelectric facility operations to ensure that generation and mechanical equipment conform to applicable regulations or standards. Direct operations, maintenance, or repair of hydroelectric power facilities.

Methane/Landfill Gas Collection System Operators. Direct daily operations, maintenance, or repair of landfill gas projects, including maintenance of daily logs, determination of service priorities, and compliance with reporting requirements. Track volume and weight of landfill waste. Recommend or implement practices to reduce turnaround time for trucks in and out of landfill site. Prepare reports on landfill operations and gas collection system productivity or efficiency. Diagnose or troubleshoot gas collection equipment and programmable logic controller (PLC) systems. Coordinate the repair, overhaul, or routine maintenance of diesel engines used in landfill operations.

Read meters, gauges, or automatic recording devices at specified intervals to verify gas collection systems operating conditions. Supervise landfill, well field, and other subordinate employees. Prepare and manage landfill gas collection system budgets. Prepare soil reports as required by regulatory or permitting agencies. Oversee landfill gas collection system construction, maintenance, and repair activities. Optimize gas collection landfill operational costs and productivity consistent with safety and environmental rules and regulations. Monitor landfill permit requirements for updates. Operate computerized control panels to manage gas compression operations. Monitor gas collection systems emissions data, including biomethane or nitrous oxide levels. Maintain records for landfill gas collection systems to demonstrate compliance with safety and environmental laws, regulations, or policies. Inspect landfill or conduct site audits to ensure adherence to safety and environmental regulations. Implement landfill operational and emergency procedures. Develop or enforce procedures for normal operation, start-up, or shutdown of methane gas collection systems. Evaluate landfill gas collection service requirements to meet operational plans and productivity goals. Oversee gas collection landfill operations, including leachate and gas management or rail operations. Monitor and control liquid or gas landfill extraction systems.

Quality Control Systems Managers. Plan, direct, or coordinate quality assurance programs. Formulate quality control policies and control quality of laboratory and production efforts. Stop production if serious product defects are present. Review and approve quality plans submitted by contractors. Review statistical studies, technological advances, or regulatory standards and trends to stay abreast of issues in the field of quality control. Generate and maintain quality control operating budgets. Evaluate new testing and sampling methodologies or technologies to determine usefulness. Coordinate the selection and implementation of quality control equipment such as inspection gauges. Collect and analyze production samples to evaluate quality. Audit and inspect subcontractor facilities including external laboratories. Verify that raw materials, purchased parts or components, in-process samples, and finished products meet established testing and inspection standards. Review quality documentation necessary for regulatory submissions and inspections. Review and update standard operating procedures or quality assurance manuals. Produce reports regarding nonconformance of products or processes, daily production quality, root cause analyses, or quality trends. Participate in the development of product specifications. Monitor development of new products to help identify possible problems for mass production. Instruct vendors or contractors on quality guidelines, testing procedures, or ways to eliminate deficiencies. Identify quality problems or areas for improvement and recommend solutions. Instruct staff in quality control and analytical procedures. Identify critical points in the manufacturing process and specify sampling procedures to be used at these points. Document testing procedures, methodologies, or criteria. Direct the tracking of defects, test results, or other regularly reported quality control data. Create and implement inspection and testing criteria or procedures. Confer with marketing and sales departments to define client requirements and expectations.

7. Management Analysts

Personality Type:
Investigative–Enterprising–Conventional

Earnings: $75,250
Growth: 23.9%
Annual Openings: 30,650

Most Common Education/Training Level:
Work experience in a related occupation

Conduct organizational studies and evaluations, design systems and procedures, conduct work simplifications and measurement studies, **and prepare operations and procedures manuals to assist management in operating more efficiently and effectively. Includes program analysts and management consultants.** Gather and organize information on problems or procedures. Analyze data gathered and develop solutions or alternative methods of proceeding. Confer with personnel concerned to ensure successful functioning of newly implemented systems or procedures. Develop and implement records management program for filing, protection, and retrieval of records and assure compliance with program. Review forms and reports and confer with management and users about format, distribution, and purpose and to identify problems and improvements. Document findings of study and prepare recommendations for implementation of new systems, procedures, or organizational changes. Interview personnel and conduct on-site observation to ascertain unit functions; work performed; and methods, equipment, and personnel used. Prepare manuals and train workers in use of new forms, reports, procedures, or equipment according to organizational policy. Design, evaluate, recommend, and approve changes of forms and reports. Plan study of work problems and procedures, such as organizational change, communications, information flow, integrated production methods, inventory control, or cost analysis. Recommend purchase of storage equipment and design area layout to locate equipment in space available.

8. Sales Managers

Personality Type: Enterprising–Conventional

Earnings: $96,790
Growth: 14.9%
Annual Openings: 12,660

Most Common Education/Training Level:
Work experience in a related occupation

Direct the actual distribution or movement of products or services to customers. Coordinate sales distribution by establishing sales

Enterprising

territories, quotas, and goals, and establish training programs for sales representatives. Analyze sales statistics gathered by staff to determine sales potential and inventory requirements and monitor customer preferences. Resolve customer complaints regarding sales and service. Monitor customer preferences to determine focus of sales efforts. Direct and coordinate activities involving sales of manufactured products, services, commodities, real estate or other subjects of sale. Determine price schedules and discount rates. Review operational records and reports to project sales and determine profitability. Direct, coordinate, and review activities in sales and service accounting and recordkeeping, and in receiving and shipping operations. Confer or consult with department heads to plan advertising services and to secure information on equipment and customer specifications. Advise dealers and distributors on policies and operating procedures to ensure functional effectiveness of business. Prepare budgets and approve budget expenditures. Represent company at trade association meetings to promote products. Plan and direct staffing, training, and performance evaluations to develop and control sales and service programs. Visit franchised dealers to stimulate interest in establishment or expansion of leasing programs. Confer with potential customers regarding equipment needs and advise customers on types of equipment to purchase. Oversee regional and local sales managers and their staffs. Direct clerical staff to keep records of export correspondence, bid requests, and credit collections, and to maintain current information on tariffs, licenses, and restrictions. Direct foreign sales and service outlets of an organization. Assess marketing potential of new and existing store locations, considering statistics and expenditures.

9. Social and Community Service Managers

Personality Type: Enterprising–Social

Earnings: $56,600
Growth: 13.8%
Annual Openings: 4,820

Most Common Education/Training Level:
Work experience in a related occupation

Plan, organize, or coordinate the activities of a social service program or community outreach organization. Oversee the program or organization's budget and policies regarding participant involvement, program requirements, and benefits. Work may involve directing social workers, counselors, or probation officers. Evaluate the work of staff and volunteers to ensure that programs are of appropriate quality and that resources are used effectively. Provide direct service and support to individuals or clients, such as handling a referral for child advocacy issues, conducting a needs evaluation, or resolving complaints. Recruit, interview, and hire or sign up volunteers and staff. Establish and maintain relationships with other agencies and organizations in community to meet community needs and to ensure that services are not duplicated. Establish and oversee administrative procedures to meet objectives set by boards of directors or senior management. Direct activities of professional and technical staff members and volunteers. Plan and administer budgets for programs, equipment and support services. Participate in the determination of organizational policies regarding such issues as participant eligibility, program requirements, and program benefits. Prepare and maintain records and reports, such as budgets, personnel records, or training manuals. Research and analyze member or community needs to determine program directions and goals. Implement and evaluate staff, volunteer, or community training programs. Represent organizations in relations with governmental and media institutions. Act as consultants to agency staff and other community programs regarding the interpretation of program-related federal, state, and county regulations and policies. Speak to community groups to explain and interpret agency purposes, programs, and policies. Direct fundraising activities and the preparation of public relations materials. Analyze proposed legislation, regulations, or rule changes to determine how agency services could be impacted.

10. Transportation, Storage, and Distribution Managers

Personality Type: Enterprising–Conventional

Earnings: $79,490
Growth: –5.3%
Annual Openings: 2,740

Most Common Education/Training Level:
Bachelor's or higher degree plus work experience

Plan, direct, or coordinate transportation, storage, or distribution activities in accordance with governmental policies and regulations. No task data available.

Job Specializations

Storage and Distribution Managers. Plan, direct, and coordinate the storage and distribution operations within organizations or the activities of organizations that are engaged in storing and distributing materials and products. Supervise the activities of workers engaged in receiving, storing, testing, and shipping products or materials. Plan, develop, and implement warehouse safety and security programs and activities. Review invoices, work orders, consumption reports, and demand forecasts to estimate peak delivery periods and to issue work assignments. Schedule and monitor air or surface pickup, delivery, or distribution of products or materials. Interview, select, and train warehouse and supervisory personnel. Confer with department heads to coordinate warehouse activities, such as production, sales, records control, and purchasing. Respond to customers' or shippers' questions and complaints regarding storage and distribution services. Inspect physical conditions of warehouses, vehicle fleets

and equipment, and order testing, maintenance, repair, or replacement as necessary. Develop and document standard and emergency operating procedures for receiving, handling, storing, shipping, or salvaging products or materials. Examine products or materials to estimate quantities or weight and type of container required for storage or transport. Issue shipping instructions and provide routing information to ensure that delivery times and locations are coordinated. Negotiate with carriers, warehouse operators and insurance company representatives for services and preferential rates. Examine invoices and shipping manifests for conformity to tariff and customs regulations. Prepare and manage departmental budgets. Prepare or direct preparation of correspondence, reports, and operations, maintenance, and safety manuals. Arrange for necessary shipping documentation, and contact customs officials to effect release of shipments. Advise sales and billing departments of transportation charges for customers' accounts. Evaluate freight costs and the inventory costs associated with transit times to ensure that costs are appropriate. Participate in setting transportation and service rates.

Transportation Managers. Plan, direct, and coordinate the transportation operations within an organization or the activities of organizations that provide transportation services. Analyze expenditures and other financial information to develop plans, policies, and budgets for increasing profits and improving services. Set operations policies and standards, including determination of safety procedures for the handling of dangerous goods. Plan, organize and manage the work of subordinate staff to ensure that the work is accomplished in a manner consistent with organizational requirements. Negotiate and authorize contracts with equipment and materials suppliers, and monitor contract fulfillment. Collaborate with other managers and staff members to formulate and implement policies, procedures, goals, and objectives. Monitor spending to ensure that expenses are consistent with approved budgets. Supervise workers

Enterprising

assigning tariff classifications and preparing billing. Promote safe work activities by conducting safety audits, attending company safety meetings, and meeting with individual staff members. Direct investigations to verify and resolve customer or shipper complaints. Direct procurement processes including equipment research and testing, vendor contracts, and requisitions approval. Recommend or authorize capital expenditures for acquisition of new equipment or property to increase efficiency and services of operations department. Monitor operations to ensure that staff members comply with administrative policies and procedures, safety rules, union contracts, and government regulations. Direct activities related to dispatching, routing, and tracking transportation vehicles such as aircraft and railroad cars. Direct and coordinate, through subordinates, activities of operations department to obtain use of equipment, facilities, and human resources. Conduct employee training sessions on subjects such as hazardous material handling, employee orientation, quality improvement and computer use. Prepare management recommendations, such as proposed fee and tariff increases or schedule changes. Implement schedule and policy changes.

Health Information Systems Administration

Personality Type:
Enterprising–Social–Conventional

Useful Facts About the Major

Prepares individuals to plan, design, and manage systems, processes, and facilities used to collect, store, secure, retrieve, analyze, and transmit medical records and other health information used by clinical professionals and health-care organizations.

Related CIP Program: 51.0706 Health Information/Medical Records Administration/Administrator

Specializations in the Major: Management, information technology.

Typical Sequence of College Courses: English composition, introduction to computer science, college algebra, oral communication, introduction to psychology, accounting, introduction to business management, statistics for business and social sciences, epidemiology, introduction to medical terminology, financial management of health care, human resource management in health care facilities, legal aspects of health care, American health-care systems, introduction to health records, health data and analysis, clinical classification systems, fundamentals of medical science, health data research, seminar (reporting on research).

Typical Sequence of High School Courses: Algebra, English, geometry, trigonometry, pre-calculus, biology, chemistry, computer science, office computer applications, public speaking, foreign language, social science.

Career Snapshot

Health information systems are needed for much more than billing patients or their HMOs. Many medical discoveries have been made when researchers have examined large collections of health information. Therefore, health information systems administrators must know about the health-care system, about various kinds of diseases and vital statistics, about the latest database technologies, and about how researchers compile data to test hypotheses. Some people enter this field with a bachelor's degree, whereas others get a bachelor's degree in another field (perhaps related to health, information systems, or management) and complete a post-graduate certification program.

Useful Averages for the Related Jobs

- ❋ Annual Earnings: $82,000
- ❋ Growth: 16.0%
- ❋ Openings: 9,940
- ❋ Self-Employed: 6.0%
- ❋ Verbal Skill Rating: 69
- ❋ Math Skill Rating: 58

Other Details About the Related Jobs

Career Cluster: 08 Health Science. **Career Pathways:** 08.1 Therapeutic Services; 08.2 Diagnostics Services; 08.3 Health Informatics.

Skills: Science, operations analysis, management of material resources, systems evaluation, management of personnel resources, management of financial resources, negotiation, instructing. **Work Conditions:** Indoors; sitting; exposed to disease or infections; exposed to radiation; close to co-workers; wear specialized protective or safety equipment; cramped work space, awkward positions; hazardous conditions.

Related Jobs

Medical and Health Services Managers

Personality Type:
Enterprising–Social–Conventional

Earnings: $81,850
Growth: 16.0%
Annual Openings: 9,940

Most Common Education/Training Level:
Bachelor's or higher degree plus work experience

Plan, direct, or coordinate medicine and health services in hospitals, clinics, managed care organizations, public health agencies, or similar organizations. Direct, supervise and evaluate work activities of medical, nursing, technical, clerical, service, maintenance, and other personnel. Establish objectives and evaluative or operational criteria for units they manage. Direct or conduct recruitment, hiring and training of personnel. Develop and maintain computerized record management systems to store and process data such as personnel activities and information, and to produce reports. Develop and implement organizational policies and procedures for the facility or medical unit. Conduct and administer fiscal operations, including accounting, planning budgets, authorizing expenditures, establishing rates for services, and coordinating financial reporting. Establish work schedules and assignments for staff, according to workload, space and equipment availability. Maintain communication between governing boards, medical staff, and department heads by attending board meetings and coordinating interdepartmental functioning. Monitor the use of diagnostic services, inpatient beds, facilities, and staff to ensure effective use of resources and assess the need for additional staff, equipment, and services. Maintain awareness of advances in medicine, computerized diagnostic and treatment equipment, data processing technology, government regulations, health insurance changes, and financing options. Manage change in integrated health care delivery systems, such as work restructuring, technological innovations, and shifts in the focus of care. Prepare activity reports to inform management of the status and implementation plans of programs, services, and quality initiatives. Plan, implement and administer programs and services in a health care or medical facility, including personnel administration, training, and coordination of medical, nursing and physical plant staff.

Job Specialization

Clinical Nurse Specialists. Plan, direct, or coordinate daily patient care activities in a clinical practice. Ensure adherence to established

Enterprising

clinical policies, protocols, regulations, and standards. Collaborate with other health care professionals and service providers to ensure optimal patient care. Provide specialized direct and indirect care to inpatients and outpatients within a designated specialty such as obstetrics, neurology, oncology, or neonatal care. Observe, interview, and assess patients to identify care needs. Read current literature, talk with colleagues, or participate in professional organizations or conferences to keep abreast of developments in nursing. Monitor or evaluate medical conditions of patients in collaboration with other health care professionals. Develop or assist others in development of care and treatment plans. Develop, implement, or evaluate standards of nursing practice in specialty area such as pediatrics, acute care, and geriatrics. Plan, evaluate, or modify treatment programs based on information gathered by observing and interviewing patients, or by analyzing patient records. Make clinical recommendations to physicians, other health care providers, insurance companies, patients, or health care organizations. Identify training needs or conduct training sessions for nursing students or medical staff. Maintain departmental policies, procedures, objectives, or infection control standards. Evaluate the quality and effectiveness of nursing practice or organizational systems. Present clients with information required to make informed health care and treatment decisions. Instruct nursing staff in areas such as the assessment, development, implementation and evaluation of disability, illness, management, technology, or resources. Perform discharge planning for patients. Direct or supervise nursing care staff in the provision of patient therapy. Develop nursing service philosophies, goals, policies, priorities, or procedures. Coordinate or conduct educational programs or in-service training sessions on topics such as clinical procedures.

Human Resources Management

Personality Type:
Enterprising–Social–Conventional

Useful Facts About the Major

Prepares individuals to manage the development of human capital in organizations and to provide related services to individuals and groups.

Related CIP Program: 52.1001 Human Resources Management/Personnel Administration, General

Specializations in the Major: Job analysis, compensation/benefits, labor relations, training.

Typical Sequence of College Courses: English composition, business writing, introduction to psychology, principles of microeconomics, principles of macroeconomics, calculus for business and social sciences, statistics for business and social sciences, introduction to management information systems, introduction to accounting, legal environment of business, principles of management and organization, operations management, strategic management, business finance, introduction to marketing, organizational theory, human resource management, compensation and benefits administration, training and development, employment law, industrial relations and labor management.

Typical Sequence of High School Courses: English, algebra, geometry, trigonometry, science, foreign language, computer science, public speaking.

Career Snapshot

Human resource managers are responsible for attracting the right employees for an organization, training them, keeping them productively employed, and sometimes severing the relationship through outplacement or retirement. Generalists often enter the field with a bachelor's degree, although specialists may find a master's degree (or perhaps a law degree) advantageous. Generalists most often find entry-level work with small organizations. There is a trend toward outsourcing many specialized functions, such as training and outplacement, to specialized service firms.

Useful Averages for the Related Jobs

- ✱ Annual Earnings: $49,000
- ✱ Growth: 26.7%
- ✱ Openings: 12,528
- ✱ Self-Employed: 1.5%
- ✱ Verbal Skill Rating: 65
- ✱ Math Skill Rating: 44

Other Details About the Related Jobs

Career Cluster: 04 Business, Management, and Administration. **Career Pathway:** 04.3 Human Resources.

Skills: Science, service orientation, operations analysis, speaking, social perceptiveness, management of personnel resources, writing, active listening. **Work Conditions:** Indoors; sitting.

Related Jobs

1. Compensation and Benefits Managers

Personality Type:
Enterprising–Conventional–Social

Earnings: $88,050
Growth: 8.5%
Annual Openings: 1,210

Most Common Education/Training Level: Bachelor's or higher degree plus work experience

Plan, direct, or coordinate compensation and benefits activities and staff of an organization. Advise management on such matters as equal employment opportunity, sexual harassment and discrimination. Direct preparation and distribution of written and verbal information to inform employees of benefits, compensation, and personnel policies. Administer, direct, and review employee benefit programs, including the integration of benefit programs following mergers and acquisitions. Plan and conduct new employee orientations to foster positive attitude toward organizational objectives. Plan, direct, supervise, and coordinate work activities of subordinates and staff relating to employment, compensation, labor relations, and employee relations. Identify and implement benefits to increase the quality of life for employees, by working with brokers and researching benefits issues. Design, evaluate and modify benefits policies to ensure that programs are current, competitive and in compliance with legal requirements. Analyze compensation policies, government regulations, and prevailing wage rates to develop competitive compensation plan. Formulate policies, procedures and programs for recruitment, testing, placement, classification, orientation, benefits and compensation, and labor and industrial relations. Mediate between benefits providers and employees, such as by assisting in handling employees' benefits-related questions or taking suggestions. Fulfill all reporting requirements of all relevant government rules and regulations, including the Employee Retirement Income Security Act (ERISA). Maintain records and compile statistical reports concerning personnel-related data such as hires, transfers, performance appraisals, and absenteeism rates. Analyze statistical data and reports to identify and determine causes of personnel problems and develop recommendations for improvement of organization's personnel policies and practices. Develop methods to improve employment policies, processes, and practices, and recommend changes to management.

Enterprising

2. Compensation, Benefits, and Job Analysis Specialists

Personality Type: Conventional–Enterprising

Earnings: $55,620
Growth: 23.6%
Annual Openings: 6,050

Most Common Education/Training Level:
Bachelor's degree

Conduct programs of compensation and benefits and job analysis for employer. May specialize in specific areas, such as position classification and pension programs. Ensure company compliance with federal and state laws, including reporting requirements. Evaluate job positions, determining classification, exempt or non-exempt status, and salary. Plan, develop, evaluate, improve, and communicate methods and techniques for selecting, promoting, compensating, evaluating, and training workers. Prepare occupational classifications, job descriptions and salary scales. Provide advice on the resolution of classification and salary complaints. Advise managers and employees on state and federal employment regulations, collective agreements, benefit and compensation policies, personnel procedures and classification programs. Prepare reports, such as organization and flow charts, and career path reports, to summarize job analysis and evaluation and compensation analysis information. Perform multifactor data and cost analyses that may be used in areas such as support of collective bargaining agreements. Assess need for and develop job analysis instruments and materials. Observe, interview, and survey employees and conduct focus group meetings to collect job, organizational, and occupational information. Assist in preparing and maintaining personnel records and handbooks. Research job and worker requirements, structural and functional relationships among jobs and occupations, and occupational trends. Administer employee insurance, pension and savings plans, working with insurance brokers and plan carriers. Negotiate collective agreements on behalf of employers or workers, and mediate labor disputes and grievances. Research employee benefit and health and safety practices and recommend changes or modifications to existing policies. Analyze organizational, occupational, and industrial data to facilitate organizational functions and provide technical information to business, industry, and government. Advise staff of individuals' qualifications.

3. Employment, Recruitment, and Placement Specialists

Personality Type:
Enterprising–Social–Conventional

Earnings: $46,200
Growth: 27.9%
Annual Openings: 11,230

Most Common Education/Training Level:
Bachelor's degree

Recruit and place workers. No task data available.

Job Specializations

Employment Interviewers. Interview job applicants in employment office and refer them to prospective employers for consideration. Search application files, notify selected applicants of job openings, and refer qualified applicants to prospective employers. Contact employers to verify referral results. Record and evaluate various pertinent data. Inform applicants of job openings and details such as duties and responsibilities, compensation, benefits, schedules, working conditions, and promotion opportunities. Contact employers to solicit orders for job vacancies, determining their requirements and recording relevant data such as job descriptions. Perform reference and background checks on applicants. Interview job applicants to match their qualifications with employers' needs, recording and evaluating applicant experience, education, training, and skills.

Review employment applications and job orders to match applicants with job requirements, using manual or computerized file searches. Select qualified applicants or refer them to employers, according to organization policy. Provide background information on organizations with which interviews are scheduled. Instruct job applicants in presenting a positive image by providing help with resume writing, personal appearance, and interview techniques. Maintain records of applicants not selected for employment. Evaluate selection and testing techniques by conducting research or follow-up activities and conferring with management and supervisory personnel. Search for and recruit applicants for open positions through campus job fairs and advertisements. Administer assessment tests to identify skill building needs. Hire workers and place them with employers needing temporary help. Refer applicants to services such as vocational counseling, literacy or language instruction, transportation assistance, vocational training and child care. Conduct workshops and demonstrate the use of job listings to assist applicants with skill building. Conduct or arrange for skill, intelligence, or psychological testing of applicants and current employees.

Personnel Recruiters. Seek out, interview, and screen applicants to fill existing and future job openings and promote career opportunities within an organization. Interview applicants to obtain information on work history, training, education, and job skills. Review and evaluate applicant qualifications or eligibility for specified licensing, according to established guidelines and designated licensing codes. Screen and refer applicants to hiring personnel in the organization, making hiring recommendations when appropriate. Contact applicants to inform them of employment possibilities, consideration, and selection. Conduct reference and background checks on applicants. Advise managers and employees on staffing policies and procedures. Inform potential applicants about facilities, operations, benefits, and

job or career opportunities in organizations. Prepare and maintain employment records. Perform searches for qualified candidates according to relevant job criteria, using computer databases, networking, Internet recruiting resources, cold calls, media, recruiting firms, and employee referrals. Hire applicants and authorize paperwork assigning them to positions. Establish and maintain relationships with hiring managers to stay abreast of current and future hiring and business needs. Maintain current knowledge of Equal Employment Opportunity (EEO) and affirmative action guidelines and laws, such as the Americans with Disabilities Act (ADA). Advise management on organizing, preparing, and implementing recruiting and retention programs. Arrange for interviews and provide travel arrangements as necessary. Recruit applicants for open positions, arranging job fairs with college campus representatives. Evaluate recruitment and selection criteria to ensure conformance to professional, statistical, and testing standards, recommending revision as needed. Supervise personnel clerks performing filing, typing and recordkeeping duties. Serve on selection and examination boards to evaluate applicants according to test scores, contacting promising candidates for interviews.

4. Training and Development Managers

Personality Type: Enterprising–Social

Earnings: $88,090
Growth: 11.9%
Annual Openings: 1,010

Most Common Education/Training Level:
Bachelor's or higher degree plus work experience

Plan, direct, or coordinate the training and development activities and staff of organizations. Conduct orientation sessions and arrange on-the-job training for new hires. Evaluate instructor performance and the effectiveness of training programs, providing recommendations for improvement. Develop testing and evaluation

Enterprising

procedures. Conduct or arrange for ongoing technical training and personal development classes for staff members. Confer with management and conduct surveys to identify training needs based on projected production processes, changes, and other factors. Develop and organize training manuals, multimedia visual aids, and other educational materials. Plan, develop, and provide training and staff development programs, using knowledge of the effectiveness of methods such as classroom training, demonstrations, on-the-job training, meetings, conferences, and workshops. Analyze training needs to develop new training programs or modify and improve existing programs. Review and evaluate training and apprenticeship programs for compliance with government standards. Train instructors and supervisors in techniques and skills for training and dealing with employees. Coordinate established courses with technical and professional courses provided by community schools and designate training procedures. Prepare training budget for department or organization.

5. Training and Development Specialists

Personality Type: Social–Artistic–Conventional

Earnings: $52,120
Growth: 23.3%
Annual Openings: 10,710

Most Common Education/Training Level: Bachelor's degree

Conduct training and development programs for employees. Keep up with developments in area of expertise by reading current journals, books and magazine articles. Present information, using a variety of instructional techniques and formats such as role playing, simulations, team exercises, group discussions, videos and lectures. Schedule classes based on availability of classrooms, equipment, and instructors. Organize and develop, or obtain, training procedure manuals and guides and course materials such as handouts and visual materials.

Offer specific training programs to help workers maintain or improve job skills. Monitor, evaluate and record training activities and program effectiveness. Attend meetings and seminars to obtain information for use in training programs, or to inform management of training program status. Coordinate recruitment and placement of training program participants. Develop alternative training methods if expected improvements are not seen. Evaluate training materials prepared by instructors, such as outlines, text, and handouts. Assess training needs through surveys, interviews with employees, focus groups, or consultation with managers, instructors or customer representatives. Screen, hire, and assign workers to positions based on qualifications. Select and assign instructors to conduct training. Devise programs to develop executive potential among employees in lower-level positions. Design, plan, organize and direct orientation and training for employees or customers of industrial or commercial establishment. Negotiate contracts with clients, including desired training outcomes, fees and expenses. Supervise instructors, evaluate instructor performance, and refer instructors to classes for skill development. Monitor training costs to ensure budget is not exceeded, and prepare budget reports to justify expenditures. Refer trainees to employer relations representatives, to locations offering job placement assistance, or to appropriate social services agencies if warranted.

International Business

Personality Type: Investigative–Artistic–Social

Useful Facts About the Major

Prepares individuals to manage international businesses and/or business operations.

Related CIP Program: 52.1101 International Business/Trade/Commerce

Specializations in the Major: A particular aspect of business, a particular part of the world.

Typical Sequence of College Courses: English composition, business writing, introduction to psychology, foreign language, principles of microeconomics, principles of macroeconomics, calculus for business and social sciences, statistics for business and social sciences, introduction to management information systems, introduction to accounting, international management, legal environment of business, principles of management and organization, operations management, international economics, business finance, introduction to marketing, organizational behavior, human resource management, international finance.

Typical Sequence of High School Courses: English, algebra, geometry, trigonometry, science, foreign language, geography, computer science, public speaking.

Career Snapshot

The global economy demands businesspeople who are knowledgeable about other cultures. This major prepares you to work in businesses here and abroad and in the government agencies that deal with them. In addition to studying standard business subjects, you'll probably study or intern abroad to become proficient in a foreign language and gain a global perspective. The work usually requires a lot of travel and a sensitivity to cultural differences.

Useful Averages for the Related Jobs

- ✱ Annual Earnings: $121,000
- ✱ Growth: –0.7%
- ✱ Openings: 23,805
- ✱ Self-Employed: 10.8%
- ✱ Verbal Skill Rating: 58
- ✱ Math Skill Rating: 63

Other Details About the Related Jobs

Career Clusters: 04 Business, Management, and Administration; 07 Government and Public Administration; 10 Human Services; 16 Transportation, Distribution, and Logistics. **Career Pathways:** 04.1 Management; 07.1 Governance; 07.3 Foreign Service; 07.6 Regulation; 10.3 Family and Community Services; 16.2 Logistics, Planning, and Management Services.

Skills: Management of financial resources, management of material resources, management of personnel resources, operations analysis, systems analysis, systems evaluation, persuasion, negotiation. **Work Conditions:** Indoors; in a vehicle; sitting.

Related Jobs

1. Chief Executives

Personality Type: Enterprising–Conventional

Earnings: $160,720
Growth: –1.4%
Annual Openings: 11,250

Most Common Education/Training Level: Bachelor's or higher degree plus work experience

Determine and formulate policies and provide the overall direction of companies or private and public sector organizations within the guidelines set up by a board of directors or similar governing body. Plan, direct, or coordinate operational activities at the highest level of management with the help of subordinate executives and staff managers. Direct and coordinate an organization's financial and budget activities in order to fund operations, maximize investments, and increase efficiency. Confer with board members, organization officials, and staff members to discuss issues, coordinate activities, and resolve problems. Analyze operations to evaluate performance of a company and its staff in meeting objectives and to determine areas of potential cost reduction,

Enterprising

program improvement, or policy change. Direct, plan, and implement policies, objectives, and activities of organizations or businesses in order to ensure continuing operations, to maximize returns on investments, and to increase productivity. Prepare budgets for approval, including those for funding and implementation of programs. Direct and coordinate activities of businesses or departments concerned with production, pricing, sales, and/or distribution of products. Negotiate or approve contracts and agreements with suppliers, distributors, federal and state agencies, and other organizational entities. Review reports submitted by staff members in order to recommend approval or to suggest changes. Appoint department heads or managers and assign or delegate responsibilities to them. Direct human resources activities, including the approval of human resource plans and activities, the selection of directors and other high-level staff, and establishment and organization of major departments. Preside over or serve on boards of directors, management committees, or other governing boards. Prepare and present reports concerning activities, expenses, budgets, government statutes and rulings, and other items affecting businesses or program services. Establish departmental responsibilities and coordinate functions among departments and sites. Implement corrective action plans to solve organizational or departmental problems.

Job Specialization

Chief Sustainability Officers. Communicate and coordinate with management, shareholders, customers, and employees to address sustainability issues. Enact or oversee a corporate sustainability strategy. Identify educational, training, or other development opportunities for sustainability employees or volunteers. Identify and evaluate pilot projects or programs to enhance the sustainability research agenda. Conduct sustainability- or environment-related risk assessments. Create and maintain sustainability

program documents, such as schedules and budgets. Write project proposals, grant applications, or other documents to pursue funding for environmental initiatives. Supervise employees or volunteers working on sustainability projects. Write and distribute financial or environmental impact reports. Review sustainability program objectives, progress, or status to ensure compliance with policies, standards, regulations, or laws. Formulate or implement sustainability campaign or marketing strategies. Research environmental sustainability issues, concerns, or stakeholder interests. Evaluate and approve proposals for sustainability projects, considering factors such as cost effectiveness, technical feasibility, and integration with other initiatives. Develop sustainability reports, presentations, or proposals for supplier, employee, academia, media, government, public interest, or other groups. Develop, or oversee the development of, sustainability evaluation or monitoring systems. Develop, or oversee the development of, marketing or outreach media for sustainability projects or events. Develop methodologies to assess the viability or success of sustainability initiatives. Monitor and evaluate effectiveness of sustainability programs. Direct sustainability program operations to ensure compliance with environmental or governmental regulations. Develop or execute strategies to address issues such as energy use, resource conservation, recycling, pollution reduction, waste elimination, transportation, education, and building design.

2. General and Operations Managers

Personality Type:
Enterprising–Conventional–Social

Earnings: $92,650
Growth: −0.1%
Annual Openings: 50,220

Most Common Education/Training Level:
Bachelor's or higher degree plus work experience

Plan, direct, or coordinate the operations of companies or public- and private-sector organizations. Duties and responsibilities include formulating policies, managing daily operations, and planning the use of materials and human resources, but are too diverse and general in nature to be classified in any one functional area of management or administration, such as personnel, purchasing, or administrative services. Includes owners and managers who head small business establishments whose duties are primarily managerial. Direct and coordinate activities of businesses or departments concerned with the production, pricing, sales, or distribution of products. Manage staff, preparing work schedules and assigning specific duties. Review financial statements, sales and activity reports, and other performance data to measure productivity and goal achievement and to determine areas needing cost reduction and program improvement. Establish and implement departmental policies, goals, objectives, and procedures, conferring with board members, organization officials, and staff members as necessary. Determine staffing requirements, and interview, hire and train new employees, or oversee those personnel processes. Monitor businesses and agencies to ensure that they efficiently and effectively provide needed services while staying within budgetary limits. Oversee activities directly related to making products or providing services. Direct and coordinate organization's financial and budget activities to fund operations, maximize investments, and increase efficiency. Determine goods and services to be sold, and set prices and credit terms, based on forecasts of customer demand. Manage the movement of goods into and out of production facilities. Locate, select, and procure merchandise for resale, representing management in purchase negotiations. Perform sales floor work such as greeting and assisting customers, stocking shelves, and taking inventory. Develop and implement product marketing strategies including advertising campaigns and sales promotions. Plan and direct activities such as sales promotions, coordinating with other department heads as required. Direct non-merchandising departments of businesses, such as advertising and purchasing. Recommend locations for new facilities or oversee the remodeling of current facilities. Plan store layouts, and design displays.

Law

Personality Type: Enterprising–Investigative

Useful Facts About the Major

Prepares individuals for the independent professional practice of law, for taking state and national bar examinations, and for advanced research in jurisprudence.

Related CIP Program: 22.0101 Law (LL.B, J.D.)

Specializations in the Major: Environmental law, international and comparative law, intellectual property, family law, litigation.

Typical Sequence of College Courses: English composition, oral communication, introduction to political science, introduction to philosophy, American history, foreign language, civil procedure, constitutional law, contracts, criminal law, legal communication, legal research, legal writing, property, torts, criminal procedures, evidence, professional responsibility, trusts and estates.

Typical Sequence of High School Courses: Algebra, English, foreign language, social science, history, geometry, public speaking.

Career Snapshot

Lawyers enter their occupation by completing four years of college, three years of law school, and then passing the bar exam. The undergraduate major may be almost anything that contributes to skills in writing and critical thinking. Often the undergraduate major helps open doors to the kinds of careers that will be options after law school—for

Enterprising

example, a bachelor's degree in a business field may help prepare for a career in tax law, labor relations law, or antitrust law. Graduates of law school can expect keen competition for positions as lawyers. Most openings are expected to be for staff lawyers rather than self-employed lawyers. There is a wide gap in earnings, work hours, and stress between lawyers who work in high-powered industries such as finance and those who work in public-interest jobs. Some law school graduates take business and government jobs where they use knowledge of law but do not practice it.

Useful Averages for the Related Jobs

- ❋ Annual Earnings: $112,000
- ❋ Growth: 13.0%
- ❋ Openings: 24,392
- ❋ Self-Employed: 25.9%
- ❋ Verbal Skill Rating: 84
- ❋ Math Skill Rating: 43

Other Details About the Related Jobs

Career Cluster: 12 Law, Public Safety, Corrections, and Security. **Career Pathway:** 12.5 Legal Services.

Skills: Persuasion, negotiation, speaking, writing, critical thinking, judgment and decision making, active learning, active listening. **Work Conditions:** Indoors; sitting; in a vehicle.

Related Jobs

Note: All of the related jobs are often filled by law school graduates. However, several of them do not require a law degree for entry.

1. Administrative Law Judges, Adjudicators, and Hearing Officers

Personality Type:
Enterprising–Investigative–Social

Earnings: $83,920
Growth: 8.0%
Annual Openings: 380

Most Common Education/Training Level: First professional degree

Conduct hearings to decide or recommend decisions on claims concerning government programs or other government-related matters and prepare decisions. Determine penalties or the existence and the amount of liability or recommend the acceptance or rejection of claims or compromise settlements. Prepare written opinions and decisions. Review and evaluate data on documents such as claim applications, birth or death certificates, and physician or employer records. Research and analyze laws, regulations, policies, and precedent decisions to prepare for hearings and to determine conclusions. Confer with individuals or organizations involved in cases to obtain relevant information. Recommend the acceptance or rejection of claims or compromise settlements according to laws, regulations, policies, and precedent decisions. Explain to claimants how they can appeal rulings that go against them. Monitor and direct the activities of trials and hearings to ensure that they are conducted fairly and that courts administer justice while safeguarding the legal rights of all involved parties. Authorize payment of valid claims and determine method of payment. Conduct hearings to review and decide claims regarding issues such as social program eligibility, environmental protection, and enforcement of health and safety regulations. Rule on exceptions, motions, and admissibility of evidence. Determine existence and amount of liability according to current laws, administrative and judicial precedents, and available evidence. Issue subpoenas and administer oaths in preparation for formal hearings. Conduct studies of appeals procedures in field agencies to ensure adherence to legal requirements and to facilitate determination of cases.

2. Arbitrators, Mediators, and Conciliators

Personality Type: Social–Enterprising

Earnings: $52,770
Growth: 13.9%
Annual Openings: 320

Most Common Education/Training Level:
Bachelor's degree

Facilitate negotiation and conflict resolution through dialogue. Resolve conflicts outside of the court system by mutual consent of parties involved. Conduct studies of appeals procedures in order to ensure adherence to legal requirements and to facilitate disposition of cases. Rule on exceptions, motions, and admissibility of evidence. Review and evaluate information from documents such as claim applications, birth or death certificates, and physician or employer records. Organize and deliver public presentations about mediation to organizations such as community agencies and schools. Prepare written opinions and decisions regarding cases. Prepare settlement agreements for disputants to sign. Use mediation techniques to facilitate communication between disputants, to further parties' understanding of different perspectives, and to guide parties toward mutual agreement. Notify claimants of denied claims and appeal rights. Analyze evidence and apply relevant laws, regulations, policies, and precedents in order to reach conclusions. Conduct initial meetings with disputants to outline the arbitration process, settle procedural matters such as fees, and determine details such as witness numbers and time requirements. Confer with disputants to clarify issues, identify underlying concerns, and develop an understanding of their respective needs and interests. Participate in court proceedings. Arrange and conduct hearings to obtain information and evidence relative to disposition of claims. Recommend acceptance or rejection of compromise settlement offers. Research laws, regulations, policies, and precedent decisions to prepare for hearings. Set up appointments for parties to meet for mediation. Authorize payment of valid claims. Determine existence and amount of liability according to evidence, laws, and administrative and judicial precedents. Issue subpoenas and administer oaths to prepare for formal hearings. Interview claimants, agents, or witnesses to obtain information about disputed issues.

3. Judges, Magistrate Judges, and Magistrates

Personality Type: Enterprising–Social

Earnings: $112,830
Growth: –2.6%
Annual Openings: 500

Most Common Education/Training Level:
Bachelor's or higher degree plus work experience

Arbitrate, advise, adjudicate, or administer justice in a court of law. May sentence defendant in criminal cases according to government statutes. May determine liability of defendant in civil cases. May issue marriage licenses and perform wedding ceremonies. Instruct juries on applicable laws, direct juries to deduce the facts from the evidence presented, and hear their verdicts. Sentence defendants in criminal cases on conviction by jury according to applicable government statutes. Rule on admissibility of evidence and methods of conducting testimony. Preside over hearings and listen to allegations made by plaintiffs to determine whether the evidence supports the charges. Read documents on pleadings and motions to ascertain facts and issues. Interpret and enforce rules of procedure or establish new rules in situations where there are no procedures already established by law. Monitor proceedings to ensure that all applicable rules and procedures are followed. Advise attorneys, juries, litigants, and court

Enterprising

personnel regarding conduct, issues, and proceedings. Research legal issues and write opinions on the issues. Conduct preliminary hearings to decide issues such as whether there is reasonable and probable cause to hold defendants in felony cases. Write decisions on cases. Award compensation for damages to litigants in civil cases in relation to findings by juries or by the court. Settle disputes between opposing attorneys. Supervise other judges, court officers, and the court's administrative staff. Impose restrictions upon parties in civil cases until trials can be held. Rule on custody and access disputes and enforce court orders regarding custody and support of children. Grant divorces and divide assets between spouses. Participate in judicial tribunals to help resolve disputes. Perform wedding ceremonies.

4. Law Clerks

Personality Type:
Conventional–Investigative–Enterprising

Earnings: $38,390
Growth: 13.9%
Annual Openings: 1,080

Most Common Education/Training Level:
Bachelor's or higher degree plus work experience

Assist lawyers or judges by researching or preparing legal documents. May meet with clients or assist lawyers and judges in court. Search for and study legal documents to investigate facts and law of cases, to determine causes of action and to prepare cases. Prepare affidavits of documents and maintain document files and case correspondence. Review and file pleadings, petitions and other documents relevant to court actions.

5. Lawyers

Personality Type: Enterprising–Investigative

Earnings: $113,240
Growth: 13.0%
Annual Openings: 24,040

Most Common Education/Training Level:
Bachelor's or higher degree plus work experience

Represent clients in criminal and civil litigation and other legal proceedings, draw up legal documents, and manage or advise clients on legal transactions. May specialize in a single area or may practice broadly in many areas of law. Represent clients in court or before government agencies. Select jurors, argue motions, meet with judges and question witnesses during the course of a trial. Present evidence to defend clients or prosecute defendants in criminal or civil litigation. Interpret laws, rulings and regulations for individuals and businesses. Study Constitution, statutes, decisions, regulations, and ordinances of quasi-judicial bodies to determine ramifications for cases. Present and summarize cases to judges and juries. Prepare legal briefs and opinions, and file appeals in state and federal courts of appeal. Analyze the probable outcomes of cases, using knowledge of legal precedents. Examine legal data to determine advisability of defending or prosecuting lawsuit. Evaluate findings and develop strategies and arguments in preparation for presentation of cases. Advise clients concerning business transactions, claim liability, advisability of prosecuting or defending lawsuits, or legal rights and obligations. Gather evidence to formulate defense or to initiate legal actions, by such means as interviewing clients and witnesses to ascertain the facts of a case. Negotiate settlements of civil disputes. Prepare and draft legal documents, such as wills, deeds, patent applications, mortgages, leases, and contracts. Confer with colleagues with specialties in appropriate areas of legal issue to establish and verify bases for legal proceedings. Supervise legal assistants. Perform administrative and management functions related to the practice of law. Probate wills and represent and advise executors and administrators of estates. Search for and examine public and other legal records to write opinions or establish ownership. Act as agent, trustee, guardian, or executor for businesses or individuals. Help develop federal and state programs, draft and interpret laws and legislation, and establish enforcement procedures.

Management Information Systems

Personality Type:
Enterprising–Conventional–Investigative

Useful Facts About the Major

Prepares individuals to provide and manage data systems and related facilities for processing and retrieving internal business information; to select systems and train personnel; and to respond to external data requests.

Related CIP Program: 52.1201 Management Information Systems, General

Specializations in the Major: Accounting, network programming, security and disaster recovery.

Typical Sequence of College Courses: English composition, business writing, introduction to psychology, principles of microeconomics, principles of macroeconomics, calculus for business and social sciences, statistics for business and social sciences, introduction to management information systems, introduction to accounting, legal environment of business, principles of management and organization, operations management, strategic management, business finance, introduction to marketing, database management systems, systems analysis and design, decision support systems for management, networks and telecommunications.

Typical Sequence of High School Courses: English, algebra, geometry, trigonometry, science, foreign language, computer science.

Career Snapshot

The management information systems major is considered a business major, which means that students get a firm grounding in economics, accounting, business law, finance, and marketing, as well as the technical skills needed to work with the latest business computer systems. Students may specialize in MIS at either the bachelor's or master's level and may combine it with a degree in a related business field, such as accounting or finance, or in computer science. The job outlook is very good.

Useful Averages for the Related Jobs

* Annual Earnings: $106,000
* Growth: 14.6%
* Openings: 11,712
* Self-Employed: 3.4%
* Verbal Skill Rating: 61
* Math Skill Rating: 63

Other Details About the Related Jobs

Career Clusters: 04 Business, Management, and Administration; 08 Health Science; 11 Information Technology; 15 Science, Technology, Engineering, and Mathematics. **Career Pathways:** 04.1 Management; 04.3 Business Analysis; 04.4 Business Analysis; 08.3 Health Informatics; 11.1 Network Systems; 11.2 Information Support Services; 11.3 Interactive Media; 11.4 Programming and Software Development; 15.2 Science and Mathematics.

Skills: Programming, management of financial resources, systems evaluation, management of material resources, technology design, operations analysis, equipment selection, troubleshooting. **Work Conditions:** Indoors; sitting.

Enterprising

Related Jobs

1. Computer and Information Systems Managers

Personality Type:
Enterprising–Conventional–Investigative

Earnings: $113,720
Growth: 16.9%
Annual Openings: 9,710

Most Common Education/Training Level:
Bachelor's degree

Plan, direct, or coordinate activities in such fields as electronic data processing, information systems, systems analysis, and computer programming. Manage backup, security and user help systems. Consult with users, management, vendors, and technicians to assess computing needs and system requirements. Direct daily operations of department, analyzing workflow, establishing priorities, developing standards and setting deadlines. Assign and review the work of systems analysts, programmers, and other computer-related workers. Stay abreast of advances in technology. Develop computer information resources, providing for data security and control, strategic computing, and disaster recovery. Review and approve all systems charts and programs prior to their implementation. Evaluate the organization's technology use and needs and recommend improvements, such as hardware and software upgrades. Control operational budget and expenditures. Meet with department heads, managers, supervisors, vendors, and others, to solicit cooperation and resolve problems. Develop and interpret organizational goals, policies, and procedures. Recruit, hire, train and supervise staff, or participate in staffing decisions. Review project plans to plan and coordinate project activity. Evaluate data processing proposals to assess project feasibility and requirements. Prepare and review operational reports or project progress reports. Purchase necessary equipment.

2. Computer Programmers

Personality Type: Investigative–Conventional

Earnings: $70,940
Growth: –2.9%
Annual Openings: 8,030

Most Common Education/Training Level:
Bachelor's degree

Convert project specifications and statements of problems and procedures to detailed logical flow charts for coding into computer language. Develop and write computer programs to store, locate, and retrieve specific documents, data, and information. May program Web sites. Correct errors by making appropriate changes and rechecking the program to ensure that the desired results are produced. Conduct trial runs of programs and software applications to be sure they will produce the desired information and that the instructions are correct. Write, update, and maintain computer programs or software packages to handle specific jobs such as tracking inventory, storing or retrieving data, or controlling other equipment. Write, analyze, review, and rewrite programs, using workflow chart and diagram, and applying knowledge of computer capabilities, subject matter, and symbolic logic. Perform or direct revision, repair, or expansion of existing programs to increase operating efficiency or adapt to new requirements. Consult with managerial, engineering, and technical personnel to clarify program intent, identify problems, and suggest changes. Perform systems analysis and programming tasks to maintain and control the use of computer systems software as a systems programmer. Compile and write documentation of program development and subsequent revisions, inserting comments in the coded instructions so others can understand the program. Prepare detailed workflow charts and diagrams that describe input, output, and logical operation, and convert them into a series of instructions coded in a computer language. Consult with and assist computer operators or system analysts to define and resolve problems in running computer programs. Investigate whether networks, workstations, the central processing unit of the system, or peripheral equipment are responding to a program's instructions. Assign, coordinate, and review work and activities of programming personnel. Write or contribute to instructions or manuals to guide end users. Train subordinates in programming and program coding. Collaborate with computer manufacturers and other users to develop new programming methods.

3. Database Administrators

Personality Type: Conventional–Investigative

Earnings: $71,550
Growth: 20.3%
Annual Openings: 4,440

Most Common Education/Training Level:
Bachelor's or higher degree plus work experience

Coordinate changes to computer databases; test and implement the databases, applying knowledge of database management systems. May plan, coordinate, and implement security measures to safeguard computer databases. Develop standards and guidelines to guide the use and acquisition of software and to protect vulnerable information. Modify existing databases and database management systems or direct programmers and analysts to make changes. Test programs or databases, correct errors and make necessary modifications. Plan, coordinate and implement security measures to safeguard information in computer files against accidental or unauthorized damage, modification or disclosure. Approve, schedule, plan, and supervise the installation and testing of new products and improvements to computer systems such as the installation of new databases. Train users and answer questions. Establish and calculate optimum values for database parameters, using manuals and calculator. Specify users and user access levels for each segment of database.

Develop data model describing data elements and how they are used, following procedures and using pen, template or computer software. Develop methods for integrating different products so they work properly together such as customizing commercial databases to fit specific needs. Review project requests describing database user needs to estimate time and cost required to accomplish project. Review procedures in database management system manuals for making changes to database. Work as part of a project team to coordinate database development and determine project scope and limitations. Select and enter codes to monitor database performance and to create production database. Identify and evaluate industry trends in database systems to serve as a source of information and advice for upper management. Write and code logical and physical database descriptions and specify identifiers of database to management system or direct others in coding descriptions. Review workflow charts developed by programmer analyst to understand tasks computer will perform, such as updating records. Revise company definition of data as defined in data dictionary.

Public Relations

Personality Type: Enterprising–Artistic–Social

Useful Facts About the Major

Focuses on the theories and methods for managing the media image of a business, organization, or individual and the communication process with stakeholders, constituencies, audiences, and the general public; and prepares individuals to function as public relations assistants, technicians, and managers.

Related CIP Program: 09.0902 Public Relations/ Image Management

Specializations in the Major: Management, creative process, new media.

Enterprising

Typical Sequence of College Courses: English composition, oral communication, introduction to marketing, introduction to economics, principles of public relations, communications theory, public relations message strategy, communication ethics, public relations media, public relations writing, public relations techniques and campaigns, organizational communications, mass communication law, introduction to communication research, visual design for media.

Typical Sequence of High School Courses: English, algebra, foreign language, art, literature, public speaking, social science.

Career Snapshot

Public relations specialists work for business, government, and nonprofit organizations and encourage public support for the employer's policies and practices. Often several "publics" with differing interests and needs have to be targeted with different messages. The work requires an understanding of psychology, the business and social environments, effective writing, and techniques used in various media for persuasive communications. A bachelor's degree is good preparation for an entry-level job in this competitive field, and an internship or work experience is an important advantage. On-the-job experience may lead to a job managing public relations campaigns; a master's degree can speed up the process of advancement.

Useful Averages for the Related Jobs

- ❋ Annual Earnings: $54,000
- ❋ Growth: 23.1%
- ❋ Openings: 13,762
- ❋ Self-Employed: 4.5%
- ❋ Verbal Skill Rating: 74
- ❋ Math Skill Rating: 45

Other Details About the Related Jobs

Career Clusters: 03 Arts, Audio/Video Technology, and Communications; 04 Business, Management, and Administration; 08 Health Science; 10 Human Services; 14 Marketing, Sales, and Service. **Career Pathways:** 03.5 Journalism and Broadcasting; 04.1 Management; 04.5 Marketing; 08.3 Health Informatics; 10.5 Consumer Services Career; 14.1 Management and Entrepreneurship.

Skills: Operations analysis, negotiation, social perceptiveness, systems evaluation, writing, persuasion, speaking, time management. **Work Conditions:** Indoors; sitting; in a vehicle.

Related Jobs

1. Advertising and Promotions Managers

Personality Type:
Enterprising–Artistic–Conventional

Earnings: $82,370
Growth: –1.7%
Annual Openings: 1,050

Most Common Education/Training Level:
Bachelor's or higher degree plus work experience

Plan and direct advertising policies and programs or produce collateral materials, such as posters, contests, coupons, or giveaways, to create extra interest in the purchase of a product or service for a department, for an entire organization, or on an account basis. Prepare budgets and submit estimates for program costs as part of campaign plan development. Plan and prepare advertising and promotional material to increase sales of products or services, working with customers, company officials, sales departments and advertising agencies. Assist with annual budget development. Inspect layouts and advertising copy and edit scripts, audio and video tapes, and other promotional material for adherence to specifications. Prepare and negotiate advertising and sales contracts. Identify and develop contacts for promotional campaigns and industry programs that meet identified buyer targets such as dealers, distributors, or consumers. Gather and organize information to plan advertising campaigns. Confer with department heads or staff to discuss topics such as contracts, selection of advertising media, or product to be advertised. Confer with clients to provide marketing or technical advice.

Job Specialization

Green Marketers. Create and implement methods to market green products and services. Prepare renewable energy communications in response to public relations or promotional inquiries. Monitor energy industry statistics or literature to identify trends. Maintain portfolios of marketing campaigns, strategies, and other marketing products or ideas. Generate or identify sales leads for green energy. Devise or evaluate methods and procedures for collecting data, such as surveys, opinion polls, and questionnaires. Conduct market simulations for wind, solar, or geothermal energy projects. Write marketing content for green energy web sites, brochures or other communication media. Revise existing marketing plans or campaigns for green products or services. Monitor energy market or regulatory conditions to identify buying or other business opportunities. Identify marketing channels for green energy products or services. Develop communications materials, advertisements, presentations, or public relations initiatives to promote awareness of, and participation in, green energy initiatives. Consult with clients to identify potential energy efficiency opportunities or to promote green energy alternatives.

2. Public Relations Managers

Personality Type: Enterprising–Artistic

Earnings: $89,690
Growth: 12.9%
Annual Openings: 2,060

Most Common Education/Training Level:
Bachelor's degree

Plan and direct public relations programs designed to create and maintain a favorable public image for employer or client or, if engaged in fundraising, plan and direct activities to solicit and maintain funds for special projects and nonprofit organizations. Establish and maintain effective working relationships with clients, government officials, and media representatives and use these relationships to develop new business opportunities. Write interesting and effective press releases, prepare information for media kits and develop and maintain company internet or intranet web pages. Identify main client groups and audiences, determine the best way to communicate publicity information to them, and develop and implement a communication plan. Assign, supervise and review the activities of public relations staff. Develop and maintain the company's corporate image and identity, which includes the use of logos and signage. Respond to requests for information about employers' activities or status. Direct activities of external agencies, establishments and departments that develop and implement communication strategies and information programs. Manage communications budgets. Draft speeches for company executives, and arrange interviews and other forms of contact for them. Evaluate advertising and promotion programs for compatibility with public relations efforts. Manage special events such as sponsorship of races, parties introducing new products, or other activities the firm supports to gain public attention through the media without advertising directly. Facilitate consumer relations, or the relationship between parts of the company such as the managers and employees, or different branch offices. Formulate policies and procedures related to public information programs, working with public relations executives. Establish goals for soliciting funds, develop policies for collection and safeguarding of contributions, and coordinate disbursement of funds. Produce films and other video

Enterprising

products, regulate their distribution, and operate film library. Confer with labor relations managers to develop internal communications that keep employees informed of company activities.

3. Public Relations Specialists

Personality Type: Enterprising–Artistic–Social

Earnings: $51,960
Growth: 24.0%
Annual Openings: 13,130

Most Common Education/Training Level:
Bachelor's or higher degree plus work experience

Engage in promoting or creating goodwill for individuals, groups, or organizations by writing or selecting favorable publicity material and releasing it through various communications media. May prepare and arrange displays and make speeches. Respond to requests for information from the media or designate another appropriate spokesperson or information source. Study the objectives, promotional policies and needs of organizations to develop public relations strategies that will influence public opinion or promote ideas, products and services. Plan and direct development and communication of informational programs to maintain favorable public and stockholder perceptions of an organization's accomplishments and agenda. Establish and maintain cooperative relationships with representatives of community, consumer, employee, and public interest groups. Prepare or edit organizational publications for internal and external audiences, including employee newsletters and stockholders' reports. Coach client representatives in effective communication with the public and with employees. Confer with production and support personnel to produce or coordinate production of advertisements and promotions. Confer with other managers to identify trends and key group interests and concerns or to provide advice on business decisions. Arrange public appearances, lectures, contests, or exhibits for clients to increase product and service awareness and to promote goodwill. Consult with advertising agencies or staff to arrange promotional campaigns in all types of media for products, organizations, or individuals. Purchase advertising space and time as required to promote client's product or agenda. Prepare and deliver speeches to further public relations objectives. Plan and conduct market and public opinion research to test products or determine potential for product success, communicating results to client or management.

Conventional Majors

Accounting

Personality Type:
Conventional–Enterprising–Investigative

Useful Facts About the Major

Prepares individuals to practice the profession of accounting and to perform related business functions.

Related CIP Program: 52.0301 Accounting

Specializations in the Major: Cost accounting, auditing, accounting computer systems, taxation, forensic accounting, financial reporting.

Typical Sequence of College Courses: English composition, business writing, introduction to psychology, principles of microeconomics, principles of macroeconomics, calculus for business and social sciences, statistics for business and social sciences, introduction to management information systems, introduction to accounting, legal environment of business, principles of management and organization, operations management, strategic management, business finance, introduction to marketing, cost accounting, auditing, taxation of individuals, taxation of corporations, partnerships and estates.

Typical Sequence of High School Courses: English, algebra, geometry, trigonometry, science, foreign language, computer science.

Career Snapshot

Accountants maintain the financial records of an organization and supervise the recording of transactions. They provide information about the fiscal condition and trends of the organization, and figures for tax forms and financial reports. They advise management and therefore need good communication skills. A bachelor's degree is sufficient preparation for many entry-level jobs, but some employers prefer a master's degree. Accountants with diverse skills may advance to management after a few years. The job outlook is generally good.

Useful Averages for the Related Jobs

* Annual Earnings: $60,000
* Growth: 21.5%
* Openings: 50,818
* Self-Employed: 7.9%
* Verbal Skill Rating: 59
* Math Skill Rating: 67

Other Details About the Related Jobs

Career Clusters: 04 Business, Management, and Administration; 06 Finance; 07 Government and Public Administration. **Career Pathways:** 04.2 Business, Financial Management, and Accounting; 06.1 Financial and Investment Planning; 06.2 Business Financial Management; 06.3 Banking and Related Services; 07.5 Revenue and Taxation.

Skills: Mathematics, systems analysis, management of financial resources, operations analysis, systems evaluation, critical thinking, writing, active learning. **Work Conditions:** Indoors; sitting.

Related Jobs

1. Accountants and Auditors
Personality Type:
Conventional–Enterprising–Investigative

Earnings: $60,340
Growth: 21.6%
Annual Openings: 49,750

Most Common Education/Training Level:
Bachelor's degree

Examine, analyze, and interpret accounting records for the purpose of giving advice or preparing statements. Install or advise on systems of recording costs or other financial and budgetary data. No task data available.

Job Specializations

Accountants. Analyze financial information and prepare financial reports to determine or maintain record of assets, liabilities, profit and loss, tax liability, or other financial activities within an organization. Prepare, examine, or analyze accounting records, financial statements, or other financial reports to assess accuracy, completeness, and conformance to reporting and procedural standards. Report to management regarding the finances of establishment. Establish tables of accounts and assign entries to proper accounts. Develop, implement, modify, and document recordkeeping and accounting systems, making use of current computer technology. Compute taxes owed and prepare tax returns, ensuring compliance with payment, reporting or other tax requirements. Maintain or examine the records of government agencies. Advise clients in areas such as compensation, employee health care benefits, the design of accounting or data processing systems, or long-range tax or estate plans. Develop, maintain, and analyze budgets, preparing periodic reports that compare budgeted costs to actual costs. Provide internal and external auditing services for businesses or individuals. Analyze business operations, trends, costs, revenues, financial commitments, and obligations, to project future revenues and expenses or to provide advice. Advise management about issues such as resource utilization, tax strategies, and the assumptions underlying budget forecasts. Represent clients before taxing authorities and provide support during litigation involving financial issues. Prepare forms and manuals for accounting and bookkeeping personnel, and direct their work activities. Appraise, evaluate, and inventory real property and equipment, recording information such as the description, value and location of property. Survey operations to ascertain accounting needs and to recommend, develop, or maintain solutions to business and financial problems. Serve as bankruptcy trustees or business valuators.

Auditors. Examine and analyze accounting records to determine financial status of establishment and prepare financial reports concerning operating procedures. Collect and analyze data to detect deficient controls; duplicated effort; extravagance; fraud; or non-compliance with laws, regulations, and management policies. Prepare detailed reports on audit findings. Supervise auditing of establishments and determine scope of investigation required. Report to management about asset utilization and audit results and recommend changes in operations and financial activities. Inspect account books and accounting systems for efficiency, effectiveness, and use of accepted accounting procedures to record transactions. Examine records and interview workers to ensure recording of transactions and compliance with laws and regulations. Examine and evaluate financial and information systems, recommending controls to ensure system reliability and data integrity. Review data about material assets, net worth, liabilities, capital stock, surplus, income, and expenditures. Confer with company officials about financial and regulatory matters. Examine whether the organization's objectives are reflected in its management activities and whether employees understand the objectives. Prepare, analyze, and verify annual reports, financial statements, and other records, using accepted accounting and statistical procedures to assess financial condition and facilitate financial planning. Inspect cash on hand, notes receivable and payable, negotiable securities, and canceled

Conventional

checks to confirm records are accurate. Examine inventory to verify journal and ledger entries. Direct activities of personnel engaged in filing, recording, compiling, and transmitting financial records. Conduct pre-implementation audits to determine whether systems and programs under development will work as planned. Audit payroll and personnel records to determine unemployment insurance premiums, workers' compensation coverage, liabilities, and compliance with tax laws.

2. Budget Analysts

Personality Type:
Conventional–Enterprising–Investigative

Earnings: $66,660
Growth: 15.1%
Annual Openings: 2,230

Most Common Education/Training Level:
Bachelor's degree

Examine budget estimates for completeness, accuracy, and conformance with procedures and regulations. Analyze budgeting and accounting reports for the purpose of maintaining expenditure controls. Direct the preparation of regular and special budget reports. Consult with managers to ensure that budget adjustments are made in accordance with program changes. Match appropriations for specific programs with appropriations for broader programs, including items for emergency funds. Provide advice and technical assistance with cost analysis, fiscal allocation, and budget preparation. Summarize budgets and submit recommendations for the approval or disapproval of funds requests. Seek new ways to improve efficiency and increase profits. Review operating budgets to analyze trends affecting budget needs. Perform cost-benefit analyses to compare operating programs, review financial requests, or explore alternative financing methods. Interpret budget directives and establish policies for carrying out directives. Compile and analyze accounting records

and other data to determine the financial resources required to implement a program. Testify before examining and fund-granting authorities, clarifying and promoting the proposed budgets.

3. Credit Analysts

Personality Type: Conventional–Enterprising

Earnings: $57,470
Growth: 15.0%
Annual Openings: 2,430

Most Common Education/Training Level:
Bachelor's degree

Analyze current credit data and financial statements of individuals or firms to determine the degree of risk involved in extending credit or lending money. Prepare reports with this credit information for use in decision-making. Analyze credit data and financial statements to determine the degree of risk involved in extending credit or lending money. Generate financial ratios, using computer programs, to evaluate customers' financial status. Prepare reports that include the degree of risk involved in extending credit or lending money. Consult with customers to resolve complaints and verify financial and credit transactions. Compare liquidity, profitability, and credit histories of establishments being evaluated with those of similar establishments in the same industries and geographic locations. Review individual or commercial customer files to identify and select delinquent accounts for collection. Confer with credit association and other business representatives to exchange credit information. Complete loan applications, including credit analyses and summaries of loan requests, and submit to loan committees for approval. Analyze financial data such as income growth, quality of management, and market share to determine expected profitability of loans. Evaluate customer records and recommend payment plans based on earnings, savings data, payment history, and purchase activity.

4. Financial Examiners

Personality Type: Enterprising–Conventional

Earnings: $71,750
Growth: 41.2%
Annual Openings: 1,600

Most Common Education/Training Level:
Bachelor's degree

Enforce or ensure compliance with laws and regulations governing financial and securities institutions and financial and real estate transactions. May examine, verify correctness of, or establish authenticity of records. Investigate activities of institutions in order to enforce laws and regulations and to ensure legality of transactions and operations or financial solvency. Review and analyze new, proposed, or revised laws, regulations, policies, and procedures in order to interpret their meaning and determine their impact. Plan, supervise, and review work of assigned subordinates. Recommend actions to ensure compliance with laws and regulations or to protect solvency of institutions. Examine the minutes of meetings of directors, stockholders, and committees in order to investigate the specific authority extended at various levels of management. Prepare reports, exhibits, and other supporting schedules that detail an institution's safety and soundness, compliance with laws and regulations, and recommended solutions to questionable financial conditions. Review balance sheets, operating income and expense accounts, and loan documentation in order to confirm institution assets and liabilities. Review audit reports of internal and external auditors in order to monitor adequacy of scope of reports or to discover specific weaknesses in internal routines. Train other examiners in the financial examination process. Establish guidelines for procedures and policies that comply with new and revised regulations and direct their implementation. Direct and participate in formal and informal meetings with bank directors, trustees, senior management, counsels, outside accountants, and consultants in order to gather information and discuss findings. Verify and inspect cash reserves, assigned collateral, and bank-owned securities in order to check internal control procedures. Review applications for mergers, acquisitions, establishment of new institutions, acceptance in Federal Reserve System, or registration of securities sales in order to determine their public interest value and conformance to regulations and recommend acceptance or rejection.

5. Tax Examiners, Collectors, and Revenue Agents

Personality Type: Conventional–Enterprising

Earnings: $48,550
Growth: 13.0%
Annual Openings: 3,520

Most Common Education/Training Level:
Bachelor's degree

Determine tax liability or collect taxes from individuals or business firms according to prescribed laws and regulations. Collect taxes from individuals or businesses according to prescribed laws and regulations. Maintain knowledge of tax code changes and of accounting procedures and theory to properly evaluate financial information. Maintain records for each case, including contacts, telephone numbers, and actions taken. Confer with taxpayers or their representatives to discuss the issues, laws, and regulations involved in returns and to resolve problems with returns. Contact taxpayers by mail or telephone to address discrepancies and to request supporting documentation. Send notices to taxpayers when accounts are delinquent. Notify taxpayers of any overpayment or underpayment and either issue a refund or request further payment. Conduct independent field audits and investigations of income tax returns to verify information or to amend tax liabilities. Review filed tax returns to determine whether claimed tax credits and deductions are allowed by law. Review selected tax returns to determine the nature and extent of audits to be performed on them. Enter tax return information into computers for processing. Examine accounting systems and records to determine whether accounting methods used were appropriate and in compliance with statutory provisions. Process individual and corporate income tax returns and sales and excise tax returns. Impose payment deadlines on delinquent taxpayers and monitor payments to ensure that deadlines are met. Check tax forms to verify that names and taxpayer identification numbers are correct, that computations have been performed correctly, or that amounts match those on supporting documentation. Examine and analyze tax assets and liabilities to determine resolution of delinquent tax problems. Recommend criminal prosecutions or civil penalties. Determine appropriate methods of debt settlement, such as offers of compromise, wage garnishment, or seizure and sale of property.

Actuarial Science

Personality Type:
Conventional–Investigative–Enterprising

Useful Facts About the Major

Focuses on the mathematical and statistical analysis of risk, and their applications to insurance and other business management problems.

Related CIP Program: 52.1304 Actuarial Science

Specializations in the Major: Insurance, investment.

Typical Sequence of College Courses: Calculus, linear algebra, advanced calculus, introduction to computer science, introduction to probability, introduction to actuarial mathematics, mathematical statistics, applied regression, actuarial models, introduction to accounting, principles of microeconomics, principles of macroeconomics, financial management, programming in C++,

investment analysis, price theory, income and employment theory.

Typical Sequence of High School Courses: English, algebra, geometry, trigonometry, science, precalculus, calculus, computer science.

Career Snapshot

Actuarial science is the analysis of mathematical data to predict the likelihood of certain events, such as death, accident, or disability. Insurance companies are the main employers of actuaries; actuaries determine how much the insurers charge for policies. The usual entry route is a bachelor's degree, but actuaries continue to study and sit for exams to upgrade their professional standing over the course of 5 to 10 years. The occupation is expected to grow at a good pace, and there will probably be many openings for those who are able to pass the series of exams.

Useful Averages for the Related Jobs

* Annual Earnings: $87,000
* Growth: 21.4%
* Openings: 1,000
* Self-Employed: 0.0%
* Verbal Skill Rating: 61
* Math Skill Rating: 97

Other Details About the Related Jobs

Career Cluster: 06 Finance. **Career Pathway:** 06.4 Insurance Services.

Skills: Mathematics, management of financial resources, systems evaluation, systems analysis, programming, judgment and decision making, operations analysis, complex problem solving. **Work Conditions:** Indoors; sitting.

Related Jobs

Actuaries

Personality Type:
Conventional–Investigative–Enterprising

Earnings: $87,210
Growth: 21.4%
Annual Openings: 1,000

Most Common Education/Training Level:
Bachelor's or higher degree plus work experience

Analyze statistical data, such as mortality, accident, sickness, disability, and retirement rates, and construct probability tables to forecast risk and liability for payment of future benefits. May ascertain premium rates required and cash reserves necessary to ensure payment of future benefits. Ascertain premium rates required and cash reserves and liabilities necessary to ensure payment of future benefits. Determine or help determine company policy, and explain complex technical matters to company executives, government officials, shareholders, policyholders, or the public. Design, review and help administer insurance, annuity and pension plans, determining financial soundness and calculating premiums. Analyze statistical information to estimate mortality, accident, sickness, disability, and retirement rates. Provide advice to clients on a contract basis, working as a consultant. Collaborate with programmers, underwriters, accounts, claims experts, and senior management to help companies develop plans for new lines of business or improving existing business. Provide expertise to help financial institutions manage risks and maximize returns associated with investment products or credit offerings. Construct probability tables for events such as fires, natural disasters, and unemployment, based on analysis of statistical data and other pertinent information. Determine equitable basis for distributing surplus earnings under participating insurance and annuity contracts in mutual companies.

Testify before public agencies on proposed legislation affecting businesses. Determine policy contract provisions for each type of insurance. Testify in court as expert witness or to provide legal evidence on matters such as the value of potential lifetime earnings of a person who is disabled or killed in an accident. Explain changes in contract provisions to customers. Manage credit and help price corporate security offerings.

Business Management

See **Enterprising**

Computer Science

See **Investigative**

Finance

Personality Type:
Conventional–Enterprising–Investigative

Useful Facts About the Major

Prepares individuals to plan, manage, and analyze the financial and monetary aspects and performance of business enterprises, banking institutions, or other organizations.

Related CIP Program: 52.0801 Finance, General

Specializations in the Major: Securities analysis, corporate finance, public finance.

Typical Sequence of College Courses: English composition, business writing, introduction to psychology, principles of microeconomics, principles of macroeconomics, calculus for business and social sciences, statistics for business and social sciences, introduction to management information systems, introduction to accounting, legal environment of business, principles of management and organization, operations management, strategic management, business finance, introduction to marketing, corporate finance, money and capital markets, investment analysis.

Typical Sequence of High School Courses: English, algebra, geometry, trigonometry, science, foreign language, computer science.

Career Snapshot

Finance is the study of how organizations acquire funds and use them in ways that maximize their value. The banking and insurance industries, as well as investment service companies, employ graduates of this field. A bachelor's degree is good preparation for entry-level jobs. Because quantitative skills are very important in finance, firms sometimes employ graduates of engineering or science majors. Jobs with Wall Street firms may continue to experience some instability as the risk-taking culture bounces back from recession.

Useful Averages for the Related Jobs

- ❋ Annual Earnings: $81,000
- ❋ Growth: 16.1%
- ❋ Openings: 14,512
- ❋ Self-Employed: 6.0%
- ❋ Verbal Skill Rating: 66
- ❋ Math Skill Rating: 71

Other Details About the Related Jobs

Career Clusters: 04 Business, Management, and Administration; 06 Finance. **Career Pathways:** 04.2 Business, Financial Management, and Accounting; 06.1 Financial and Investment Planning; 06.2 Business Financial Management; 06.3 Banking and Related Services.

Skills: Management of financial resources, systems analysis, mathematics, systems evaluation, operations analysis, judgment and decision making, writing, persuasion. **Work Conditions:** Indoors; sitting.

Related Jobs

1. Budget Analysts

Personality Type:
Conventional–Enterprising–Investigative

Earnings: $66,660
Growth: 15.1%
Annual Openings: 2,230

Most Common Education/Training Level:
Bachelor's or higher degree plus work experience

Examine budget estimates for completeness, accuracy, and conformance with procedures and regulations. Analyze budgeting and accounting reports for the purpose of maintaining expenditure controls. Direct the preparation of regular and special budget reports. Consult with managers to ensure that budget adjustments are made in accordance with program changes. Match appropriations for specific programs with appropriations for broader programs, including items for emergency funds. Provide advice and technical assistance with cost analysis, fiscal allocation, and budget preparation. Summarize budgets and submit recommendations for the approval or disapproval of funds requests. Seek new ways to improve efficiency and increase profits. Review operating budgets to analyze trends affecting budget needs. Perform cost-benefit analyses to compare operating programs, review financial requests, or explore alternative financing methods. Interpret budget directives and establish policies for carrying out directives. Compile and analyze accounting records and other data to determine the financial resources required to implement a program. Testify before examining and fund-granting authorities, clarifying and promoting the proposed budgets.

2. Credit Analysts

Personality Type: Conventional–Enterprising

Earnings: $57,470
Growth: 15.0%
Annual Openings: 2,430

Most Common Education/Training Level:
Bachelor's or higher degree plus work experience

Analyze current credit data and financial statements of individuals or firms to determine the degree of risk involved in extending credit or lending money. Prepare reports with this credit information for use in decision-making. Analyze credit data and financial statements to determine the degree of risk involved in extending credit or lending money. Generate financial ratios, using computer programs, to evaluate customers' financial status. Prepare reports that include the degree of risk involved in extending credit or lending money. Consult with customers to resolve complaints and verify financial and credit transactions. Compare liquidity, profitability, and credit histories of establishments being evaluated with those of similar establishments in the same industries and geographic locations. Review individual or commercial customer files to identify and select delinquent accounts for collection. Confer with credit association and other business representatives to exchange credit information. Complete loan applications, including credit analyses and summaries of loan requests, and submit to loan committees for approval. Analyze financial data such as income growth, quality of management, and market share to determine expected profitability of loans. Evaluate customer records and recommend payment plans based on earnings, savings data, payment history, and purchase activity.

3. Financial Analysts

Personality Type:
Conventional–Investigative–Enterprising

Earnings: $73,670
Growth: 19.8%
Annual Openings: 9,520

Most Common Education/Training Level:
Bachelor's degree

Conduct quantitative analyses of information affecting investment programs of public or private institutions. Assemble spreadsheets and draw charts and graphs used to illustrate technical reports, using computer. Analyze financial information to produce forecasts of business, industry, and economic conditions for use in making investment decisions. Maintain knowledge and stay abreast of developments in the fields of industrial technology, business, finance, and economic theory. Interpret data affecting investment programs, such as price, yield, stability, future trends in investment risks, and economic influences. Monitor fundamental economic, industrial, and corporate developments through the analysis of information obtained from financial publications and services, investment banking firms, government agencies, trade publications, company sources, and personal interviews. Recommend investments and investment timing to companies, investment firm staff, or the investing public. Determine the prices at which securities should be syndicated and offered to the public. Prepare plans of action for investment based on financial analyses. Evaluate and compare the relative quality of various securities in a given industry. Present oral and written reports on general economic trends, individual corporations, and entire industries. Contact brokers and purchase investments for companies according to company policy. Collaborate with investment bankers to attract new corporate clients to securities firms.

4. Financial Managers

Personality Type: Enterprising–Conventional

Earnings: $101,190
Growth: 7.6%
Annual Openings: 13,820

Most Common Education/Training Level:
Bachelor's degree

Plan, direct, and coordinate accounting, investing, banking, insurance, securities, and other financial activities of a branch, office, or department of an establishment. No task data available.

Job Specializations

Financial Managers, Branch or Department. Direct and coordinate financial activities of workers in a branch, office, or department of an establishment, such as branch bank, brokerage firm, risk and insurance department, or credit department. Establish and maintain relationships with individual and business customers and provide assistance with problems these customers may encounter. Examine, evaluate, and process loan applications. Plan, direct, and coordinate the activities of workers in branches, offices, or departments of such establishments as branch banks, brokerage firms, risk and insurance departments, or credit departments. Oversee the flow of cash and financial instruments. Recruit staff members and oversee training programs. Network within communities to find and attract new business. Approve or reject, or coordinate the approval and rejection of, lines of credit and commercial, real estate, and personal loans. Prepare financial and regulatory reports required by laws, regulations, and boards of directors. Establish procedures for custody and control of assets, records, loan collateral, and securities in order to ensure safekeeping. Review collection reports to determine the status of collections and the amounts of outstanding balances. Prepare operational and risk reports for management analysis. Evaluate financial reporting systems, accounting and collection procedures, and investment activities and make recommendations for changes to procedures, operating systems, budgets, and other financial control functions. Plan, direct, and coordinate risk and insurance programs of establishments to control risks and losses. Submit delinquent accounts to attorneys or outside agencies for collection. Communicate with stockholders and other investors to provide information and to raise capital. Evaluate data pertaining to costs in order to plan budgets. Analyze and classify risks and investments to determine their potential impacts on companies. Review reports of securities transactions and price lists in order to analyze market conditions. Develop and analyze information to assess the current and future financial status of firms.

Treasurers and Controllers. Direct financial activities, such as planning, procurement, and investments, for all or part of an organization. Prepare and file annual tax returns or prepare financial information so that outside accountants can complete tax returns. Prepare or direct preparation of financial statements, business activity reports, financial position forecasts, annual budgets, and/or reports required by regulatory agencies. Supervise employees performing financial reporting, accounting, billing, collections, payroll, and budgeting duties. Delegate authority for the receipt, disbursement, banking, protection, and custody of funds, securities, and financial instruments. Maintain current knowledge of organizational policies and procedures, federal and state policies and directives, and current accounting standards. Conduct or coordinate audits of company accounts and financial transactions to ensure compliance with state and federal requirements and statutes. Receive and record requests for disbursements; authorize disbursements in accordance with policies and procedures. Monitor financial activities and details such as reserve levels to ensure that all legal and regulatory requirements are met. Monitor and evaluate the performance of accounting and other financial staff; recommend and implement personnel actions such as promotions and dismissals. Develop and maintain relationships with banking, insurance, and non-organizational accounting personnel in order to facilitate financial activities.

Coordinate and direct the financial planning, budgeting, procurement, or investment activities of all or part of an organization. Develop internal control policies, guidelines, and procedures for activities such as budget administration, cash and credit management, and accounting. Analyze the financial details of past, present, and expected operations in order to identify development opportunities and areas where improvement is needed. Advise management on short-term and long-term financial objectives, policies, and actions.

5. Loan Officers

Personality Type:
Conventional–Enterprising–Social

Earnings: $54,880
Growth: 10.1%
Annual Openings: 6,880

Most Common Education/Training Level:
Bachelor's degree

Evaluate, authorize, or recommend approval of commercial, real estate, or credit loans. Advise borrowers on financial status and methods of payments. Includes mortgage loan officers and agents, collection analysts, loan servicing officers, and loan underwriters. Meet with applicants to obtain information for loan applications and to answer questions about the process. Approve loans within specified limits and refer loan applications outside those limits to management for approval. Analyze applicants' financial status, credit, and property evaluations to determine feasibility of granting loans. Explain to customers the different types of loans and credit options that are available, as well as the terms of those services. Obtain and compile copies of loan applicants' credit histories, corporate financial statements, and other financial information. Review and update credit and loan files. Review loan agreements to ensure that they are complete and accurate according to policy. Compute payment schedules. Stay abreast of new types of loans and other financial services and products to better meet customers' needs. Submit applications to credit analysts for verification and recommendation. Handle customer complaints and take appropriate action to resolve them. Work with clients to identify their financial goals and to find ways of reaching those goals. Confer with underwriters to aid in resolving mortgage application problems. Negotiate payment arrangements with customers who have delinquent loans. Market bank products to individuals and firms, promoting bank services that may meet customers' needs. Supervise loan personnel. Set credit policies, credit lines, procedures, and standards in conjunction with senior managers. Provide special services such as investment banking for clients with more specialized needs. Analyze potential loan markets and develop referral networks to locate prospects for loans. Prepare reports to send to customers whose accounts are delinquent and forward irreconcilable accounts for collector action. Arrange for maintenance and liquidation of delinquent properties. Interview, hire, and train new employees. Petition courts to transfer titles and deeds of collateral to banks.

6. Personal Financial Advisors

Personality Type:
Enterprising–Conventional–Social

Earnings: $68,200
Growth: 30.1%
Annual Openings: 8,530

Most Common Education/Training Level:
Bachelor's degree

Advise clients on financial plans, using knowledge of tax and investment strategies, securities, insurance, pension plans, and real estate. Duties include assessing clients' assets, liabilities, cash flows, insurance coverages, tax statuses, and financial objectives to establish investment strategies. Prepare and interpret for clients information such as investment performance reports, financial document summaries, and income projections. Recommend strategies clients can use to achieve their financial goals and objectives, including specific recommendations in such areas as cash management, insurance coverage, and investment planning. Build and maintain client bases, keeping current client plans up-to-date and recruiting new clients on an ongoing basis. Devise debt liquidation plans that include payoff priorities and timelines. Implement financial planning recommendations, or refer clients to someone who can assist them with plan implementation. Interview clients to determine their current incomes, expenses, insurance coverages, tax statuses, financial objectives, risk tolerances, and other information needed to develop financial plans. Monitor financial market trends to ensure that plans are effective, and to identify any necessary updates. Explain and document for clients the types of services that are to be provided, and the responsibilities to be taken by personal financial advisors. Explain to individuals and groups the details of financial assistance available to college and university students, such as loans, grants, and scholarships. Guide clients in the gathering of information such as bank account records, income tax returns, life and disability insurance records, pension plan information, and wills. Analyze financial information obtained from clients to determine strategies for meeting clients' financial objectives. Meet with clients' other advisors, including attorneys, accountants, trust officers, and investment bankers, to fully understand clients' financial goals and circumstances. Answer clients' questions about the purposes and details of financial plans and strategies. Open accounts for clients, and disburse funds from account to creditors as agents for clients. Authorize release of financial aid funds to students.

International Business

See **Enterprising**

Management Information Systems

See **Enterprising**

Marketing

Personality Type: Enterprising–Conventional

Useful Facts About the Major

Prepares individuals to undertake and manage the process of developing consumer audiences and moving products from producers to consumers.

Related CIP Program: 52.1401 Marketing/Marketing Management, General

Specializations in the Major: Marketing research, marketing management.

Typical Sequence of College Courses: English composition, business writing, introduction to psychology, principles of microeconomics, principles of macroeconomics, calculus for business and social sciences, statistics for business and social sciences, introduction to management information systems, introduction to accounting, legal environment of business, principles of management and organization, operations management, strategic management, business finance, introduction to marketing, marketing research, buyer behavior, decision support systems for management, marketing strategy.

Typical Sequence of High School Courses: English, algebra, geometry, trigonometry, science, foreign language, computer science.

Career Snapshot

Marketing is the study of how buyers and sellers of goods and services find one another, how businesses can tailor their offerings to meet demand, and how businesses can anticipate and influence demand. It uses the findings of economics, psychology, and sociology in a business context. A bachelor's degree is good preparation for a job in marketing research. Usually some experience in this field is required before a person can move into a marketing management position. Job outlook varies, with some industries looking more favorable than others.

Useful Averages for the Related Jobs

* Annual Earnings: $107,000
* Growth: 12.2%
* Openings: 7,639
* Self-Employed: 4.7%
* Verbal Skill Rating: 68
* Math Skill Rating: 50

Other Details About the Related Jobs

Career Clusters: 04 Business, Management, and Administration; 10 Human Services; 14 Marketing, Sales, and Service. **Career Pathways:** 04.1 Management; 04.5 Marketing; 10.5 Consumer Services Career; 14.1 Management and Entrepreneurship; 14.2 Professional Sales and Marketing; 14.4 Marketing Communications and Promotion; 14.5 Marketing Information Management and Research.

Skills: Management of financial resources, operations analysis, management of material resources, persuasion, management of personnel resources, systems evaluation, negotiation, systems analysis. **Work Conditions:** Indoors; sitting; in a vehicle.

Related Jobs

1. Advertising and Promotions Managers
Personality Type:
Enterprising–Artistic–Conventional

Earnings: $82,370
Growth: –1.7%
Annual Openings: 1,050

Most Common Education/Training Level:
Bachelor's or higher degree plus work experience

Plan and direct advertising policies and programs or produce collateral materials, such as posters, contests, coupons, or giveaways, to create extra interest in the purchase of a product or service for a department, for an entire organization, or on an account basis. Prepare budgets and submit estimates for program costs as part of campaign plan development. Plan and prepare advertising and promotional material to increase sales of products or services, working with customers, company officials, sales departments and advertising agencies. Assist with annual budget development. Inspect layouts and advertising copy and edit scripts, audio and video tapes, and other promotional material for adherence to specifications. Prepare and negotiate advertising and sales contracts. Identify and develop contacts for promotional campaigns and industry programs that meet identified buyer targets such as dealers, distributors, or consumers. Gather and organize information to plan advertising campaigns. Confer with department heads or staff to discuss topics such as contracts, selection of advertising media, or product to be advertised. Confer with clients to provide marketing or technical advice.

Job Specialization

Green Marketers. Create and implement methods to market green products and services. Prepare renewable energy communications in response to public relations or promotional inquiries. Monitor energy industry statistics or literature to identify trends. Maintain portfolios of marketing campaigns, strategies, and other marketing products or ideas. Generate or identify sales leads for green energy. Devise or evaluate methods and procedures for collecting data, such as surveys, opinion polls, and questionnaires. Conduct market simulations for wind, solar, or geothermal energy projects. Write marketing content for green energy web sites, brochures or other communication media. Revise existing marketing plans or campaigns for green products or services. Monitor energy market or regulatory conditions to identify buying or other business opportunities. Identify marketing channels for green energy products or services. Develop communications materials, advertisements, presentations, or public relations initiatives to promote awareness of, and participation in, green energy initiatives. Consult with clients to identify potential energy efficiency opportunities or to promote green energy alternatives.

2. Marketing Managers

Personality Type: Enterprising–Conventional

Earnings: $110,030
Growth: 12.5%
Annual Openings: 5,970

Most Common Education/Training Level:
Bachelor's or higher degree plus work experience

Determine the demand for products and services offered by firms and their competitors and identify potential customers. Develop pricing strategies with the goal of maximizing firms' profits or shares of the market while ensuring that firms' customers are satisfied. Oversee product development or monitor trends that indicate the need for new products and services. Develop pricing strategies, balancing firm objectives and customer satisfaction. Identify, develop, and evaluate marketing strategy, based on knowledge of establishment objectives, market characteristics, and cost and markup factors. Evaluate the financial aspects of product development, such as budgets, expenditures, research and development appropriations, and return-on-investment and profit-loss projections. Formulate, direct and coordinate marketing activities and policies

to promote products and services, working with advertising and promotion managers. Direct the hiring, training, and performance evaluations of marketing and sales staff and oversee their daily activities. Negotiate contracts with vendors and distributors to manage product distribution, establishing distribution networks and developing distribution strategies. Compile lists describing product or service offerings. Consult with product development personnel on product specifications such as design, color, and packaging. Use sales forecasting and strategic planning to ensure the sale and profitability of products, lines, or services, analyzing business developments and monitoring market trends. Select products and accessories to be displayed at trade or special production shows. Confer with legal staff to resolve problems, such as copyright infringement and royalty sharing with outside producers and distributors. Coordinate and participate in promotional activities and trade shows, working with developers, advertisers, and production managers, to market products and services. Advise business and other groups on local, national, and international factors affecting the buying and selling of products and services. Initiate market research studies and analyze their findings. Consult with buying personnel to gain advice regarding the types of products or services expected to be in demand. Conduct economic and commercial surveys to identify potential markets for products and services.

3. Sales Managers

Personality Type: Enterprising–Conventional

Earnings: $96,790
Growth: 14.9%
Annual Openings: 12,660

Most Common Education/Training Level:
Bachelor's or higher degree plus work experience

Direct the actual distribution or movement of products or services to customers. Coordinate sales distribution by establishing sales

territories, quotas, and goals, and establish training programs for sales representatives. Analyze sales statistics gathered by staff to determine sales potential and inventory requirements and monitor customer preferences. Resolve customer complaints regarding sales and service. Monitor customer preferences to determine focus of sales efforts. Direct and coordinate activities involving sales of manufactured products, services, commodities, real estate or other subjects of sale. Determine price schedules and discount rates. Review operational records and reports to project sales and determine profitability. Direct, coordinate, and review activities in sales and service accounting and recordkeeping, and in receiving and shipping operations. Confer or consult with department heads to plan advertising services and to secure information on equipment and customer specifications. Advise dealers and distributors on policies and operating procedures to ensure functional effectiveness of business. Prepare budgets and approve budget expenditures. Represent company at trade association meetings to promote products. Plan and direct staffing, training, and performance evaluations to develop and control sales and service programs. Visit franchised dealers to stimulate interest in establishment or expansion of leasing programs. Confer with potential customers regarding equipment needs and advise customers on types of equipment to purchase. Oversee regional and local sales managers and their staffs. Direct clerical staff to keep records of export correspondence, bid requests, and credit collections, and to maintain current information on tariffs, licenses, and restrictions. Direct foreign sales and service outlets of an organization. Assess marketing potential of new and existing store locations, considering statistics and expenditures.

Pharmacy

See **Investigative**

Public Administration

Personality Type:
Enterprising–Conventional–Social

Useful Facts About the Major

Prepares individuals to serve as managers in the executive arm of local, state, and federal government; and focuses on the systematic study of executive organization and management.

Related CIP Program: 44.0401 Public Administration

Specializations in the Major: Policy analysis, program management, economic development, finance and budgeting, personnel and labor relations.

Typical Sequence of College Courses: English composition, oral communication, accounting, introduction to business management, American government, state and local government, college algebra, introduction to economics, organizational behavior, statistics for business and social sciences, organizational theory, introduction to psychology, urban politics, public policy making process, public finance and budgeting, political science research methods, planning and change in public organizations, seminar (reporting on research).

Typical Sequence of High School Courses: Algebra, English, foreign language, social science, trigonometry, history, public speaking, computer science.

Career Snapshot

The public sector includes many kinds of agencies, working in the fields of health, law enforcement, environmental protection, transportation, and taxation, to name just a few. Because of this variety of fields, graduates who have been trained in administrative skills (perhaps at the master's level) often find it helpful to combine that background with specific training in another field, such as health, science, engineering, or accounting. Public administration programs usually include internships that give students actual experience working in a public agency.

Useful Averages for the Related Jobs

* Annual Earnings: $95,000
* Growth: –0.1%
* Openings: 53,888
* Self-Employed: 2.0%
* Verbal Skill Rating: 50
* Math Skill Rating: 64

Other Details About the Related Jobs

Career Clusters: 04 Business, Management, and Administration; 07 Government and Public Administration; 10 Human Services; 16 Transportation, Distribution, and Logistics. **Career Pathways:** 04.1 Management; 07.1 Governance; 07.3 Foreign Service; 07.6 Regulation; 07.7 Public Management and Administration; 10.3 Family and Community Services; 16.1 Transportation Operations; 16.2 Logistics, Planning, and Management Services.

Skills: Management of material resources, management of financial resources, operations analysis, management of personnel resources, systems analysis, negotiation, coordination, systems evaluation. **Work Conditions:** Indoors; sitting; in a vehicle; walking and running; high places.

Related Jobs

1. Administrative Services Managers

Personality Type: Enterprising–Conventional

Earnings: $75,520
Growth: 12.5%
Annual Openings: 8,660

Most Common Education/Training Level: Work experience in a related occupation

Plan, direct, or coordinate supportive services of an organization, such as recordkeeping, mail distribution, telephone operator/receptionist, and other office support services. May oversee facilities planning and maintenance and custodial operations. Direct or coordinate the supportive services department of a business, agency, or organization. Prepare and review operational reports and schedules to ensure accuracy and efficiency. Set goals and deadlines for the department. Acquire, distribute and store supplies. Analyze internal processes and recommend and implement procedural or policy changes to improve operations, such as supply changes or the disposal of records. Plan, administer and control budgets for contracts, equipment and supplies. Monitor the facility to ensure that it remains safe, secure, and well-maintained. Hire and terminate clerical and administrative personnel. Oversee the maintenance and repair of machinery, equipment, and electrical and mechanical systems. Oversee construction and renovation projects to improve efficiency and to ensure that facilities meet environmental, health, and security standards, and comply with government regulations. Conduct classes to teach procedures to staff. Participate in architectural and engineering planning and design, including space and installation management. Manage leasing of facility space. Dispose of, or oversee the disposal of, surplus or unclaimed property.

2. Chief Executives

Personality Type: Enterprising–Conventional

Earnings: $160,720
Growth: –1.4%
Annual Openings: 11,250

Most Common Education/Training Level: Bachelor's or higher degree plus work experience

Determine and formulate policies and provide the overall direction of companies or private and public sector organizations within the guidelines set up by a board of directors or similar governing body. Plan, direct, or coordinate operational activities at the highest level of management with the help of subordinate executives and staff managers. Direct and coordinate an organization's financial and budget activities in order to fund operations, maximize investments, and increase efficiency. Confer with board members, organization officials, and staff members to discuss issues, coordinate activities, and resolve problems. Analyze operations to evaluate performance of a company and its staff in meeting objectives and to determine areas of potential cost reduction, program improvement, or policy change. Direct, plan, and implement policies, objectives, and activities of organizations or businesses in order to ensure continuing operations, to maximize returns on investments, and to increase productivity. Prepare budgets for approval, including those for funding and implementation of programs. Direct and coordinate activities of businesses or departments concerned with production, pricing, sales, and/or distribution of products. Negotiate or approve contracts and agreements with suppliers, distributors, federal and state agencies, and other organizational entities. Review reports submitted by staff members in order to recommend approval or to suggest changes. Appoint department heads or managers and assign or delegate responsibilities to them. Direct human resources activities, including the approval of human resource plans and activities, the selection of directors and other high-level staff, and establishment and organization of major departments. Preside over or serve on boards of directors, management committees, or other governing boards. Prepare and present reports concerning activities, expenses, budgets, government statutes and rulings, and other items affecting businesses or program services. Establish departmental responsibilities and coordinate functions among departments and sites. Implement corrective action plans to solve organizational or departmental problems.

Job Specialization

Chief Sustainability Officers. Communicate and coordinate with management, shareholders, customers, and employees to address sustainability issues. Enact or oversee a corporate sustainability strategy. Identify educational, training, or other development opportunities for sustainability employees or volunteers. Identify and evaluate pilot projects or programs to enhance the sustainability research agenda. Conduct sustainability- or environment-related risk assessments. Create and maintain sustainability program documents, such as schedules and budgets. Write project proposals, grant applications, or other documents to pursue funding for environmental initiatives. Supervise employees or volunteers working on sustainability projects. Write and distribute financial or environmental impact reports. Review sustainability program objectives, progress, or status to ensure compliance with policies, standards, regulations, or laws. Formulate or implement sustainability campaign or marketing strategies. Research environmental sustainability issues, concerns, or stakeholder interests. Evaluate and approve proposals for sustainability projects, considering factors such as cost effectiveness, technical feasibility, and integration with other initiatives. Develop sustainability reports, presentations, or proposals for supplier, employee, academia, media, government, public interest, or other groups. Develop, or oversee the development of, sustainability evaluation or monitoring systems. Develop, or oversee the development of, marketing or outreach media for sustainability projects or events. Develop methodologies to assess the viability or success of sustainability initiatives. Monitor and evaluate effectiveness of sustainability programs. Direct sustainability program operations to ensure compliance with environmental or governmental regulations. Develop or execute strategies to address issues such as energy use, resource conservation, recycling, pollution reduction, waste elimination, transportation, education, and building design.

3. Emergency Management Specialists

Personality Type: Social–Enterprising

Earnings: $52,590
Growth: 21.7%
Annual Openings: 560

Most Common Education/Training Level:
Bachelor's or higher degree plus work experience

Coordinate disaster response or crisis management activities, provide disaster-preparedness training, and prepare emergency plans and procedures for natural (e.g., hurricanes, floods, earthquakes), wartime, or technological (e.g., nuclear power plant emergencies, hazardous materials spills) disasters or hostage situations. Keep informed of activities or changes that could affect the likelihood of an emergency, as well as those that could affect response efforts and details of plan implementation. Propose alteration of emergency response procedures based on regulatory changes, technological changes, or knowledge gained from outcomes of previous emergency situations. Maintain and update all resource materials associated with emergency preparedness plans. Develop and maintain liaisons with municipalities, county departments, and similar entities to facilitate plan development, response effort coordination, and exchanges of personnel and equipment. Keep informed of federal, state, and local regulations affecting emergency plans and ensure that plans adhere to these regulations. Prepare emergency situation status reports that describe response and recovery efforts, needs, and preliminary damage assessments.

4. General and Operations Managers

Personality Type:
Enterprising–Conventional–Social

Earnings: $92,650
Growth: –0.1%
Annual Openings: 50,220

Most Common Education/Training Level:
Work experience in a related occupation

Plan, direct, or coordinate the operations of companies or public- and private-sector organizations. Duties and responsibilities include formulating policies, managing daily operations, and planning the use of materials and human resources, but are too diverse and general in nature to be classified in any one functional area of management or administration, such as personnel, purchasing, or administrative services. Includes owners and managers who head small business establishments whose duties are primarily managerial. Direct and coordinate activities of businesses or departments concerned with the production, pricing, sales, or distribution of products. Manage staff, preparing work schedules and assigning specific duties. Review financial statements, sales and activity reports, and other performance data to measure productivity and goal achievement and to determine areas needing cost reduction and program improvement. Establish and implement departmental policies, goals, objectives, and procedures, conferring with board members, organization officials, and staff members as necessary. Determine staffing requirements, and interview, hire and train new employees, or oversee those personnel processes. Monitor businesses and agencies to ensure that they efficiently and effectively provide needed services while staying within budgetary limits. Oversee activities directly related to making products or providing services. Direct and coordinate organization's financial and budget activities to fund operations, maximize investments, and increase efficiency. Determine goods

Conventional

and services to be sold, and set prices and credit terms, based on forecasts of customer demand. Manage the movement of goods into and out of production facilities. Locate, select, and procure merchandise for resale, representing management in purchase negotiations. Perform sales floor work such as greeting and assisting customers, stocking shelves, and taking inventory. Develop and implement product marketing strategies including advertising campaigns and sales promotions. Plan and direct activities such as sales promotions, coordinating with other department heads as required. Direct non-merchandising departments of businesses, such as advertising and purchasing. Recommend locations for new facilities or oversee the remodeling of current facilities. Plan store layouts, and design displays.

5. Legislators

Personality Type: Enterprising–Social

Earnings: $18,810
Growth: 0.7%
Annual Openings: 1,970

Most Common Education/Training Level:
Work experience in a related occupation

Develop laws and statutes at the federal, state, or local level. Attend receptions, dinners, and conferences to meet people, exchange views and information, and develop working relationships. Analyze and understand the local and national implications of proposed legislation. Represent their government at local, national, and international meetings and conferences. Promote the industries and products of their electoral districts. Oversee expense allowances, ensuring that accounts are balanced at the end of each fiscal year. Organize and maintain campaign organizations and fundraisers in order to raise money for election or re-election. Evaluate the structure, efficiency, activities, and performance of government agencies. Establish personal offices in local districts or states and manage office staff. Encourage and support party candidates for

political office. Conduct "head counts" to help predict the outcome of upcoming votes. Speak to students to encourage and support the development of future political leaders. Alert constituents of government actions and programs by way of newsletters, personal appearances at town meetings, phone calls, and individual meetings. Write, prepare, and deliver statements for the Congressional Record. Vote on motions, amendments, and decisions on whether or not to report a bill out from committee to the assembly floor. Serve on commissions, investigative panels, study groups, and committees in order to examine specialized areas and recommend action. Develop expertise in subject matters related to committee assignments. Appoint nominees to leadership posts or approve such appointments. Determine campaign strategies for media advertising, positions on issues, and public appearances. Debate the merits of proposals and bill amendments during floor sessions, following the appropriate rules of procedure. Seek federal funding for local projects and programs.

6. Postmasters and Mail Superintendents

Personality Type:
Enterprising–Conventional–Social

Earnings: $58,770
Growth: –15.1%
Annual Openings: 520

Most Common Education/Training Level:
Work experience in a related occupation

Direct and coordinate operational, administrative, management, and supportive services of a U.S. post office or coordinate activities of workers engaged in postal and related work in assigned post office. Organize and supervise activities such as the processing of incoming and outgoing mail. Direct and coordinate operational, management, and supportive services of one or a number of postal facilities. Resolve customer complaints. Hire and train employees and evaluate their performance. Prepare employee work schedules.

Negotiate labor disputes. Prepare and submit detailed and summary reports of post office activities to designated supervisors. Collect rents for post office boxes. Issue and cash money orders. Inform the public of available services and of postal laws and regulations. Select and train postmasters and managers of associate postal units. Confer with suppliers to obtain bids for proposed purchases and to requisition supplies; disburse funds according to federal regulations.

7. Social and Community Service Managers

Personality Type: Enterprising–Social

Earnings: $56,600
Growth: 13.8%
Annual Openings: 4,820

Most Common Education/Training Level:
Bachelor's or higher degree plus work experience

Plan, organize, or coordinate the activities of a social service program or community outreach organization. Oversee the program or organization's budget and policies regarding participant involvement, program requirements, and benefits. Work may involve directing social workers, counselors, or probation officers. Evaluate the work of staff and volunteers to ensure that programs are of appropriate quality and that resources are used effectively. Provide direct service and support to individuals or clients, such as handling a referral for child advocacy issues, conducting a needs evaluation, or resolving complaints. Recruit, interview, and hire or sign up volunteers and staff. Establish and maintain relationships with other agencies and organizations in community to meet community needs and to ensure that services are not duplicated. Establish and oversee administrative procedures to meet objectives set by boards of directors or senior management. Direct activities of professional and technical staff members and volunteers. Plan and administer budgets for

programs, equipment and support services. Participate in the determination of organizational policies regarding such issues as participant eligibility, program requirements, and program benefits. Prepare and maintain records and reports, such as budgets, personnel records, or training manuals. Research and analyze member or community needs to determine program directions and goals. Implement and evaluate staff, volunteer, or community training programs. Represent organizations in relations with governmental and media institutions. Act as consultants to agency staff and other community programs regarding the interpretation of program-related federal, state, and county regulations and policies. Speak to community groups to explain and interpret agency purposes, programs, and policies. Direct fundraising activities and the preparation of public relations materials. Analyze proposed legislation, regulations, or rule changes to determine how agency services could be impacted.

8. Transportation, Storage, and Distribution Managers

Personality Type: Enterprising–Conventional

Earnings: $79,490
Growth: –5.3%
Annual Openings: 2,740

Most Common Education/Training Level:
Bachelor's or higher degree plus work experience

Plan, direct, or coordinate transportation, storage, or distribution activities in accordance with governmental policies and regulations. No task data available.

Job Specializations

Storage and Distribution Managers. Plan, direct, and coordinate the storage and distribution operations within organizations or the activities of organizations that are engaged in storing and distributing materials and products. Supervise the activities of workers engaged in receiving, storing, testing, and shipping products or materials. Plan, develop, and implement warehouse safety and security programs and activities. Review invoices, work orders, consumption reports, and demand forecasts to estimate peak delivery periods and to issue work assignments. Schedule and monitor air or surface pickup, delivery, or distribution of products or materials. Interview, select, and train warehouse and supervisory personnel. Confer with department heads to coordinate warehouse activities, such as production, sales, records control, and purchasing. Respond to customers' or shippers' questions and complaints regarding storage and distribution services. Inspect physical conditions of warehouses, vehicle fleets and equipment, and order testing, maintenance, repair, or replacement as necessary. Develop and document standard and emergency operating procedures for receiving, handling, storing, shipping, or salvaging products or materials. Examine products or materials to estimate quantities or weight and type of container required for storage or transport. Issue shipping instructions and provide routing information to ensure that delivery times and locations are coordinated. Negotiate with carriers, warehouse operators and insurance company representatives for services and preferential rates. Examine invoices and shipping manifests for conformity to tariff and customs regulations. Prepare and manage departmental budgets. Prepare or direct preparation of correspondence, reports, and operations, maintenance, and safety manuals. Arrange for necessary shipping documentation, and contact customs officials to effect release of shipments. Advise sales and billing departments of transportation charges for customers' accounts. Evaluate freight costs and the inventory costs associated with transit times to ensure that costs are appropriate. Participate in setting transportation and service rates.

Transportation Managers. Plan, direct, and coordinate the transportation operations within an organization or the activities of organizations that provide transportation services. Analyze expenditures and other financial information to develop plans, policies, and budgets for increasing profits and improving services. Set operations policies and standards, including determination of safety procedures for the handling of dangerous goods. Plan, organize and manage the work of subordinate staff to ensure that the work is accomplished in a manner consistent with organizational requirements. Negotiate and authorize contracts with equipment and materials suppliers, and monitor contract fulfillment. Collaborate with other managers and staff members to formulate and implement policies, procedures, goals, and objectives. Monitor spending to ensure that expenses are consistent with approved budgets. Supervise workers assigning tariff classifications and preparing billing. Promote safe work activities by conducting safety audits, attending company safety meetings, and meeting with individual staff members. Direct investigations to verify and resolve customer or shipper complaints. Direct procurement processes including equipment research and testing, vendor contracts, and requisitions approval. Recommend or authorize capital expenditures for acquisition of new equipment or property to increase efficiency and services of operations department. Monitor operations to ensure that staff members comply with administrative policies and procedures, safety rules, union contracts, and government regulations. Direct activities related to dispatching, routing, and tracking transportation vehicles such as aircraft and railroad cars. Direct and coordinate, through subordinates, activities of operations department to obtain use of equipment, facilities, and human resources. Conduct employee training sessions on subjects such as hazardous material handling, employee orientation, quality improvement and computer use. Prepare management recommendations, such as proposed fee and tariff increases or schedule changes. Implement schedule and policy changes.

APPENDIX A

Resources for Further Exploration

The facts and pointers in this book provide a good beginning to the subject of college majors and related jobs that may suit your personality. If you want additional details, we suggest you consult some of the resources listed here.

Facts About Majors and Careers

College Majors Handbook with Real Career Paths and Payoffs, by Neeta P. Fogg, Ph.D.; Paul E. Harrington, Ed.D.; and Thomas F. Harrington, Ph.D. (JIST): This book, based on a U.S. Census Bureau study of 150,000 college graduates, describes 60 majors and the courses they require; discusses jobs that graduates actually obtain; and gives information on employers, tasks, and salaries.

"What Can I Do With A Major In..." at the website of University of North Carolina at Wilmington: http://uncw.edu/stuaff/career/Majors.

The College Entrance Examination Board website: Describes college majors and the careers related to them at www.collegeboard.com/csearch/majors_careers/profiles.

Occupational Outlook Handbook (or the *OOH*) (JIST): Updated every two years by the U.S. Department of Labor, this book provides descriptions for more than 300 major jobs covering about 90 percent of the workforce.

O*NET Dictionary of Occupational Titles (JIST): The only printed source of the more than 900 jobs described in the U.S. Department of Labor's Occupational Information Network database. It covers all the jobs in the book you're now reading, but it offers more topics than I was able to fit here.

Educational and Career Decision Making and Planning

50 Best Jobs for Your Personality, by Michael Farr and Laurence Shatkin, Ph.D. (JIST): This book is built around the same Holland personality types as the book you're now reading and includes lists and descriptions of high-paying and high-growth jobs linked to those personality types.

Best Resumes for College Students and New Grads, by Louise M. Kursmark (JIST): Containing sample resumes and more, this book describes the skills and attributes that employers find valuable in the workplace and shows how to demonstrate them in writing.

200 Best Jobs for College Graduates, by Michael Farr and Laurence Shatkin, Ph.D. (JIST): Identify jobs that may be right for you with more than 60 "best jobs" lists, based on earnings, growth, openings, education, interests, and more, and then browse more than 200 information-packed job descriptions.

College Success Guide, by Karine Blackett and Patricia Weiss (JIST): This book is designed to walk you through the 12 keys that make students successful in college and life. The authors have used statistics and student feedback to formulate the lessons that prepare you for college.

Community College Companion, by Mark C. Rowh (JIST): Enrollment at community colleges is booming, and they are a popular route to a four-year degree as well. This book can help you make the most of the community college experience by showing you how to pick the right program, juggle classes and other responsibilities, and succeed academically. Includes information on the transfer process and developing a career plan.

College Major Quizzes, by John Liptak, Ed.D. (JIST): The 12 assessments in this book help you explore your options, evaluate the merits of each, and choose the college program that fits you and your career goals best. The quizzes are easy to take, score, and interpret, and each chapter contains checklists and activities to help you make the most of your results.

APPENDIX B

Majors Sorted by Three-Letter Personality Code

This list can identify the best college majors in this book that may appeal to you. It is organized by the one-, two-, and three-letter RIASEC personality codes assigned to majors. (Learn about these codes in Part I).

If you are aware of your dominant personality type (see Part II), you may find it helpful to make a note of all majors that have RIASEC codes beginning with the letter for your dominant type. If you are aware of one or more additional personality types that you resemble, you may want to pay special attention to the majors that share their second or third RIASEC codes (either or both) with you. You may also find it useful to consider majors that have your dominant personality type as their second or third RIASEC code. For example, if you describe yourself as IR, you may want to look not only at majors coded IR (such as Biochemistry) or IR_ (such as Computer Engineering, coded IRC), but also at the major that has R as its first code, Civil Engineering (coded RIE).

This listing is based on the coding used by the O*NET database of the U.S. Department of Labor to classify the occupations related to the majors. Other publishers may not create the exact same set of linkages between RIASEC codes and majors or occupations. For example, some sales jobs that are coded as Social by Psychological Assessment Resources, Inc., the publisher of the Self-Directed Search, are coded as Enterprising by O*NET.

Here is a reminder of the personality type that each code letter represents:

R = Realistic

I = Investigative

A = Artistic

S = Social

E = Enterprising

C = Conventional

RIASEC Code	College Major	RIASEC Code	College Major
RIC	Civil Engineering	SI	Occupational Therapy
IR	Geology	SIR	Chiropractic
IR	Geophysics	SIR	Physical Therapy
IR	Microbiology	SIR	Physician Assisting
IR	Oceanography	SIA	African-American Studies
IR	Veterinary Medicine	SIA	American Studies
IRS	Dentistry	SIA	Area Studies
IRE	Aeronautical/Aerospace Engineering	SIA	Speech-Language Pathology and Audiology
IRC	Computer Engineering	SIA	Women's Studies
IRC	Environmental Science	SA	Humanities
IAR	Biochemistry	SAE	Communications Studies/Speech
ISR	Medicine	SAC	Elementary Education
ISR	Optometry	SE	Physical Education
IEC	Economics	EI	Biology
ICR	Computer Science	EI	Botany
ICS	Pharmacy	EI	Law
ARE	Graphic Design, Commercial Art, and Illustration	EIR	Bioengineering
AIE	Architecture	EAS	Public Relations
AS	Chinese	ESC	Health Information Systems Administration
AS	Classics	ESC	Human Resources Management
AS	French	EC	Business Management
AS	German	EC	Marketing
AS	Japanese	ECI	Management Information Systems
AS	Modern Foreign Language	ECS	International Business
AS	Russian	ECS	Public Administration
AS	Spanish	CEI	Accounting
AE	Interior Design	CEI	Finance
SI	Graduate Study for College Teaching	CIE	Actuarial Science
SI	Nursing (R.N. Training)		

APPENDIX C

The Career Clusters and Pathways

As the introduction explains, the career cluster scheme was developed by the U.S. Department of Education's Office of Vocational and Adult Education. Each career cluster contains two or more career pathways that are linked to educational programs and occupations. In the descriptions of majors in Part IV, you'll find the clusters and pathways for the jobs related to each major. We thought you would want to see the complete career cluster taxonomy so you would have a sense of the detailed pathways belonging to these clusters. In some cases, the pathway titles resemble titles of college majors or specializations within majors, so the pathways may suggest areas of employment related to a major that interests you.

In the career cluster taxonomy, the clusters have two-digit code numbers; the pathways have four-digit code numbers beginning with the code number for the cluster in which they are classified. Following are the 16 career clusters and 71 career pathways. You should understand that some states and school systems use modified versions of this taxonomy.

01 Agriculture, Food, and Natural Resources
    01.1 Food Products and Processing Systems
        Agricultural Business and Economics
        Agronomy and Crop Science
        Animal Science
        Food Science
        Graduate Study for College Teaching
    01.2 Plant Systems
        Agricultural Business and Economics
        Agronomy and Crop Science
        Animal Science
        Biochemistry
        Economics

Family and Consumer Sciences
Food Science
Graduate Study for College
  Teaching
Soil Science
01.3 Animal Systems
  Agricultural Business and
    Economics
  Agronomy and Crop Science
  Animal Science
  Family and Consumer Sciences
  Food Science
  Graduate Study for College
    Teaching
  Veterinary Medicine
01.4 Power Structure and Technical Systems
  Graduate Study for College
    Teaching
01.5 Natural Resources Systems
  Agricultural Business and
    Economics
  Agronomy and Crop Science
  Animal Science
  Economics
  Environmental Science
  Forestry
  Graduate Study for College
    Teaching
  Parks and Recreation Management
  Wildlife Management
  Zoology
01.6 Environmental Service Systems
  Occupational Health and
    Industrial Hygiene
01.7 Agribusiness Systems
  Agricultural Business and
    Economics
  Animal Science
  Family and Consumer Sciences
  Food Science
  Graduate Study for College
    Teaching
  Graphic Design, Commercial Art,
    and Illustration

Industrial Design
Journalism and Mass
  Communications
02 Architecture and Construction
  02.1 Design/Pre-Construction
    Aeronautical/Aerospace
      Engineering
    Agricultural Engineering
    Architecture
    Bioengineering
    Chemical Engineering
    Civil Engineering
    Computer Engineering
    Electrical Engineering
    Graduate Study for College
      Teaching
    Industrial Engineering
    Interior Design
    Landscape Architecture
    Materials Science
    Mechanical Engineering
    Metallurgical Engineering
    Petroleum Engineering
  02.2 Construction
    Business Management
    Mechanical Engineering
    Operations Management
  02.3 Maintenance/Operations
03 Arts, Audio/Video Technology, and
      Communications
  03.1 Audio and Video Technology and Film
    Art
    Art History
    Dance
    Drama/Theater Arts
    Film/Cinema Studies
    Graduate Study for College
      Teaching
    Graphic Design, Commercial Art,
      and Illustration
    History
    Industrial Design
  03.2 Printing Technology
    Art

Graduate Study for College
Teaching
Graphic Design, Commercial Art,
and Illustration
03.3 Visual Arts
Art
Graduate Study for College
Teaching
Graphic Design, Commercial Art,
and Illustration
Industrial Design
Interior Design
03.4 Performing Arts
Art
Communications Studies/Speech
Dance
Drama/Theater Arts
Family and Consumer Sciences
Film/Cinema Studies
Graduate Study for College
Teaching
Graphic Design, Commercial Art,
and Illustration
Journalism and Mass
Communications
Music
03.5 Journalism and Broadcasting
Communications Studies/Speech
Drama/Theater Arts
English
Family and Consumer Sciences
Film/Cinema Studies
Graduate Study for College
Teaching
Journalism and Mass
Communications
Public Relations
03.6 Telecommunications
Film/Cinema Studies
04 Business, Management, and Administration
04.1 Management
Advertising
Business Management
Communications Studies/Speech
Computer Science

Economics
Family and Consumer Sciences
Graduate Study for College
Teaching
Industrial Engineering
International Business
International Relations
Management Information Systems
Marketing
Mechanical Engineering
Operations Management
Public Administration
Public Relations
Transportation and Logistics
Management
04.2 Business, Financial Management, and
Accounting
Accounting
Astronomy
Biochemistry
Biology
Botany
Chemistry
Finance
Geology
Geophysics
Graduate Study for College
Teaching
Industrial Engineering
Mathematics
Microbiology
Oceanography
Physics
Statistics
Zoology
04.3 Human Resources
Graduate Study for College
Teaching
Human Resources Management
Industrial and Labor Relations
04.4 Business Analysis
Astronomy
Biochemistry
Biology
Botany

Chemistry
Computer Science
Geology
Geophysics
Industrial Engineering
Management Information Systems
Mathematics
Microbiology
Oceanography
Operations Management
Physics
Statistics
Zoology
04.5 Marketing
Advertising
Communications Studies/Speech
Graduate Study for College
Teaching
Marketing
Public Relations
04.6 Administrative and Information
Support
05 Education and Training
05.1 Administration and Administrative
Support
Graduate Study for College
Teaching
Physical Education
05.2 Professional Support Services
Graduate Study for College
Teaching
Library Science
05.3 Teaching/Training
Astronomy
Business Education
Chemistry
Chinese
Classics
Dietetics
Early Childhood Education
Elementary Education
Family and Consumer Sciences
French

German
Graduate Study for College
Teaching
History
Industrial/Technology Education
Japanese
Library Science
Modern Foreign Language
Parks and Recreation Management
Physical Education
Physics
Russian
Secondary Education
Spanish
Special Education
06 Finance
06.1 Financial and Investment Planning
Accounting
Finance
Graduate Study for College
Teaching
06.2 Business Financial Management
Accounting
Finance
06.3 Banking and Related Services
Accounting
Finance
06.4 Insurance Services
Actuarial Science
Graduate Study for College
Teaching
Insurance
07 Government and Public Administration
07.1 Governance
Business Management
Graduate Study for College
Teaching
International Business
International Relations
Journalism and Mass
Communications
Operations Management
Political Science

Public Administration

Transportation and Logistics
Management

07.2 National Security

07.3 Foreign Service

Business Management

International Business

International Relations

Public Administration

Transportation and Logistics
Management

07.4 Planning

Graduate Study for College
Teaching

07.5 Revenue and Taxation

Accounting

07.6 Regulation

Business Management

International Business

International Relations

Public Administration

Transportation and Logistics
Management

07.7 Public Management and
Administration

Business Management

Public Administration

08 Health Science

08.1 Therapeutic Services

Biochemistry

Chiropractic

Dentistry

Dietetics

Graduate Study for College
Teaching

Health Information Systems
Administration

Hospital/Health Facilities
Administration

Medicine

Microbiology

Nursing (R.N. Training)

Occupational Health and
Industrial Hygiene

Occupational Therapy

Optometry

Pharmacy

Podiatry

Psychology

Speech-Language Pathology and
Audiology

Veterinary Medicine

08.2 Diagnostics Services

Graduate Study for College
Teaching

Health Information Systems
Administration

Hospital/Health Facilities
Administration

Medical Technology

Medicine

Physician Assisting

08.3 Health Informatics

Art

Communications Studies/Speech

Computer Engineering

Computer Science

English

Family and Consumer Sciences

Graduate Study for College
Teaching

Graphic Design, Commercial Art,
and Illustration

Health Information Systems
Administration

Hospital/Health Facilities
Administration

Journalism and Mass
Communications

Management Information Systems

Occupational Health and
Industrial Hygiene

Orthotics/Prosthetics

Physical Therapy

Psychology

Public Relations

08.4 Support Services

Agricultural Business and
Economics

Animal Science

Dietetics

Family and Consumer Sciences

Graduate Study for College
Teaching

08.5 Biotechnology Research and
Development

Computer Engineering

Computer Science

Graduate Study for College
Teaching

Graphic Design, Commercial Art,
and Illustration

Pharmacy

09 Hospitality and Tourism

09.1 Restaurants and Food/Beverage
Services

Hotel/Motel and Restaurant
Management

09.2 Lodging

Hotel/Motel and Restaurant
Management

09.3 Travel and Tourism

Hotel/Motel and Restaurant
Management

09.4 Recreation, Amusements and
Attractions

Agricultural Business and
Economics

Animal Science

Family and Consumer Sciences

Hotel/Motel and Restaurant
Management

10 Human Services

10.1 Early Childhood Development and
Services

Agricultural Business and
Economics

Animal Science

Early Childhood Education

Family and Consumer Sciences

Graduate Study for College
Teaching

10.2 Counseling and Mental Health
Services

Graduate Study for College
Teaching

Medicine

Music

Parks and Recreation Management

Philosophy

Psychology

Religion/Religious Studies

Social Work

10.3 Family and Community Services

Agricultural Business and
Economics

Animal Science

Business Management

Family and Consumer Sciences

Graduate Study for College
Teaching

International Business

International Relations

Public Administration

Social Work

Sociology

Transportation and Logistics
Management

Urban Studies

10.4 Personal Care Services

10.5 Consumer Services Career

Agricultural Business and
Economics

Animal Science

Business Management

Chinese

Classics

Communications Studies/Speech

Family and Consumer Sciences

French

German

Graduate Study for College
Teaching

Japanese

Journalism and Mass
Communications

Marketing

Modern Foreign Language
Public Relations
Russian
Spanish
Special Education

11 Information Technology
    11.1 Network Systems
        Art
        Computer Engineering
        Computer Science
        Graduate Study for College
           Teaching
        Graphic Design, Commercial Art,
           and Illustration
        Industrial Design
        Management Information Systems
        Operations Management
    11.2 Information Support Services
        Computer Engineering
        Computer Science
        Graduate Study for College
           Teaching
        Graphic Design, Commercial Art,
           and Illustration
        Management Information Systems
        Operations Management
    11.3 Interactive Media
        Computer Engineering
        Computer Science
        Graphic Design, Commercial Art,
           and Illustration
        Management Information Systems
    11.4 Programming and Software
        Development
        Aeronautical/Aerospace
           Engineering
        Agricultural Engineering
        Architecture
        Bioengineering
        Chemical Engineering
        Civil Engineering
        Computer Engineering
        Computer Science
        Electrical Engineering
        Graduate Study for College
           Teaching

Graphic Design, Commercial Art,
    and Illustration
Industrial Engineering
Landscape Architecture
Management Information Systems
Materials Science
Mechanical Engineering
Metallurgical Engineering
Petroleum Engineering

12 Law, Public Safety, Corrections, and Security
    12.1 Correction Services
        Graduate Study for College
           Teaching
        Social Work
    12.2 Emergency and Fire Management
        Services
    12.3 Security and Protective Services
        Criminal Justice/Law Enforcement
        Graduate Study for College
           Teaching
    12.4 Law Enforcement Services
        Criminal Justice/Law Enforcement
        Graduate Study for College
           Teaching
    12.5 Legal Services
        Agricultural Business and
           Economics
        Animal Science
        Family and Consumer Sciences
        Graduate Study for College
           Teaching
        Law
    12.6 Inspection Services

13 Manufacturing
    13.1 Production
        Business Management
        Mechanical Engineering
        Operations Management
    13.2 Manufacturing Production Process
        Development
        Agricultural Business and
           Economics
        Animal Science
        Environmental Science
        Family and Consumer Sciences
        Food Science

13.3 Maintenance, Installation, and Repair
    Agricultural Business and
      Economics
    Animal Science
    Computer Engineering
    Computer Science
    Family and Consumer Sciences
    Interior Design
13.4 Quality Assurance
    Occupational Health and
      Industrial Hygiene

14 Marketing, Sales, and Service
  14.1 Management and Entrepreneurship
    Advertising
    Business Management
    Family and Consumer Sciences
    Graduate Study for College
      Teaching
    Marketing
    Public Relations
  14.2 Professional Sales and Marketing
    Family and Consumer Sciences
    Hotel/Motel and Restaurant
      Management
    Insurance
    Interior Design
  14.3 Buying and Merchandising
    Insurance
  14.4 Marketing Communications and
      Promotion
    Business Management
    Family and Consumer Sciences
    Marketing
  14.5 Marketing Information Management
     and Research
    Economics
    Family and Consumer Sciences
    Graduate Study for College
      Teaching
    Marketing

15 Science, Technology, Engineering, and
    Mathematics
  15.1 Engineering and Technology
    Aeronautical/Aerospace
      Engineering
    Agricultural Engineering
    Architecture
    Bioengineering
    Business Management
    Chemical Engineering
    Civil Engineering
    Computer Engineering
    Computer Science
    Electrical Engineering
    Graduate Study for College
      Teaching
    Graphic Design, Commercial Art,
      and Illustration
    Industrial Engineering
    Landscape Architecture
    Materials Science
    Mechanical Engineering
    Metallurgical Engineering
    Petroleum Engineering
  15.2 Science and Mathematics
    Aeronautical/Aerospace
      Engineering
    Agricultural Engineering
    Anthropology
    Archeology
    Architecture
    Art History
    Astronomy
    Biochemistry
    Bioengineering
    Biology
    Botany
    Chemical Engineering
    Chemistry
    Civil Engineering
    Classics
    Computer Engineering
    Computer Science

Dietetics
Economics
Electrical Engineering
Geography
Geology
Geophysics
Graduate Study for College
  Teaching
Graphic Design, Commercial Art,
  and Illustration
History
Industrial Engineering
International Relations
Landscape Architecture
Management Information Systems
Materials Science
Mathematics
Mechanical Engineering
Medicine
Metallurgical Engineering
Microbiology
Oceanography
Petroleum Engineering
Physics
Political Science
Sociology
Soil Science
Statistics
Urban Studies
Wildlife Management
Zoology

16 Transportation, Distribution, and Logistics
  16.1 Transportation Operations
      Business Management
      Dietetics
      Operations Management
      Public Administration
      Transportation and Logistics
        Management
  16.2 Logistics, Planning, and Management
      Services
      Business Management
      International Business
      International Relations
      Operations Management
      Public Administration
      Transportation and Logistics
        Management
  16.3 Warehousing and Distribution Center
      Operations
      Operations Management
      Transportation and Logistics
        Management
  16.4 Facility and Mobile Equipment
      Maintenance
  16.5 Transportation Systems/Infrastructure
      Planning, Management, and
      Regulation
  16.6 Health, Safety, and Environmental
      Management
      Environmental Science
  16.7 Sales and Service

APPENDIX D

Definitions of Skills Used in Descriptions of Majors

In the Part IV descriptions of majors, you can see the top skills required by the jobs related to each major. Because some of the skill names may not be completely familiar to you, I present here the definitions of all the skills referred to in this book. Note that not every skill included in the O*NET database is included in this book; among college-level jobs, certain skills tend to dominate.

Skill Name	Definition
Active Learning	Working with new material or information to grasp its implications.
Active Listening	Listening to what other people are saying and asking questions as appropriate.
Complex Problem Solving	Identifying complex problems, reviewing the options, and implementing solutions.
Coordination	Adjusting actions in relation to others' actions.
Critical Thinking	Using logic and analysis to identify the strengths and weaknesses of different approaches.
Equipment Maintenance	Performing routine maintenance and determining when and what kind of maintenance is needed.
Equipment Selection	Determining the kind of tools and equipment needed to do a job.
Installation	Installing equipment, machines, wiring, or programs to meet specifications.
Instructing	Teaching others how to do something.
Judgment and Decision Making	Weighing the relative costs and benefits of a potential action.
Learning Strategies	Using multiple approaches when learning or teaching new things.

(continued)

(continued)

Skill Name	Definition
Management of Financial Resources	Determining how money will be spent to get the work done and accounting for these expenditures.
Management of Material Resources	Obtaining and seeing to the appropriate use of equipment, facilities, and materials needed to do certain work.
Management of Personnel Resources	Motivating, developing, and directing people as they work; identifying the best people for the job.
Mathematics	Using mathematics to solve problems.
Monitoring	Assessing how well one is doing when learning or doing something.
Negotiation	Bringing others together and trying to reconcile differences.
Operation and Control	Controlling operations of equipment or systems.
Operation Monitoring	Watching gauges, dials, or other indicators to make sure a machine is working properly.
Operations Analysis	Analyzing needs and product requirements to create a design.
Persuasion	Persuading others to approach things differently.
Programming	Writing computer programs for various purposes.
Quality Control Analysis	Evaluating the quality or performance of products, services, or processes.
Reading Comprehension	Understanding written sentences and paragraphs in work-related documents.
Repairing	Repairing machines or systems, using the needed tools.
Science	Using scientific methods to solve problems.
Service Orientation	Actively looking for ways to help people.
Social Perceptiveness	Being aware of others' reactions and understanding why they react the way they do.
Speaking	Talking to others to effectively convey information.
Systems Analysis	Determining how a system should work and how changes will affect outcomes.
Systems Evaluation	Looking at many indicators of system performance and taking into account their accuracy.
Technology Design	Generating or adapting equipment and technology to serve users' needs.
Time Management	Managing one's own time and the time of others.
Troubleshooting	Determining what is causing an operating error and deciding what to do about it.
Writing	Communicating effectively with others in writing as indicated by the needs of the audience.

Index

A

C